The Best Gardens
in Italy A Traveller's
Guide

Was it, in short, ever well to be elsewhere
when one might be in Italy?

Edith Wharton

The Best Gardens in Italy
A Traveller's Guide

Kirsty McLeod

Photographs by Primrose Bell

Introduction by Robin Lane Fox

F

FRANCES LINCOLN LIMITED

PUBLISHERS

Quarto is the authority on a wide range of topics.
Quarto educates, entertains and enriches the lives of
our readers—enthusiasts and lovers of hands-on living.
www.quartoknows.com

Frances Lincoln Limited
4 Torriano Mews
Torriano Avenue
London NW5 2RZ
www.franceslincoln.com

MIX
Paper from
responsible sources
FSC® C013604
www.fsc.org

Page 1 Villa del Balbianello
Pages 2–3 Villa Arvedi
Right Villa Capponi
Pages 6–7 Villa Massei

Contents

Introduction by Robin Lane Fox

Italian gardens underlie so much of the style of gardens in the rest of Europe, and in the United States. Those formal ground plans, green parterres of glistening box, clipped topiary, fountains and flowery meadows all go back to the inspiring example of ancient Roman and Renaissance art and authors. The foundations of French gardens' formal style are Italian and with the added impetus of French palaces and the splendour of Louis XIV they were copied at so many of the minor courts elsewhere in Europe, from Germany to pre-revolutionary Russia. Even in the 1970s, in California, the Getty Museum chose the historic pattern of a Roman peristyle for its architecture and accompanying garden. The best of modern 'English style' adapts informal planting to a formal plan, whether at Hidcote Manor or Sissinghurst Castle, but ultimately its formal bones are clones of Italy's ancestors. How has this legacy developed within Italy itself?

In the 1880s, at a time when a fashion for Italianate villas had already begun on America's East Coast, historic Italian gardens were restudied briefly by the American landscape artist Charles Platt. Other authors followed, including the novelist Edith Wharton and the obsessive Sir George Sitwell, who travelled in Italy and took notes on more than two hundred Italian formal gardens while recovering from a nervous breakdown. In the early 1960s, Georgina Masson returned to the challenge and hit on several old ground plans in outlying parts of Italy which the English had never seen: her big illustrated book opened the eyes of a new wave of travellers. In the 1980s Italian gardens became a magnet for discerning travel guides and groups. England's National Gardens Scheme then began to interest Italian owners and an Italian garden circuit started to develop. Even in red-hot August, readers of my weekly column in the *Financial Times* now bombard me with requests for gardens to visit in Italy while on holiday.

This rise of 'garden-visiting' in Italy is not something I had foreseen. In 1972 it had been a struggle to find any book except Masson's on gardens which were visitable. I remember pleading in the nearby bar to gain access to the Castello Ruspoli in Vignanello, said to have one of the finest surviving Renaissance box parterres in Italy. Eventually an elderly lady let me in and pointed out the family tree hanging gloomily in the hallway. Most of the branch-lines ended in a smudge of blood, indicating that surviving Ruspoli were now extremely rare. The big parterre seemed likely to follow them. It was largely untrimmed and the underlying formality was difficult to see. The heavy old door of the castle closed behind me and I never imagined that I would be reading, forty years later, illustrated chapters about the Ruspoli parterre in all its neat, fresh glory. Its remarkable gardener Santino has transformed the look of the parterre with love and skill and, as a true plantsman, grows onions alongside his lemons to keep them healthy. With the help of EU funds, the present occupant, Claudia Ruspoli, has turned this great surviving garden into an historic landmark.

I certainly never imagined I would be reading about it in anything like this stunning book by Kirsty McLeod and Primrose Bell. Some local guides to 'gardens open' exist, especially in Tuscany, but this book is a revelation on a different scale. It covers the entire peninsula and is based everywhere on personal research and patient visiting. It is illustrated by over 450 evocative photographs by Primrose Bell. A labour indeed, and also one of persistent love as each garden has had to be seen in season. Clearly, it rests on years of travel to gardens all over Italy, so many of which have eluded foreign visitors. It will shape my travels for years to come. Kirsty McLeod is an accomplished author who writes, as usual, with style and elegance, drawing us in to the long histories of each garden but never daunting us with too much fact for the sake of telling all she knows. This book does not only fill a gap. It opens a panorama of gardens which are unknown to outsiders and it will remain invaluable long after publication. It is a milestone in the study of the subject.

Of course the set-pieces are all here, whether the Villa Lante at Bagnaia or the water gardens of Tivoli's Villa d'Este. Even in these much-studied sites this book follows an informed, perceptive line which is not to be extracted from glossy guides on sale at the gate. Entry after entry confronts us with the extraordinarily long history to which Italian gardens are heirs, whether at Rome's Villa Madama, where Raphael's new awareness of the younger Pliny's ancient letter about his garden was so important for the design, or at outlying sites, unknown to me before, like the Castello di Grazzano Visconti near Piacenza, where the 'high-walled, four-square keep contained within battlemented towers and surrounded by a defensive moat' goes back to the fourteenth century, long before its first major restoration in 1910. Since 2005, the present Visconti owners have been busily replanting and redesigning, while opening their historic home to visitors.

The most fascinating aspect of this book is its eye-opening awareness of all the gardening and restyling which Italian owners have undertaken during the past twenty years. The old books of Platt, Wharton and even Masson gave an impression of a classic tradition in Italy whose formal gardens were slumbering in isolation while nothing much was happening around them. This book shows that the story never stops. Garden lovers and visitors need to attend carefully to all it has to say about initiatives of recent years.

At Santa Maria in Portella near Todi, there are spectacular roses nowadays among the olive trees and at La Ferriera in the Maremma, wonderful roses are followed by magnificent drifts of blue agapanthus. In the 1990s the garden at La Pescigola in Tuscany was covered in brambles and known locally as the Sleeping Beauty. Since 2000 the owners have been planting lavishly, beginning with a birthday present of thirty thousand daffodils in four hundred varieties, many of which are rare and ignored elsewhere. Primroses and violets are the new spring glory of a place which Kirsty McLeod describes as having an approach drive which 'must be one of the most beautiful anywhere'. I cannot wait to see it again.

Between the Arno and the heights of San Miniato, the Bardini garden in Florence is on ground with a history of cultivation throughout seven centuries. Since 2000 it has had a transformative replanting and rearrangement. Now, more than sixty fine varieties of hydrangea brighten up the summer and there are big groups of such English favourites as *Campanula persicifolia* 'Chettle Charm'. Over in the Marches, the fascinating Borgo Storico Seghetti Panichi has also taken on a new life. The great plantings here were the work of the famous German botanist and architect Ludwig Winter in 1875. Much of his framework survives and has been given new life by two keen family members, Giulia Panichi Pignatelli and her daughter Stefania, heads of the recent garden conservation society for the Marches. They have introduced 'bioenergetic' planting, with therapeutic effects reflected in their skincare products. The energy flows into their gardening. At the Castello di Vasanello near Viterbo the severe castle dates back to 1285 but the latest owner, the archaeologist Elena Misciatelli, has been restoring the overgrown garden for the past seven years. She, too, is a keen herb-grower and has introduced a neat plan based on an ancient map for St Gall, a Benedictine monastery, in AD 795. She began by seeking repose in the garden 'to refresh me and give me strength for the rest' but it looks to me as if her lovely plantings have been her occupational therapy instead.

Down in Sicily the garden at Il Biviere has been justly praised, the personal creation of Miki Borghese, one of Italy's most thoughtful plantswomen. On the bleakest of sites she has made a great garden round her world-wide choice of architectural plants. Kirsty McLeod and Primrose Bell have been there, of course, but they have also penetrated Puglia in search of other spiky garden planting in the hottest of zones. No other guide to Italy ever looks so far or so closely at the south.

Not long ago a dear Italian friend came for the weekend in summer and picked and arranged my flowers. When I asked her to stay longer, 'Only animals', she told me, 'live in the country.' This book shows how wrong she is. In Italy there are far more gardens and gardeners than she ever imagined and not all of them are within earshot of an urban café.

Map of Italy

LOMBARDY
Villa Cicogna Mozzoni
Giardino della Villa Bagatti Valsecchi
Villa del Balbianello
Villa d'Este
Villa Carlotta
Villa Melzi d'Eril
Il Pizzo
Villa Cipressi
Giardino di Villa Monastero
Villa Sommi Picenardi
Villa Borromeo Visconti Litta
Giardino Botanico André Heller
Isola del Garda
I Giardini di Limoni

TRENTINO
Castel Trauttmansdorff
Parco nell'Ombra del Paradeis

FRIULI
Castello di Duino
Castello di Miramare

VENETO
Giardino di Pojega a Villa Rizzardi
Villa Arvedi
Parco Giardino Sigurta
Giardino Giusti
Villa da Schio
Villa Trissino Marzotto
Ca' Marcello
Orto Botanico di Padova
Villa Nazionale Pisani
Villa Barbarigo-Pizzoni Ardemani
Villa Emo

PIEDMONT
Castello di Agliè
Villa Rossi
Castello di Pralormo
Giardino di Villa San Remigio
Ente Giardini Botanici di Villa Taranto
Isola Bella
Isola Madre
Giardino Botanico Alpinia

EMILIA ROMAGNA
Castello di Grazzano Visconti

LE MARCHE
Villa Giardino Buonaccorsi
Giardino Sgariglia
Borgo Storico Seghetti Panichi

UMBRIA
Il Giadorto
Villa Aureli
Orto e Giardino di Barbanera
Santa Maria in Portella

LIGURIA
La Mortola: Giardini Botanici Hanbury
Villa Boccanegra: Giardino Piacenza
Villa Gavotti della Rovere
La Cervara

PUGLIA
La Cutura

TUSCANY
La Pescigola
Villa Grabau
Villa Oliva-Buonvisi
Il Giardino di Palazzo Pfanner
Villa Bernardini
Parco Villa Reale di Camigliano
Villa Torrigiani di Camigliano
Villa Massei
Giardini di Agrumi e Orti Urbani di Buggiano Castello
Storico Giardino Garzoni
Giardino di Boboli
Giardino Bardini
Giardino Torrigiani
Giardino di Palazzo Corsini al Prato
Villa Capponi
Giardino dell'Iris
Villa Le Balze
Villa La Pietra
Villa Peyron al Bosco di Fontelucente
Giardini di Villa Gamberaia
Villa I Tatti
Villa della Petraia
Villa Medicea di Castello
Villa Guicciardini Corsi Salviati
Poggio Torselli
Vignamaggio
Giardino di Bibbiani
L' Apparita
Badia a Coltibuono
Castello di Brolio
Castello di Celsa
Villa di Geggiano
Il Bosco della Ragnaia
La Foce
Valle Pinciole
Giardini di Villa Cetinale
La Porrona
Il Giardino di Orlando
Il Giardino Corsini: Orto Botanico della Casa Bianca
La Ferriera

LAZIO
Castello Ruspoli-Vignanello
Sacro Bosco di Bomarzo
Palazzo Farnese di Caprarola
Villa Lante
Giardino del Castello Orsini di Vasanello
Palazzo Patrizi
Il Palazzo del Quirinale
Giardini Vaticani
Villa Giulia
Villa Madama
Villa Medici
Villa Wolkonsky
San Liberato
Villa d'Este a Tivoli
Parco Villa Gregoriana
Parco di Villa Belvedere Aldobrandini
Giardini di Castel Gandolfo
Giardini della Landriana
Il Giardino di Ninfa
Il Giardino di Torrecchia Vecchia

CAMPANIA
Parco della Reggia di Caserta
Giardino dei Duchi Guevara di Bovino
Il Chiostro di Santa Chiara
La Mortella
Villa San Michele
Villa Cimbrone
Villa Rufolo

SICILY
Orto Botanico di Palermo e Villa Giulia
Giardino della Kolymbetra
Giardino di Villa Trinità
Il Giardino del Biviere: Villa Borghese
San Domenico
Racalia

VALLE D'AOSTA

TRENTINO

FRIULI

LOMBARDY

VENETO

MILAN

VENICE

TURIN

PIEDMONT

GENOA

EMILIA ROMAGNA

LIGURIA

FLORENCE

TUSCANY

LE MARCHE

UMBRIA

ABRUZZO

ROME

LAZIO

MOLISE

CAMPANIA

NAPLES

PUGLIA

BASILICATA

CALABRIA

SICILY

PIEDMONT

Piedmont – from *ad pedem montium*, meaning 'at the foot of the mountains' – is one of the most northerly regions of Italy. It is a land of lakes and mountains, good food, truffles and award-winning wines. The Alps rear along its border, home to national parks which boast many rare species of mountain flowers. The ancient pilgrims' route from Canterbury to Rome also passed through Piedmont along the Valley of the Abbeys. The region has no coastline but includes the western shore of Lake Maggiore, with many famous gardens containing exotics which flourish in the lake's microclimate.

Piedmont was part of the ancient territory of Savoy, whose ruling house was to provide the Kings of Italy after Unification. The region's great gardens naturally reflected a French influence. Their wide tree-lined avenues, parterres of *broderie* and orange trees in Versailles planters were typically French, as was the vastness and monumentality of their structure. These qualities were perhaps less suited to northern Italy's terrain than to the flat, forested lands of France.

Piedmont's capital, Turin, ringed by a picturesque amphitheatre of snow-capped peaks, sees itself still as a gateway between northern and southern Europe.

Castello di Agliè

The magnificent Castello di Agliè was built around the nucleus of a medieval castle owned by the San Martino di Agliè family. Between 1642 and 1667 Filippo di San Martino di Agliè, a classical scholar and student of architecture, astronomy and mathematics, transformed his family's rugged fortress and laid out the garden on the three levels we see today. After his death in 1667 all work stopped. Filippo not only studied architecture, which made him well qualified to undertake these renovations, but also began the works at a time when architecture and gardens were beginning to be seen as a metaphor for power, something this gifted polymath clearly understood. A 1682 engraving from the two-volume *Theatrum Sabaudiae*, a celebration of the Savoy state, shows a grand residence much like what is here today, encircled by magnificent formal Italian gardens, each centred on a pool surrounded by an intricate parterre. The garden was linked to the castle on various levels by staircases and doors. It boasted massive walls and a virtuoso display of terraces, balustrades, colonnades, vaulted arches and suspended hanging gardens as well as the more usual statues, pools and fountains. Little of the seventeenth-century garden remains, although the terraced structure has survived.

On the grand south façade of the castle a symmetrical double staircase leads down to a circular pool. In the seventeenth century this pool dominated a formal garden and was surrounded by clipped trees. Transformed into an English garden in the nineteenth century, it now has an air of forgotten grandeur. A few massive trees – *Fagus sylvatica* 'Pendula', sequoia, cedars and *Magnolia grandiflora* – have the air of survivors in a diminished landscape.

The box parterre garden on the south-west side, though changed, is the only formal garden remaining from the seventeenth-century layout. A complex play of box hedging surrounds an elliptical pool. The brick wall supporting the overlooking hanging garden is pierced by a nymphaeum with a grotesque marble mask. A *Cycas revoluta* on the terrace above acts as a punctuation mark, and beyond the green treetops is a superb panorama of snowy peaks.

The terrace leading to the hanging garden contains a *limonaia* with a series of frescoed rooms, carefully restored. Birds soar in blue skies; turbaned Moors ride dolphins and sea creatures; herms hold up arches; urns, birdcages and flower baskets appear among painted trelliswork. The last and largest room is kept cool and airy with colonnades of columns and an interior fountain. Doors open on to a *giardino pensile* (hanging garden), where lemons and potted cycads stand against the seventeenth-century marble balustrade. Wisteria and Banksian roses clothe the castle walls, and in the corner a graceful dovecote in faded brick frames the superb view to the Gran Paradiso peak and the Graian Alps.

In 1765 Carlo Emmanuele III of Savoy gave the castle to Benedetto Maria Maurizio, the youngest and favourite of his ten children. A second stage of transformation now began to make the castle fit for a ducal summer residence. Ignazio Birago di Borgaro refurbished the building and created a great square connecting the castle to the village (1766–77). Michel Benard transformed the layout around the existing seventeenth-century central

Page 11 Overlooking Lake Maggiore from Isola Bella.
Right, above The south front of Castello di Agliè across the circular pool.
Right, below The box parterre beneath the *giardino pensile*.

axis into a grander eighteenth-century formal design with extensive vistas towards the surrounding landscape, and created the Fountain of the Four Rivers to replace what had been a simple semicircular pool. This monumental horseshoe-shaped fountain, sculpted by the Collino brothers and containing gods and sea creatures, is now cut adrift by the nineteenth-century road that divides the park. The road (1881) gave access to the great square linking the castle to the village, at the cost of cutting through the park: the two parts are connected by an underpass.

The park was redesigned again in 1830–40, supposedly by Xavier Kurten, gardener to the court of Savoy. Rigid formality was abandoned in favour of woods, clearings and winding paths. Rustic bridges spanned canals, and cottages decorated islands in ornamental lakes. The romantic repertoire extended well beyond the garden to the rest of the estate.

The condition of the park declined during the early twentieth century. Canals and fountains became clogged; trees were felled. After the Second World War, the castle passed from the royal house of Savoy into the ownership of the state. Restoration was delayed until the 1980s. The pleasure grounds are now a peaceful place to walk, with the sound of running water accompanying the path, past a mill and through woods of evergreen and deciduous trees. A great meadow opens out behind the fountain. There is the feeling of a vanished world, a world of bewigged dukes and extravagantly coiffed, beribboned ladies, with an accompanying sense of gentle melancholy.

Left, above The restored frescoed *limonaia*.
Left, below Arched windows lead out to the *giardino pensile*.
Right, above The Fountain of the Four Rivers, sculpted by the Collino brothers.

Villa Rossi

On the outskirts of Venaria Reale and with a view over an amphitheatre of Alpine peaks, eighteenth-century Villa Rossi was originally the house of the Superintendent of the Royal Palace. In the nineteenth century it came into the ownership of the Rossi di Montelera, the distinguished Torinese family who went on to found the Martini & Rossi drinks company. When the present owner inherited the estate from his grandparents, the property had been abandoned for twenty years. Young, knowledgeable and energetic, he immediately began a programme of renovation, far-sightedly restoring the garden at the same time as rescuing the house.

As was the Italian custom, the nineteenth-century Rossi lived mostly in nearby Turin, using the villa for day visits or as a retreat in the heat of summer. The carriages in which they bowled back and forth still sit in one of the outlying barns, one fitted with a box to carry plants back to the family's town house. Arriving at the villa, the carriages would have drawn to a halt in the grand central courtyard. This courtyard, now beautifully restored, exemplifies the care and attention to detail found throughout Villa Rossi. Garden designer Peter Curzon has re-cobbled the courtyard in a series of interlocking squares. Big, square Versailles planters hold tall *Malus* 'Red Sentinel' and swelling domes of osmanthus, rather than the usual box and bay. Beside the front door *Hydrangea aspera* subsp. *sargentiana* and *Hosta* 'Halcyon' are crammed together in huge tubs.

Faced with a tangle of approach roads to the courtyard, Peter Curzon simplified and formalized the layout with a circle leading to an elegant gravelled exedra. Scalloped bowls from Haddonstone stand in front of the exedra's hornbeam hedge: they contain *Cornus alba* 'Sibirica', another example of imaginative planting. The statues of the Four Seasons which outline the circle were bought recently by the owner to replace others stolen during the long years of abandonment.

Inevitably after such neglect, Peter Curzon's first task was to thin out the trees, creating a green framework for the garden, which gives just the right amount of dappled shade. Through the trees, avenues lead off towards views of distant mountains, or, closer to hand, to a new eye-catcher – a copper obelisk made at the villa.

The lake, re-excavated, extended and bordered with stones, is surrounded by agapanthus, daylilies and drifts of liriope and lily-of-the-valley. In spring, branches of white spirea brush the surface of the water, where white waterlilies are planned. On the newly created island young oaks have been planted and a classically pillared and pedimented duck house awaits new occupants. A copper-roofed boathouse, also made at the villa, is supported on chestnut beams. Beside the lake an aviary with heatable nesting boxes has been designed to house ornamental fowl. Through it flows one of the many rills in the garden, this one designed to keep the birds' drinking water clean. Originally, underground channels criss-crossed the garden, bringing water from the mountains to the fields. Destroyed by tree roots, these channels have been reinstated as pebble-lined streams. From the lake, water is pumped in a closed system to feed a rocky cascade in the woods. This has also been restored, its grottoes re-excavated and its precarious pile of giant boulders carefully replaced.

The south-facing façade of the villa is sheltered by two *Magnolia grandiflora*, which cast shade over the side beds. In one, *Bergenia* 'Silberlicht' grows with camassias and *Spiraea prunifolia* in a colour scheme of blue, white and pink. Camellias and hydrangeas populate the other, shadier side, where winter jasmine (*J. nudiflorum*) flourishes against the wall and deciduous *Ceanothus* 'Gloire de Versailles' manages to survive the harsh winters. On this sunnier side of the garden Peter Curzon has made full use of *Rosa* × *odorata* 'Mutabilis', which flowers valiantly throughout the

intense summer heat. Other roses tend to stop flowering in July and begin again with the cooler weather in September.

A balustraded double staircase set with urns leads down to a swimming pool set in a grassy terrace. A line of fastigiate hornbeams and, to the side, a fine stand of horse chestnuts frame the view over the town to the magnificent peaks. Paulownias and *Styphnolobium japonicum* (syn. *Sophora japonica*) relish the strong sunlight, while a grotto in the staircase wall offers a cool, watery retreat. The lowest terrace, the newest extension to the garden, has been designed as an ornamental orchard to replace the hillside with fruit trees which once was here. Original and witty touches

include espaliered quince and jujube on the retaining wall, and cherry and thornless blackberry espaliered along a fence. Two classical gazebos are topped with zinc silhouettes of Zephyr and Flora, once again designed and made at the villa.

This gentle and sensitive reawakening of an historic garden is the result of enthusiastic teamwork on the part of the two gardeners, informed by Peter Curzon's botanical knowledge and inspired by the young owner's input and affection for his family home. Plans are afoot to develop the second courtyard opening off the first and develop more gardens around it, taking advantage of the sublime view over green treetops to the snow-capped Alps.

Far left The re-excavated lake is surrounded by the sword-like leaves of agapanthus and daylilies. An elegant duck house has been placed on the newly created island.
Left A balustraded double staircase leads down to the swimming pool set in a grassy terrace.
Above Looking up to the villa with its enclosed terraced garden.

Castello di Pralormo

Fifty thousand bulbs are planted each October round the ancient, rosy-brick castle of the Counts of Pralormo, which since the thirteenth century has looked across from its hilltop towards Monte Rosa, Monte Bianco and a glittering horizon of Alpine peaks. Countess Consolata di Pralormo began the tradition of bulb planting ten years ago after holidaying in Keukenhof in Holland. Each spring since she has revisited the Dutch bulb fields to choose new and unusual tulips, as well as hyacinths and muscari, to plant under the cedars, limes and holm oaks of Xavier Kurten's romantic English park. Kurten, a Prussian botanist and architect, was the Director of the Gardens of the court of Savoy. Brought in during the nineteenth-century transformation of the castle into a grand country house, Kurten placed trees to reveal fine views of the peaks, laid out the winding paths and planted the magnificent cedars, Atlas, deodar and cedar of Lebanon, which still frame the castle.

Each year, the countess presents last year's tulip bulbs to the villagers of Pralormo, several of whom come in to help with ten days of intensive bulb planting. The result of all this hard work is Messer Tulipano, a spring festival unique in Italy, dedicated to the tulip in all its glorious variety – single, Lily-flowered, Viridiflora, Parrot tulips, multi-flowered tulips, double peony tulips, fringed and species.

The countess has a sure eye for unusual colour contrasts, blending reds, purples and pinks successfully. Sultry 'Queen of Night' glows against ivory and fuchsia-pink, goblet-shaped 'Marilyn'; pale violet tulips are set off by the deep red flowers of 'Contessa di Pralormo'. The colour schemes, new each year, are carefully designed to fit in with flowering dates. Early flowering cream tulips in March may be followed by the purple and cream-streaked blooms of 'Shirley'. Then both may be trumped by the Single Late doge-purple 'Recreado'.

The tulip beds curve in sinuous sweeps under the trees, edged by wavy ribbons of blue muscari or purple violas. Narcissi light up the undergrowth and throughout April, lilacs and 100-year-old pink tree peonies, 'Duchesse de Morny' – planted to remind a homesick Pralormo bride of her home in Nice – blossom luxuriantly. In summer, martagon lilies colonize the woods.

Accompanying the tulip festival is a multitude of stalls set up in the stables and selling seeds, herbs, honey and natural products. The path to the stable courtyard passes the pretty Olive Garden, enclosed by a living-willow lattice fence. Its olive trees are encircled by white daisies and around the central pool pots of daisies mingle with tulips of the palest pink. Two years ago the castle, too, opened to the public, showing off its ancient kitchen and the embroidered covers for which Piedmont castles are famous. Replacing silk, these embroidered cottons date back to the early seventeenth century, each great house boasting its own design.

Sixty thousand people now visit Pralormo annually, most between the end of March and the beginning of May, to see this spectacle, described as 'a living catalogue of tulips'. The festival's huge success is a tribute to Contessa Consolata's energy and commitment. Now, having found drawings inside the castle which point to the existence of a green theatre here, she has plans to restore it.

Right, above A newly introduced tulip.
Right, below Drifts of tulips spread under the trees as far as the eye can see.

Giardino di Villa San Remigio

Villa San Remigio has a dream-like quality. History has stopped here, and the world created by its remarkable owners is slowly dying. Their vision – the vision of a musician married to a painter – was to make a garden on the most beautiful corner of the lake: 'a dream that we shared during our youth, planned during our adolescence, and carried out when we got married'. Their garden, despite its columns and terraces, its statues and mosaic-tiled niches, is no classical Italian garden, or even a reconstruction of one. This is a northerner's dream of what Italy should be, a fantastical and quixotic reinterpretation where theatricality reigns, scalloped shell seats and basins abound, goddesses drive shell chariots through fountain pools, and the different garden rooms are themed according to moods – melancholy, happiness, love, memories. There is even a Garden of Sighs, where hypericum grows to take away low spirits.

The story behind Villa San Remigio is as romantic as the garden itself. In 1860 a British diplomat, Peter Browne, came to the Castagnola hill in search of land, preferably a natural ledge above the lake, on which to build a summer house. The hill, as its name suggests, was completely covered by chestnuts, but he managed to reach the top, where he could enjoy the astounding views. Here, on 8 hectares/20 acres, he built a simple Swiss chalet which became the summer home of the Brownes. For ten years their only neighbours were a family of Neapolitan nobility, the Marchesi della Valle di Casanova, who had built a house alongside the twelfth-century Romanesque church. The families became close: one generation intermarried; and in the next, Silvio and Sophie, first cousins and inseparable childhood companions, fell in love.

Below and right Terraces dotted with columns, statues, urns and shell seats ascend the hill towards the villa.

They married in 1896, by then both well into their thirties, after years of parental opposition on the grounds of their close blood tie. It was 1903 when Silvio and Sophie transformed the modest chalet into a palatial residence, and 1905 when they began work on the magnificent terraces that form the backbone of the garden. Almost from its completion the garden was open to the public.

From the bottom of the slope near the entrance lodge there is splendid vista of these terraces, crowned with statues and wound about with billowing mounds of *Rosa banksiae*, ascending the hill up to the house. At the foot of the steps, the first garden, the Garden of Melancholy, is planted sombrely with evergreens. Still pools reflect the dark shapes of conifers and camphor trees. Box topiary and domes of *Osmanthus heterophyllus* surround a mosaic nymphaeum with a statue of Hercules.

The curved sweeping steps leading to the next terrace signify a change of mood. In the centre Venus rides her shell chariot. Around her, *broderie* outlined in box are filled with pink roses and bright summer flowers. A splendid *Cryptomeria japonica* overhangs one side.

A sundial marks the centre of the third terrace, the Terrace of the Hours. To the front, life-sized on the balustrade, stand Orazio Marinali's baroque statues of Roman gods. At the back, behind a tamarisk and unusual palms, is the Winter Garden, carved like a grotto out of the rock. A stream runs

through it and ferns luxuriate in the moist shade. Remarkably, a mineral in the rocks has turned *Begonia rex* an extraordinary vivid blue.

On another slope, the sentimental Garden of Sighs celebrates love in a baroque medley of love knots and 'flames' of love, picked out in mosaic in a curved exedra with statues in niches, reminiscent of the semicircle at Villa Aldobrandini (see page 205). Represented in medallions here, Silvio and Sophie did indeed lead a charmed life, she painting in her studio, he a pupil of Liszt. Together they entertained poets and painters, took nostalgic walks in their English woods and oversaw a workforce of sixty gardeners ready to implement their most ambitious plans.

Young as they were, the couple planned for their creation to last. Sadly, this did not happen. The grand terraces are crumbling now, the balustrades collapsing, the shell seats cracked, the steps eroding away. It all adds to an enjoyable air of ghostly romance and gentle, melancholic decay.

Below Venus rides her shell chariot across a pool.

Ente Giardini Botanici di Villa Taranto

LAKE MAGGIORE, PIEDMONT

Left High mountains provide a backdrop for the garden.

In his 1954 book *The Villa Taranto: A Scotsman's Garden in Italy*, published by *Country Life*, Captain Neil McEacharn told the story of how he came to buy Villa Taranto. Returning by train from Venice to England, he read in *The Times* an advertisement for a villa for sale on Lake Maggiore. Promptly abandoning his sleeping berth, he jumped off the train when it came to a stop at Pallanza. He never looked back. What appealed to him were not only the villa's position but the opportunity to buy adjoining land. Villa Taranto would end up with 40.5 hectares/100 acres, with 8 kilometres/5 miles of roadway and another 8 kilometres/5 miles of dry-stone walls.

It is to Charles Quest-Ritson and his book *The English Garden Abroad* that we owe most of what we know about this rich and determined man, who was driven by the desire to make a statement with his garden. 'As some men might spend their money on racing stables,' he wrote, 'or other costly sports, I have made these gardens my occupation and my adventure.'

The Villa Taranto garden is on the north side of Lake Maggiore, 32 kilometres/20 miles from the Swiss border, at an altitude of 305 metres/1,000 feet and with high mountains all around. The temperature here varies greatly – from heavy and lasting winter snowfalls to summer heat reaching 35°C/95°F in the shade. Rainfall is high at over 230 centimetres/90 inches, falling mostly in the spring and autumn.

In these surroundings and conditions, McEacharn set out to recreate the natural woodland garden of his Scottish childhood. Although Villa Taranto was next door to San Remigio (see page 17), with a garden gate between them to which both owners had a key, McEacharn was not an admirer of Italian formality. Italian gardens, he considered, lacked colour: they had no green lawns and not enough flowers. Villa Taranto's original garden he had declared 'a horror, with badly designed Italian formal gardens and endless dreadful statues'. His first task, therefore, was to plant silver birches, bought in at 3.5 metres/12 feet high. In these birch woods, rhododendrons and azaleas would flourish, with masses of bluebells and primulas, followed by foxgloves and lily-of-the-valley.

Villa Taranto is best reached by boat: from Pallanza it is a ten-minute ride. One of the recommended times to visit is late April, when 80,000 tulips are in bloom against a flowering backdrop of rhododendrons, magnolias and azaleas.

The scale of Villa Taranto is extraordinary, as is its standard of upkeep. Sixteen gardeners keep it in perpetual perfection, with a special lawn kept in reserve as a resource for patching areas of grass gone brown. Besides the big set-pieces such as the Terraced Gardens and the Water Gardens, there are imaginative small corners – here a tree fern valley, there a hosta and hydrangea walk. In one of the most magical parts of the garden, dahlias are planted out, not in regimented straight lines but as the captain decreed, in the Dahlia Forest. The sensation of meandering along winding paths through a jungle of 350 different species and varieties of dahlia, including the towering *Dahlia imperialis*, is unique. The dahlias are planted out in mid-May: within the space of a week, they are all in. Near them is the Curiosity Border of unusual plants, including 5-metre/16-foot-high *Telanthophora grandifolia* (syn. *Senecio grandifolius*) and the bashful sensitive plant (*Mimosa pudica*), which folds its leaves inwards when touched. Near by in a small tank, floating roots and all, is *Pistia stratiotes*, often known as the water lettuce.

In the greenhouses is one of the garden's biggest crowd-pullers – a pool filled with the great floating saucers of *Victoria amazonica*, the giant Amazon waterlily. The largest of all aquatic plants, its leaves can reach 3 metres/10 feet across and are able to bear the weight of a small child. Like the slightly smaller *V. cruziana*, also grown here, its flowers open at dusk and during the course of the night turn from white into pink. They die after two or three days.

Planted near the greenhouses is the rare tree *Emmenopterys henryi* from China. Not often seen even now outside south-east Asia, these trees, which can live up to 1,000 years and reach 45 metres/147 feet in height, were first introduced to Europe in 1907. It was not until 1971 that the specimen here first flowered: it was the first flowering seen in Europe.

From the top of the steps near the serpentine Lotus Pond, you can see the vast expanse of the Terrace Gardens, with the modern water staircase surrounded by brilliant spring and summer bedding. The restful Blue Garden close by complements a view of far-off mountain peaks. Palms and banana palms grow in the middle distance.

In deliberate contrast to the public grandeur of the Terrace Gardens, Captain McEacharn created the Valletta, a romantic secret valley, spanned by a dry stone bridge and cut by the *scalpellini*, the stone-cutters who worked here by the hundred. Here grow plants that thrive on humidity and shade. Huge paulownias stand by the bridge; graceful, yellow *Caesalpinia pulcherrima* spreads its ferny branches; and in spring, *Davidia involucrata* waves its snowy white 'handkerchiefs' or bracts.

Charles Quest-Ritson describes Neil McEacharn as a gardener among botanists and a botanist among gardeners. Never happier than when in his nursery, he grew from seed or acclimatized thousands of plants. In his experimental beds, he fostered plants grown from seeds sent in from all over the world, 90 per cent of them, he claimed, never before grown in Italy. By the early 1950s the Seed Room in the *villetta* (which also housed Villa Taranto's reference library), contained more than 1,400 boxes of seeds. Especially tender plants would be overwintered in little houses, made by the captain's carpenters. Each spring, he would drive around the grounds in the small van he named the *giardinetta*, supervising the planting out of thousands of plants.

A passionate collector of plants, the captain was also generous with his finds, giving away seeds, cuttings and plants to public and private gardens and supplying the War Graves Commission. He had always intended his garden to be open to the public. Twenty years after the first plants went in, he offered it to the Italian state. Villa Taranto is now run by a private trust in which the province and the state are represented.

Villa Taranto receives 150,000 visitors a year but such is its scale that it is possible to stay off the beaten track on quiet paths wandering through fine specimens of trees. Among the groves of cornus, stewartia, sweet-smelling edgeworthia and thirty species of magnolia is an acer walk containing strawberry-red *A. palmatum* 'Captain McEacharn'. A datura bed and a bank of stately white *Cardiocrinum giganteum* are among other arresting sights.

Captain McEacharn is buried in a mausoleum in his garden. *Itea ilicifolia*, with its long pendant racemes of greenish-white flowers, weeps gently near by.

Top In a secluded corner of the garden a large pool holds aquatic plants.
Bottom The Valletta: a secret valley spanned by a dry-stone bridge.

Isola Bella

Left Parterres de broderie on the southern terrace, overlooking the waters of sunny Lake Maggiore.

This celebrated seventeenth-century island garden floats like a galleon on the waters of Lake Maggiore, its great pyramid of terraces rising at the southern end to mimic a vessel's flat-topped stern. That this effect was intended can be deduced from Marc'Antonio dal Re's early eighteenth-century engraving, which includes the never-completed north of the island, extended to form a pointed prow. As Georgina Masson points out, this print shows the garden as more or less bare, with a few trees planted to conceal the fact that the Borromeo palazzo was built off-centre to the main garden axis. However skilfully disguised, such irregularity was not a desirable effect in seventeenth-century garden design, but the uneven shape of the island meant that the imposing T-shaped palace is misaligned, occupying an asymmetrical position on Isola Bella's north-western corner. Yet so ingenious was architect Angelo Crivelli in disguising this that from the topmost terrace of the garden high above the lake there is the sensation of being at the helm of a stately craft sailing straight ahead, perhaps towards the Hesperides.

The garden was begun in 1631 and built over forty years. Neither Count Carlo Borromeo III, who commissioned it, nor the Milanese architect Crivelli, to whom he entrusted the design, lived to see its completion. Count Carlo was the nephew of the cardinal-saint Carlo Borromeo and husband to Isabella d'Adda, after whom the island – originally Isola Isabella – was named. To Crivelli, a relative unknown, fell the preliminary hard labour of levelling the rock and building massive vaults to support the terracing. Bishop Gilbert Burnet, who visited Isola Bella in 1685, reported that 'The whole Island is a garden . . . and because the figure of

the Island was not made regular by Nature they have built great Vaults and Portica's along the Rock . . . and so they have brought it into a regular form by laying earth over these Vaults.' Tons of this earth, as well as tufa, pink Baveno granite and enormous blocks of dressed stone, all had to be shipped in by boat. When Carlo III died, his son Vitaliano Borromeo took on the project, bringing in experts such as Carlo Fontana and the Milanese church architect Francesco Castelli. The garden's progress is chronicled by letters between Vitaliano and his brother Cardinal Giberto, who wrote anxiously from Rome about details such as the size of the statues.

To a certain extent, the lack of plants seen in dal Re's 1726 engraving of Isola Bella must reflect his own eighteenth-century taste. In 1663, Borromeo records tell us, 100 terracotta pots bearing the family crest were ordered for the garden, while citrus, box, cypress and, more unusually, elegant vegetable plots were planted. By 1739 when the Burgundian scholar and politician Charles de Brosses came, pots of flowers had appeared on the balustrades, while the terraces sported trellises hung with oranges, jasmine and pomegranates. Baedeker in 1882 noted the addition of cedars, magnolias, laurels, 'magnificent oleanders and other luxuriant products of the south', and by the time Edith Wharton visited at the turn of the century, every path, every balustrade, every stairway was wreathed in flowers. Today, the garden, one of the best kept in Italy, still guards a heritage of magnificent trees, including at the entrance a huge, ancient camphor tree (*Cinnamomum camphora*), partnered by the false camphor (*C. glanduliferum*). Without overwhelming the dramatic architecture, rare and tender plants crowd the lower terraces. A wall of

the unicorn, heraldic symbol of the Borromeo, which prances on the skyline. The granite and pebble-encrusted façade is studded with niches containing statues of gods and goddesses. Other niches are hung with enormous scallop shells. In the central niche a giant carved out of tufa pays homage to Verbano, while to each side, rows of pebbled pilasters are topped with *putti*, each in a different pose.

Flights of steps at each side lead up to the highest point on the island, a balustraded terrace 37 metres/121 feet above the lake. The topmost of ten rising terraces that narrow successively in a pyramidal shape, this unique and commanding viewing platform serves as the poop of Angelo Crivelli's imaginary galleon. Framed by urns, obelisks and allegorical figures, it is dominated by Carlo Simonetta's *putto* bearing the unlikely emblem 'Humilitas', the motto of the Borromeo family.

To the south of the platform, parterres of *broderie* can be seen, as the terraces, softened by oleander and decked with campsis and roses, descend gently towards the lake. Of the two hexagonal towers, now housing a café and bookshop, one was originally the pump-house for the reservoir concealed behind the water theatre.

camellias is underplanted with showy *Bletilla striata*; the sensitive plant (*Mimosa pudica*) is interestingly placed beside a path. Cannas and musa add their spiky exoticism, and tamarind, myrtles, mimosas and oleander bloom in lush profusion.

Six heavily mosaiced ornamental grottoes in the vaults beneath the palace lead out to the Courtyard of Diana, where twin staircases rising up to the garden level cleverly disguise the change of axis. Emerging on to a terrace shaded by camphor trees, where Isola Bella's famous white peacocks strut and swagger, you are drawn inexorably forwards by the sight of Carlo Fontana's fantastical water theatre. It is an extraordinary spectacle, its soaring height exaggerated by the plumed obelisks framing

Not everyone has fallen for Isola Bella's bravura theatricality. English visitors to the Borromean Islands tended to prefer Isole Madre (see page 23) with its lush planting and more natural, English landscaping. Dorothy Wordsworth, sister of the romantic poet, dismissed Isola Bella as 'the peak of absurdity, a garden not of flowers but of stone'. The painter William Brockedon thought it 'the extravagance of a rich man with the taste of a confectioner'. Even Baedeker considered it 'in questionable taste'. But these were views informed by nineteenth-century romanticism. The seventeenth century had more robust ideas about man's place in the cosmos. Not only were man's achievements glorious, but to celebrate them allowed for self-glorifying imagery; while to enjoy and revel in them required grandiose water features, and ever higher, more dizzyingly dramatic terracing. Gilbert Burnet, a well-travelled, well-educated man of his times, marvelled at Isola Bella, writing in the book he published in 1687 that 'perhaps the whole world has nothing like it'. Such praise ensured Isola Bella five-star billing among the Grand Tourists who followed him.

Above Mosaic ornamental grottoes beneath the palace lead out to the Courtyard of Diana.
Below Allegorical figures, obelisks and urns decorate Angelo Crivelli's ten steeply rising terraces.

Isola Madre

According to head gardener Gianfranco Giustina, there is a difference in temperature of four or five degrees Centigrade between Isola Bella and Isola Madre. 'Isola Bella is in the shade of a mountain,' he says. 'In winter at 2.30 or so the sun is gone, but on Isola Madre it shines all day.'

Because of this smiling climate and its relatively flat surfaces, Isola Madre was the first of the Borromean Islands to be settled, long before its more famous sister. In 1501 Lancellotti Borromeo built a simple house on top of a Roman fort: with its vines and orchards and hunting woods, the island was used as a larder for the family. By the mid-1500s the simple house had been rebuilt as a grand Renaissance villa. Leandro Alberti's survey of its 'agreeable garden' mentions 550 grape vines, 9 walnut and 4 fig trees as well as cherries, quince, apple and pomegranate. Oranges and lemons had been imported. John Evelyn, sailing past in 1646, praised 'walks set all about with Oranges and Citron trees'. These terraces can be clearly seen in a mid-eighteenth-century painting by Antonio Joli, before the nineteenth-century fashion for English ornamental parks swept them away.

John Evelyn credited 'the reflection from the Water' for 'rendring the place very warme', a theory Signor Giustina agrees with. 'Warmth rising from the lake enables us to combine the plants you would expect here – acers, magnolias, camellias, rhododendrons – with exotics like musa, bougainvillea, hibiscus and palms.'

Stepping off the boat on the southern side of the island, you walk straight down Viale Africa, with its casuarina, myrtles and mimosa trees. A wisteria pergola is laden with fragrant blossom in drooping clusters of white, purple, pink and violet. Many of the twenty-three different varieties were gifted by horticulturalist Sir Peter Smithers from his private botanic garden high above Lake Lugano: Sir Peter believed that the pleasure of owning a beautiful plant was not complete until it had been shared with friends. A camellia 'wall' includes plants dating back to the 1800s, introduced by the Rovelli brothers, who had a nursery at Pallanza. An 1845 catalogue they compiled about plants on the Borromean

Islands listed over five hundred varieties of camellia. The camellias begin flowering here in January.

Some of the oldest trees are on this side of the island, including *Taxodium distichum* and the once star attraction, a 200-year-old *Cupressus cashmeriana*, one of the most beautiful trees in Europe. Tragically, it toppled over in a recent storm, but the main root survived and so the gardeners have been able to train it upright again.

The Prato dei Gynerium (Pampas Grass Lawn) also has *Styrax japonicus*, tender *Magnolia macrophylla* and *Rhododendron auriculatum* with its dizzying almond smell and white flowers in mid-July. In a clearing, peacocks roam under two magnificent paulownias. Scots pines frame a view of Pallanza. A walk lined with gardenia hedging leads you down to the water through clouds of scent.

Autumn on Isola Madre burns with saffron, fiery crimson and gold, as the cornus, acers and *Ginkgo biloba* take centre stage. Before then, the island stages a lotus festival with forty exquisite lotuses displayed in pots, followed by a hibiscus festival on the front terrace near the house. Solanum, passiflora and bougainvillea compete to cover the villa. Tree ferns colonize the moat, and elephant's ears (*colocasia*) thrive in pots near cool water. The rare and showy *Franklinia alatamaha*, unknown in the wild, was brought back from the southern states of America in 1870. Also from here is the American snowdrop tree (*Halesia diptera*).

Such was the romance of this lush and exotic island that Flaubert (one of many famous visitors) imagined he could see 'a grave and gentle sultan appear from behind a bush with his . . . silk robe'. From the boat, on leaving, there is the arresting sight of the walls beneath the house cloaked in Madonna blue – agapanthus under swathes of ipomoea. For head gardener Gianfranco Giustina, this has been his kingdom for thirty years, a kingdom he shares with more than a hundred thousand annual visitors. Recently, the Borromeo family gave him charge of Isola Bella as well.

Above A white peacock roams the Prato dei Gynerium (Pampas Grass Lawn).
Left Isola Madre from the lake.

Giardino Botanico Alpinia

From the top of the twenty-minute cable-car ride from Stresa to Mottarone there is one of the most spectacular views in northern Italy: a 360-degree vista from the summit of Monte Rosa, over seven lakes, lying far below in a natural basin. Just as beautiful, though more intimate, is the view over Lake Maggiore and the Borromean Islands from halfway up. It is here, 300 metres/985 feet from the cable-car stop, that you will find the Alpinia Botanic Garden.

Basking in the sunshine on a natural balcony 800 metres/2,625 feet up, this delightful botanical garden specializes in species from the alpine and sub-alpine zone of the Alps, as well as some from the Caucasus, China and Japan – around a thousand species in all. Founded in 1934, it is still lovingly maintained, with neatly kept beds contained within rocky outcrops, fed by a natural spring. Hamid, the curator, lives on the spot and does all the work himself with one assistant.

The garden is a miniature paradise of gentians, helianthemums, aquilegias, primulas, saxifrages, heuchera, sedums, dianthus, alliums, thymes and *Alchemilla alpina*. These are adaptable plants: survivors, they have strong roots to bind themselves to the thin mountain soil, or they bend in the wind to withstand gales. Small fleshy or hairy leaves conserve water in high winds and hot sunlight. Dwarf, creeping growth habits enable them to withstand crushing by snow. There are plants with spreading root systems, which search out nutrients and moisture, and plants that, for protection, cover themselves with thorns or downy hair.

A winding path leads past a hut, with a map of the panorama of alpine peaks on the horizon, up to grassy slopes with azaleas, birches, larches and pines. Behind the garden is a pine forest. It is still up here, with a sensation of floating above the world.

Above and left
Beds of alpine plants contained within rocky outcrops.

LOMBARDY

The northern Italian region of Lombardy borders Switzerland. As well as its alpine north, Lombardy contains the 'smiling landscape' of the Italian lakes, blessed with their own much milder microclimate. It also comprises huge, flat plains – as if, fancied John Evelyn, 'Nature had here swept up the rubbish of the earth into the Alps to form and clear the Plains of Lombardy.'

Such varied geography and climate gave rise to differing styles of gardens, from the lemon groves and exotic gardens flourishing on the shores of the lakes, to sixteenth-century gardens reflecting the long reach and architectural influence of Renaissance Rome. Lombardy, close as it was to Italy's borders, felt the impact of changing fashions in the eighteenth and nineteenth centuries, when enthusiasm for 'English' parks and the new romantic landscape style swept away many much older gardens. Edith Wharton was one who mourned. 'The fury of modern horticulture,' she wrote in 1904, had 'swept over Lombardy like a tidal wave, obliterating terraces and grottoes, substituting winding paths for pleached alleys, and transforming level box parterres into rolling lawns . . .'

Villa Cicogna Mozzoni

The balustraded fishponds to one side of the parterre are not only decorative but were once stewponds holding fish for the household. The balustrades, says Count Jacopo, were originally terracotta. In the late eighteenth century, stone was substituted from the quarries at Viggiù. The tufa wall behind is decorated with busts and statues of Diana and Hercules dated 1701.

Set into the side of a steep hill, the garden is on three main levels, its proportions finely calculated. 'From every level of the house, you are looking out at a different garden,' Count Jacopo says. 'Axes run through the house; house and garden work miraculously well together.' The *piano nobile* opens on to a long terrace running along the rear of the villa. This terrace links the various areas of the garden both physically and visually, and offers views of the mountains and even, on a clear day, of Lake Lugano. At its centre, opposite the windows of the main salon, rises the garden's famous water staircase, probably of sixteenth-century origin. A hundred and fifty steps lead uphill on either side of a rill, which flows down past two reclining nymphs into a basin decorated with a mask. This, says Count Jacopo, is supposedly the devil capturing the water for the underworld.

The staircase is a minor masterpiece, perfectly proportioned for the scale of the garden. At its top, beyond the pavilion, lies an English romantic park with origins in the early nineteenth century. Towards the bottom, another terrace cut into the hillside contains mostly blue and white flowers – irises, Japanese anemones, *Phlox paniculata* 'Blue Paradise', *Aster* 'Little Carlow'. The planting is based on old photographs and the present Contessa Cicogna Mozzoni's memories.

Count Jacopo rents out greenhouses in exchange for work on the garden. Deeply attached to his ancestral family home, he greatly enjoys showing visitors around. 'I am nearly always here. This is my life.'

Frescoed inside and out, most notably in the loggias of the graceful courtyard, this exquisite hunting lodge has kept intact all its Renaissance character. In the fifteenth century the Mozzoni came to hunt bears and boar here in the wooded foothills of the Viggiù Alps. With them they brought illustrious guests, such as Galeazzo Maria Sforza, the powerful Duke of Milan. In 1476, contemporary chroniclers tell us, the young duke's life was saved by Agostino Mozzoni and one of his hunting dogs, who together diverted an attacking bear. The dog is immortalized in stone here at the villa. For the Mozzoni, the duke's lucky escape and his evident gratitude brought them privileges and tax exemptions, all of which made the family rich. Between 1530 and 1560 the hunting lodge was enlarged and given a Renaissance makeover by Ascanio Mozzoni, a cultivated scholar and poet who had visited Roman and Florentine villas and gardens. It was his daughter Angiola who married Giovanni Pietro Cicogna; their descendants still live here today. This long family continuity has helped to preserve Villa Cicogna Mozzoni virtually unchanged.

The house is in the shape of a classic 'U', its two arcaded arms reaching out to enclose a courtyard leading on to the Italian Garden. This allows for a typical Renaissance interplay between garden and house; this is further aided by frescoed trellises bearing fruit and flowers, which cover the ceilings and arches of the arcades. These intricate frescoes of vines, flowers and citrus fruits were painted around 1580 by the Campi brothers of Cremona. As Count Jacopo Cicogna Mozzoni points out, they incorporate the same vistas of mountains and lake as can be seen from various viewpoints in the property. Villa and garden flow into each other, with the balustrade of the Italian Garden reproduced in paint up the house's grand staircase, and the pavilion at the top of the water staircase embroidered on the state bed. In the loggias, some of the frescoes were discovered relatively recently, having been whitewashed as a barrier against infection when the villa served as a quarantine hospital during an outbreak of plague. In its colourful fecundity, the painted trellising recalls the swags of flowers and fruit in Raphael's loggia at Rome's Villa Farnesina, the work of his pupils Giulio Romano, and the countryman Giovanni da Udine.

Page 25 Villa del Balbianello from Lake Como.
Above, left Balustraded fishponds and parterres lead out from the arcaded courtyard of Villa Cicogna Mozzoni.
Below Frescoed trellises bearing fruit and flowers cover the ceilings and arches of the arcades.

Top Early eighteenth-century busts sit in niches in the tufa wall.
Bottom A stone fish swims in one of the balustraded fishponds.

Giardino della Villa Bagatti Valsecchi

LAKE COMO, LOMBARDY

The house is entered from the lovely Piazza Comunale with its *graffito* decoration and inscribed exhortation to the vistor to 'rest a while in beautiful Cardano'. The Bagatti family inherited it when a relative, the last Baron Galbiati, died childless in 1896. The present owner, Baron Pier Fausto Bagatti Valsecchi, is an architect with a great enthusiasm for houses and gardens. His grandparents added on to the house – another storey, two loggias and a tower; their reason is self-explanatory when you walk through the house to its other side.

Here is a romantic landscape straight out of a painting: 366 metres/1,200 feet up and hanging over a deep ravine, the house looks across at woods of larch, pine and fir, backed by high, jagged peaks. A bridge crosses the dizzying drop of the ravine to a 15-hectare/37-acre arboretum park, which Baron Galbiati 'improved' in the nineteenth century by cutting down chestnut trees and planting conifers, in order to evoke the scenery of the high mountains. Other members of his family devised the romantic scheme, adding a bridge over the rushing stream, and woodland paths up to a belvedere looking out

over Lake Como. A tunnel was cut through the rock from which to admire the waterfalls. The park reflects the nineteenth-century liking for tamed wilderness with just a frisson of the wild. Expeditions were mounted here, and tea in the woods, says the present Baron, 'was a ceremonial affair'.

The Old Garden, near the house, was embellished by the Baron's father, Pasino Bagatti Valsecchi, a former president of the Lombard Horticultural Society, who took out a formal pool and fountain, and naturalized the space with rocks. He planted *Cedrus deodara* and maples, with cotoneaster and *Chamaecyparis obtusa* 'Nana' and 'Crippsii' down the ravine. This vertical rock garden, fenced off for safety, is tended by men on ropes.

The New Garden, designed on a neighbouring slope by the baron's father, was added to bit by bit, as gradually more land became available. Reached by steps from the loggia, it is terraced in the manner of the local agriculture near by. The first level, a meadow, has an English border designed to flower in August and September, the bright flowers in striking contrast to the dark woods behind.

The levels are linked by La Scala Fiorita (The Flowering Stairway), from whose stone walls spill achillea, phlox and lavender, with santolina and other sun-loving silver plants. Helianthemums, verbena, catmint and sedums spring up, among an array of colourful annuals.

On the very top level, shaped like a ship's prow, is a conifer bed among rocks brought from Lake Como. Three cypresses stand on the summit and the view stretches along a line of mountain peaks all the way to Switzerland.

Above The romantic garden hangs over a deep ravine falling away from the house.

Villa del Balbianello

Villa del Balbianello occupies the most idyllic position on all of Lake Como. Its wooded peninsula juts out into the water almost opposite Bellagio, with breathtaking views up and down the lake in both directions. The panorama is best enjoyed from the open loggia built at the highest point by a discerning eighteenth-century cardinal. Dosso di Lavedo, as Balbianello's rugged promontory is known, was to become a favourite subject for romantic artists, who loved to paint the villa perched on top of its sheer, rocky outcrop, with the snowy peaks of the Engadine shimmering far away across the water. Stendhal took a boat trip that passed in front of Balbianello, and greatly admired the scenery, which reminded him of Scotland.

It was Cardinal Angelo Durini in 1787 who saw the potential of Dosso di Lavedo, after he had failed to buy the small, wooded isle of Comacina, the only island on the lake. The cardinal, a cultivated and worldly prelate who had enjoyed a prestigious diplomatic career, was looking for a retreat where he could read, think and spend time in the company of learned friends. The quotation he borrowed from the sixteenth-century satirist Rabelais, 'Fay ce que voudras' (Do as you please), which greeted guests arriving at the portico of the stone-walled harbour, epitomized the cardinal's attitude to his retirement.

Today, as Cardinal Durini's eighteenth-century visitors did, you reach the villa, rather romantically, by boat from Lenno, arriving at a landing stage marked by four gaily painted red- and white-striped Venetian poles. As the boat rounds the promontory, the villa is in full view, gracefully descending the cliff on three levels. The lowest level, close to the little harbour, incorporates the remains of a thirteenth-century convent. Its two slender bell towers, left in place by Cardinal Durini, along with the church's façade, still point the way towards heaven. At the topmost level, flanking the airy loggia, are two rooms, a library and a music room, where the cardinal entertained.

Villa del Balbianello's garden is on difficult terrain with cold winds sweeping down the lake from the north and little cultivable soil. There is not enough space on this rocky headland for grand parterres, nor for the kind of 'English' romantic landscape that swept them away. Despite all of this, the headland appears green. In a clever play on the formality of Italian gardens, the plants – bay laurel, box, ilex, ivy, *Ficus pumila* – are clipped, pruned and trained with meticulous precision into green architecture. Even on the precipitous cliffs, box and bay laurel are shaped by hand into umbrellas, drums and globes. Regular hand-clipping has transformed mature bay laurels into a green carpet, and there are ivy garlands strung

even along the rocks. This topiary, carried out with skill and daring by gardeners propping up their ladders against the cliff face to work in the most inaccessible of places, gives Villa del Balbianello a sense of intimacy in contrast to its expansive views.

The garden evolved like this as a result of one twentieth-century owner's desire to have uninterrupted views of the lake. Except for Cardinal Durini, Count Guido Monzino was perhaps Villa del Balbianello's most famous resident. The count was an explorer and alpinist, with expeditions to the North Pole and Everest to his credit. During the 1970s, he scrupulously restored the villa, added a collection of important furniture and objets d'art, and created inside the house a museum of exploration and mountaineering which includes his dog sled from the journey to the North Pole and remarkable Eskimo carvings. Here, too, is Monzino's collection of books about mountaineering and polar expeditions – one of the best to be found anywhere.

To Cardinal Durini's garden Count Monzino brought a fresh, modern touch, characterized by crisp, innovative topiary. The path up from the landing stage leads past candelabra-pruned plane trees with ivy necklets. Roman statues stand in between the trees against a backdrop of well-tended lawns edged by impeccably clipped box and laurel. Colour is used sparingly in this garden, which is mostly limited to many differing shades of green. From a sunny, south-facing viewing platform shaded by pines, Isola Comacina can be seen across an expanse of clear blue water. Sheer cliffs, wooded on top, plunge down into the lake, and swans patrol the shoreline. At the top of the slope, the caretaker, Signor Antonio, lives in a little house surrounded by statues and cypresses between two of the very best views in the world.

The open-sided loggia, now used for exhibitions, has *Ficus pumila* trained up its pillars and coiled along its ochre-coloured walls. The ficus is said to be over a hundred years old. The serpent, emblem of the Visconti family, on the loggia's coat of arms recalls their purchase of Balbianello from Cardinal Durini's nephew and heir. The orientalist and scholar Giammartino Visconti was responsible for the fine ornamental balustrades that enclose the garden's terraces. On the north terrace's balustrade stands the much-photographed statue of Diana, her back with its quiver of arrows turned towards the villa, her gaze fastened on the snow-capped mountains mirrored in the lake. The great holm oak on the grassy terrace behind her was first pruned into a hemisphere on the instructions of Monzino, who wanted the view from his study to the headland of Bellagio unimpeded by foliage. He requested that the tree's shape be preserved when, in 1988, he left Villa del Balbianello with all its land and art collections to FAI (Fondo per L'Ambiente Italiano), the Italian equivalent of the National Trust. FAI has looked after the villa and its garden immaculately ever since. Guido Monzino himself is buried in an ice cave that was carved out of rocks in the garden.

Page 29 The villa perched on its rocky outcrop jutting out into Lake Como.
Above Paths wind through candelabra-pruned plane trees.
Left The open-sided loggia with *Ficus pumila* trained up the pillars offers views of the lake on both sides.

Villa d'Este

The villa, now a famous hotel, overlooking Lake Como, was built in 1568 by Tolomeo Gallio, the son of a local family, who rose to the giddy heights of Cardinal and Papal Secretary of State under Pope Gregory XIII. This was his summer residence. It has only been known as Villa d'Este since 1815, when Caroline of Brunswick, the estranged wife of the Prince Regent (later George IV), settled here in a scandalous exile. To bolster a distant connection with a d'Este ancestor she shared with her husband, Caroline renamed the villa.

Much of the sixteenth-century garden has been lost, but the graceful nymphaeum, with its twin pavilions decorated with mosaics, remains. It was designed by the villa's architect, Pellegrino di Tibaldo de' Pellegrini (1527–96), who, unusually, placed it to the side of the villa. At a time when the villa was accessible only by water, Pellegrini did not want to obstruct the view for visitors arriving at the lake shore: he wanted to give them full sight of his nymphaeum, and beyond it, the Renaissance water staircase. Nymphaeum and water staircase are magnificent in conception, although here executed on a minor scale. Both the cardinal and his architect were familiar with Rome, Pellegrini having worked and studied there. This remaining fragment of Villa d'Este's original garden has a grandeur reminiscent of the great Roman gardens, but in miniature.

Left In the nymphaeum caryatids, sporting luxuriant tufa hair and moustaches, hold up Ionic capitals. *Below* Cypresses line the Renaissance water staircase beyond Pellegrini's richly decorated nymphaeum.

The wings of the nymphaeum are richly decorated with shell work and pebble mosaics in a palette of black and white, rust and grey. Obelisks on the pavilion roofs lead the eye all the way up the cypress *viale* flanking the water staircase to the eighteenth-century temple housing a statue of Hercules at the top. Beyond is a splendid panorama of mountains. Up some steps, in the centre of the nymphaeum, is a fountain in an oval pool. On either side of the pool are niches with tufa grottoes, now planted with lantana. Around the curving walls, caryatids, sporting luxuriant tufa hair and moustaches, hold up Ionic capitals. To the sculpted bas-reliefs on mythological themes another two were added in 1985, on the themes of Love and of Solitude.

From the fountain at the top of the slope, water flows down the graceful, double water staircase, splashing into over a hundred granite basins, dating from the Renaissance period. Cypresses cast horizontal shadows across the grassy central path. To walk here in the dappled sunlight, accompanied by the sound of falling water, is still as delightful as Pellegrini must have intended it to be, four and a half centuries ago.

To the right, high up on the cliffs, is another of Villa d'Este's delights: a hillside covered in toy-town fortifications and sham ruins, linked by winding paths. There are turrets, arrow slits, arched doorways, spiral staircases and battlement walks, all accessible by a bridge which spans the road. This mock fortress was built by a young widow for her dashing second husband, one of Napoleon's generals. Fearing that he might miss the thrill of battle, she had these fortifications built on the hill overlooking the gardens. The general was so delighted with his new toy that he imported military cadets to stage mock battles there, after which dinner was served to the accompaniment of fireworks.

The magnificent plane tree on the terrace is said to be one of the oldest in Lombardy.

Villa Carlotta

Villa Carlotta is the most famous of all the villas on Lake Como. Backed by soaring mountains, and fronting a series of terraces descending to the lake, it stands on the western shore between Tremezzo and Cadenabbia and almost opposite Bellagio.

The neoclassical, cream stucco villa was actually begun in 1690 as a home for the Milanese banker Marchese Giorgio Clerici. By 1801 the house had passed out of the hands of the Clerici family and into the ambitious grasp of Gian Battista Sommariva, who paid 72,500 lire for the property. Sommariva had fought his way up from modest beginnings, and the villa was a symbol of his rise. It was also a valuable card in his game of one-upmanship with his rival, Francesco Melzi, whose own sumptuous villa was at that very moment being built on the opposite shore of Lake Como. In life, Melzi and Sommariva vied with each other in collecting plants and competed to purchase works of art. In death, lying entombed in the mausoleums both had commissioned for themselves, they still face each other across the water.

The Clerici had bequeathed to Sommariva the baroque garden, rising with its terraces and staircases from the shoreline. An eighteenth-century writer mentions the fishpond, with its statue of Arion, son of Neptune, being saved by a dolphin. This jaunty little statue survives, surrounded by encircling curlicues of box, all that remains of a decorative *broderie* parterre that once stretched all along this terrace. Now clipped thickets of laurel serve to protect the garden from the road.

Sommariva preserved these baroque terraces with their citrus fruit espaliers, and extended the estate by buying agricultural land. The paths that linked the baroque garden with his olive groves, *orto* and vineyards later became the main axes of the nineteenth-century landscape garden with its flowering shrubs.

This romantic landscape was largely the creation of a German prince, the Duke of Saxe-Meiningen, whose wife, Charlotte of Prussia, was given the villa in 1850 as a wedding present from her mother. We are told that the young couple loved to entertain, transporting their guests to picnics and outings around the lake in splendid ducal barges decked in green and white livery. The monogrammed 'C' on the elegant entrance gates, much admired by Edith Wharton, may stand for the original owners, the Clerici. However, the ducal crown means that more probably it commemorates Charlotte (Carlotta), after whom the villa is named.

Princess Charlotte died in childbirth at twenty-four. Her widower, Duke George, a passionate botanist, oversaw the extravagant transformation of the park, adding large numbers of botanical exotics to the collection of rhododendrons and azaleas begun by Sommariva. The duke aimed to harmonize the baroque elements with his vast, richly romantic, flowering park. Shrubs, climbers and brightly coloured perennials were planted in lush profusion, overhanging the famous terraces. Now potted red geraniums climb the steps and roses swathe the balustrades. Still here, though, are the citrus tunnels that were a hallmark of the early garden. Covered with a polytunnel in winter, the citrus trees, planted in the ground, manage to bear crops of orange, grapefruit, lemon and lime.

At the back of the villa, 9-metre/30-foot-high hedges of camellias, edged with *Ophiopogon jaburan*, weave a tapestry of reds and pinks in spring, while banks of brilliantly coloured azaleas line the winding paths. In summer, to follow these paths leading horizontally across the garden is to

venture into an exotic, tropical world. Orchids from the jungles of Brazil and Mexico dangle in baskets from the branches of pines. Anthuriums, crotons, clivias and the shrimp plant (*Justicia brandegeeana*) mingle with lilies and amaryllis under palms. Cacti, yuccas and succulents such as the giant *Euphorbia candelabrum* colonize one rocky slope, while on another Duke George's rock garden is a riot of spring colour. Further on, the Bamboo Forest, with its pools and waterfalls, holds twenty-two different types of bamboo.

The cool, green Tree Fern Valley is a natural ravine, in whose sheltered depths dicksonias and different species of cyathea unfurl their tender fronds. This great spectacle owes much to the hard work of Villa Carlotta's gardeners: each spring every tree fern is moved in its pot from the shelter of the greenhouse to be planted out in this secluded valley. Each autumn, every plant is carefully moved back again.

Rivalling the Tree Fern Valley for romance is Villa Carlotta's Rhododendron Wood, planted, probably by Duke George, with *R. arboreum*, first discovered in Kashmir in 1796 and introduced into Europe in the early nineteenth century. This enchanted wood, carpeted in pink, fallen petals and with the sculptural, bare trunks of the rhododendron trees twisting sinuously overhead, is underplanted with hydrangeas and glossy, green clumps of *Aspidistra elatior*.

Villa Carlotta's park is a dendrologist's paradise. Its magnificent tree collection includes vast, towering liriodendron and wellingtonia, spreading oriental planes, weeping and purple beeches, stately *Parrotia persica*, colourful liquidambar and floriferous magnolias and paulownias.

In the Vecchio Giardino (Old Garden) on the other side of the villa, a path overhung by *Podocarpus totara* and scented by the heavily fragrant edgeworthia leads towards the Waterfall of the Dwarfs. These grotesque, miniature figures are a relic from the Saxe-Meiningens. Araucaria and *Cinnamomum camphora* can be found near by.

Open from mid-March until November, Villa Carlotta attracts over 150,000 visitors a year. Its gardens, as well as being botanically varied, are immaculately kept. In summer the hedges are clipped every two to four weeks and a gardener on permanent duty with a leaf-blower ensures that not a stray leaf is out of place.

Opposite, top The statue of Arion, son of Neptune, being saved by a dolphin, at the entrance to Villa Carlotta.
Opposite, bottom Citrus tunnels, a hallmark of the early garden, have now been reintroduced.
Above, left A view of the lake through the lush planting.
Above, right One of the grotesques in the Waterfall of the Dwarfs.

Villa Melzi d'Eril

This serene, white neoclassical villa right by the waterfront is one of the most iconic images of Lake Como. It was designed around 1808 by Giacondo Albertolli to the requirements of a discerning and powerful client, Francesco Melzi d'Eril, friend of Napoleon and vice-president of the short-lived Italian Republic founded by the Emperor. It was from Napoleonic France that Melzi learned his neoclassical taste. The Duke of Lodi, as Melzi became, wished for a villa of sober elegance and architectural purity, so as not to detract from the natural beauty of the site. In choosing the latest fashion for his house and garden, he may also have been influenced by his rivalry with Gian Battista Sommariva of Villa Carlotta (see page 32), who must have watched with mixed feelings as this splendid new villa rose up from its foundations to dominate his own view across the lake.

Completed between 1811 and 1815, the landscape garden at Villa Melzi was entirely planned, down to the placing of the statues, by the architect Luigi Canonica and the botanist Luigi Villoresi. In this, the first garden on the lake to be designed in the new English style, major earthworks were undertaken to create the appropriate romantic vistas and distinctive views. By levelling some areas and building up others, the architects aimed to give the illusion of distance and create an impression that the park was larger than it actually was. For example, a main axis leads from the waterline to a viewpoint high above the villa: this slope is criss-crossed by winding stone paths. The old public road along the lake was replaced by an impressive private drive, lined by plane trees trained into graceful umbrella shapes. This method of pruning, which allows glimpses of the lake from higher

Top The serene neoclassical Villa Melzi d'Eril rises from the shore of the lake.
Bottom Palms and clipped domes of laurel set in grass stretch behind the house.

up in the garden, was brought to Italy from France, where it is thought to have been adopted to shade Napoleon's troops from the sun. Between the villa and the lake is a magnificent terrace with columns, pools and statues behind a marble balustrade. Further along, green grassy slopes lead directly down to the shoreline. Here, without fences or barriers, the lake, a calm, mirrored surface, is an integral part of the design.

The villa and its grounds were designed as a self-sustaining entity, with woods and vineyards to serve the house. These vineyards have now disappeared but were known to the father of Count Lodovico Gallarati Scotti, a descendant of Francesco Melzi. Count Gallarati Scotti now oversees the care of the garden, with the help of Nino, the 'unequalled gardener' at Villa Melzi for almost fifty years. This important landscape is immaculately kept.

Count Lodovico points out the great cedar by the house as one of the first trees to be planted. By 1821, it was accompanied by 'rare foreign plants, fragrant shrubs and flowers of all kinds'. Giant redwoods, tulip trees (*Liriodendron tulipifera*) and camphor trees joined a *Ginkgo biloba* planted around 1820. A visit by Maximilian von Habsburg, Emperor of Mexico, saw the distinctive, long-needled pine *P. montezumae* introduced by the lake. The nineteenth-century taste for eclectic exoticism is displayed in the Oriental Garden, alight in October with the brilliant hues of acers. A stone bridge overhangs a secluded pool; camellias are reflected in its dark, unruffled surface. A bamboo grove on the other side of the garden is echoed inside the house by a room full of bamboo furniture, collected during the nineteenth-century craze for all things oriental. The twentieth century also left its mark on the garden through the introduction of massed rhododendrons and azaleas, ordered during the 1950s from English nurseries. During Duke Tommaso Gallarati Scotti's time as the Italian Ambassador in London, he had developed a liking for these plants. A walk by the lake is now lined with red and white azaleas. More colour is provided by a rockery created on the slope behind the house and planted with seasonal bedding. Near by, the original, terraced greenhouses are faced with flowering quince. Cypresses, palms and clipped domes of laurel set in the grass act as a calming foil to all the vibrant colours.

Canonica and Villoresi planned the garden as an unfolding drama, with different moods, light and shade, moments of delight and elements of surprise. In the shelter of trees and along the shore, the architects placed statues and monuments, including sphinxes from Egypt and sarcophagi and busts from ancient Rome. A statue of Melzi himself, surrounded by cypresses, gazes approvingly on his villa. The nineteenth-century blue and white Moorish pavilion, or kiosk, by the water's edge contains statues of Dante and Beatrice, by Giovanni Battista Comolli, of 1810. These were moved to the kiosk from inside the house. Liszt, a frequent visitor to the garden, would compose music here.

Stendhal stayed at the villa just after its completion, professing himself charmed by his days on the lake. Napoleon, too, may well have come here, as friend and patron to Francesco Melzi. His portrait by Andrea Appiani is kept inside the villa.

Left, above Architect Luigi Canonica planned the garden down to the placing of every statue.
Left, below The blue and white Moorish pavilion perches by the water's edge.

Il Pizzo

Villa Pizzo's gardens stretch over 1 kilometre/0.6 miles along Lake Como's western lake-shore. Sheltered by the Bay of Cernobbio, they bask in hot sun, yet much of the garden is green and secluded, the result of nineteenth-century landscape planting. The villa was built in the mid-sixteenth century by the Muggiasca, a family of rich Como silk merchants, on what had been a peasant's smallholding. The figs and olives that grow at the garden's working end are a reminder of the garden's origins.

The Muggiasca managed to hold on here for 300 years until the family died out, and the villa was bought in 1842 by the Austrian viceroy, Archduke Rainieri, as a summer residence. His head gardener, Ettore Villoresi, did much of the specimen planting, overseeing a staff of thirty gardeners; there are now two at Villa Pizzo. *Magnolia grandiflora*, *Cinnamomum camphora*, *Lagerstroemia indica*, *Fagus sylvatica* 'Pendula', sequoia, plane trees, ginkgos and holm oaks are all relics of his time. However, the towering 30-metre/98-foot *Cupressus sempervirens* by the lake predate the Austrians by a century or more. One of the garden's cypresses is thought to date to 1600.

Uniquely among the Como villas, visitors are guided on a 1-kilometre/0.6-mile shoreline walk, on a path which opens up to exhilarating views of the lake, only to retreat again into shady thickets of woodland. A castellated Moorish folly marks the spot where olives and wines were once sent by chute down to boats moored on the water. Here the wind whistles down from the Austrian peaks in the mornings, and blows the other way up the lake in the afternoons. Towards the end, the walk becomes wilder. Oregano, marjoram and box grow on the cliffs, along with tumbling Banksian roses that scent the path, and the only sound is the waves lapping against the Cernobbio promontory.

Around the house Count Pizzo has transformed the formal gardens with much English-style planting. *Rosa* × *odorata* 'Mutabilis' grows in a circle of box; paths are edged neatly with convallaria; pale pink geraniums grow alongside blue ceonothus, and, the *pièce de résistance*, a glorious garland of Banksian roses is held aloft by a line of *putti*.

Left and above Statues are dotted along the shoreline walk.

Villa Cipressi

Strung like a necklace around the villa, the flowering terraces of Villa Cipressi's century-old gardens descend in gentle tiers towards the lake. On the lowest level, a long walk weaves between palms and a rich curtain of purple wisteria towards iron gates leading to a landing stage. A tamarisk reaches down to trail its frondy fingers in the water.

The villa is now a hotel and conference centre, but a joint ticket can be bought for entrance to its gardens and those of Villa Monastero, a short walk away. Entrance is through a side door in the hotel, which leads out on to a terrace with dazzling views of the bay, and of the picturesque façade of Villa Monastero, a former Cistercian convent. As you follow the path down this rocky promontory, next to the wisteria-clad balustrade, the views become wider and even more panoramic. Framing the vistas are the cypress trees from which the villa gets its name.

On the terrace directly in front of the hotel, a spreading frangipani tree scents the whole area. A double staircase leading further down is shaded by *Osmanthus fragrans* trees. From this vantage point, four more wisteria-hung terraces are visible, connected by a series of gently winding paths, ramps and steps. Two paths lead off on each side, past jasmine,

more wisteria and hedges of box. To the left, another double staircase is overhung with oleanders. Down a further staircase, in the shade of cypress trees, is a grotto housing a terracotta statue. Rusticated with tufa, and cloaked in ivy, violets and wild strawberries, it is a romantic spot.

On the shadier side of the garden, hydrangeas, aspidistras and bamboos shelter under the canopy of holm oaks. Another walk is dramatically planted with agaves, phormiums and dasylirions, with erigeron spilling out of a nearby wall. Elsewhere, musa and *Cycas revoluta* add to the garden's air of rich exoticism.

The path to Villa Monastero, heady with the scent of wisteria in April and May, passes a huge *Magnolia grandiflora* and pomegranate and persimmon trees. By the boathouse stands a towering copper beech.

Left Wisteria-covered steps leading up to a higher terrace.
Below A view across the lake to the distant hills, from the lowest terrace.
Bottom Ferns and erigeron sprout from rocky walls.

Giardino di Villa Monastero

Villa Monastero, as its name suggests, was originally a medieval Cistercian convent, dating from around 1200 and dedicated to St Mary Magdalene. When the convent closed in the mid-sixteenth century and the last six sisters living here were transferred elsewhere, the building became a villa, the property of the noble Mornico family. Lelio Mornico, who inherited from his father Paolo this house by the lake, obviously loved the family's new acquisition and went to great efforts to improve it; we are told that 'he turned the Lake into a garden'. In recognition of this, the house, held by the Mornico from 1569 to 1862, was known as Villa Leliana for many years.

In the late nineteenth and early twentieth centuries, the villa was transformed by the then owner, the shipowner Walter Kees, in an eclectic mix of styles, periods and different architectural elements. A harmonious Renaissance loggia was added on the waterfront, flanked by *tortile* columns facing out over the lake. Elsewhere, a Moorish pavilion acted as a coffee house, and a Corinthian-columned classical temple housed statues. The most valuable work introduced by Kees was Giovanni Battista Comolli's sculpted group *The Clemency of Titus*. Many of the exotic plants were brought in at this time: palms, agaves and yuccas, as well as the great trees – camphor, cedars, Montezuma pines, and the century-old *Magnolia grandiflora*, which overhangs the water.

The gardens, long and narrow, are laid out between the mountains and the lake, opening out on to various terraces, avenues and parterres. Much of the path is balustraded, and urns and statues are dotted around among the architectural shapes of succulents and palms. To the left, the shoreline curves a protective arm around the grounds.

The entrance path winds down past cordylines and windmill palms (*Chamaerops excelsa*), their trunks linked to one another by swags of roses. Fan palms (*Chamaerops humilis*), date palms (*Phoenix dactylifera*) and the Mexican blue palm (*Brahea armata*) are planted with *Agave americana* and *A. salmiana* var. *ferox* to form an exotic jungle.

Further on, the *tempietto* at the top of the slope is reached by a gracefully curving double staircase. There are charming statues of a hunter and huntress with a hunting dog. The path then opens out into a box-edged parterre, with oleanders lining the waterfront. Here are the ruins of a thirteenth-century Cistercian church, its Tuscan granite columns lying where they were found in the parterre. Past the loggia hung with wisteria, a citrus avenue leads into a tropical glade of palms, agaves, yuccas and phormiums. A lofty *Jubaea chilensis* dwarfs the primitive shapes of *Cycas revoluta*. The wisteria-clad steps at the end lead up to a broad terrace offering spectacular views of the lake. Near by is a group of spring-flowering Judas trees (*Cercis siliquastrum*).

The garden seems to meander on for ever, past more balustrades and statues, past a curved parterre outlined in myrtle, past dasylirions planted in a starburst cluster. *Rosa banksiae* tumbles over a pergola walk; bignonia climbs up a cypress tree; wisteria and oleanders line the water's edge. At the very end, leading to the Moorish pavilion, is an old cypress avenue. These trees predate the nineteenth-century renovations to the garden.

Since 1953 the villa itself has been an international conference centre for high-level academic conferences. Part of it is also set aside as a museum.

Left The lakeside Villa Monastero was originally a Cistercian convent.
Right A previous owner, Walter Kees, furnished the garden with a collection of antiquities and architectural curiosities.
Below Steps lead up to a broad terrace offering spectacular views of the lake.

Villa Sommi Picenardi

LECCO, LOMBARDY

The nucleus of the villa is an ancient watchtower on the corner joining the family apartments with the delightfully frescoed fourteenth-century wine press and granary. In the late seventeenth century a family of local nobility, the Sala, built themselves the house when they made this the centre of their agricultural estate. The watchtower is a medieval survival, marking the nearby border between the territories of Milan and Venice. The present owners, the Sommi Picenardi family, think that the Sala, who could trace their ancestry back a thousand years, were one of the first families to explore their genealogy by making a family tree. The Sommi Picenardi emblem, the unicorn, is much in evidence, even picked out in topiary in the courtyard.

Originally, the courtyard at the front of the villa was closed, but the wall was demolished in the nineteenth century to make a much more fashionable *giardino inglese*. An oil painting dated 1859, which is inside the villa, shows two *Platanus orientalis* sited near the villa: one splendid specimen survives. Near by in the park are a venerable cedar of Lebanon and a magnificent *Fagus sylvatica* var. *heterophylla* 'Aspleniifolia', the fern-leaved beech, flourishing in the fertile soil. Water rushing down from the hills is plentiful here and was used to make the lake, where *Taxodium distichum* grows.

The hall, stuccoed with trophies representing the country pastimes of hunting, music and gardening, runs from the front of the villa to the back, where it overlooks the charming Italian Garden with its terracing and central staircase ascending the slope. The small scale of this *giardino segreto* is ideally suited to the small green hills that are a backdrop to the villa. From the large windows of the *piano nobile*, the garden can be viewed like a stage set.

The Italian Garden's double staircase is studded with coloured mosaics in exuberant Roman style, a rare sight in Lombardy. Graceful stone garlands hang from the balustrades in a foretaste of eighteenth-century elegance. These are echoed by swags of real roses, which link the pedestals of the statues on the top terrace. Further up the hill, stone figures once lined the steep steps, but empty spaces now mark where they have been stolen from. In the not-so-distant past, the children of the family were given 1,000 lire to scrub the statues with brushes; now experts come to clean them. The garden was restored at some point, and the flat, grassy parterre, with its central pool in which miniature bronze seahorses prance, may be a sympathetic later addition.

To one side of the villa is the Theatre Garden, made in the 1930s, with 'curtains' of clipped hornbeam creating a green proscenium arch.

Villa Sommi Picenardi is a miraculous survival: a family house still lived in yet unchanged, and sprinkled with the dust of history. During the Second World War it escaped the pillaging of its contents through the quick thinking of the present marchese's great-grandfather, who used the nuns who had been evacuated into a wing of the villa as a ruse to declare the estate Vatican property. The Germans obeyed the notice he had pinned hastily to the gates, and marched on.

Alessandra Sommi Picenardi was a passionate Anglophile and a leading breeder of Airedales, whose proud achievement was the first non-English Crufts 'Best in Show'. Her sons have inherited her love of dogs and of their delightful family home .

Right The double staircase of the Italian Garden is studded with colourful mosaics in the Roman style.

Villa Borromeo Visconti Litta

The industrial suburb of Lainate is an unusual place to find one of the most important nymphaea in northern Italy. Easy to miss, this unmarked treasure is marooned in the middle of a rather scruffy municipal park. The delightful, many-roomed nymphaeum, encrusted with mosaics and concealing many hidden water jokes, was created by Count Pirro I Visconti, then aged twenty, around 1585. It took ten years for the university-educated count to complete this delicious 'place of coolness' in the midst of a field on his agricultural estate, and twenty years to effect its restoration, which was not completed until around 2000. The credit for saving such a unique building goes to the comune of Lainate, helped by the region of Lombardy and public and private money. Now 25,000 visitors a year come from all over Italy. Local volunteer guides will proudly show you around.

Count Pirro I Visconti was a banker with money to indulge his wide interest in the arts. Having visited Villa d'Este and Villa Lante (pages 31 and 182), he determined to bring together the best artists in Lombardy to create his own playful 'place of enchantment'. Among those Count Pirro called upon were architect Martino Bassi and sculptor Francesco Brambilla, both of whom worked on the Duomo in Milan. 890 metres/2,920 feet of lead piping were ordered to carry water from a 20-metre/66-foot-high water tower to feed the many fountains, waterfalls and jets, as well as fifty-three hidden *giochi d'acqua* (water jokes), which duly sprayed and

soaked Count Pirro's guests. The system drew inspiration from the ideas of the military engineer Captain Agostino Ramelli, who was in the service first of Gian Giacomo de' Medici and later Henri III of France. In 1588 Ramelli published an illustrated folio volume of his 'diverse and artifactitious' machines, a classic work of Renaissance engineering, including designs, real and imaginary, for pumps and fountains, and mechanisms for raising water.

Pirro's main purpose in building the nymphaeum was to display his vast collection of minerals, fossils, coins, sacred relics, antiquities, automata, and even paintings and bronzes. Leonardo's *Madonna Litta* is supposed to have hung here for a time, along with works by Correggio and Bronzino. For many years Lainate was known as the *villa delle meraviglie* (villa of marvels), in recognition of Pirro's wish to astonish and awe his visitors. The rooms leading off on either side of Bassi's graceful central rotunda are like empty jewel caskets, awaiting the return of the count's treasures.

Bassi designed the nymphaeum as a rectangle with, at its centre, an octagonal rotunda. With open porticos at its southern and northern ends, the rotunda, known as the Hall of the Four Winds, is crowned by a

Below The ornate statue-studded façade of the sixteenth-century nymphaeum.

polygonal lantern. Symmetrical wings housing the collection rooms are faced with tufa and travertine, mosaics and stucco stalactites. Water pours down the façade and allegorical statues of rivers stand in niches.

The water jokes were controlled by water attendants, hidden behind the walls. The fun starts outside the building in the Giardino dei Giochi, with jets spraying the steps and drenching the nearby seat. Inside, in the Hall of the Four Winds, to step on to the central iron plate is to invite a soaking.

This domed central atrium was named after four bronze statues representing the winds, which were once housed in niches in each corner. Above them, in more niches lined with travertine, Brambilla's figures of the Four Seasons still look down from their lofty perches under the dome's painted sky. They are distinguishable by the crowns they wear – flowers, fruit, ears of corn or laurel. All the statues in the nymphaeum were of classical or mythological figures. A trompe-l'oeil balustrade runs round the inside of the dome; the walls are a riot of rocaille work, shells and pebbled mosaics. Venus and Mercury preside over the doorways that lead to the side rooms.

Even without Pirro's treasures, these rooms are an artistic treasure chest, their walls, ceilings and floors decorated with swirling black and white mosaics in complicated arabesques and floral and geometric patterns. Griffins, satyrs, centaurs and strange, bestial figures frolic within the intricate compositions. The mosaics were the work of Bolognese artist Camillo Procaccini, who was to become well known in Lombardy for his sacred works in churches, and in the cathedrals of Piacenza and Milan. Here at Lainate, under the eye of his patron, Count Pirro, he achieved a late Renaissance masterpiece of the profane. The decorations seem to have been inspired by a theme of movement and metamorphosis: a man is given the limbs of an animal, while an animal is subsumed into the trunk of a tree. To execute his fantastical designs, Procaccini used pebbles of black limestone and white quartz, and in some rooms actually painted the pebbles, using a new and unusual technique. All the mosaics have been faithfully and carefully restored by hand.

To restore the numerous, playful water games, the comune had to reinstate a thousand water jets. In a ten-year marathon of restoration they took up the mosaic floors and re-laid them by hand in order to renew pipes for the hydraulics. The works in the mysterious little Egg Room were particularly delicate and complicated to restore. In this room, named after a charming, gilded-metal, nineteenth-century automaton of a hen, water falling into a marble basin triggers the jet, which holds her 'egg'

Top Niches housing statues of classical and mythological figures are set in the rocaille-covered walls.
Below The underground grotto gallery in the nymphaeum.
Bottom The evocative figure of Silence, also known as The Lady with the Veil, reclines by the Galatea Fountain.

suspended in the air. Other water jets soak the room on cue, making it 'rain' on unwary guests – except in one corner where, presumably, Count Pirro stood, dry shod, to enjoy the fun.

A buried, semicircular grotto gallery is covered with shells and stalactites, a home for Venus, who bathes in water gushing from the roof. More water spurts from the floor or trickles down the walls, misting the room. In Count Pirro's magical 'kingdom of water', only the unrestored Court of the Rain is now dry and silent. Once, water falling down the walls here created, at the pull of a lever, drizzle, mist, downpours – all the different kinds of rain.

To the north of the nymphaeum, facing the fine, original Renaissance façade, is the striking Galatea Fountain by the eighteenth-century artist Donato Carabella. Among eight statues in white Carrara marble are two masterpieces: the figures of Sleep and of Silence (also known as The Lady with the Veil).

Giardino Botanico André Heller   LAKE GARDA, LOMBARDY

This garden, begun in 1910 and crammed with plants from every continent, is the extraordinary creation of Dr Arthur Hruska, botanist and dentist to Tsar Nicholas II. Drawn by the beauty of Lake Garda, Hruska bought parcels of vineyards from local farmers, deciding to recreate here the alpine landscape of his beloved Dolomites as a habitat for alpine flora. He ended up with 2,000 species – a verdant mix of alpine, subtropical and even desert plants. The Austrian artist André Heller, who bought the garden in 1988, described it as a place of 'edelweiss amidst orchid meadows; tree ferns several metres high next to pomegranate . . . streams and waterfalls', the latter created by Hruska with water channelled in from a mountain brook. And then there were the crags. Built of tufa, covered with stone, the man-made peaks imitate in miniature much-loved mountains from the Dolomite range. Pines, rhododendrons and every kind of rock plant have colonized their vertiginous slopes, finding water deep inside clefts and crevices.

If the entrance to the garden is somewhat garish, a splendid araucaria points the way to what is to come. The sound of falling water leads to a pool spanned by a bamboo and wood bridge, arched with oleander and a cascade of roses. The pool is set in a velvety green carpet of plants – *Musa* x *paradisiaca*, *Zantedeschia aethiopica*, astilbes and majestic royal ferns (*Osmunda regalis*). Ganesh, the Hindu elephant god, peers from among the leaves.

A shady path winds gently uphill beside a mountain stream lined with maidenhair ferns and huge-leaved *Colocasia esculenta*. In the dim light under the trees all is cool and green, until suddenly at the top of some steps the view opens out on to a spectacle of brilliant colour. The seasonal planting here is riotous: bright pink impatiens grows under *Acer palmatum* var.*dissectum* 'Garnet'. Banks of hot-coloured azaleas glow in tones of spice and amber.

But it was the Alpine Garden that claimed Dr Hruska's heart, and this remains the much-loved focus of the garden. It is a charming sight, its diminutive Dolomitic crags smothered with valerian, saxifrages, campanula, aubrieta, alchemilla, primroses and gentians. Rocky steps wind in between and up the mounds, the tallest of which overlooks the lake. Another crag is subtly planted with white snapdragons, evening primroses, grey-leaved verbascums and white *Cerastium tomentosum* among its ferns. Everywhere, there is the heady scent of wild roses.

At the back of the garden the stream that crosses the lawn is bordered by hostas in the shade of palms. Here thrives a tropical area with *Washingtonia filifera*, *Chamaerops humilis*, dracaena, *Cycas revoluta* and a clutch of agaves.

The graceful bamboo forests that make up the Indian section of the garden are among the most beautiful anywhere, lushly underplanted with *Acanthus mollis*, ferns and broad-leaved *Ruscus hypoglossum*. Beyond them is a bridge with two masks spitting out water at unwary passers-by. On the route downhill, an ancient wisteria has curved and twisted its sinewy arms around the path: it has right of way. Near by, an ivy tunnel is complemented by a green border planted within an outcrop of rock – hellebores, painted ferns and the black lilyturf *Ophiopogon planiscapus* 'Nigrescens'. Elsewhere in the garden, orchids, waterlilies and swathes of Tibetan primroses all add their distinctive beauty.

This is not a neat garden but a luxuriant one, voluptuously overflowing with plants. It contains month-by-month interest, with summer-flowering geraniums and roses taking over from the rhododendrons, azaleas and magnolias of spring. André Heller has also introduced sculptures and contmporary art installations to create talking points around the garden.

Right The mysterious, lushly underplanted bamboo forest.
Far right The Alpine Garden with its diminutive Dolomitic crags.

Isola del Garda

Lapped by the clear waters of the lake and ringed by distant views of snow-capped mountains, long, narrow Isola del Garda is half natural, half man-made. In 1870 the Duke and Duchess De Ferrari, ancestors of the present owners, acquired the island and brought rubble and earth from the mainland to create another low-lying island linked to the first. They then transformed the existing 'decorous' villa into a fairytale, white palazzo in the Venetian-gothic style the Duchess loved. The eighty-four-roomed Villa Borghese Cavazza with its lancet windows, ogee arches, spires, trefoils and gothic tower took thirteen years to finish, with marble and sandstone laboriously carted in from Vicenza. Despite the effort it took to build it, the Duke and his wife confined their visits to the summer, retreating to their tower to catch the breezes blowing from the mountains down the lake. The Duchess, a lover of all things Venetian, embellished her park with islets and little bridges, and began the planting of exotic trees which her daughter Anna Maria would continue on a far grander scale. Most of the trees on the island are not visible in the early photographs, and were planted in the early 1900s by Anna Maria and her husband, Prince Scipione Borghese. A great philanthropist, Anna Maria nursed victims of the First World War and the Spanish flu epidemic. In 1924 she drowned in the lake. Her great-granddaughter Alberta Cavazza now organizes tours of the island. She is one of seven siblings who administer the Cavazza estates, which span one of the most beautiful promontories of the lake. This is very much a family enterprise: six of the family still live on the island, which became their full-time home in the 1960s.

Boats from the mainland dock at a toy port built in military style with a little tower. This port is the legacy of the Lechi brothers, one of whom was a general during the Napoleonic Wars. Under the ownership of Count Luigi Lechi in the early nineteenth century, the island became a favourite with writers and musicians, including Donizetti and the opera singer Adelaide Malanotte, Rossini's muse.

On the north of the island are caves cut out of the rock, once lived in by Franciscan monks retreating from the world in prayer and contemplation. St Francis himself is supposed to have set up this hermitage when he visited the island in 1221. In 1227 St Anthony of Padua came to meet his brothers and find peace and solace in the solitude. Almost a century later, Dante, himself a Franciscan tertiary, supposedly visited the mystical 'Island of the Monks'; a century on, St Bernard of Siena built the austere, fifteenth-century Franciscan monastery which still stands, now smothered by a tumbling Banksian rose. The Franciscans left other legacies on the island – olive trees, some sixteenth century, and the cultivation of citron and lemons, which still flourish, espaliered against the stone wall that protects the north of the island in its sheltering embrace.

Top The castellated Venetian-gothic palazzo, surrounded by its gardens, seen from the lower terrace.
Bottom Swans glide among the swamp cypresses in the wilder reaches of the park.

On the shoreline along the banks of the lake, pomegranates, persimmons, olives and jujubes grow with palms and agaves among clipped domes of topiary. From the greenhouses, there is a dramatic view past palms and soaring cypresses to the topmost terrace. A walnut tree hangs over the ascending steps. The lower gardens were made from what had been a First World War vegetable garden; in 1915 the ancient Franciscan monastery housed pigs and chickens. Alberta's father's marriage to Charlotte Chetywnd-Talbot, daughter of the Earl of Shrewsbury, accounts for these gardens' gentle, ice-cream-coloured, English style. Pink **Bonica** roses line the garden paths; *Geranium* 'Johnson's Blue', old-fashioned pinks, campanula and forget-me-nots flower among the clipped holm oaks, box hedging and Celtic-knot box parterre.

The more formal upper terraces opening out from the house were established by the Lechi family in the nineteenth century. In 1870 there was a lemon garden here, overlooking the lake, containing 300 potted lemon trees. These were replaced by a topiary design in box, picking out the eagles and dragons that form part of the family crest. Elsewhere, stately Canary Island palms stand next to box and grass enclosures, and agaves grow against the rocky back wall of a columned arcade. The view from the house sweeps across the Italian Garden, and down over the lower terraces, sloping gently to the shore of the lake. The park and garden were designed to be seen not only from the upper terraces but also from the water during the lake-crossing to the island.

While the original island preserves a mild climate, never dropping below zero, the second island is colder, more exposed to the lake's sudden storms. This wilder part of the park adds to its air of mysterious romance,

with the dark woods full of birdsong and populated by pine, acacia, magnolia, oak and plane. Two hundred and twenty species of birds fly free here, and red squirrels roam the treetops. White peacocks and white dogs are a long-lived tradition of the island, as is the hospitality offered by the family (including wine and olive oil from the estate) at the end of each tour.

Above The dramatic gothic architecture is softened by lush planting.
Left Roses, clipped holm oaks and palms grow alongside a curving box parterre.

I Giardini di Limoni

Along the western shores of Lake Garda, against a backdrop of mountains and facing towards the sun, lemons have been cultivated since the thirteenth century, when they are said to have been introduced by Franciscan monks living in Gargnano. This story seems to be borne out by the thirteenth-century cloister of the church of San Francesco in Gargnano, which has columns decorated with citrus leaves and fruit, carved in exquisite detail.

The lemon farmers supplemented their own poor, stony soil with earth brought by boat from the eastern, shady side of the lake. Soil was not their only challenge. For hundreds of years their lemon groves were the most northerly in the world. Growing so far north, the fruit needed protection from the frosts. It was for this reason that, mainly in the seventeenth and eighteenth centuries, the lemon houses were put up: temporary greenhouses to house the lemons from November to March. In September 1786 Goethe noticed them from his boat on the lake. 'We passed in front of Limone where the terraced gardens planted with lemon trees have a very prosperous and beautiful appearance. The garden is made of rows of white square pillars, placed at regular distance from each other and climbing up the terraced mountain. Very strong beams are placed on top of the pillars to cover the trees during winter. There was nothing better than observing and contemplating this pleasant view while sailing by ...'

Goethe's view is very different today. The lemon gardens are empty, their terraces abandoned – 'like ruins of temples ... as if they remained from some great race that had once worshipped here', wrote D.H. Lawrence when he saw them. The bare, white pillars remain, rising in tiers up the green mountainsides, like ghostly fingers pointing at the sky. The cypresses planted as windbreaks march in vertical rows alongside them.

Over the last ten years, a ruined lemon house in the old village of Limone sul Garda has been restored as a living museum named La Limonaia del Castel. Here, among the lemons, limes, tangerines and clementines that have been planted, visitors can see how the growers worked night and day to protect their precious crops against the threats of frost and humidity. The protection they used was moveable and temporary: every door, chestnut roof beam, wooden ceiling plank and glass pane was numbered, so that it could be taken down quickly at the end of March, with the arrival of the migrant birds. In winter, inside the lemon houses, it was cold and dim, the aim being to keep the lemons dormant and thus resistant to frost. The ceilings were high to allow air to circulate, and the walls on three sides thick to protect the shallow-rooted citrus from winter winds. Thus carefully sheltered, and grown in earth fertilized with horse and sheep manure, mixed with cinders and pressed grapes, the citrus trees often endured for more than a century, with mature trees able to bear 600 fruits a year.

Another lemon museum worth visiting is the Ecomuseo Limonaia Pra'dela Fam, where a reconstructed greenhouse houses eighty citrus trees – lemons, mandarins and bergamot – brought in from nurseries in Liguria.

Lemon production along the shores of Lake Garda was at its height in the first half of the nineteenth century. It is estimated that at one point there were 4,000 fields of lemons here on the sunny side of the lake, with citron and oranges grown as well, and tangerines introduced later. Lemons were exported to Germany, Austria, Poland, England and Russia, bringing a good income to the lake's fishermen and peasant farmers. Wrapped in tissue paper and carefully placed in wooden crates, they were shipped by boat to the port of Desenzano at the foot of the lake, from where they were sent

on by rail to London or St Petersburg. The Garda lemons were especially prized for their thick, glossy rind, aromatic flavour and durability, which helped keep them useable up to six months after harvesting.

In the early eighteenth century the Bettoni company entered the lemon trade, and soon had agents throughout Italy and northern Europe. The family's profits paid for a splendid villa, the Villa Bettoni at Gargnano, whose eighteenth-century baroque garden is not open to the public but can be viewed from the road from behind a wrought-iron screen. Against a backdrop of mountains, the garden is an ornate architectural composition, with a double staircase, criss-crossing ramps, statue-studded niches, fountains and balustrades, all linking a series of terraces with lemon gardens. Behind, the park with its fine old trees rises towards the hills. The gates are opened for a plant fair at the beginning of May.

When the collapse in lemon production came it was sudden, precipitated by a disease in 1855 which ruined many local families. In the south, the burgeoning Sicilian lemon industry was more economic by far to run than the high-maintenance Lake Garda lemons, with their costly lemon houses demanding both upkeep and year-round manpower. During the First World War the wooden roofing of the lemon houses was requisitioned to build trenches. A further blow was the discovery of synthetic citric acid.

With their communities in crisis, many former lemon growers were forced to find factory work, or even to emigrate. It was not until 1931, when the road linking these isolated lakeside villages was finally in place, that they discovered a new future: tourism.

Above Part of a restored *limonaia* in the museum.

TRENTINO

Trentino-Alto Adige is perhaps the least Italian of Italy's regions. Bordering Austria, it is a mountainous region dominated by the saw-toothed ridges and jagged peaks of the Dolomites. Vines grow in the gravelly moraine at the foot of the mountains.

Trentino–Alto Adige is an autonomous region. Its southern part, Trentino, is markedly more Italian than the northern Alto Adige, also known as Südtyrol. Place names tend to have both German and Italian spellings here, and *würst* is as popular as spaghetti in the spick and span medieval villages and towns. Castles and onion-domed churches dot the landscape of upland meadows, valleys, apple orchards and alpine lakes.

In 1803 the territory came under the rule of the Habsburgs and was annexed to the province of Tyrol. It became part of Italy in 1919, after the First World War. In 1939 a large segment of the population emigrated north across the border. It was not until 1992 that the final measures were implemented that made this an automonous region of Italy.

The region includes the northernmost tip of Lake Garda, with its own microclimate which allows it to grow lemons at the northernmost point in Europe. There are many mountain parks containing alpine flora and, in the Val d'Ultimo, 1,000-year-old birch trees.

Castel Trauttmansdorff

In a spectacular setting, Castel Trauttmansdorff sits in a sunny natural amphitheatre against a backdrop of the snowy peaks of the South Tyrol. Historically and climatically it is a paradox. This is Italy, but until 1919 the area was part of Austria, a legacy which survives in pin-neat Tyrolean villages and the prevalence of German speakers. Despite being so near the Alps, the castle's position on a sheltered, sun-baked ledge gives it a dry, sub-Mediterranean climate, allowing the cultivation of Italy's northernmost olive trees, along with a 150-year-old tradition of growing exotics. The garden, proudly owned by the province of Bolzano and beautifully run by the Laimburg Research Centre for Agriculture and Forestry, was opened in 2001. In 2005 it was chosen as Italy's Most Beautiful Garden and, a year later, as one of the top six Gardens of Europe. The Touriseum in the grounds tells the story of 200 years of alpine tourism.

Trauttmansdorff is famous as the garden of glaciers and palms, much visited for its historic viewing platform of the high Alpine peaks, as well as for its flowering terraces, kept immaculately in constant bloom, and its pyrotechnic display of autumn colours. But this is also a botanic garden with a serious educational purpose, a walk-in encyclopaedia of plants. Organized thematically by habitat, the garden aims to show how man has transformed the natural landscape by cultivating, collecting, introducing and using plants. It is on an epic scale: there are twenty-six full-time gardeners, eighty different landscapes or gardens, an artificial stream, 7 kilometres/4½ miles of paths and 700,000 plants.

The garden is organized into four garden worlds: the Forests

of the World with its miniature forests from the Americas and Asia; the Mediterranean Sun Gardens; the Water and Terraced Gardens; and the landscapes of South Tyrol, containing the region's indigenous plant species.

The Japanese section of the Forests of the World contains examples of loquat, *Daphniphyllum macropodum*, *Kadsura japonica*, *Aralia elata*, the Japanese horse chestnut (*Aesculus turbinata*), the Japanese evergreen rose (*Rosa wichurana*) and *Cinnamomum camphora* – rare so far north. There are 385 different rhododendrons and 50 different species of bamboo. Alongside the botany is cultural history: we learn of *hanami*, the annual cherry blossom viewing, of the Japanese garden as a contemplative setting for the tea ceremony, and of the cultivation of rice, 'bread of the east', for 5,000 years.

In the lush and sheltered Valley of the Ferns, the mild, generally frost-free winters enable *Wollemia nobilis* (a joint project with the Australians) to thrive. In this area are the world's first emerging plants – living fossils such as the dawn redwood, cycas, araucaria, *Ginkgo biloba*, dicksonia and 200 species of ferns. In the background, a waterfall splashes and a fossil 90 million years old is displayed.

In contrast to the cool green of the shaded forests, the Sun Gardens on the southern slopes below the castle are ablaze with colour. Here there is another microclimate, with a winter temperature fully five degrees

Centigrade higher than elsewhere. So steep are some of the gradients that bulbs such as alliums (here with santolina) are planted in mesh by gardeners roped for safety. In spring the trademark of Trauttsmandorff is its tulips, and in the Flowering Meadow marble-white 'Maureen' glows against inky 'Queen of Night'. Later, dicentra, poppies and iris bloom, with *Gaura lindheimeri* and *Verbena bonariensis* following in summer.

The planting at Trauttmansdorff is a virtuoso display: pink *Albizia julibrissin* underplanted with a lavender field; *Cornus florida* f. *rubra* and *Rosa glauca* against a grey teucrium hedge; anemones and myosotis winking, jewel bright, under a Judas tree; crown imperials towering among white tulip beds; blowsy mounds of *Rosa banksiae* billowing over the top terrace. There is even a garden of poisonous plants, the Forbidden Garden.

In the Mediterranean section the olive, the pomegranate and the fig, the most antique cultivated trees in the Mediterranean, reign supreme. Under the olives mass lime-yellow *Euphorbia characias* subsp. *wulfenii*. A sloping field of barley is covered in July by dwarf sunflowers. In spring all the tones of blue are here in myosotis, viola, iris, *Phlox* 'Chattahoochee' and trailing bright blue rosemary.

In 1870–71 'Sissi', the Empress Elisabeth of Austria, wintered at the castle and created the terraced paths for her daily promenades. These wind downhill past an oleander forest and a white wisteria pergola, through an Australian wood of mimosa, eucalyptus and acacia, and along a walk lined with *Clematis armandii* to the lake. Here tropical lotus flowers grow in heated water, separated from the water lilies of the temperate zone, and in spring all the differently coloured iris dance along the shoreline. A floating stage hosts concerts. This is a botanical garden like no other.

Page 47 The woodland garden of Parco nell'Ombra del Paradeis.
Left Pink tulips line a stream running through the garden, against the backdrop of the Tyrolean Alps.
Above, left The Japanese Garden.
Above, right Anemones and myosotis encircle a Judas tree.

Parco nell'Ombra del Paradeis

Alois Lageder's family grow wine here on the gravelly moraine at the foot of the majestic Fenner mountain. Wine makers around Bolzano for 150 years, in 1991 they added Casòn Hirschprunn to their estates. With the grapes came a house, part-medieval, part-Renaissance and once the country home of the Bishop of Trento. And with the house, choked by undergrowth and overgrown with trees, was an abandoned garden. The garden, now restored, is named after a vineyard above the tiny village of Magrè in South Tyrol. Together, the vineyards and the stylish, modern *enoteca* near the Renaissance house and its new garden make up this harmonious and exceptional estate.

A visionary and innovative wine maker, Alois Lageder also has a passion for art and a discerning eye. He waited eight years to replant the garden at Casòn Hirschprunn until a chance meeting with Don Leevers – landscape designer and former owner of the influential nursery at Venzano – convinced him that he had found the right person for the rescue operation. Don's special interest is plants for shade and here he found the perfect sylvan setting for his favourites. The woodland floor is carpeted with them – heuchera, tiarella, bergenia, Japanese anemones, epimedium, polygonatum; even primroses and cowslips flourish in the improved soil and newly raised tree canopy.

Left A blue rosemary flashes colour against the courtyard wall. *Below* The woodland, romantically planted with shade-loving plants.

The garden was first planted in 1880, enjoyed a brief flowering and then all but disappeared. Don has reinstated the original central box avenue, its formality a deliberate contrast with the romantic mood elsewhere. Paths meander off under the trees on either side. The planting is subtle and restrained – violas overlooked by nodding dicentras, white rhodohypoxis and pink *Convallaria majalis* var. *rosea*. Great attention is paid to leaf differentiation, Don's intention being that 'You should bask in all the different greens.' Martagon lilies and *Lilium candidum* provide points of light. *Geranium macrorrhizum* 'Ingwersen's Variety' colonizes the deepest shade.

Nick, the English gardener, grows as much as possible from seed: cyclamen, hellebores, hostas, golden *Paeonia mlokosewitschii* – the Caucasian peony, also known as Molly the Witch – and showy *P. ostii*, first introduced by Don. *Hydrangea quercifolia* 'Harmony', with its voluptuous white blooms, has taken magnificently from cuttings.

Shrubs, mostly white, anchor the garden, the viburnums – *V. judii*, *V. burkwoodii*, *V. opulus* 'Roseum' and *V. plicatum* 'Cascade' – a sober backdrop to such show-stoppers as the fragrant white woodland *Paeonia obovata* var. *alba*; the aristocratic giant lily *Cardiocrinum giganteum*; and a very particular form of *Magnolia sieboldii*, its paper-white flowers blotched with striking crimson stamens.

The woodland garden connects with the house through a rose garden of David Austin roses in a colour palette ranging from pink through to orange, chosen to reflect the nearby Dolomite peaks bathed in the rosy light of the setting sun. A huge tamarisk arches against the courtyard wall. Vivid blue rosemary in cream urns splashes the ancient stone walls with colour.

VENETO

The powerful Republic of Venice generated the wealth which gave rise to many great villas and gardens, built over a period from the fifteenth to the eighteenth centuries. These country villas, created by the great Venetian families, later enabled them to enjoy the *villeggiatura* – the annual summer retreat from the city. In 1645 John Evelyn journeyed down the Brenta Canal in a boat pulled by horses and marvelled at 'both sides deliciously planted with country villas and gentleman's retirements. Gardens planted with Oranges, Figs and other fruit, belonging to the Venetians.' These villas stood, for the most part, on flat land at the centre of their agricultural estates. Their gardens aimed to provide pleasant views to compensate for the monotony of the surrounding farmland. Venetian gardens were also a setting for the constant entertainment which came to characterize the *villeggiatura*. They were furnished with loggias, temples and belvederes, decorated with fishponds and peopled with statues from the workshops of Orazio Marinali and Antonio Bonazza, carved in stone from the Berici and Euganean Hills. Statues were to become one of the main elements of Venetian garden ornamentation: they portrayed dwarfs, peasants, mythological and Arcadian figures, gods from Olympus and well-loved characters from the *commedia dell'arte*.

Giardino di Pojega a Villa Rizzardi VERONA, VENETO

In 1650 Count Carlo Rizzardi purchased the property of Pojega, when it was already an established wine estate with its villa. A hundred years later, his descendant, Antonio Rizzardi, created the famous garden of Pojega with its unique green amphitheatre. In this, he was helped by the architect-engineer Luigi Trezza.

Begun in 1783, Trezza's garden is often considered to be the last flowering of the classical Italian style. His design, consisting of four drawings, is in the Civic Library in Verona. The garden is rectangular and on a slope, its backbone consisting of three parallel horizontal lines cut into the hill: at the top, the *bosco*; on the middle level, a cypress *viale* linking the villa to the famous Green Theatre; on the lowest level, a hornbeam avenue. On the cross-axis, another cypress avenue runs from the highest point of the garden – a hexagonal belvedere – to the lowest, where the hornbeam avenue ends in rotunda. Throughout, views of the garden and landscape are revealed by carefully framed openings through the trees.

Trezza's patron, Antonio Rizzardi, is known to have been inspired by woodcut illustrations in the mysterious and anonymous 1499 *Hypnerotomachia Poliphili*, which show, in a famous example of early printing, a garden landscape containing amphitheatres and avenues, classical ruins and statues, grottoes and fountains, arbours and pergolas – a landscape where nature is subject to the rules of geometry, and plants themselves are used as elements of architecture. Count Rizzardi, who was well travelled

and cultivated, also wanted to include elements of the informal English style fashionable in the late eighteenth century. Moreover, through his journeys abroad, he had developed a passion for unusual plants. All these influences combined to make the garden at Villa Rizzardi. It is, says the present countess, Maria Cristina Rizzardi, 'a lovely mix of a spectacular Italian concept with views and perspectives, and the romantic idea of *boschetto* and *tempietto*'. A keen gardener herself, she likes to keep the garden 'a little bit loose, natural and unmanicured: it is, after all, a garden in the country.'

The entrance to the garden leads through ancient hornbeams into a wood, in which mysterious stone animals lurk among ruscus and fan palms (*Trachycarpus fortunei*), a memento of the exotics once planted here, no doubt to remind Count Rizzardi of his travels. In the midst of the wood is a Roman 'ruin' – an exquisite, round *tempietto*, open to the sky and roofed only by a tracery of foliage, which forms a green vault overhead.

The Green Theatre at Villa Rizzardi is one of the finest in Italy. The fact that it was not completed till 1796 reflects Trezza's resolve to find the best possible site for it. Dug out of the hillside, the space is organized, as in ancient Greek amphitheatres, to make the most of the views and the contours of the land. Seven tiers of turf seats, separated by box (now overgrown), are intersected by three flights of steps in stone. At the top in hornbeam niches

stand the 'likenesses of ancients' mentioned in Trezza's plan – mythological characters from Greek theatre, sculpted by Pietro Muttoni.

The side door of the villa looks on to a parterre with spouting fountains and then beyond, down the dappled length of the hornbeam avenue. (These are hop hornbeams, *Ostrya carpinifolia*, with leaves like the common hornbeam and fruit resembling hops.) It is positioned so that in the middle of the day the sun strikes the centre of the grass sward running down the centre of the avenue. The trees are contained within a low box hedge and edged with convallaria.

Trezza completed work on Villa Rizzardi during the course of the French Revolution, a time of anxiety and unease for the whole European aristocracy. Yet in contrast to the prevailing fashion in gardens for English naturalism and romanticism, his plan harks back to the formality and grandeur of the *ancien régime*.

Page 51 Giardino Giusti, studded with Lorenzo Muttoni's statues
Opposite The cypress *viale* (*above*) links Villa Rizzardi with its Green Theatre (*below*), one of the finest in Italy.
Below, left The woodland *tempietto*, open to the sky.
Below, right An opening in a rustic stone wall offers a glimpse of the surrounding countryside.

Villa Arvedi

Despite its ochre-washed, baroque grandeur, Villa Arvedi is very much a working farm, set in an agricultural landscape of vineyards and olive groves, next to a huddle of its own farm buildings and granaries. It is probable that olives have been harvested and pressed here for as many as eight centuries, with oxen walking in circles to work the olive press until the advent of steam. The tall chimney still visible to the side of the villa was used for creating steam power, which drove the machines until electricity took over. There are three thousand olives now on the estate, many of the trees centuries old. Wine has been produced here since the fifteenth century, and liqueurs are also bottled here from lemons and citrons grown on the estate.

The approach is typical of many Venetian villas, with a central axis running from the house across the garden to the fields beyond. However, this axis was changed in the nineteenth century to create a curve at the bottom of the drive leading to the gatehouse. This enables the villa to be seen across a patchwork of vineyards, fruit trees and topiary, and skilfully enhances the perspective. From its commanding position backing on to a steep hill of woods and olive groves, the villa dominates the landscape. It is flanked by two square dovecotes, to which it is linked by terraces extending from the *piano nobile*. The drive is lined with box topiary and persimmon trees, their showy golden fruit an arresting sight in late autumn. In May the olive trees float in a cloud of blue and yellow iris behind the ordered rows of vines.

Edith Wharton, when she made the trip out from Verona, found 'a beautiful old house standing above a terrace-garden planted with an elaborate *parterre de broderie*'. Best viewed from above, this swirling, intricate parterre, divided by a central basin into two fan shapes gracefully delineated in box, beautifully complements the house and is unique in Italy. Tests have established that the box, once thought to be modern, is 250 years old; the parterre has survived unchanged since its inception. Domes of clipped box and vertical cypresses stand sentinel among the coiling arabesques. Gravel and earth provide the insets. An eighteenth-century fresco inside the villa shows the parterre laid out geometrically with square compartments, surrounded by lemon trees. Count Paolo Arvedi considers this a design for a project that was never realized. The box is cut once a year by five gardeners, who start in June and finish in September. Low walls enable the parterre to blend with the hills behind and the vineyards and fruit orchards in front, making a garden that, as Geoffrey Jellicoe wrote, 'claims the country for its own'.

At the back of the villa is a courtyard laid out as a curved hemisphere with a circular lawn. Facing the villa's rear façade, the baroque chapel of San Carlo stands on a terraced platform, reached by a balustraded double staircase. This chapel, still used by the family on Sundays, is supposed to have been built to commemorate the visit of San Carlo Borromeo in the mid-sixteenth century, during his journey north to attend the Council of Trent. The ornate, curved outline contrasts with the slender, pencil spires of dark cypress on the hill behind. From the chapel there is a view through the main salon of the villa, out of the front door, across the garden parterre, all the way to the hills across the valley. In the foreground, on the lawn in front of the chapel, is the statue of a headless lion. Count Paolo Arvedi thinks it was decapitated by his father experimenting with gunpowder.

The villa, in its present form, was built to the design of the sculptor and architect G.B. Bianchi in the mid-1650s to replace an earlier house,

possibly the 'battlemented palace' in 'an estate with . . . wine and oil presses' referred to in 1432. The Arvedi family, originally from Hungary, came to Verona to join the silk industry and bought the villa from the Allegri in 1824. They still own it and twenty members of the family live on the estate. Inside the magnificently frescoed rooms of the villa is a collection of machines for silk printing – hand stamps and wood and copper rollers.

In the nineteenth century Count Paolo's ancestress Lucidalba Arvedi, who founded a religious order, took exception to the villa's 'pagan' statuary. Mythological statues in the courtyard and on the balustrade were removed and disposed of in the river. Some were later rediscovered here, retrieved and subsequently reinstated in their original places.

Above The drive leading to the villa is lined with box topiary and persimmon trees.
Below The celebrated box *parterre de broderie*, much admired by Edith Wharton. It is believed to be 250 years old.

Parco Giardino Sigurta

This vast garden-park belonging to the Sigurta family owes its existence to a serendipitous visit to the area by Carlo Sigurta in 1941. On a mission to buy a buggy – petrol being short in wartime – he ended up buying land here at the foot of these morainal hills close to Lake Garda. It took nearly forty years and access to a water supply to turn this arid landscape into the flowering parkland it is today. The park opened to the public in 1978. It now contains eighteen lakes, forty thousand box trees, groves of maple, avenues of pine and birch, a kilometre/0.6 mile-long rose avenue and several water gardens.

This is gardening on a grand scale. A million tulips flower each spring and have naturalized on the grassy slopes in a firework display of yellow, orange and red. Elsewhere, cyclamen-pink tulips glow against purple-black 'Queen of Night'. The Dutch contribute many unusual bulbs to Sigurta, as does the Iris Society of Florence. Thousands of irises line the kilometres of paths and avenues in wavy ribbons of blue, yellow and purple.

Sigurta treads the balance between garden and park. It was Carlo Sigurta who laid out the park, diverting water from the River Mincio under rights dating back to 1766. He built on the foundations of what was once an historic garden surrounding Villa Maffei (now private), built in Palladian style in 1693. The estate here was splendid enough for Napoleon III to choose it for his headquarters during the war of 1859.

The thousands of centuries-old box trees for which Sigurta is famous were transplanted by the family to new locations in the park. Trimmed very lightly, these ancient trees have been allowed to grow into strange and surreal shapes – living sculptures, Carlo Sigurta proudly called them. Planted companionably in the grass, or adjacent to and seeming to lean against the trees, these characterful box shapes have the eerie air of spectators, watching the visitors.

Sigurta is not a garden for understated displays of good taste in pastel shades. Planted by Enzo Sigurta, a psychiatrist with an interest in the effects of colour, it combines sweeping emerald lawns with planting in brilliant hues. Abundance is the key here. The garden does not have just one acer: it has every variety save one. It does not have a few cotinus: it has vast clumps of cotinus like hazy, purple woodland. The showpieces of the garden, guaranteed to last the year, are the five great flowerings: tulips followed by irises, then roses, waterlilies and finally waves of blue and purple asters.

The park offers constant interest: a fern path, a belvedere with a vista of the Alps, a medicinal herb garden, a dog cemetery and a path studded with drinking fountains, lined with narcissi, followed by iris and lilies, and shaded by poplars and silver birch. Among the buildings are a neo-gothic church, a miniature gothic *castelletto* and the most sublime eye-catcher possible: the silhouette of the fourteenth-century Scala castle, outside the grounds but approached by a kilometre-long avenue of roses, and reflected among the waterlilies growing in the sixteenth-century stone basin of Sigurta's Aquatic Garden.

Immaculately kept and much loved by the family, of whom Giuseppe and Magda Sigurta are the latest members to work here, the Sigurta gardens are a tour de force.

Top The fourteenth-century Scala castle, reflected in Sigurta's Aquatic Garden.
Centre Parco Sigurta's living sculptures in clipped box.
Bottom An ancient stone lion stands guard in the herb garden.

Giardino Giusti

A weary Grand Tourist, shaken by the arduous crossing through the Brenner Pass over the Alps, might have made his way down the Adige valley to Verona, where, in the heart of the city, he would have found this harmonious Renaissance garden, one of the oldest in northern Italy. Thomas Coryat, whose 1611 travel book *Coryat's Crudities* was an early influence on the Grand Tour, had praised the Giusti garden as 'a second paradise . . . beautified with many curious knots, fruits of divers sorts and two rowes of lofty cypresse trees, three and thirty in ranke'. The garden became a fixture on the itinerary of the Tour, along with Verona's Roman amphitheatre and Romeo and Juliet's supposed balcony. John Evelyn, travelling in Italy to escape the upheavals of England's Civil War, saw from the garden 'a pleasant prospect of Mantua and Parma, though at great distance'. He also admired 'the goodliest cypress, I fancy, in Europe . . . a prodigious tree'.

The Giusti garden has been visited by the public ever since the Renaissance garden was created around 1570 by Agostino Giusti, Knight of the Venetian Republic and Gentleman-in-Waiting to the Grand Duke of Tuscany. The Giusti, originally a Tuscan family, took refuge in Verona, as Dante did, to escape the Guelph–Ghibelline conflict. Acute politically as well as commercially, they found favour with the Venetian overlords of Verona.

The Giusti origins in Tuscany explain the fact that this is not a Venetian garden. Rather, it has all the hallmarks – box, fountains, a maze, closed perspectives – of a central Italian design. Agostino Giusti, an ambitious and cultivated man, was a follower of fashion, as shown by his taste for much-prized Roman antiquities. His garden in Verona was calculated to make a statement by emulating, as far as it could, the gardens of Rome and Florence. Over the centuries, certain details have changed, but the Giusti garden still retains the definitive elements of a Renaissance garden, with its geometrical layout outlined in box, its statues of pagan deities and its grotto carved out of the tufa rock and faced by a terrifying *mascherone*. This mask is redolent of the Mouth of Hell at Bomarzo (see page 179), which it post-dates, thinks Count Nicolò Giusti, the co-owner of the garden, by perhaps ten years. From its position high on the cliff face, the mask was intended to loom over the lower garden and frighten visitors. It was also an allusion to the Renaissance belief that Reason, the achievement of Man, remained at the mercy of unpredictable and hostile Nature. In 1581 at a staging of Torquato Tasso's pastoral drama *Aminta*, the *mascherone* was made to spit fire, and strange music was heard. Inside, the grotto was decorated with shells, coral, mother-of-pearl, and distorting mirrors to confuse the unwary.

In 1615 when Agostino Giusti died, his son Giovan Giacomo inherited the garden, managing to increase its water supply by gaining permission to divert water from a nearby stream. As a result, additional fountains were built to a more sophisticated design. In the early 1700s, perhaps as a tribute to their famous garden, the Giusti were granted the charming epithet 'del Giardino' after their title.

The garden, approached through the *palazzo* built by the Giusti family, is on two levels, contrastingly formal and wild and differentiated by light

Left The coiling arabesques of Luigi Trezza's French-influenced parterres.

and shade. From the gate, the main axis follows the famous cypress *viale*, source of wonder and awe to generations of visitors. Goethe was one who marvelled at Giardino Giusti's cypresses, deciding that 'a tree whose every branch, from the lowest to the highest, aspires to heaven and which may live 300 years deserves to be venerated.' The poet picked some twigs to make up a bouquet with flowering capers, which he then carried through the streets, 'to the astonishment of the Veronese people'.

A print by Volkamer of 1714 shows the parterres on either side of the cypress avenue planted in complex geometrical patterns of Renaissance perfection, each square outlined by cypresses. This layout was changed in the eighteenth century by the architect Luigi Trezza, who introduced to the parterres a French-influenced design of sweeping circles and horseshoe shapes. The cypresses were removed to open up views over the garden from the palazzo, and graceful statues by Lorenzo Muttoni were installed.

The garden already had a maze, which had famously foxed the brilliant Charles de Brosses in 1736. In his diary he recorded the incident: 'I got lost in the maze, and I was an hour wandering in the blazing sun, and would have still been there, had I not been taken out by one of the people of the place.' This maze, redone by Trezza in 1786, has in recent years been replanted once again.

As Georgina Masson commented, no Italian garden was less suited to the landscape style than Giardino Giusti. Yet landscaped it was in the nineteenth century, and with gusto. Trezza's maze was abolished, and the upper terraces became hillside walks, planned as an itinerary offering magnificent views over Verona. The winding path uphill, softened by an effective planting scheme of lamium, ruscus and acanthus, leads to the cliff-face tower, with the internal staircase linking the two levels of the garden.

In 1892, when it was visited by the American landscape architect Charles Platt, author of an early book on Italian gardens and prominent in the early twentieth-century American Renaissance movement, the romanticized garden was overgrown. He described it as a 'great tangle ... Few of the old fountains are running, many of them being filled up with earth and planted with flowers ... It was very difficult ... to get a view which seemed to give a true impression of the place.' An immense cedar still stands as a survivor from the romantic period.

As the result of the single-minded commitment to the garden of their ancestors shown by co-owners Count Nicolò Giusti and Countess Alessandra Giusti, what Count Nicolò describes as 'a keen-minded historical restoration' has taken place, with expert advice from architect Pier Fausto Bagatti Valsecchi. The lower garden has been returned to its former crisp formality; in 2005 they introduced the lemon trees – 'not only Tuscan but also local' – pictured in Volkamer's print. Now immaculately kept, and once again providing a cherished green sanctuary amidst the city hubbub and bustle, the Giusti garden retains all its solemn loveliness.

Right, above Roman antiquities were much prized during the Renaissance.
Right, below Graceful statues by Lorenzo Muttoni decorate the garden.

Villa da Schio

South of Vicenza and laid out at the foor of the Berici Hills, the terraced eighteenth-century gardens of Villa da Schio, decked with charming statues by Orazio Marinali, have a romantic, almost feminine appeal. While acknowledging this, the owner, ex-engineer Count Giulio da Schio ,explains that he is more interested in the mechanics of how the garden works. He cleaned the statues himself, having gained permission from the notoriously protective authorities, whom he persuaded to come to Costozza di Longare to provide him with a crash course in restoration.

Count Giulio's father's discovery of medieval terracotta drainpipes on the site proves the existence of a much earlier house, now vanished. The present garden's structure (unchanged – even the statues are in their original positions) is the result of remodelling at the beginning of the eighteenth century by Giuseppe Trento and Valeria Fieramosca, although the terracing of this sunny, south-facing site may have served originally to grow fruit and vegetables for the villa's table.

The garden has been described as 'like a vast conservatory', with its statues, grottoes and staircase aligned mostly along a central axis, leaving more room for plants. Intimate in size, it is also not square as it appears from the bottom, but slanted, something only visible from the top of the slope. From the road, the effect is of a delightful perspective garden, with its central staircase and five formal terraces ascending gently up the slope of the Berici Hills.

'The garden started with Neptune,' says Count Giulio, and indeed, behind the fountain of Neptune is a lion's head dating to the 1600s. This and part of a pavilion – the House of the Winds – are all that remain of what was reportedly a lavish park with an aviary and wild animal enclosure.

Marinali's famous dwarfs line the staircase leading up to the main villa's conservatory (originally part of a *limonaia*) with its 100-year-old *Ficus pumila*. Sheltering under the roof here are the two original dwarfs; the rest are copies. Marinali himself lived in a curious, small building higher up the slope, reached through woodland carpeted with violets. Hewn partly from the rock, it is still known as Marinali's Grotto. Here at Costozza, he was close to the quarries of white Vicenza stone from which he carved his graceful gods and shepherdesses and figures from the *commedia dell'arte*.

On the top terrace Marinali's masterful Neptune brandishes his trident over Flora and her lover Zephyrus, who rise from beds of *Iris japonica* 'Variegata' outlined in stone – the pattern copied from that of a 1700 silver plate given to the count's father as a wedding present. From her rustic niche, Venus presides over the next level, where the old greenhouses have given way to a simple box *allée*. This was the first statue that Count da Schio cleaned and, along the way, re-plumbed: the water spurting from the goddess's nipples no longer travels through lead pipes.

Ten thousand visitors come to this delightful garden each year, five thousand of them for the highly regarded May Plant Fair.

Opposite Orazio Marinali's statues sculpted in white Vicenza stone.
Below, left Venus in her rustic niche, water spouting from her nipples.
Below, right Copies of Marinali's famous dwarfs line the staircase leading to the conservatory. The topmost two are original.

Villa Trissino Marzotto

There are two villas here, built by different branches of the powerful Trissino clan, a family of German origin who settled in this part of the Veneto at the beginning of the eleventh century. The feudal stronghold built by the Trissino Baston was transformed into a villa in the more peaceable eighteenth century. It is visible from some way off, perched on its rocky crag, dominating the Agno valley and with the village of Trissino, famous for its jewellery workshops, spread out beneath it.

The commission for designing the villa and its garden was given in 1722 to the baroque architect Francesco Muttoni. Working in Vicenza, he was well known to the eighteenth-century admirers of Palladio who flocked to the city. Muttoni made drawings of Palladio's buildings for an English aristocratic patron and collaborated in republishing an edition of Palladio's work.

Muttoni's original drawings show the scale and scope of what was envisaged here, which was nothing less than to flatten the crag and tame a rocky cliff into a vast, terraced garden. Linked on different levels by ramps, staircases, tunnels and courtyards, it was also adorned with belvederes to take advantage of the panoramic hill-top views.

Sadly, the garden at Trissino was never finished. Muttoni's plans, meticulously coloured in to show which parts of his scheme had been executed, demonstrate that even after twenty-five years of work, he died in 1748 with only a small part of his great project realized. The imposing triple gate, a rococo masterpiece fantastically decorated with scrolls, pinnacles, flaming torches and armorial insignia, and with niches for statues, opens on to the muted fragment which is all that remains of Muttoni's grand design.

The upper villa opens out on to a large, grassy courtyard, its retaining wall studded with statues in rusticated niches and festooned with crimson 'Cocktail' roses. At the far end, the wall supports a raised area, which was Muttoni's resourceful and practical solution to the difficult terrain: this hanging *manège* or *cavallerizza* for schooling horses used the rock as its foundation. The horses reached it by means of a hidden ramp, while their riders ascended a staircase concealed in a belvedere shaped like a minaret. The *cavallerizza* was linked to the *piano nobile* of the villa by a path along the top of the courtyard wall.

Below, a long terrace is lined with lemon pots interspersed with statues. This terrace walk ends in a belvedere parterre garden where stone-edged beds depict the Trissino crest. The solidity of the encircling trees, which have grown to their full height, detracts from the dizzying sense of hanging in space which Muttoni must originally have envisaged.

Further down the hill and reached by a woodland walk through ancient holm oak, lime and chestnut, the roofless and abandoned secondary villa was home to another branch of the family, the Trissino Riale. Two disastrous fires broke out here, the first in 1841. Shortly after it had been rebuilt, the villa went up in flames once more. It now stands doorless, its scars hidden by greenery, its shutters hanging loose, its graceful windows crudely bricked up.

Despite its ruined state, the burnt-out villa exerts a powerful presence, for under its eyeless gaze stands an assembly of some of the finest statues in the Veneto, created in 1715 in *pietra tenera*, a soft limestone, by the sculptor Orazio Marinali. These elegantly pastoral figures of shepherdesses and hunters in eighteenth-century dress throng the grassy terrace below the villa. Clustering on the balustrades and encircling the central octagonal pool, they stand as if waiting for an unseen orchestra to strike up – and for the Venetian aristocrats who once roamed these gardens, gossiping, admiring the view and watching the fountains play, to return again to Trissino. It is a poignant and romantic sight.

There is no archival evidence that Muttoni also designed this lower garden but the baroque splendour of the entrance gates suggests that this may have been the case.

Criss-crossing the parkland and woods are 5 miles (8 kilometres) of paths. Stands of majestic trees open on to meadows of wild flowers, including carpets of cyclamen. There is a cemetery in the grounds and long-dead Trissinos are buried in a ruined chapel reached through the long grass.

By the end of the war Trissino was in a perilous state. In 1950 Count Giannino Marzotto, an entrepreneur and racing driver, bought the estate and restored the upper villa and the grounds. Count Marzotto, the saviour of Trissino, died in 2012. The villa has been inherited by his three daughters.

Opposite The eighteenth century octagonal pool, set in grass, surrounded by statues by Orazio Marinali.
Left Swathed in greenery, the roofless ruin of Villa Trissino Riale overlooks its intact garden.
Below These statues from 1715 are among the finest in the Veneto.

Ca' Marcello

The stately white villa is an eighteenth-century revival of the Palladian style, the original sixteenth-century building having been refashioned in the 1700s on a more monumental scale. The graceful, arcaded *barchesse* wings (*barco* meaning an arch in Venetian dialect) date back to the original house. Two hundred years later, when the imposing new façade of *marmrino* (Venetian plaster), designed by Francesco Maria Preti, was applied, the wings were joined to the pedimented central block.

The Marcello, a noble, military family, have provided two doges and can trace their lineage back to AD 982. They have owned the villa since it was built, apart from an interval of nearly a hundred years beginning in 1725, when it was suddenly and disastrously lost at a game of cards. In 1821 they managed to buy it back again. There are, says Count Jacopo Marcello, fewer than ten of the many thousand Venetian villas built that remain in the hands of the original family.

As the expert John Dixon Hunt has pointed out, early Venetian villas were not the sort of humanist retreats from the city where civilized men retired to enjoy the secluded pleasures of writing, reading and conversation in surroundings chosen to reflect the new-found Renaissance delight in nature and landscape. Such villas existed elsewhere in Italy in more scenic territory. In Venice the history of villas is the history of agriculture. The villas were situated mainly on flat terrain in the centre of their own demesnes. Flanked by its *barchesse*, in which to store crops, the Venetian villa was surrounded by its own cultivated fields, and thus served as the beating heart and management centre of a busy agricultural estate. Even the layout reflected this: a long straight avenue led up to the villa from the nearest road, and it continued on the other side of the villa for perhaps several kilometres until it reached the boundary of the property. This avenue would then often become the central axis of the garden.

To Ca' Marcello the journey from Venice might take a day, depending on water levels in the marshland. The family, when they arrived each summer to run their property, would have had to be self-sustaining. In the *barchesse* the first floor was used to store grain and tobacco, to be sold twice a week in the hall downstairs. This essentially practical and rural way of life continued, as in many other villas, up until the Second World War.

The Marcello archive disappeared in a fire, leaving much to speculation. A garden is not thought to have existed here until the eighteenth century, when the house was impressively renovated for large-scale entertaining. In front of the villa the Italian Garden holds eighteenth- and nineteenth-century statuary of mythological figures, centred around a fountain and simple grass parterres. On each side the gate piers are surmounted by statues of the Four Seasons, with Winter depicted as an old man and Summer grasping a scythe. This austerely elegant layout was put in place in the twentieth century to replace a fussier, nineteenth-century composition. The more recent introduction of soft powder-blue plumbago in pots successfully lightens the severity of the stone.

Over the past ten years the Marcello family have restored their park, in which majestic 300-year-old liriodendron and hornbeam survive from the original *bosco*. Nineteenth-century convallaria-lined paths wind under venerable specimens of plane and beech, and statues appear at the end of dappled paths. Approached by a lime avenue, the picturesque sixteenth-century dovecote is contemporary with the first house, and once housed

pigeons, a Venetian delicacy. The birds were also used as carrier pigeons, which took messages to Venice – a mode of communication the Germans adopted enthusiastically when they commandeered the villa during the First World War. As late as the 1920s, the dovecote also contained silkworms, bred to provide silk for the house.

The rear façade of Ca' Marcello retains its Renaissance style with an appearance of sober simplicity. The large arched window and door, allowing air to circulate through high vaulted rooms, demonstrate the benefits of peace under the powerful Venetian Republic: Venetian villas did not have to protect themselves. Set out here, each on its own pillar, are the villa's famous miniature statues of six monkey musicians, playing a variety of instruments from accordion to tambourine. The conductor is in the middle, baton raised. These statues, as well as others of dwarfs placed along the canal, date back to the seventeenth century. The canal stretching from the back of the house was dug originally to make bricks for the villa. Then, with Venetian practicality, it became a fishpond and finally, a decorative feature of the garden. Near by, the family have planted to expand the park and made a white garden near a walk with vines.

For all its magnificence, Ca' Marcello is still very much a family home, with Count Jacopo or Count Vettor, his father, personally welcoming visitors. A football pitch in the park was made for the Marcello brothers' childhood games; elsewhere, the family keep chickens, ducks, geese and rabbits. And somewhere in the grounds is a stone lion spattered with crimson paint. This lion was painted red by the Marcello boys as a prank in their youth: it has proved impossible to clean.

Opposite, above Francesco Maria Preti's imposing eighteenth-century façade.
Opposite, below The Italian Garden, with simple grass parterres laid out around a fountain.
Left Dappled woodland paths wind through the park.
Below, left The statue of Summer with her scythe, on one of the gate piers of the Italian Garden.
Below, centre One of the famous miniature statues of monkey musicians, dating back back to the seventeenth century.
Below, right The stone lion streaked with red paint.

Orto Botanico di Padova

Founded in 1545 and a World Heritage Site since 1997, this is the oldest university botanical garden in the world to have remained *in situ*. (Pisa, founded in 1544, is an older garden but was relocated.) Miraculously, the Padua Orto Botanico has also preserved its original layout, surviving unchanged, except in detail, for over 450 years.

The idea for the garden was conceived in response to the growing scientific interest in plant classification and plant remedies during the sixteenth century, which aimed to rectify the mistakes caused by faulty identification of plants. Francesco Bonafede, holder of the first chair in botany (Lectrum Simplicium) at Padua University, first posited the idea of a garden of simples (medicinal herbs), where his students could identify and study living plants; in 1545 the Venetian Republic ratified this plan. Daniele Barbaro, a scholarly Venetian nobleman and polymath with an interest in medicine and medicinal botany, has been credited with supervising the botanic garden's planning and construction. The architect Andrea Moroni from Bergamo was also involved.

The site chosen for the *orto* was on land owned by a Benedictine monastery. The trapezoid shape of the plot was to influence the garden's eventual design. In 1552 a circular enclosing wall had to be built to protect the growing collection of plants from thieves, who came by night despite heavy penalties, including imprisonment and exile. Within these protective walls, the overall design for the *hortus cinctus* was of a circle containing a square. This square was partitioned into smaller squares by two main intersecting paths, and then further subdivided into beds laid out in complex, decorative geometric patterns. More beds formed the outside circle, each numbered on a master plan to identify its plants. Later, fountains were added and an irrigation supply ensured.

In the early 1700s, four gateways were put in place, their piers topped with stone vases containing wrought-iron sprays of flowering plants. The wall was adorned with a balustrade of Istrian stone, and busts were placed there of curators of the garden. In the nineteenth century, the greenhouses and a botanical theatre were built, and half-length portraits of eminent botanists such as Carl Linnaeus joined the busts of the curators. Yet apart from these minor changes, two plans – one dated 1654 and now in the

Above Some of the large collection of succulents in the Orto Botanico.

Uffizi collection, the other a lithograph of 1835 – show the design of the garden substantially unaltered.

John Evelyn toured the garden in 1645 during a visit to 'this flourishing and ancient University'. Having seen 'the garden of simples, rarely furnished with plants', he 'gave the order to the gardener to make me a collection of them for an *hortus hyemalis*', which he later showed to Samuel Pepys. Pepys admired the 'leaves laid up in a book of several plants kept dry, which preserve colour, however, and look very finely, better than any Herball'. After seeing this treasure, he confided to his diary that his friend Evelyn suffered from 'a little conceitedness' but could be allowed it, 'being a man so much above others'.

In 1786 Goethe famously visited Padua and saw the fan palm (*Chamaerops humilis* var. *arborescens*) planted here in 1585 and still alive today, protected by a glasshouse. The structure of the plant so fascinated Goethe that it inspired him to think, 'It might be possible to derive all plant forms from one original plant.' The palm is referred to in his celebrated scientific treatise *The Metamorphosis of Plants*. In articulating a view of the homologous nature of plants, Goethe was, in 1790, anticipating the theory of evolution.

The Orto Botanico was continually enlarged with plants from far-flung corners of the globe, benefiting from the long reach of the Venetian Empire. Among the plants it is supposed to have introduced into Europe are the tulip tree (*Liriodendron tulipifera*), the Himalayan cedar (*Cedrus deodara*) and lilac (*Syringa vulgaris*). Freesias, bleeding heart (*Lamprocapnos spectabilis* syn. *Dicentra spectabilis*), morning glory and sunflowers are among the common favourites supposed to have taken root here first. Rhubarb was brought to Europe through the Orto Botanico.

The purpose of the garden has always been to educate. Its stone-edged beds are meticulously maintained, its plants carefully labelled. Even at

weekends, there are many gardeners watering. Between the north and south gates, next to the circular wall, are the medicinal plants, which recall the garden's first purpose. Herbs with historic healing associations are planted here, and so are plants containing compounds now used by the pharmaceutical industry. Yew (*Taxus baccata*) is one of these.

A source of delight to the schoolchildren who linger, enthralled, near by is the collection of poisonous plants, a more recent innovation in the garden. Datura, oleander, convallaria, amaryllis, delphiniums and autumn crocuses are among nature's villains, identified according to their toxicity by the number of black crosses on their labels. Elsewhere are aquatic plants, including the giant Amazon waterlily (*Victoria amazonica*), a section of indigenous plants from the nearby Euganean Hills and an itinerary for the blind with textured and scented plants in pots and labelled in Braille.

The *orto* contains a ginkgo from 1750, and a *Magnolia grandiflora*, probably planted in 1786 and considered to be the oldest in Europe. Outside the walls of the *hortus cinctus* is an arboretum, designed in the second half of the eighteenth century and romanticized with a miniature hill and winding paths. Among its great trees are sequoia, cedar, liquidambar, the American persimmon (*Diospyros virginiana*) and, planted in 1680, a huge, hollow-trunked oriental plane (*Platanus orientalis*). Most striking of all is a tree from Europe, *Fagus sylvatica* 'Pupurea Tricolor', shimmering, pink edged, in the light.

Above and left Aquatic plants in stone-edged pools.

Villa Nazionale Pisani

From the sixteenth century, Venetian noble families would escape from the summer heat in the city to their country villas, which stretched, surrounded by gardens and orchards, along the banks of the Brenta Canal. The nobles would be rowed from St Mark's across the lagoon in comfortable covered barges, called *burchielli*. Arriving at Fusina – still a ferry terminal today – they would transfer to a boat, which was pulled by horses along the Brenta. The villas, at first utilitarian farmhouses, were gradually aggrandized in the seventeenth and eighteenth centuries to suit the *villeggiatura* – the festive merry-go-round of summer entertainment wittily observed by the Venetian playwright Carlo Goldoni. Goldoni described Villa Pisani in the eighteenth century as a place of 'great fun, served meals, dance and shows'.

The simple late sixteenth-century house owned by the Pisani family was demolished in 1720 to make way for the monumental 114-room mansion, now a national museum, which dominates the riverbank today. More palace than villa, it was the brainchild of Alvise Pisani (1664–1741), Venetian ambassador to Versailles, where Louis XIV, the Sun King, granted him the honour of standing as godfather to his son. Returning from France in 1704, Alvise, with his brother Almorò, held high office in Venice. Backed by the large fortune amassed by the Pisani family, both brothers aspired to the position of doge. (Alvise would achieve it in 1735.) It was no doubt with an eye to the pomp and ceremony such a prominent position would involve that they undertook the renovations to the villa.

Surprisingly, the gardens were laid out before the vast house was built. Count Girolamo Frigimelica had been granted the commission for both in 1719. His garden plan was implemented but the house, redesigned more grandly by Francesco Maria Preti after Alvise became doge, had to be fitted into the space Frigimelica had originally left for it. The French influence of le Nôtre, an unsurprising reminder of Alvises's time in France, is evident in the broad central axis. Transverse *allées* radiate off this central vista, creating perspectives. Some of them end in woodland, while others continue out into the surrounding landscape through decoratively carved wrought-iron gates and windows cut into the boundary wall. Immediately behind the villa, Frigimelica had laid out a grand *broderie* parterre. The pleasing substitution of the glorious sheet of water which sweeps down the central perspective today did not happen until 1911, and then for practical rather than aesthetic reasons. The villa was being used as an engineering school at the time and the great canal was built to carry out naval experiments. At the end of the canal is Frigimelica's restored, peach-coloured stable block, crowned with urns and statues, its curved wings, like an exedra, forming a theatrical backdrop to the grand central vista. On the walls inside the open arched loggias is a delicate, nineteenth-century decoration of birds perched on a trellis of reeds and morning glory. The actual stables are pillared in pink Verona stone and adorned with statuettes of prancing horses.

The right-hand side of the park is furnished with a variety of architectural features, including the much-photographed Maze, one of the best preserved in Italy. Frigimelica designed the tower with its external spiral staircase. Two laughing *putti* stand at the Maze's entrance gate and the tower is crowned appropriately with a statue of Minerva, goddess of reason. The Maze has been restored many times and was mainly composed

Right, above The Maze, one of the best preserved in Italy, with Frigimelica's tower.
Right, below Six paths, each offering a different perspective, intersect at the exedra.

of hornbeam in the nineteenth century. It was last replanted with box in the 1970s.

Six paths intersect at the white-walled, eighteenth-century exedra, each offering a different perspective. A winding staircase concealed in a turret leads to a balustraded terrace with statues supposedly by the Venetian sculptor Giovanni Bonazza. Alongside stands the head gardener's house and near by grow magnificent lime trees, planted by Napoleon's gardeners in the early nineteenth century for shade.

Having bought the villa from the by now impoverished Pisani, the Emperor presented it to his stepson, Eugène de Beauharnais. He laid out the Citrus Arboretum, one of the most delightful parts of the garden. In the seventeenth century citrus cultivation had flourished in the great aristocratic villas of the Veneto. Count Frigimelica himself had envisaged the construction of two citrus houses near to the exedra. Walled, with a gate guarded by two stone dogs, the Orangerie Parterre originally contained seven citrus houses and over four hundred potted citrus. After 1815 and the advent of the Habsburgs, the citrus collection grew under the stewardship of a botanically minded viceroy, expanding until it reached a total of over a thousand plants. In the late nineteenth century, the greenhouses also contained camellias and ninety-seven pots of pineapples. Remnants of old heating equipment are still preserved, along with a list of the citrus varieties compiled by a nineteenth-century head gardener.

Reassembled today, the citrus collection stands in geometrical precision on its rediscovered stone pedestals, facing out towards long avenues with statues effectively placed against green hedging. The airy, brick-floored *limonaia* has a workmanlike appeal and houses an assortment of ladders, tools, wheeled stands and painted carts. This working part of the garden is beautifully kept by the villa's gardeners, who display flowering plants on a stand outside their tool shed. The flower borders against the rose-covered outside walls are planted subtly with a wave of blue delphiniums, perovskia, lupins and clematis, shading into grey artemisia. Just outside the walls of the arboretum, *Taxodium distichum* grows beside the lily-filled moat of the Coffee House.

To the west of the stables in the left-hand part of the garden is a small, romantic wood begun during Napoleon's time and finished by the Austrians. Paths wind through thick undergrowth and busts, set in the ground, peer out from underneath curtains of ivy. A satyr grins underneath a yew and broken torsos of statues adorn the mound covering the nineteenth-century ice house. Ceres, goddess of agriculture, surveys the wood from the top of the hill.

Far right, top The *limonaia*, with its collection of historic gardening tools.
Far right, centre A composition in differing shapes and shades of green.
Far right, bottom Fragments of statues set in a romantic wood.

Villa Barbarigo-Pizzoni Ardemani PADUA, VENETO

'Consider', wrote Geoffrey Jellicoe and John Shepherd in 1925, 'an amphitheatre of hills, the ends linked by a great avenue flung across the valley, and in this valley an arrangement of lesser avenues furnished with all the delights of an Italian garden, box hedges, lemon trees, sculpture, pools and fountains, and you have an impression of the gardens at Valsanzibio.'

Villa Barbarigo-Pizzoni Ardemani – known to Shepherd and Jellicoe as Villa Dona Dalle Rose – is also known by its place name, Valsanzibio. This is a corruption of Valle di San Eusebio, meaning the expanse of shallow water across which boats sailed to enter at the villa's imposing watergate. The garden is one of the most beautiful, as well as one of the most intricate and unspoiled, among Venetian baroque gardens. Its design is deceptively simple, arranged around the principal defining axis that was a feature of Italian baroque garden design. The long axis continues up a cypress avenue, climbing the hill behind the villa. In front, it takes the form of a lengthy *tapis vert*, punctuated by fountains and enclosed by high beech hedges. A cross-axis, running east to west, takes water as its inspiration. A series of pools, fountains and cascades, unique in the Veneto, carry the eye in a *prospettiva d'acqua*, which rises up gently towards the wooded, green Euganean Hills. This hilly landscape is not terraced, as in Tuscany or Rome, but has been left to become a natural element in the composition. Beside the two main axes, the garden was divided up into compartmentalized squares or rectangles, each with its own character or theme.

Over this straightforward design was laid a complex iconography. The garden carried a Christian message, promulgated in an itinerary full of symbolic meaning. The itinerary, represented in fountains, inscriptions, around sixty statues and even water jokes, is a journey from the pagan to the Christian world, as well as an account of man's progress towards his own perfectibility and salvation. Villa Barbarigo itself – although aggrandized in a decorative and idealized painting done in the seventeenth century – was 'surprisingly small', in Geoffrey Jellicoe's words, 'and never more than a shelter in which to live for the gardens'.

The Barbarigo, an important family of the Venetian nobility, retreated from plague-stricken Venice to this estate south of Padua in 1630, when the Black Death was rampaging across the city, killing 12,000 Venetians in one month. At Valsanzibio, a modest *giardino segreto* near the house was surrounded by a practical country garden of woods, orchards and fishponds. It was the next generation in the shape of two Barbarigo brothers, Gregorio and Antonio, who around 1660 conceived this elaborate garden. It is generally said to have been completed by 1669, but documents held in Venice's Museo Correr show that its development went on for many years. In 1678 iron supports were ordered for the statues; in 1717 extra land was bought to provide rights over a stream and drainage ditch to replenish the water used in the garden.

Gregorio (1625–97) was the older son, but he gave up his inheritance to join the priesthood. As Bishop of Padua and friend of the Cardinal Secretary of State, Fabio Chigi, he was summoned to the Vatican when, in 1655, Chigi was elected as Pope Alexander VII. Gregorio became Cardinal Barbarigo in 1660, and was closely associated with the stern Counter Reformation ideals laid down in the previous century by the Council of Trent. Personally ascetic, he is supposed, according to Catholic tradition, to have sold his furniture, his clothes and even his bed to help the poor. In 1960 he was canonized. Throughout the process of planning and making the garden, the cardinal consulted closely with Antonio, his more worldly brother, who held the high office, second only to the doge, of Procurator of St Mark's. During his period in Rome Cardinal Barbarigo had dealings with Luigi Bernini, sculptor, engineer and pupil of Gian Lorenzo Bernini, his more famous brother. In 1660 Luigi Bernini was commissioned to draw up a plan for the gardens at Valsanzibio.

The present-day entrance is near the stately watergate called Diana's Gate and dedicated to the sport of hunting. Diana, goddess of the hunt, stands on top, flanked by her dogs and other pagan deities. On either side of the central arch, bas-reliefs carved in stone display lifelike rabbits,

Above, left The stately watergate is dedicated to the sport of hunting.
Above, right The Fountain of the Winds, part of the *prospettiva d'acqua*.

deer and duck, hanging as if in a game larder. Elsewhere are carved fox heads, wild boar and the trophies of the chase – arrows and bows, a quiver and hunting horns, all linked decoratively by rope. This graceful pavilion, Diana's domain, signifies the fallibility of the pagan world, and represents the starting point of the soul's journey through Christianity to salvation. So minutely observed is the symbolism that, as Helena Attlee has pointed out, Diana's mastiff dogs have their heads turned away from the Protestant north to face south towards Rome and the Vatican.

Behind the watergate stretches the shimmering expanse of the *prospettiva d'acqua*, where swans and ducks swim lazily on the calm, mirrored surface of the pools. Reclining, bearded sea gods and water nymphs deck the pools, and ahead are the rocky silhouette and cascade of the Fountain of the Winds. Around the circular Fountain of the Rainbow sit four mischievous *putti*, spraying jets and dangling their chubby feet in the water. To one side, behind a hedge, an intricate, allegorical maze shows visitors the many paths through life, and confronts them with the choice of a route to Virtue. Beyond the Maze, in the woods, the Hermitage represents, perhaps, the cardinal's desire to escape the Vatican and lead a life of Christian retreat.

At the Pila Fountain, where a figure of a woman with rabbits by her feet charmingly symbolizes human fertility, the main avenue turns right towards the house. On one side the monumental, winged statue of Time is a reminder of human mortality; he is crushed by the weight of age on his shoulder. Across the avenue, surrounded by a moat, is the enchanting Rabbit's Island. This conceit, taken from the Romans, who kept rabbits in walled gardens with deep foundations, echoes the Pila Fountain in celebrating the constraints of Time defeated by the continuity of successive generations. On the island, the attractive little stone tower of the aviary has been restored; a stone hawk hovers overhead, guarding the budgerigars inside. An engraving by Vincenzo Campana shows the island in the eighteenth century, densely populated by live rabbits. There are still rabbits here today, mingling with the stone rabbits, their features eroded and barely discernible, which cluster by the water's edge.

The main path brings us through a series of *giochi d'acqua*, each with a precise symbolic meaning, to steps at the end. These steps are inscribed with a poem, of which the last line of the last verse marks the end of the garden's allegorical journey: 'The hell is there and here is Paradise.'

In front of the villa is the curious Fountain of the Mushroom, standing for Revelation; it is surrounded by figures in stone, symbolizing the rewards both of the garden itself and of its spiritual destination. In this *giardino segreto* sheltered by the villa, eighteenth-century members of the Barbarigo family indulged their love of rare and exotic plants, stimulated by the example of Padua's exceptional botanic garden near by (see page 64). The Barbarigo family died out in 1804. In 1929 the villa became the property of the Pizzoni Ardemani, since when three generations of that family have cared for this exceptional place. The damage caused in the Second World War has been repaired, and the fishponds, water cascades, fountains and water jokes which give Valsanzibio its special character have been restored. This paradisiacal garden of the Barbarigo has come alive again.

Right, above The Fountain of the Rainbow, with seated *putti*.
Right, below A stone hawk hovers above the aviary on Rabbit's Island.

Villa Emo

The garden at Villa Emo is a glorious mix: partly, as one would expect, a recreation of a sixteenth-century Veneto garden, but with vibrant English flower borders thrown in for good measure.

Bordering the banks of the Battaglia Canal, the white-stuccoed villa is a graceful and imposing cube with a double staircase leading up to a vast classical portico on the *piano nobile*. It is easy to imagine the impression it would have made in 1588 as it rose from its foundations. To the humanist scholars of the Renaissance, Andrea Palladio's architecture marked a resurgence of the classical spirit, evoking echoes of a lost and golden age. Palladio himself was, with his sons, a frequent visitor to classical sites, where he undertook surveys of Roman buildings, enabling him to reprise the porticos and pediments of the temples of ancient Rome in Venetian domestic architecture. In fact, Villa Emo is the work not of Palladio but of his accomplished pupil Vincenzo Scamozzi, who published his own late Renaissance work on the theory of architecture.

In accordance with Palladian principles, the main reception rooms open off a central hall, here beautifully frescoed with paintings of the Four Seasons. From these rooms the view is unchanged, with the ancient, conically shaped Euganean Hills as backdrop. These hills were home to Petrarch, the first person since antiquity to express his love for landscape and the countryside, and, already in the 1300s, a gardener as we would recognize it, who kept a day book recording the success and failure of his plants.

The garden was restored in the 1960s by the present owner's mother, Countess Giuseppina Emo Capodilista, who found, in what were cornfields, the outline of an historic garden. This outline was later confirmed by an eighteenth-century plan discovered in the family archives. At the front, overlooked from the villa's *piano nobile*, is a box *broderie* parterre with interlaced initials picked out in gravel from the hills. This parterre was one of the four elements common to Venetian gardens that the countess set out to reinstate, two of the others being an orchard and a hornbeam tunnel.

The most important discovery was the two long, rectangular fish pools that flank the house, rare survivals of a once common Veneto tradition. Their brick walls, reclaimed intact from the mud, still include the recesses in which young carp could breed and shelter. Now huge carp once again patrol the ponds and freshwater mussels have been sighted.

Countess Marina Emo has added a love of plants to her mother's successful restoration. A wildflower meadow adjoins the garden, overlooked by beds of standard Iceberg roses. Elsewhere, Paul Neyron roses succeed tulips as bedding-out. The countess plants her tulips in pasta colanders, for protection and for easy lifting.

At the back of the villa the countess has placed a large, horizontal coat of arms to replace a pool in the centre of the lawn. 'Too big,' she laughingly admits. 'But at least our arms are two discreet stripes. Imagine if it had been a dragon.'

The English borders are Countess Marina's great achievement – a fireworks display of the colour she loves. Blue iris contrasts with orange roses. In early summer the palette is dreamy – blue, pink and white, brightened with flashes of clear yellow. Here are familiar English favourites: lychnis, phlox, lupins, poppies, alchemilla, tradescantia and peonies, enabled to survive in the hot sun by a network of subterranean springs. Roman pipelines, too, still carry underground water. Later, the colours darken as *Buddleja* 'Black Knight', aconitum and purple Michaelmas daisies take over.

At the end, silhouetted against the hills, is the hornbeam tunnel, added in the 1970s, its open mouth an invitation into the coolness inside. The lower temperature here enables all sorts of woodland plants to grow. Snowdrops, bluebells, fritillaries, Peruvian scillas and even primroses thrive.

Countess Marina now lives in the villa's stables, once home to the horses that pulled barges all the way to Venice. Close at hand, past a paulownia leaning over a fish pool, is one of the most magical parts of this garden, a *Taxodium distichum* avenue. Underplanted with *Iris japonica*, it holds two statues, bought locally and nicknamed, for their facial appearance, Glenn Ford and Doris Day. 'They were just growing lichen when I went away to Rome,' says the countess, 'and while I was away, they cleaned them.'

Above, left Vicenzo Scamozzi's Villa Emo, overlooking the box parterre with its interlaced initials.
Above, right One of the long rectangular fish pools, recently re-excavated and home to carp and freshwater mussels.

FRIULI

Rarely visited by tourists and off the beaten path, the region of Friuli–Venezia Giulia occupies Italy's far-eastern corner. The derivation of its name – Friuli (from *Foro Julio*) and Giulia (referring to Caesar) – points to its importance to the Roman Empire: the area was a vital outpost against marauding barbarians and it is rich in Roman remains, including the exquisite fourth-century mosaics at Aquileia.

Friuli's strategic geographical position at the crossroads of Latin, German and Slavic cultures has meant that rival powers have tussled over this comparatively narrow strip of land. It has frequently been invaded and overrun – by the Huns, the Goths, the Lombards and later the Nazis – and has come under the rule of the Venetian Republic, Napoleonic France and, in the nineteenth century, the Habsburg Empire. Only after the capital, cosmopolitan Trieste, was reunited with Italy in 1954 could the autonomous region of Friuli–Venezia Giulia be established in 1963. It still bears many signs of Austrian and Slavic influence.

Castello di Duino

Crouched on a rocky spur high above the Gulf of Trieste, the fifteenth-century castle at Duino is the seat of the princely Torre e Tasso (Thurn und Taxis) family, once Hereditary Postmasters to the Holy Roman Emperor. There are two castles on this promontory: Dante is supposed to have stayed at the older eleventh-century castle, whose picturesque ruins cling to the rocks far below. The 'new' clifftop castle is itself built on a Roman military site. A stone, placed here in the third century, commemorates Emperor Diocletian's visit to this remote outpost of the Roman Empire.

The castle gardens, carved out of the cliffs on many different levels, are looked after faithfully by Nino, gardener here for over fifty years. They are trim and neat with seasonal plantings of myosotis and begonias in the Pool Garden, and *Canna indica*, hydrangeas and impatiens in riotous shades along the moat. Wisteria clambers over the low wall leading up to the castle gateway, while clipped Boston ivy (*Parthenocissus tricuspidata* 'Veitchii') softens the massive blocks of stone. From his small greenhouse Nino provides the cuttings and seedlings – salvias, geraniums, centranthus – for all these splashes of colour.

The Carso, a rock band which stretches from here all the way round the Dalmatian coast to Greece, is criss-crossed at Duino by streams, which bring water to the garden. Ancient trees provide shade, including a 400-year-old cork oak (*Quercus suber*). A thick band of trees – holm oak, cypress and laurel – protects the garden from the ferocious wind, the bora, which roars through this corner of Italy.

Each year 65,000 visitors come here and walk the sea wall girdling the castle to admire the dizzying views of sea and sky. A 400-year-old bridge spans a ravine where agaves grow and irises flower in spring among the rocks. Seagulls nest in these cliffs, wheeling and diving over the terrace, which juts out vertiginously over a sheer drop to the water. Somewhere down below, reached by a woodland path, is the family's private beach.

In 1916 the castle, Austrian territory in the First World War, was bombarded by the Italians from the spit of land opposite. From 1943 to 1945 it housed the Kriegsmarine (the Navy of the Third Reich), who, fearful of an Allied naval attack, built an enormous bunker deep underground, using forced labour. This historical curiosity is now open to the public. When the British did come, it was by road. They did not leave until 1954. For the intervening nine years the prince was shut out of his castle while it was requisitioned by the British military authorities. During visits to his ancestral home, he was forced to pitch a tent in the old castle ruins.

After this the castle remained closed until 2003. During its nineteenth-century heyday Mark Twain had been a guest at Duino, as had Franz Liszt and Johann Strauss. The German poet Rainer Maria Rilke composed here his *Duino Elegies*, later translated into English by Vita Sackville-West. And from along the coast at nearby Miramare, Archduke Maximilian and his bride, Charlotte of Belgium, chose this peerless spot, with its rocky outcrops, its towering trees, its flower-decked terraces and vast horizons, for their honeymoon.

Page 71 The ruined eleventh-century Castello di Duino, perched on a rocky promontory above the Gulf of Trieste.
Left The later Castello di Duino towers above the pool garden.

Castello di Miramare

Above The Castello di Miramare, clad in white Istrian limstone, faces out to sea.

This is the home built for a young couple, Maximilian of Habsburg and his beloved wife, Charlotte of Belgium, during the happiest days of their tragically foreshortened marriage. Younger sibling of the future Emperor Franz Joseph, 'Max', as he was known within his family, was very different from his older brother. Sensitive, a lover of nature and a collector of antiquities, the twenty-three-year-old archduke had already travelled widely in the Mediterranean when he decided in 1855 to build a castle on a rocky spur jutting out into the Adriatic Sea near Trieste, and to reclaim the barren promontory for a botanical park.

The fairytale castle, clad in white Istrian limestone, perches on top of a strong, defensive wall, facing squarely out to sea. This, and the cabin-like intimacy of the couple's private rooms on the ground floor, was designed to give the impression of being on board a ship afloat, no doubt reminding the archduke of days spent at sea with the Austrian fleet. On Christmas Day 1860, with the state apartments still unfinished, the archducal couple finally took possession of their home. 'Miramar is a delicious position,' wrote Charlotte in the summer of 1861. 'We have

splendid apartments, warm in spring, fresh in summer, with the murmur of the sea in the background and the fishermen's boats passing.' A narrow balustraded walk encircles the castle on the seaward side. Maximilian found that 'dear, tranquil Miramare', where 'the blue sea murmured around me', was the place where his soul, too, was restored and his energy replenished.

Maximilian and Charlotte journeyed to Miramare by train and, while the castle was being completed, stayed at the eccentric, miniature *castelleto*. The rocky shoreline yielded no space for a wide and princely entrance road. Instead, a holm oak avenue was planted from the castellated entrance gate, and the railings embellished with pineapples, Maximilian's emblem and a symbol of richness and prosperity. Maximilian also aggrandized the harbour with terracing and an elaborate double staircase. A third-century BC granite sphinx which guards the end of the harbour quay is the only one of Maximilian's Egyptian antiquities to survive at Miramare.

The magnificent parterre with its terraces sweeping down to the sea was also laid out according to Maximilian's plan. For statuary, he turned to the Berlin firm Moritz Geiss. They made copies of ancient statues housed in Berlin's museums in zinc, a material thought to be able to withstand the salt and harsh winters of the Gulf of Trieste. In Maximilian's time, the parterre was less conventional than it is today, and included tall, tropical species like yuccas, araucarias and palms.

In 1859–60 Maximilian had joined a scientific expedition to Brazil, sending seeds and rhizomes back to the hothouses at the Schönbrunn Palace in Vienna, and eventually publishing a book about the new and fascinating plants the expedition discovered. From now on, whenever he was abroad, he indulged his habit of buying large quantities of trees, plants and seeds, which were sent first to Schönbrunn and then to Miramare. Firs from Spain and the Himalayas, cedars from North Africa and the Lebanon, cypresses from California and Mexico, all found their way to Maximilian's burgeoning garden.

Work on the park had also started: in 1859 Anton Jelinek, who was to become Maximilian's trusted gardener, had been appointed to oversee the design and planting. Maximilian, with his serious interest in botany, was very much involved. With typical sensitivity, he did not choose to emulate the vast and monumental park at Schönbrunn, preferring a more intimate layout of romantic, winding paths and secluded woodland, planted to imitate nature. At the same time, the park was to be a botanical laboratory where plants from all over the world, even exotics, had to withstand the gusty bora wind sweeping the Adriatic, as well as survive the bitter Trieste winters. To aid them, tender plants were first acclimatized by a spell in the castle orangeries, and then protected from gales by the tall, wind-resistant black pine of Austria (*Pinus nigra* var. *austriaca*), planted in belts as windbreaks. Groves of these beautiful trees can be found covering the rise to the east of the castle.

The archduke and his gardener inherited bare, rocky slopes on the promontory but managed to build up an arboretum of over 300 different species of tree, of which about 120 survive. Between 1859 and 1864, twenty reports attest to the difficulties the two men faced and the failures they endured, including the demise of Maximilian's plan for a more Mediterranean, citrus-dominated garden.

The area to the north of the castle still holds most of the exotic trees. Notable is a 40-metre/130-foot *Sequoiadendron giganteum* and two redwoods, *Sequoia sempervirens*. A cluster of Californian incense cedars (*Calocedrus decurrens*) stands out, as do the striking, red-barked strawberry trees (*Arbutus unedo*), here grown to a splendid size. There is a huge ginkgo, Himalayan and Atlantic cedars, and from the New World Monterey and digger (*Pinus sabineana*) pines. Originating from the conifer forests of the Sierra Nevada, the incense cedars would have made a huge impact when seen here in the mid-nineteenth century.

Maximilian was able to send plants and seeds back from the New World because in 1863 he had been proclaimed Emperor of Mexico. In 1864 he renounced his claim to the Austrian throne and he and Charlotte set sail for Vera Cruz. Behind the naïve young archduke's acceptance of this poisoned chalice lay the machinations of Napoleon III, who was in Mexico in search of mineral wealth and to recover unpaid debts. By crowning a puppet emperor, Napoleon saw a way to strike a blow at the republican movement in Mexico and bolster the European presence. Franz Joseph saw the chance to use his younger brother to restore glory to the Habsburg name.

Within two years the political situation had deteriorated so badly that Charlotte left Maximilian and returned to Europe, visiting the Pope to

solicit aid for her beleaguered husband. It was all in vain. The French, who had crowned Maximilian, cynically abandoned him by withdrawing their troops at the end. Maximilian was shot with his generals by the Mexican republican government on 19 June 1867, aged thirty-five. He was never to see his beloved park mature.

Immediately the news reached Paris on 1 July, a shocked Edouard Manet began the first of three large paintings of the execution, a political protest which ensured the works were never exhibited in Paris during his life.

Charlotte did not recover from this blow. Symptoms of madness appeared and after being confined at Miramare, she was taken by her family back to Belgium. The castle was used occasionally by Habsburg family members during the summer months. After the First World War and the collapse of the Austro-Hungarian Empire, Italy annexed Trieste. From 1930 to 1937 the castle was the home of Prince Amedeo of Savoy-Aosta, fox-hunting Anglophile and a cousin of Victor Emmanuel III, who went on to become Viceroy of Italian East Africa. He is commemorated – as is Maximilian – by a striking statue in the garden. The castle is now a museum.

Above A twentieth-century statue of Prince Amedeo of Savoy-Aosta.

LIGURIA

The narrow strip of land that is Liguria is squeezed between the mountains and the coast. Space is at a premium and Genoa, beloved of Byron and Shelley and once known for its gardens stretching down to the sea, the pleasure gardens of its great merchant princes, has, from the nineteenth century onwards, lost much of this heritage to insensitive overdevelopment.

Edith Wharton wrote about Genoa's Villa Doria (now Villa del Principe), where in 1521 the great Admiral Andrea Doria created a villa and garden 'to enjoy in peace the fruits of an honoured life'. When John Evelyn visited it in 1644, he found 'orange-trees, citrons and pomegranates, fountains, grots and statues' in what was described by other travellers as a fine Renaissance garden. By Wharton's time, at the beginning of the twentieth century, change had already come and part of the grounds was cut off by a railway cutting. More recently, the building of a motorway close by compounded the damage.

Liguria has a temperate climate which enables it to grow olives, flowers for export and vines on steep, stone-terraced slopes. Its rocky coastline includes the Riviera di Ponente, known for the cultivation of roses and the rugged and unspoiled landscape of the Cinque Terre. The road which hugs the coastline follows the ancient Roman Via Aurelia.

La Mortola: Giardini Botanici Hanbury

Of all the gardens in Italy, the entrance to the Hanbury Botanic Gardens is the most dramatic. Steep, its perspective is framed by the arch of the Victorian gateway and narrowed by a corridor of cypress at the top. The effect of sea and sky against the green is theatrical, almost like a stage set. Vertiginous steps lead down to the garden path, the beginning of a 91-metre/300-foot descent to the sea crashing on the rocks below. Paths wind through massed banks of scent and colour, and the combination of landscape and lush planting, all bathed in the pure Riviera light, is breathtaking.

La Mortola, as it is also called, is inextricably linked with the nineteenth-century Englishman Thomas Hanbury, whose descendants still live in a villa, a former guesthouse, on one side of the property. His unusual history is foretold by the Chinese character *fo* inscribed above the gateway. This inscription, meaning happiness, was presented to Sir Thomas by the first ambassador sent by China to the West in 1879. It is a reminder of Hanbury's past in Shanghai, where he pursued the enormous fortune in property that, fourteen years later, he would use to pay for his garden.

Of Quaker stock, Hanbury had been born into a prosperous pharmaceutical dynasty, Allen Hanbury and Barry. His brother Daniel was a scientist, a pharmacologist interested in the botanical origins of drugs. Thomas had sent back many specimens from China to be nurtured in Daniel's greenhouses in Clapham. It was Daniel, taking a 'chemist's holiday' on the Riviera, who first saw Punta della Mortola, a rocky promontory where Palazzo Orengo – a dilapidated house so old that Machiavelli was said to have stayed in it – stood among cypress and olive groves. Three years later, in 1867, Thomas Hanbury followed Daniel on holiday to Menton. He was bored and restless and hated the English winter with its fog and 'cheerless sky'. Leaving England on 9 March, by April he had bought himself the headland and the villa. He was thirty-five: forty years of gardening at La Mortola lay ahead of him.

The Hanbury brothers' plan was to create a botanical garden where exotic plants could acclimatize and live alongside indigenous species. There were disadvantages: drought, poor soil, isolation and the palazzo itself which, he confided to a friend, 'bears a striking resemblance to a barn with rooms at present'. Yet citrus, pomegranates, peaches, pears and cherries grew in the garden, and there was a palm tree by the side of the house. Soon, Daniel Hanbury would sow vibrant pink *Cistus albidus* and white *C. salviifolius*, as well as the seeds of holm oak, buckthorn and other evergreen shrubs. The first new tree to be planted was a eucalyptus and by 1880 fifty different species of eucalyptus were thriving in the garden. In 1867, Daniel oversaw the introduction of *Ceratonia siliqua* in the shape of twelve young carobs. By the shoreline, he planted the now magnificent maritime pines (*Pinus pinaster*). Succulents were a natural choice in the drought-ridden conditions and suited Thomas Hanbury's maxim: 'Never go against Nature.' For impact, Thomas Hanbury planted them not singly but in groups. The Succulent Garden at La Mortola is still a show-stopping sight: the gigantic, man-sized plants, some of them original, crowd together along rocky terraces, clinging precariously to the hillside.

For a year the two brothers gardened together, Daniel Hanbury, with his superior botanical expertise and contacts, corresponding with colleagues who would send him seeds from all over the world. From Algeria came bougainvillea; from South Africa, *Aloe ferox*. A friend brought *Clematis armandii* back from China; roses arrived from their father's garden in Clapham. In 1868 the Hanburys took on as their head gardener Ludwig Winter, whose job at the Tuileries had ended abruptly when he was sacked for whistling 'La Marseillaise' in the Empress Eugénie's presence. A young man of twenty-two, Winter was already displaying talent as a landscaper. He helped to bring structure to the burgeoning collection, transforming it into a real garden, traversed by pathways, where plants were placed

Page 75 *Cycas revoluta*, the Japanese sago palm, at La Mortola. *Opposite, left* The Viale Nuovo, laid out by Dorothy Hanbury. *Opposite, right* A Judas tree blooms in spring. *Left* Part of the Succulent Garden, laid out on the hillside.

bold gardener,' says Carolyn Hanbury, who still lives in the garden and acts as its ambassador. 'Dorothy threw colour in; she had five thousand pots.' With her liking for the Italianate style, Dorothy added pools and fountains, vistas, steps and seats. She straightened winding paths and laid out the main artery of the garden, the Viale Nuovo.

By the small belvedere at the top of the garden, the path slopes down past a venerable *Yucca elephantipes* and the fairytale, lilac-blue blossoms of jacaranda. Strelitzias with their broad, banana-like leaves and gorgeous bird-of-paradise flowers announce that this is a garden of exotics. Among the olive trees aloes grow. Clouds of white *Rosa laevigata* cover the stone walls near the Cycad Avenue. Winter's favourite palm trees hold their heads high above the villa, where Dorothy's tulips and lavender have been replaced by the succulents of Sir Thomas's time.

Dorothy's Perfumed Garden was created in 1927, though a huge specimen of red bignonia was planted earlier by Sir Thomas. Scent drifts up from a medley of herbs, scented geraniums, *Salvia mellifera*, *Calycanthus occidentalis*, *Akebia quinata* and other scented plants. Near by, unlabelled, is the sole specimen in the garden of *Rosa brunonii* 'La Mortola'.

The *giardinetti* were laid out by Dorothy in what may well be the oldest part of the garden in memory of the local men who died in the First World War. Dorothy, says Carolyn Hanbury, also planted the tree peonies, in the 1950s, although the *Araucaria cunninghamii* dates back to the time of Daniel Hanbury. Arching everywhere are huge sprays of bridal white *Spiraea cantoniensis*, while against a wall a lush bank of turn-of-the-century red climbing tea rose 'Noëlla Nabbonnand' is a tribute to Dorothy's love of colour. As Charles Quest-Ritson has pointed out in his book *The English Garden Abroad*, Dorothy's interest lay in making an ornamental flower garden at La Mortola rather than expanding the botanical collection.

In the lowest part of the garden runs a section of Roman road, the Via Aurelia, overhung by Judas trees (*Cercis siliquastrum*). Popes and kings have passed this way, and marching armies, including Napoleon's. Below, is a subtropical orchard with avocados, banana palms, kiwi fruit and feijoa, the pineapple guava from Brazil, underplanted with a blue haze of iris, *Scilla hughii* and some of the many different types of salvia which used to grow in a prized botanical grouping here. Though this collection has been dispersed, many different species of passiflora clothe the lower pergola, including the beautiful *Passiflora* 'Incense'. By the pergola is the datura copse.

Thomas Hanbury employed forty-two gardeners at La Mortola. Cecil and Dorothy retained forty, with one gardener's sole job being to pick and arrange flowers for the house. Between the wars, the garden was at its zenith. Yet Cecil and Dorothy usually only spent the winters at La Mortola, and, says Carolyn Hanbury, 'Dorothy kept her children at arm's length and didn't involve them in the garden.' After the Second World War, although the garden was open again and Winston Churchill came to paint here, there was a gradual decline. Fewer gardeners meant that Dorothy could not reverse for a second time the wartime years of neglect. In 1960, Dorothy, by then wheelchair-bound and resisting huge offers from developers, retired to the guesthouse, safeguarding La Mortola by selling the estate to the Italian state. In 1983 it was transferred to the University of Genoa, where, almost a hundred years before, Sir Thomas had founded a botanical institute.

for landscaping effect. It was Winter who took charge, alongside Daniel Hanbury, when Thomas and his new wife, Katherine, went back to China for two years. In 1871 they would return, with a shipment of cycas palms and a future curator for the garden: their baby son, Cecil.

Thomas and Daniel were not only brothers but allies, confidants and co-adventurers in the great project they had undertaken. Thomas relied on Daniel's vastly superior horticultural knowledge and shared with him a strong Quaker faith. Practical and even ruthless though the businesslike Thomas could be, he also shared with Daniel an attitude, aptly described by his biographer Alasdair Moore, that 'a botanic garden was a heady mixture of the mind, the wallet and the soul'.

It was thus an immense sadness to Thomas when Daniel, his brother and right-hand man, died in 1875 of typhoid in his fiftieth year. Three months later, Ludwig Winter left to set up a plant nursery, supported by Thomas, along the coast at Bordighera. Thomas was now alone at the helm. Nevertheless, his commitment to La Mortola ensured that Daniel's collection of 557 species in 1875 had risen to 5,800 by 1912, with detailed records of the planting still surviving in the archives of the museum in Bordighera. Among Thomas's many philanthropic projects was his 1903 gift to the Royal Horticultural Society for the purchase of land at Wisley. As this energetic, far-thinking man was fond of saying, 'It is better to wear out than to rust out.' By the turn of the century, the director of the Royal Botanic Gardens, Kew, was claiming that La Mortola had 'no rival among the principal collections of living plants in the world'. Queen Victoria visited and spent time there sketching.

In 1920 Thomas's son, Cecil, returned after the First World War to find the garden 'bare, arid . . . weedchoked' with 'stunted malformed trees and shrubs'. Fortunately, his wife, Dorothy, was a keen horticulturist, her father and brother both landscape designers. 'She was a great gardener, a

Villa Boccanegra: Giardino Piacenza

Boccanegra dates back to the seventeenth century and has had many owners, including Giuseppe Biancheri, politician, rose-grower and friend of the Hanburys at La Mortola (see page 76) and of their head gardener, the German botanist Ludwig Winter. But it is mainly associated with the Victorian gardener and self-taught botanist Ellen Willmott.

Ellen Willmott led an enviable life, able to indulge her passion for plants and gardens on a grand scale through the generosity of her father and her godmother, who sent her £1,000 on every birthday. When she bought Boccanegra in 1906, she already owned two gardens – 13.5-hectare/33-acre Warley Place, Essex, in England, where for a time she employed nearly a hundred gardeners, and Château de Tresserve in France, famous for its iris collection and its beds of over 11,000 roses. Boccanegra, although she was there only during March and April and in the winter months of November and December, offered her an irresistible opportunity to experiment with subtropical and exotic as well as Mediterranean plants.

It may well have been Thomas Hanbury who found Boccanegra for Ellen Willmott. She had already visited him at La Mortola, a couple of miles along the coast. With the house, she inherited a scorchingly hot, arid hillside sloping down to the sea and terraced with olives. Water was obviously a priority; to the west, at the upper end of the garden, there

was a sizeable water basin. Before the war, a further large tank was built out of concrete on the eastern side of the garden, at the upper end. Used to getting her own way, Miss Willmott embarked on all-out war with the Italian railway, which planned to expropriate some of her land. This war she lost, but she succeeded in screening off the railway line with eucalyptus and *Phoenix dactylifera* ordered from a Riviera nursery. All in all, over the next four years, she spent £2,000 on plants – figs, mimosa, yuccas, citrus, cedars, 300 cannas, and opuntia, agaves and aloes by the score. Some of the exotic plants survive today, as do the paths she laid out, following the natural contours of the rocks. 'My plants and my gardens come before anything in life for me,' she wrote, 'and all my time is given up to working in one garden or another, and when it is too dark to see the plants themselves, I read or write about them.' She organized the running of her three botanical gardens by despatching, from wherever she was, a stream of postcards.

Some time after buying Boccanegra, Ellen Willmott began to run out of money. She rented out Villa Boccanegra and in 1923 was forced to sell the property to an Englishman, John Tremayne. He extended the main house and made a small *laghetto* (pond). In 1956 Boccanegra was acquired by Mario Sertorio, who gave it to his wife, Emilia. In 1969, when

Opposite A variety of succulents and other plants cling to the steep sides of the garden.
Centre Paths weave through the olives.
Left Scilla peruviana, irises and agapanthus grow in blue drifts under trees.

are wound around the olive's trunk. To the right is a deep ravine with cistus, prickly pears, rosemary and *Echium fastuosum* crowding its steep sides. Neat pittosporum hedges lead to the *laghetto*, framed by four cypresses and overhung by a Judas tree (*Cercis siliquastrum*).

Boccanegra's beauty, set against a timeless backdrop of olive groves, appears natural but is the result of an inspired eye and immaculate planning. Paths weave down through the olives and under red-barked arbutus trees, among banks of myrtle and pittosporum, past groves of cycas and through blue drifts of agapanthus, irises and *Scilla peruviana*. Blowsy pink *Rosa* 'Follette' clambers up the grey olive trees, and succulents – agaves, aloes and tall-flowering yuccas – provide drama and punctuation points. Their seedlings are dug up and replanted all over the garden. Sun-loving hibiscus basks on a stone wall above the path, and sedums, lavender, pelargonium and different kinds of rosemary sprawl over the dry hillsides. Everywhere you hear the crashing sound of the sea.

Guido Piacenza's first task, on arriving in 1983, was to clear the garden of a tangle of self-seeded trees, shrubs and climbers. With no documentation available, it was up to him to lay bare the bones of the garden and try to decipher Miss Willmott's ideas. Part of her much-loved rock garden – planted with drought-resistant plants – and her succulent area had survived; her iris collection and huge range of pelargoniums had not. Like Ellen Willmott, Guido Piacenza is a plantsman. In 1986 he was joined at Boccanegra by his wife, Ursula, a scientist with a special interest in experimenting with new plants. Together, they began, successfully, to introduce Californian, South African and Australian species to the garden – plants accustomed to the Mediterranean weather pattern of dry summers alternating with winter rains. Each year, rare and interesting plants are added to the Piacenzas' collection; couriers arrive at Boccanegra bearing seeds from all corners of the globe. Yet there is only one gardener to help Ursula: he weeds, waters and repairs the dry-stone walls.

Towards the end of the garden, the mood becomes more mysterious, with cypress adding darker notes and a bridge spanning the ravine. Glimpses of the sea appear and disappear in carefully orchestrated views.

Further down, enormous agaves grow out of cracks in the rock. Down by the shore, in the working part of the garden, a citrus orchard is laid out next to a banana grove, and a *potager* flourishes. Even the testy Miss Willmott would concede that this exceptional private botanical garden is in the best of hands.

Emilia died, Boccanegra passed into the family of her sister Giuseppina, the wife of Enzo Piacenza. Enzo's father, Felice (born 1843), had created Parco Burcina in Piedmont, where, at the turn of the century, 950 hardy hybrid rhododendrons were planted. It was Harold Hillier, the famous plantsman from Winchester in England, who inspired Enzo's son Guido to start his own amateur nursery in 1970. Guido Piacenza later married a Tuscan botanist, Ursula, who looks after Boccanegra today with great knowledge and love.

Villa Boccanegra is concealed behind high gates on the Via Aurelia, now the busy coast road. Banksian roses tumble over the garden walls. These roses appear in a photograph of Giuseppe Biancheri taken at the turn of the century. The bougainvillea which covers the house's walls may be the one pictured in a *Country Life* article of November 1929. As you enter through the gates, a terrace straight ahead offers a panoramic view of the garden. A second, lower terrace has an exotic air, with a huge *Strelitzia nicolai* flourishing. *Petrea volubilis*, the sandpaper vine, billows, in a cloud of purplish blue, against a wall, and potted orchids are trained up into the branches of trees. From here, a cobbled path leads downhill through sprawling banks of scented geraniums, past an olive tree entwined in the serpentine embrace of an ancient wisteria, whose thick, gnarled branches

Villa Gavotti della Rovere

SAVONA, LIGURIA

This four-square, green-shuttered villa at Albissola, along the coast from Genoa, incorporates an earlier fifteenth-century house; the outline of its tower can still be discerned in the walls. According to tradition, the original villa was the birthplace of the della Rovere pope Julius II (1503–1513), patron of Michelangelo, who bullied the reluctant sculptor into undertaking and then completing his great work, the ceiling in the Sistine Chapel.

In the mid-1700s the villa was splendidly enlarged in the baroque style by Francesco Maria della Rovere, who became Doge of Genoa in 1765. Geralomo Brusco, architect of the Republic of Genoa, was commissioned to add two long wings, which enclose an Italian Garden. The wings support balustraded terraces, crowned with statues on mythological subjects. Two magnificent staircases in marble from Carrara sweep down and meet at a central *vasca*.

At the same time as the house was being refurbished, Francesco della Rovere undertook the drainage of the surrounding marshland, building banks and digging canals to redirect water from two rivers which flowed down into the marshes from the hills. The countryside too was reordered; local houses were dignified with painted architectural features; roads were enhanced with gates and exedras and vase-topped columns. From the terrace of his villa, Francesco Maria could look out over the Arcadian landscape he had created.

As a result of the rivers, water was an important element in the eighteenth-century garden. Sirens and dolphins were made to spurt water from marble fountains, and in a pool surrounded by a vine-clad pergola a nymph bestrides a sea monster.

The present owner, the scholarly Marchese Giovanni Maria Gavotti, explains the significance of the 250-year-old statues as a playful duel between Man and Nature, and a celebration of the qualities of both. This is exemplified by the statues of fauns, and the massive sculptural group of Hercules battling with the Nemean lion.

From the top of the staircase, the nearby *autostrada* is visible, but lower down in the Italian Garden the effect is of a secret enclave. The original marble-edged parterre contains day lilies and Japanese anemones, while hydrangeas in terracotta vases are lined up outside the twin *gallerias*. An imposing Atlas cedar and a 115-year-old magnolia are, says the marchese, 'not the trees for this garden; the planting should be low so that you can see the architecture'.

The unique glory of Villa Gavotti della Rovere is to be found inside the *gallerias*, where the Four Seasons are depicted in rich stucco in the lyrical Genoese baroque style. The stucco work is three-dimensional, of exquisite grace and delicacy. Another Arcadian fantasy, it was the imaginative creation of the Porta brothers, stucco artists from Lombardy and well known also across the Alps in Austria and Bavaria. In the room dedicated

to Spring, foliage weaves across the ceiling, blossoming branches cover the walls and *putti* hold up vases of roses. Summer is adorned with cherubs reaping grain under a sky in which birds wheel in flight among the laden branches of fruit trees. Lifelike plums, apricots, apples and wheat sheaves decorate the walls, and even the candelabra are entwined with fruit and flowers. In the hall of Autumn, the capitals of columns are entwined with bunches of grapes, while vines tangle around the windows and more *putti* frolic, this time with wine barrels. Across the Italian Garden in the opposite *galleria*, Winter is enclosed in a rocky, stalactite-encrusted cave. The grotto is lightened by mirrors, which reflect candelabra in the shape of coral branches.

Doge Francesco Maria lavished his fortune on his house and did not live to see it completed. It was his widow, Caterina, who finished the works and on her death in 1789 bequeathed the villa to her nephew. From him the property descended to the Gavotti family of Savona and Genoa, kin of the della Rovere. They have held it for the past 200 years.

Left The Italian Garden is enclosed by balustraded terraces crowned with eighteenth-century statues.
Centre Behind the shuttered doors, flanked by lemon trees, are the galleries depicting the Four Seasons.
Right An ornate door leads into the villa.

La Cervara

Built by Benedictine monks who laid the foundation stone in the summer of 1361, the abbey occupies one of the most dramatically beautiful sites in all Italy. It perches on top of a high, wooded cliff above the famous coast road between Santa Margherita and Portofino, with a view over the Gulf of Tigullio and Shelley's 'sublime' scenery. Its drive winds up the steep, wooded hill to end in a little square with a tower built in the sixteenth century as a lookout against Saracen raiders. A painted archway leads through into the cloistered inner courtyard.

There were monks living at the abbey until the beginning of the twentieth century and, though now privately owned, their monastery remains a spiritual and peaceful place. The fourteenth-century church is still consecrated; the fifteenth-century cloisters, once crudely whitewashed, are now restored to their original state. White roses are trained against the cloister walls and white violas border the trim central lawn.

The abbey has seen distinguished visitors, including Petrarch and a clutch of popes. It provided accommodation for Don John of Austria, hero of the 1571 naval battle against the Turks at Lepanto, a

victory which halted the Ottoman advance into Europe. In 1525, after his defeat by Charles V, Francis I of France was imprisoned here in a tower with a picturesque sea view. Periods of great power and riches gave way to periods of decline, and in 1937 the abbey was finally sold to become a private house. The current owner, a Milanese who took his holidays in Santa Margherita and fell in love with the building one rainy day in 1990, felt compelled to buy it, even though unsure of its future use. He has carefully restored it with the help of his daughter Chiara. La Cervara now hosts concerts, weddings, conferences and cultural events.

The monks' *orto* is now a formal Italian garden centred on a seventeenth-century marble fountain of a *putto*. The greenness of this parterre, laid out in grass and box, contrasts with the blue of the sea beyond. Previously bright with flowers, the beds here were returned to lawn because the owners considered it more peaceful and fitting for the monastic setting. Single box plants have been clipped into banded topiary domes, and lilies grow with teucrium and Japanese anemones in the subtle planting around the sides. In the gravel at the end, three magnificent stone pines stand silhouetted against the sea.

Different parts of the garden are linked with pergolas covered with plumbago, bougainvillea and sweet-smelling *Trachelospermum jasminoides*. In a shady courtyard, a massive 100-year-old wisteria entwines its branches overhead and along the walls; found in a collapsed and abandoned state, it was engineered back into place. A window in the courtyard wall captures a picture-perfect view of the bay. Elsewhere, a centuries-old false pepper tree (*Schinus molle*) droops its feathery branches; exotic *Erythrina crista-galli* adds a splash of vivid colour, and pink capers blossom in the walls. In the herb garden, potted citrus and herbs grow in box compartments round an octagonal pool. Underneath the nearby pavilion are the water tanks

originally used to collect rainwater and still used to water the garden.

La Cervara is special, not only for its contemplative atmosphere but for its position as a clifftop garden overhanging the sea. It is sensitively cared for and aims to delight visitors with successive waves of planting.

Above The formal parterre, laid out simply in box and grass, with pergolas overlooking the sea. *Left* A painted archway leads into the cloistered courtyard.

EMILIA ROMAGNA

Emilia Romagna, situated south of the Veneto, stretches from the River Po delta to the Apennines and is partly mountainous with broad valleys stretching down to the low-lying coastal plain. Here, the lagoons and marshland offer a retreat to thousands of migrating birds, a mecca for birdwatchers on boat excursions. The region's rich farmlands were once the breadbasket of the Roman Empire and its name derives from the Roman road that once ran through here – the Via Aemilia. Today, this is one of the richest, most developed regions in Europe, with the result that few historic gardens open to the public have survived. Across the broad, flat expanse of the plains rise the bell towers and cupolas of some of the most beautiful Renaissance cities in Italy – Parma, Modena and Ferrara as well as Bologna, the capital, with its university, the oldest in Europe. Yet only a few fragments of the gardens which once graced these great Renaissance duchies survive.

Castello di Grazzano Visconti PIACENZA, EMILIA ROMAGNA

Towards the end of the fourteenth century, a minor Piacenza nobleman named John Anguissola was riding high. Not only had he married Beatrice, half-sister of Gian Galeazzo Visconti, despot of Milan, but he was basking in the tyrant's favour. By the duke's hand, permission was granted to the 'eminent and beloved' pair to build a 'fortification' on the flat lands at Grazzano. As a further sign of ducal esteem, they were granted relief from taxes.

These are the historic origins of this high-walled, four-square keep contained within battlemented towers and surrounded by a defensive moat. Yet close up, there is something of the film set about the present-day building, with its outside staircase winding up from a romantic courtyard where Virginia creeper hangs in a red curtain, and at any moment Juliet might materialize at one of the arched gothic windows.

The rebuilding of the by-now abandoned castle in this romantic neo-medieval style was the achievement of Giuseppe Visconti di Modrone, who inherited Grazzano in 1910. Rich, leisured and cultivated, he made his inheritance his life's work, transforming the hovels outside the castle gates into a fantastical neo-medieval village – now a popular tourist attraction – and landscaping the extensive gardens. He also found time to produce seven children, one of whom was the film director Luchino Visconti.

For the first time, the grounds are now open to the public. It is five years since Luchino Visconti – named after his great-uncle – and his sister Verde began restoring them, advised by landscape architect Oliva di Collobiano.

The garden is part Italian formality and part English romantic park. The entrance, deliberately low key, is through a little gate opened up in the castle wall; away from the noise and hubbub of the village, the park is a tranquil, umbrous place, where great trees loom up mysteriously beside winding paths. Lacking contours for his garden, Giuseppe provided an architectural framework of evergreens, against which the native woodland – black poplar, elm, pedunculate oak – offers a continual play of light and shade. Giuseppe was also a compulsive collector of exotics – the Bhutan pine (*Pinus wallichiana*), *Styphnolobium japonicum* (syn. *Sophora japonica*), *Catalpa bignonioides*, the Persian silk tree (*Albizia julibrissin*) and many magnificent stands of cedars. These acquisitions he planted serendipitously with no overriding plan.

To the east of the castle the more formal Viale del Belvedere is centred on an Italian Garden with pergolas of white climbing roses and an elliptically

shaped pool. Around the pool a froth of white roses softens the stone – one example of this garden's sophisticated and muted planting. (Another is the row of variegated miscanthus planned for the centre of the *viale*, cleverly imitiating the play of fountains.)

Behind a yew maze, restored with seedlings gathered from the park, is a play-cottage built for Giuseppe's younger daughters. Inside, everything was tailored especially for them, including child-sized knives and forks; they could cook in their kitchen and sleep in tiny bedrooms upstairs. Luchino and Verde have surrounded the playhouse with beds of cottage-garden flowers.

The Italian Garden near the entrance front of the castle is smaller and more playful, with busts on pedestals under bowers of pink roses. Ivy swags surround it and in the middle a fountain plays. Beside the church behind another rose garden is Giuseppe's painting studio, in which he painted frescoes in medieval style for his village.

Page 83 A mossy lion guards Castello di Grazzano Visconti.
Top, left The romantic neo-medieval façade of the Castello.
Top, right The Viale del Belvedere.
Above, right Autumn in the parkland garden.

TUSCANY

'Florence could not have had a better or more delightful tyrant,' wrote the sixteenth-century historian Lodovico Guicciardini of Lorenzo the Magnificent (1449–1492). Under the firm but generally enlightened control of the Medici, who consolidated their power over the city under Cosimo de' Medici in 1434, Florence, technically a republic, flourished and expanded during a period of stability, wealth and artistic innovation.

With the expansion of the city came the desire to have a retreat from urban life, when the scorching summers made the narrow streets around the Arno unbearable. At his rural villas, built by his favoured architect Michelozzo Michelozzi, Cosimo the Elder began the Medici tradition of gardening, 'grafting and pruning with his own hand'. His grandson, Lorenzo, statesman, poet and lover of nature, would continue it, as would other members of the family. In time Florence's rich merchant class would build houses on the surrounding 'villa-clad hills'.

The concept of the rural idyll and of villa life went back to classical antiquity. Pliny the Younger, a rich and learned senator, constantly recommended 'simplicity', by which he meant a respite in the country from urban life. Here, Renaissance man, too, could rest, write and cultivate his soul. Here, he could contemplate nature and lay out a garden. 'Yesterday I came to the villa of Careggi,' Cosimo confided to the fifteenth-century Platonic scholar and humanist Marsilio Ficino, 'not so much with the idea of improving my gardens as myself.'

La Pescigola

The drive up to La Pescigola must be one of the most beautiful anywhere. Stately cypresses alternate with blocks of lavender in a charming country *viale*. As the road curves, flashes of gold light up the silvery terraces of olive trees, a glimpse of the host of 150,000 daffodils for which this garden is justly famous. On a sunny and panoramic slope, La Pescigola is surrounded by mysterious wooded hills with a distant view of snow-capped peaks. Sheep wander on the hillsides; a miniature hen 'villa' is home to chickens, doves and white peahens. A stream murmurs through holm oaks. La Pescigola, in the cool hills of northern Tuscany, is a springtime paradise.

For those used to daffodils marshalled into stiff, regimented lines, here is a lesson in planting. Seemingly natural, the daffodils cover the terraced hillsides in drifts and clumps and graceful, sinuous arabesques. Ten years ago, this garden, then covered with brambles, was known as 'the Sleeping Beauty'. Then Andrea Hedges Scrufari took it on and decided to give her husband a birthday present of 30,000 daffodils. Now 400 different varieties flourish – some old, some new, some rare, some highly scented.

The pink-washed villa, romantically neo-gothicized in the nineteenth century, is fronted by a row of magnificent Atlantic cedars. The main axis of what was the historic Italian Garden descends sedately towards the valley on this sunny south-facing hillside. A painting inside the villa on a drawing-room door may show it as it once was. Three large terraces enclosed by scalloped walls and set with statues and fountains bear terracotta vases of citrus fruit in the Tuscan style. The owners believe this to represent the 'modern garden' visited by Florentine botanist and scholar Giovanni Targioni Tozzetti during his travels in Tuscany in the mid to late 1700s. Pescigola, he wrote admiringly, 'has little to envy with the villas of Lucca or Florence'. To back this theory up, during restoration part of this original eighteenth-century garden layout was indeed uncovered.

Restored, it is now a box-edged daffodil parterre. The upper parterre, all baroque curls and *broderie*, contains white narcissi. At the lowest level, 50,000 glowing golden daffodils form a daffodil maze. Down a grassy path, lemon trees in specially commissioned terracotta pots commemorate the Lemon Garden that was once here. Once the daffodils have died away, the design of the maze remains clear, etched out with lavender; 600 plants were introduced to the garden in 2009 from the English lavender farm Norfolk Lavender.

A nineteenth-century owner, Signora Adami, created the hilltop path which runs from the villa's faded pink courtyard where narcissus bulbs and honey are sold, along with Andrea's latest venture: creams and lotions made from lavender oil, and scent distilled from perfumed daffodil varieties ('Sir Winston Churchill', 'Actaea', *Narcissus poeticus* var. *recurvus*, 'Ice Follies' and 'Erlicheer' among them). Along the path, nineteenth-century gods and emperors gaze down from their posts on a scalloped wall, while *mascheroni* spout water into eighteenth-century basins resting on neat marble feet. In flower beds at the base of the wall, 30,000 tulips in harmonious pastel shades are planned.

The slope beneath is criss-crossed by streams and stone-edged rivulets, mountain water captured in stone basins, one home to black trout, the other to two black swans. Primroses and violets thrive here. Iris and peonies line the banks. Further on, to extend the growing season, Andrea has planted camellias in different hues of pink and rose. David Austin roses – 'Malvern Hills', 'Crocus Rose' and 'The Generous Gardener' – complete the creamy palette. Nothing here is strident, the pastel colours carefully chosen by Andrea to blend with the soft-washed walls of the house.

Page 85 The view from
Villa Capponi across the
Florence skyline.
Far left Steps lead down
to the daffodil parterre.
Left The miniature hen
'villa', home to chickens,
doves and white pea hens.
Below, left to right
The daffodil parterre;
daffodils are naturalized
throughout the garden;
the drive up to the villa
is lined with cypresses,
olives and drifts of
daffodils.

At the very bottom of the slope, Andrea has made a semicircular *teatrino* of yew and ilex, peopled with statues of musicians. Further along is the newest project in this constantly evolving garden: a semicircular lake.

The Scrufari came here to visit their friends the Giustiniani who, besides La Pescigola, owned two other castles near by. 'Why don't you take it on?' they said to Andrea. 'It needs a gardener.' Fortunately, it has found one.

Villa Grabau

Stately Villa Grabau, at the foot of the Lucchesian Hills, has undergone two transformations to reach its present, serene neoclassical appearance. Originally a gothic building with lancet windows, it was redesigned in the Renaissance by the Diodati, a family of rich merchants from Lucca. They added an open loggia in the style of Villa Madama (see page 194) and Villa Farnesina in Rome. Though altered, this loggia remains, as does the Diodati coat of arms still hanging on the villa's northern façade.

In the nineteenth century the villa changed again. It was remodelled in neoclassical style and the sixteenth-century loggia was glassed in. Its new owners, the Cittadella family, were no doubt influenced by their famous neighbour, Napoleon's sister Elisa Bacciocchi, who had altered the seventeenth-century villa of the Orsetti according to neoclassical taste (see page 94).

These changes of style affect Villa Grabau's surrounding park, which contains several different gardens within its 9 hectares/22 acres. Among them are an Italian garden, an exquisite seventeenth-century lemon house, a box-hedge theatre and a fine nineteenth-century botanical garden laid out in naturalistic, English fashion. Of its great trees, many were planted by the Grabau family, who came from Hamburg in the nineteenth century. In 1868 the German banker Baron Rudolf Schwartze bought the villa for his wife, Carolina Grabau. Her direct descendants still live here.

Elegant wrought-iron gates lead into a straight drive, bordered by clipped holm oaks, which is a continuation of the old road from Lucca. As it approaches the house, this carriage drive divides to encircle the large oval lawn in front of the villa – a layout dating back to the time of the Cittadella. The drive is lined with magnificent trees, including fine examples of tulip trees (*Liriodendron tulipifera*), Douglas fir, Atlas and Himalayan cedar, Californian redwood, *Washingtonia filifera* and a striking copper beech.

At the back of the villa is a rare *Magnolia figo*, nicknamed the banana shrub for the scent of its fragrant white flowers and utilized in parts of China as a tall evergreen hedge. The only other local example is in Lucca's Botanic Garden. A pair of majestic, cone-shaped *Magnolia grandiflora* stand like sentinels beside the house, and *Campsis × tagliabuana* adds fiery colour.

The delightfully simple semicircular Italian Garden is framed by a curving *Quercus ilex* hedge, said to be a hundred years old. Above it rise the rolling hills of Lucca, on which are scattered olive trees, farms and a church spire in a classic Tuscan view. The formal garden is on two levels, separated by a balustraded retaining wall built of white marble and local Matraia stone. The wall is mosaiced with rock crystal, quartz and tufa, and set with four fountains dribbling water from grotesque masks. Two – the bronze heads of satyrs – are attributed to Pietro Tacca (1577–1640), successor to Giambologna as court sculptor to the Medici.

Steps lead to the upper terrace. Here, on twin grass ovals, stand Villa Grabau's seventy ancient lemon trees in Impruneta terracotta pots dating back to the eighteenth and nineteenth centuries. Some are stamped 'EC' for Enrico Cittadella. Others, brought here by inheritance or marriage, bear the coats of arms of the families who commissioned them. The first lemons on the trees are carefully picked off in spring to conserve the plant's energy for the main crop in September.

Miniature orange and lemon trees circle the pool at the back of the garden, which once contained a sixteenth-century grotesque sculpture in marble. This petrifying figure, part tortoise, part dragon, with an elephant's

Above, left The beautiful pink-washed seventeenth-century *limonaia*, studded with high arches and oval windows.

trunk and a human head, is reminiscent of the stone monsters at Bomarzo (see page 178). It has since been moved and now lurks along a shady path in the midst of dark and mysterious woods. Near by in a clearing, a marble table with lion's-paw feet waits as if abandoned by long-forgotten diners.

In winter the lemons shelter in a *limonaia* that must be one of the most beautiful in Italy, its pink-washed façade studded with high arches and oval windows framed with rusticated ashlar stone. Against the sturdy walls grow *Rosa* 'Climbing Peace' and *R.* 'Climbing Madame Caroline Testout' facing a *limonaia* garden planted with white flowers.

A woodland walk past bamboo, prunus and camellia groves ends in the charming Box Hedge Theatre, inspired, it is thought, by the Green Theatre at Marlia. Curving side stairs rise up each side behind the theatre's box 'wings', and a spherical box niche conceals the prompter's stand. The old box was damaged recently when a storm felled a huge *Quercus ilex*, and one section of hedging had to be replaced. Shaded by limes, the Theatre Garden is a peaceful, green retreat, with box pyramids and terracotta urns lined up behind a box hedge.

Among the exotic trees growing in the park, the rarest is *Quercus × audleyensis*, a man-made and sterile cross between the holm and common oaks. To be found on the west side of the Parco Inglese, its shiny, green leaves contrast strikingly with the blue foliage of *Cupressus arizonica*. Underneath, wild strawberries, violets and cyclamen carpet the ground.

This is a garden lovingly cared for by its owners, Dr Francesca and Federico Grabau. Each year brings a restoration project: recently, they restored eleven eighteenth-century statues, now housed for safety indoors. Villa Grabau is still very much a family home, where evidence of a young family – a football pitch occupies the field beside the entrance gates – sits alongside a serious and knowledgeable approach to conservation.

Above, left A sixteenth-century grotesque – part tortoise, part dragon, with an elephant's trunk and human head, lurks in the woods.
Above, right The bronze head of a satyr, attributed to the Medici court sculptor Pietro Tacca.
Right The interior of the *limonaia*.

Villa Oliva-Buonvisi

The Buonvisi, the original owners of the villa, were Lucca's bankers. As the silk and wool trade flourished, and merchants like Alessandro Diodati from next-door Villa Grabau (see page 88) prospered, they too grew rich. In the sixteenth century they employed agents in France, as well as in Nuremberg, Lisbon and Constantinople. The Lucchesian patrician class invested their profits in land, and the Buonvisi owned many country villas.

Since the fifteenth century these villas, around 300 of them, had been built as summer retreats encircling the town of Lucca. During the hottest months Lucca's fortunate merchants and bankers abandoned town for their country houses. From the refreshing cool of the hills, they looked across at the great walled city, immured in its hot, dusty plain. And the city looked back at them. Many urban *palazzi* had belvederes at rooftop height: airy little rooms for city-dwellers to escape to and enjoy the view.

The sixteenth-century writer Giovanni di Vicenzo Saminiati made recommendations to Lucca's new elite about their rural *palazzi*. The main façade of a villa must be 'facing the City or some other noble place fair to the eye'. The drive should be long, guiding visitors from the city from afar. It should add 'decorum and Magnificence and perspective to the Palazzo'.

The Buonvisi villa, here at San Pancrazio, was one of their most important: a harmonious example of early Renaissance architecture by the Lucca-born architect and sculptor Matteo Civitali (1436–1502). He trained in Florence and Harold Acton detected a Florentine influence in the graceful double-storey portico on the northern façade, underneath small square windows also reminiscent of Florence. Certainly, to find a portico of such soaring height, held up in this case by columns carved from single blocks of Matraia stone, is rare among Lucchesian villas.

The cypress-lined entrance avenue, which leads up to the south-facing front of the villa, also forms the central axis of the garden. Grey stone and white marble columns announce the importance of the House of Buonvisi, punctuating the wall that encircles the 5-hectare/12-acre park. Today's visitors, though, enter by a side gate, emerging on the villa's northern side – no loss when their first sight is of Civitali's beautiful, arched loggia. Across a semicircle of grass a rustic grotto of tufa, surrounded by a curving

ilex hedge, dwarfs the solitary *putto* seated under its stalactites. From here, the path continues to the western side of the villa past the splendid stables, restored by the present owners. Around a corner, seated on a wall, is a surprise: the astonishingly natural terracotta figure of an old man, his legs dangling down, his shoulders slumped as he takes his ease, his hand rummaging in a bag to pull out some snuff to enhance the moment. This is the *Pitocco*, one of the park's most original and lifelike statues. He sits with his back to what may be Lucca's oldest swimming pool, created out of an ancient basin.

Villa Oliva has an unusual layout in that its terraces are at right angles to the house, with the main entrance drive or cypress avenue forming the middle level. On the upper terrace, vestiges of the baroque layout have survived a nineteenth-century transformation. A grove of camellias leads into a *stanza di verzura*, a green 'room', formed of laurel and yew, where 'furnishings' of a table and two stone benches add to the illusion. Further along is a small ilex wood, formerly a *ragnaia*, where a statue of Diana with her quiverful of arrows alludes to past years of hunting. Near by in the *limonaia*, 120 lemon and orange trees are taken in for winter in their ancient pots. A constant restoration schedule means that these venerable pots, some still bearing the Buonvisi arms, are kept in useable condition.

Throughout the garden, cool, winding paths are embellished by flowers – spirea, *Magnolia stellata*, marguerites and geraniums – in restful green and white, while nearer the house stand enormous pots of white azaleas. An unusual feature of the garden is the hornbeam tunnel parallel to the main entrance avenue. Now a secluded and shady walk, it may originally have been used as a carriage drive.

Water, abundant in the area, was originally distributed through the garden through a series of fountains and pools, including one fed by a stepped, tufa water staircase, where terracotta *putti* ride horses with fishtails. This water staircase is illuminated at night. From a pebbled niche in the fine sixteenth-century Fontana della Sirena, a grimacing, fishtailed siren pours water into a basin from its mouth and breasts. High above, a cornice of marble masks sits under a broken pediment and at the centre is the Buonvisi coat of arms. Other masks decorating this historic fountain were defaced by German commandos during the Second World War.

Three cardinals added their lustre to the Buonvisi name, but despite all their power and riches, the family did not survive beyond 1800. The villa passed into other hands, ending up badly damaged in the Second World War. It is to the Oliva family from Genoa that we owe the successful restoration: the villa is now their summer residence. During August, concerts, operas and other cultural events take place. Concerts in aid of charities are held here weekly on Friday nights; there are exceptional acoustics in the loggia. Concert-goers can walk the lovely grounds, where architectural fragments from the original garden, some lit up at night, survive among magnificent nineteenth-century parkland trees.

Left The double-storey portico on the northern façade of the Villa Oliva-Bionvisi.
Right, above The tufa grotto's solitary *putto* faces the northern façade of the villa.
Right, below The *Pitocco*, a lifelike terracotta figure of an old man, perches on a wall.

Il Giardino di Palazzo Pfanner

The garden, a little baroque gem, sits in between the palazzo and the tree-topped ramparts of Lucca's massive, encircling city walls, from where it is visible to onlookers. Even the entrance is theatrical, the vaulted hall with its magnificent, columned open staircase, leading out, as one visitor observed, into a 'courtyard . . . [that] appears to have been built to stage shows'.

The central walk up to the splashing fountain in its octagonal pool is lined with graceful statues on mythological and allegorical themes. Around the basin are Dionysus, Mercury, Poseidon and Amphitrite. Bedding plants splash colour against the grey stone – primulas in spring, bronze cannas and scarlet geraniums in summer – framed by a green backdrop of box, magnolia and umbrella pine, and an eighteenth-century bamboo grove. Beyond the pool, the path continues with a row of potted lemons and more statues, the Four Seasons. It ends at the balustraded *limonaia*, bearing, above its central arched door, two sculpted lions and a basilisk, emblem of the Controni family, who contributed to the building of the palace.

Palazzo Pfanner was commissioned in 1660 by the Moriconi family, rich merchants of Lucca. When they emigrated to Poland, it was bought by the Controni, who had recently acquired a title to go with their splendid new palace. In 1686 the Controni added the impressive outdoor staircase with its balustrades and painted loggia, which acts as a visual link between house and garden. The garden was finished at the turn of the next century, possibly to a design by the baroque architect Filippo Juvarra, who brought his skills as a set designer to the discipline of architecture, which he studied in Rome under Carlo Fontana. The interplay between house, garden and city, and the views, both public and private, of town or home, are what make this small baroque garden so intriguing.

'The Controni family,' wrote the scholar, painter and antiquarian Georg Christoph Martini, describing Lucca, his adopted home town, 'commissioned two elegant buildings: one is close to San Frediano, has a magnificent staircase with columns and balustrades, and numerous statues adorn its garden.' Little has changed since Martini wrote his three-volume *Giornale di Viaggio* in the seventeenth century. The church of San Frediano, with its great lancet-windowed tower, still looks down on this peaceful, statue-studded, flowering oasis in the heart of Lucca.

In 1835 the Duke of Lucca decreed that the brewing of beer in the city must be overseen by a skilled German manufacturer. His call was answered by the Austrian brewer Felix Pfanner, who arrived in Lucca in 1846. Pfanner rented the lower floors of this palazzo. He placed vats in the cellar, and in the garden he set up a beer house with chairs and tables under a pergola. The venture proved so successful that eventually he could buy the palace.

The Pfanner beer house, the first of its kind in the duchy of Lucca and one of the first in Italy, closed down in 1929, but the Pfanner family still live here today. Some may recognize their garden as the one in which Isabel Archer strolled under her parasol in the film *Portrait of a Lady*. Henry James himself visited Lucca, 'that compact and admirable little city', in 1874, and experienced 'the famous promenade on the city-wall'. Walking along 'its summit planted with goodly trees', he admired the view, the 'swelling . . . bastions and outworks and little open gardens'. This charming small garden, sheltering in the lee of Lucca's great wall, must have been one of those he saw.

Right The splashing fountain in the octagonal pool, surrounded by graceful statues on mythological and allegorical themes, and by lemon trees in pots.

Villa Bernardini

Left The Green Theatre in box, dating back to the mid-eighteenth century.

Bernardino Bernardini commissioned this late Renaissance villa in 1615. His name is inscribed over the front door, and his villa has remained in the Bernardini family ever since. It was only one of eleven villas once owned by the Bernardini, an ancient family of Lucca, whose coat of arms with its crescent emblem signifies their participation in the Crusades. In 1888 Federico Bernardini was the last heir to inherit all eleven country villas and the family palazzo within the city walls. On his death the properties were divided between his sons.

It is the sense of time asleep which makes this graceful, four-square villa, backed by a wooded hill, so appealing. Little has happened inside the villa since the minor alterations made for the marriage of Francesco Bernardini to Marianna Parensi in the 1700s. The architecture is typically Lucchesian, with a front loggia – facing east so that by midday there is shade – leading to an airy reception hall connecting the front and back gardens. Hall, salons and reception rooms are filled with the family's original furniture, collected over the centuries, and much of it painted or engraved, making this a unique 'villa museum'.

The lush and leafy front garden has undergone many changes from the smaller, rather more severe walled space depicted on the 1738 map now kept inside the villa. First enlarged to accommodate *broderie* parterres, it was later naturalized into a *giardino inglese* with an open lawn broken up by bushes and trees. Two sequoia planted in the mid-1800s still dominate the heart-shaped lawn. The present owner, a botanist, has contributed many unusual trees and shrubs to emphasize seasonal colour and leaf contrast. There are thirty different acers.

The most exceptional part of the garden, however, is at the rear: the immaculately kept Green Theatre in box, dating back to the time of Marianna and Francesco Bernardini in the mid-1700s. It rises gently on three levels, following the slope of the hill behind, also part of the Bernardini estate. Clipped box spheres decorate the low hedges surrounding the horseshoe-shaped stage. Lemon trees in pots face the theatre and a low-lying *Datura meteloides* sprawls over the paving outside the house.

Inside the villa is a wooden model of a green theatre placed by a window overlooking the real *teatro di verzura*. It bears the inscription 'Parco del Palazzo F. Petri fecit'. But it is a design for a project that was never realized. Dotted with fountains and statues and with an elaborate *broderie*-style parterre, leaving little room for actual use, it was, as Massimo Bernardini explains, 'not a functional design: it was mainly to impress guests'. The villa's eighteenth-century chatelaine, Marianna Bernardini, required a more practical space in which to hold her musical soirées. She got her wish. The theatre's ample stage and good acoustics mean that it is regularly used for concerts and weddings today. Marianna's portrait still hangs inside her old home.

Parco Villa Reale di Camigliano LUCCA, TUSCANY

The Villa Reale gets its name from its royal connections. From 1805, Napoleon's sister, Elisa Bacciocchi, lived here and, as Princess of Lucca, created a miniature Ruritanian court in which Paganini was the leader of her orchestra. 'Eh, bien, mon prince,' reads the first line of *War and Peace*, which begins its story in 1805, 'so Genoa and Lucca are now no more than private estates of the Bonaparte family.' Later, after the Napoleonic period, the villa belonged for a while to Vittorio Emanuele II, who passed it to the Bourbon prince Charles of Capua, brother of the last King of the Two Sicilies. The prince had been disinherited because of his elopement in 1836 to Gretna Green in Scotland with a British beauty, Penelope Smyth: the morganatic couple are buried in the chapel in the grounds. After their son's death in 1918, the contents of Villa Reale were sold, and many of the parkland trees cut down for timber. The parents of the present owners, Count and Countess Pecci-Blunt, stepped in and bought the villa in 1924, beginning the vital task of restoration.

Elisa Bonaparte Bacciocchi was a woman of heady ambition. No sooner had she and her brother, the Emperor, forced Count Orsetti to part with the villa and its baroque garden, the ancestral home which his family had owned since 1651, than Elisa moved to annexe the neighbouring sixteenth-century palace of the bishops of Lucca, in one stroke doubling her acreage.

Elisa had grand plans for her new property, and set out to transform the Orsetti's Renaissance country house into an imposing neoclassical palace.

The entrance was aggrandized by twin neoclassical gate and guard houses. The old Tuscan *manège* in front of the villa was vastly extended to form a huge lawn, part of a fashionably romantic English park. Here, roe deer and merino sheep grazed under plantations of holm oaks, plane trees

and lime, and groves of magnolia. In the lower part of the garden a large ornamental lake was created, now home to a single, bad-tempered swan. Elisa despatched her court botanist to visit the royal gardens at Caserta, after which tulip trees, ginkgos and weeping willows were shipped in.

Elisa would probably have continued with her naturalizing 'improvements' had she not been halted by her brother's downfall and her subsequent eviction in 1814 by English troops. These tumultuous events ensured the survival of Villa Reale's fine, seventeenth-century baroque gardens, which lie alongside the villa in a series of garden rooms.

A long avenue enclosed by high holm oak hedges runs parallel to the villa: it leads to the Palazzina dell'Orologio (clockhouse) with its eighteenth-century clock tower, used by Elisa for stabling and staff. From the avenue, a gate opens into the simple, rectangular Lemon Garden, divided into four quadrants and given height by glossy, dark green, cone-shaped magnolias. At the far end of the Lemon Garden is a pool garden, described by Georgina Masson as 'surely the most magnificent garden room in Italy'. With its graceful balustrade, on which stand potted citrus trees, it reminded her of a baroque ballroom, with the glittering rectangle of water as its floor and the golden fruit of the citrus lighting up the dark green backdrop like 'so many little lamps'. Two Tuscan river gods, representing the Serchio and Arno rivers, stretch out languorously at one end, beside a curved exedra housing a statue of Leda and the swan. John Singer Sargent painted two watercolours of these river gods, reclining against a backdrop of citrus trees: they are now in the Museum of Fine Arts in Boston.

A few steps away through a circular 'anteroom', where a single jet of water shoots dramatically skywards, is Villa Reale's greatest delight, one of the finest green theatres in Italy. Here, Paganini played the violin, so brilliantly that it was whispered that he had made a pact with the devil. 'The reigning Elisa sometimes fell into a swoon at my playing,' the maestro claimed. Planted in 1652, the theatre has wings of yew and footlights of spherically clipped box; a box conductor's podium faces the stage. In niches at the back stand life-size terracotta figures from the *commedia dell'arte*, the much-loved repertory of comic characters developed in sixteenth-century Italy by travelling players. This charming theatre seems to have served as inspiration for the Green Theatre at La Pietra (see page 117), where once again live actors and lifelike sculpted figures inhabit the same stage.

The sixteenth-century Bishop's Palace is the third building on the site. This graceful Renaissance summer villa displays all the pathos of an abandoned house, its loggias and arcades deserted, its marble basins languishing upturned in the empty courtyard. A modern parterre is laid out alongside.

Acquiring the Bishop's Palace brought a great treasure to the garden in the shape of the harmonious Renaissance nymphaeum with its grotto dedicated to Pan. The nymphaeum, built in the sixteenth century as an open two-storey pavilion, is decorated in the style of the Mannerist architect Buontalenti, with pebble mosaics in arabesque designs and rough *pietra spugna* walls. *Giochi d'acqua* set in the mosaic and terracotta floor would have refreshed weary visitors resting on the stone seats on the hottest of days. In the dark recesses of the circular grotto, Pan presides under a domed roof, accompanied by sea gods.

Near by is the modern Spanish Garden designed in the 1920s by the French landscape architect Jacques Greber. Rills of water, redolent of the Alhambra, cut through green grass studded with topiary balls.

Left, above Two Tuscan river gods recline at the end of the pool in the Lemon Garden.
Left, below The celebrated Green Theatre, with terracotta figures from the *commedia dell'arte*.
Above The nymphaeum, built in the sixteenth century in the Mannerist style.

Villa Torrigiani di Camigliano

LUCCA, TUSCANY

A monumental cypress avenue leads to the ornate gates of Villa Torrigiani. From here, there is the first glimpse of the villa's extraordinary Mannerist façade, looking, as Harold Acton wrote, as if 'an intricate mask had been clapped on to a simpler frame'. Which is indeed what happened when Marchese Nicolao Santini, Lucca's ambassador to Louis XIV, remodelled the plain sixteenth-century villa of the Buonvisi into this seventeenth-century baroque showpiece. In his flamboyant makeover, lions guard the steps; busts in niches frame the central arch; there are porticos, pillars, arches, carved stucco plaques, statues in niches, and yet more statues thronging the balustrades.

If Mannerism was a capricious and irreverent deviation from accepted architectural rules, this fantastical composition seems more Mannerist than baroque. Originally surrounded by a French garden said to have been sketched out by le Nôtre on his way to see the Pope in Rome, the villa is now set off by a serene English park of spreading lawns and groves of trees. Only the seventeenth-century basins and fishponds, and the garden's hidden treasure, the delightful, sunken Garden of Flora, survived the nineteenth-century vogue for landscaping which swept these earlier gardens away.

Villa Torrigiani still belongs to the descendants of the modernizing ambassador, whose fashionable tastes and transforming plans for his villa must have been influenced by his time in France at the court of

Above A lion stands guard on the steps at the entrance to the villa.
Left Flower beds and box intermingle in this semi-formal part of the garden near the house.

the Sun King. Whether or not le Nôtre personally designed the new gardens, they were modelled on his style at Versailles. A 1797 plan inside the house pictures two large parterres of quartered sections of intricate *broderie* surrounding twin pools in front of the villa. At the rear was another, larger and grander parterre centred on a round pool, now embedded in an expansive 'English' lawn. All these parterres disappeared in the nineteenth century. The front lawn with its surviving baroque pools, also now set into grass, is framed today by four huge domes of *Magnolia grandiflora*.

To the east, the plan shows the sunken Garden of Flora, which, unlike the parterre gardens, has miraculously survived from the seventeenth century. Here, between the Grotto of the Winds at one end and the graceful, balustraded double staircase at the other, is a sunny, secret garden, originally planted with aromatic herbs. (Santini introduced the pepper plant into it.) Now in summer, the box-lined beds are a sea of blue ageratum; pots of geraniums line the staircase and *R. banksiae* 'Lutea' is among the climbers draping the walls. The cool grotto, with marble statues of the Four Winds, is decorated with tufa and black and white pebble mosaics, under a cupola crowned by Flora herself, bearing a basket of wrought-iron flowers. In the heat of the summer its dim recesses must have been a welcome retreat for Marchese Santini's illustrious guests, but the ambassador had a surprise for them.

The entire Garden of Flora is a sequence of elaborate water jokes of the kind irresistible to seventeenth-century humour, a series of *giochi d'acqua* in which guests, in all their finery, got drenched, to the hilarity of their hosts, and, imprisoned by sprays of water, found it impossible to escape. If they climbed the stairs, water jets would pursue them, shooting out of the steps and balustrades. Running down the path activated yet more spouts, until the dripping guests took refuge in the grotto. Unfortunately for them this was the trap: a curtain of water would descend, cutting off their exit. Jets shot up from the floor; water squirted from statues' mouths; and in the *coup de grâce* a torrent of water poured through the roof. It has been suggested that the enduring popularity of *giochi d'acqua* enabled Flora's garden to survive the sweeping changes in design introduced into Lucchesian gardens in the nineteenth century. But more than this, Flora's delightfully ingenious little garden stands as a testament to what may have been lost. It is still possible to experience the water jokes, now that many of the *giochi* have been carefully restored.

The water that fed the pipes for the garden was stored on the level above it in a graceful rectangular basin. Lemon pots line the stone rim; statues stand on the balustrade; lion masks trickle water into the pool; and white ducks float lazily on the surface. Behind are the beckoning *bosco* and cool walks through the shady ilex woods.

This is a garden for all seasons, with its majestic tulip trees flowering in May, followed by the magnolias in June. From November to March the camellias are in bloom, with many nineteenth-century varieties. The family's preferred name for the villa is Villa Camigliano, after the camellias which flourish here.

Top The sunken Garden of Flora has survived from the seventeenth century.
Centre and below The rectangular basin that once held the water for the *giochi d'acqua*. A marble siren looks out over the pool.

Villa Massei

Left The Orange Garden with its faded pink Renaissance nymphaeum.
Right, above An intimate corner of the garden.
Right, below The new Pergola Garden, with round brick pillars in typical Lucchese style.

In his engaging book *A Garden in Lucca*, Paul Gervais relates how he and Gil Cohen from Point Reyes, California, ended up in this classic, pink-washed Renaissance country villa outside the walled city of Lucca. Situated in the gently rolling foothills of the Monti Pisani, surrounded by dense woods of oak, ash, pine and chestnut, the villa was once the sixteenth-century hunting lodge of the Counts Sinibaldi. In the far distance, across the valley of the River Serchio, rises the rugged silhouette of the Apuan Alps, where Michelangelo searched the quarries for pure white Carrara marble.

Growing up in Massachusetts, Paul Gervais had longed for a trim, white clapboard New England house, with sturdy plank floors and 'chalky white colonial rooms'. Villa Massei, when he and Gil first saw it in 1982, was dilapidated and in urgent need of restoration. Its roof sagged. A tangle of wild clematis, self-seeded honeysuckle and wildly unkempt wisteria was choking the garden. The heart of the garden, the Renaissance grotto, or nymphaeum, was in use as a store for garden tools, making it, Paul Gervais observed, 'the most breathtakingly beautiful garden shed in all of Italy'.

Nevertheless, they bought Villa Massei, seduced by its ancient twin cypresses, its stately plane tree beside the *limonaia* and its 150-year-old *Cinnamomum camphora* tree shading the enclosed rear courtyard. And there was a stream running through the land, for irrigation. They wanted to live here, Paul Gervais later admitted, the moment they entered the gates.

Taking on a garden, let alone a garden of this size and importance, was never part of Paul and Gil's plan. Half-abandoned and gradually dissolving into shapelessness, the garden at Villa Massei clamoured for a fresh start that would still respect its age-old structure. And Paul and

Gil have achieved the perfect transformation – a brilliant reinterpretation of a Renaissance scheme, skilful in its sympathetic arrangement of space and its treatment of new and existing garden rooms, and overlaid with interesting planting. Their aim was not to challenge visitors to the garden with their originality and modernity; rather, they wanted to evoke the past, and reassure them.

In his book, Paul describes himself as a neophyte who came too late to gardening, but he then gives himself away by writing that during the making of the garden he was learning the names of a hundred plants a week. Much scholarly research went into the planning. Paul and Gil visited and studied Renaissance gardens for their principles of design and structure. They kept notes, made drawings and read widely about historic gardens and the habitats of plants.

As Paul points out, Renaissance villas generally sit on clear ground, well away from fussy planting, and often behind a wall or balustrade, which serves to enhance the house's standing. At Villa Massei, there was no such balustrade or mellow wall, only an ugly concrete, brick and cinder block parapet. To give the house dignity, the lawn on the flat terrace in front of the villa needed to be formally defined. Paul's solution, adopted after seeing the famous water cascade at Villa Aldobrandini (see page 205), was to plant shrubs to conceal the wall and, in front of them, a hedge to provide the necessary formality and frame the lawn. The terrace's geometric, clipped hedging was inspired by the shape of the beds at Villa Buonaccorsi (see page 160). The cruciform layout of the Orange Garden was suggested by the cloisters of medieval monasteries.

The approach to Villa Massei leads up a steep, traditionally Tuscan *viale* lined by cypresses. Against the northern side of the villa, in the Dolphin Court, the Dolphin Grotto houses a collection of ferns. The tender climber *Muehlenbeckia complexa* frames an arched doorway, while the long-leaved box, *Buxus linearifolia*, droops beguilingly from terracotta vases.

Leading off from the lawn on the other side of the villa is Paul and Gil's new Pergola Garden, created out of a field. The long pergola, with its round brick pillars in typical Lucchese style, is made to look even longer by the hedge lining the path, an idea inspired by the Giardini Botanici Hanbury (see page 76). The round brick columns with simple flat capitals uphold a living green roof. In the borders alongside, the planting has been planned in shades of burnt caramel and cream. Pincushions of *Santolina pinnata* and the sword-like leaves of *Sisyrinchium striatum* 'Aunt May' mingle with *Potentilla fruticosa* 'Daydawn' and tawny orange *Kniphofia* 'Toffee Nosed'. *Papaver pilosum* var. *spicatum* and *P. atlanticum* contribute notes of apricot and orange, and the thick bronze foliage of *Haloragis erecta* 'Wellington Bronze' strikes a deeper chord. The inspiration for the pool at the end of the walk came from Villa Grabau (see page 88).

Steep steps lined with bay laurel hedges lead to a series of 'garden rooms', echoing the layout of green rooms at Le Balze and La Landriana (see pages 115 and 209). In the pastoral cherry orchard, an avenue of cherries marches towards an urn circled by deep blue *Iris germanica*. Yellow and white narcissi flower here in spring, while the retaining wall is rimmed with 1,000 snow-white bearded irises. The Italian Garden, planted in 1991, was the first 'room' to be furnished; its thick box hedging is laid out in angled, almost interlocking beds. Shady and secret,

it nevertheless has far-reaching views over the valley to the mountains. The old shepherd's hut near by has been made into an attractive guesthouse, fronted by a terrace planted with diamonds of rosemary and clumps of pinks. Pots of agapanthus line the wall and a pair of bitter orange trees provide height. Steps lead up to the informal and understated Pool Garden, scented by oleander and full of sun-loving cistus, euphorbia, erigeron, lavender and different kinds of rosemary.

Most beautiful of all is the Orange Garden, enclosed on one side by the restored loggia, while on the other stands the exquisite Renaissance temple nymphaeum or grotto – 'the garden's destination,' says Paul. Its faded pink façade, with square relief columns topped by Ionic capitals, glows in the gloom cast by an ancient camphor tree. A wisteria walk, underplanted with ferns, leads to the temple, and the white blooms of *Hydrangea quercifolia* in pots lighten the shade. Having experimented with wild strawberries in the box parterre, Paul settled for simple grass beds containing vases of mophead *Citrus* × *microcarpa* The formality is softened by lavender and white 'Sea Foam' roses billowing from the back wall.

Villa Massei reflects Paul Gervais's very Italian love of symmetry and architecture, but it also benefits from a knowledgeable use of unusual plants and some stunningly original touches. In his book, Paul amusingly recounts his early mistakes, including a neighbour's horror on seeing lines of newly planted red salvias. Be that as it may, this late-blooming gardener has achieved perfection here.

Giardini di Agrumi e Orti Urbani di Buggiano Castello

PISTOIA, TUSCANY

The medieval hilltop village of Buggiano Castello is visible from far off, down in the plain. Uniquely, its ancient houses are painted a deep Pompeian red – 'Buggiano red', as it is known: the estate colour of the Sermolli family, local landowners whose historic Villa Sermolli dominates Buggiano.

The village benefits from a microclimate. Perched neatly on a south-facing ledge, sheltered by encircling hills, it faces marshland 10 kilometres/6 miles away, which helps temper the climate. There is no frost or snow and the temperature hovers five degrees Centigrade higher than in the plain. Documentary evidence shows that citrus gardens have flourished here since the 1400s: nowadays Buggiano is known as the Borgo degli Agrumi.

Hidden away behind high stone walls, the villagers' small plots traditionally combined vegetables, medicinal herbs and citrus fruit – espaliered to maximize space. Many century-old lemons survive, planted in the ground and grown huge and luxuriant against the sun-warmed walls.

The fourteen gardens open to the public have romantic names. Giardino Antiqui Profumi, scented by huge pots of gardenia and shaded by mimosa and a laden grapefruit tree, takes its name from a forty-year-old double pink peony inherited from the owner's grandmother, whose garden this once was. Armonie di Verde's cool, green terraces, shaded by a magnificent camphor tree, harbour roses, hydrangea and jasmine in pots as well as 110 azaleas collected by the owner, fondly called the 'Mayor of Buggiano'. There is a 'wood' of camellias, including one growing as a tree. Calla lilies gleam in corners, lighting up the different shades of green. Villa Sermolli's Giardino Barocco is the largest and grandest of the gardens with three terraces and a courtyard in which the Chusan palm (*Trachycarpus fortunei*) and the Canary Island date palm (*Phoenix canariensis*) surround an octagonal pool. Yucca, agaves and forty-year-old specimens of the sago palm (*Cycas revoluta*) add yet more exoticism.

The cobbled streets of Buggiano are colourful with oleander and pomegranates, huge cacti and laden citrus trees. Clementines, mandarins and grapefruit grow, along with the bitter orange (*Citrus × aurantium* Sour Orange Group) used for marmalade – all fruiting profusely through Buggiano's mild winters. By the ancient walls are tiny vegetable plots. Pots of flowers and climbers enliven every wall.

It is Professor Franchi, a long-time resident of Buggiano, who deserves the credit for opening up these hidden treasures to the world. Now two thousand people come on two consecutive Sundays in April and May to stroll the streets, admire the gardens, listen to music from the harp and the flute, and sample the food on offer – orange and lemon tarts and cakes, limoncello of every description, including one with basil and another made from citrus leaves. The entrance fees go to the town towards the restoration of various monuments in Buggiano.

Right and opposite Citrus gardens of every description flourish throughout Buggiano Castello.

Storico Giardino Garzoni

PISTOIA, TUSCANY

Left The Viale delle Palme, from which the staircase rises to the Viale degli Imperatori on the next level.
Opposite, above One of the terracotta busts of Roman emperors.
Opposite, below left Stone figures recline amidst the play of water.
Opposite, below right One of Diodati's shell seats.

The magnificent seventeenth-century palazzo villa was erected, probably from 1633, over the foundations of the medieval castle of Collodi. Built to withstand attack, the castle commanded the top of a precipitous cliff, with the village of Collodi huddled for safety around its defensive walls. When, in more peaceable times, the villa rose in its place, there was no space for a garden to be made around the house. The architect's solution was to lay it out on an adjoining hillside: a bridge was thrown to span the steep gorge that separated this hillside from the villa. Thus linked to the house, the spectacular baroque garden could unfold dramatically down the slope – in a manner, Georgina Masson observes, more usually associated with Rome. The first account of the garden is found in a work by the Lucchese poet Francesco Sbarra called *Le pompe di Collodi*, dating back to 1652. Villa Garzoni's bridge, the terracing, the labyrinth and wood with its network of parallel paths are all carefully described in it. All still exist: a 1680 map demonstrates that the seventeenth-century garden layout has survived essentially unchanged. As Shepherd and Jellicoe observed when making their survey of it in the 1920s, it was the limitations of the site that inspired this garden's beautiful shape.

The Garzoni were a family from Peschia, who had suffered the confiscation of their property during the Guelph–Ghibelline conflicts of the Middle Ages. They fled to this stronghold on the Lucca boundary, as near as was safe to their old home. An early seventeenth-century owner, Marchese Romano Garzoni, was the originator of this garden, which took 170 years to complete. It was not until 1786 that the innovative Lucchese architect Ottaviano Diodati came on the scene, providing the statues, the

fountain basins, the Green Theatre and the *parterres de broderie*, which replaced a large lawn at the base of the hill. A complex hydraulic system made possible a water staircase and numerous *giochi d'acqua*.

From the bottom of the hill the garden rises, like a theatrical *mise-en-scène*, outlined against the green backdrop of a wooded hill. To the left the silhouette of the vast palazzo rears up against the sky. With its great staircases creating a perspective effect, its terracotta statues and its water staircase rising up to the giant figure of Fame at the top, the prospect reveals an exuberant and flamboyant example of baroque garden architecture.

In the *broderie* parterre garden, coloured sand has been used to fill in some of the curling box arabesques, an effect described by eighteenth-century visitors. Other beds, planted with pansies, hyacinths and crocuses in spring, swirl and spiral around two large pools, from which 12.25-metre/40-foot jets of water shoot skywards, and black and white swans swim, untroubled, alongside the garden's menagerie of topiary birds and animals. Further up the slope, in a second parterre garden, the Garzoni coat of arms is picked out in coloured pebbles.

From this parterre, the imposing double staircase, embellished with terracotta statues and set with terracotta balustrades, rises in tiers. It is flanked to left and right by terraces, and on their retaining walls are espaliered citrus, recently replaced just as they were in the seventeenth century. Up the first flight of steps is the Viale delle Palme, punctuated by palm trees planted in the early twentieth century. A grotto with stone seating round its walls is at the centre of the terrace. Cool and inviting, it was designed to tempt unwary visitors, who then found themselves trapped inside by a curtain of spray. In his watery cave, lined with *spugne* (artificial stalactites), Neptune rides a sea monster surrounded by mermen and water nymphs.

The elegant Viale degli Imperatori on the next level is named after the terracotta busts of Roman emperors which gaze down haughtily from their niches in the hedge. At one end of this terrace is Diodati's Green Theatre, adorned with statues of the Muses, Tragedy and Comedy. Diodati's terracotta shell seats still await a vanished audience. The architect also introduced the terracotta monkeys that frolic near by on the staircase balustrade.

Above the terraces, the double water staircase climbs a steep slope through the *bosco*, marking the passage from the formal to the wild garden. At the top of the cascade, the monumental, running figure of Fame blows into a conch shell, sending an arc of water into the pool at her feet. Further down, giant statues representing the rivers of Florence and Lucca recline on either side, and strange birds pour water from their beaks. Behind Fame is the bath house where the Garzoni family bathed in marble bathrooms, with dressing rooms and a richly decorated salon attached. An orchestra played, and male and female bathers laughed and gossiped behind decorous screens.

The garden was restored on the basis of the documented descriptions available. A new education centre presents the history of these striking baroque gardens through documents, film and photographs.

Giardino di Boboli

Left The balustraded Vasca dell'Isola.
Right The Neptune Fountain.

Eleanor of Toledo married Duke Cosimo I de'Medici in 1539. Her portrait by Bronzino in the Uffizi shows her in sumptuous bronze brocade and strung with pearls, her small son by her side. In 1550 Eleanor bought the Pitti Palace, an unfinished building designed by Brunelleschi for Luca Pitti, which then became the official residence of the Medici. Its rough hillside of agricultural land, the Orto de' Pitti, would be made into a garden worthy of the royal couple. The name Boboli, indicating 'wooded areas', had been associated with this part of Florence since the Middle Ages, a farming family, the Borgholi, owning some of the land. According to one of Italy's most famous ghost stories, a Borgholi farmer still wanders the hillsides of the Boboli and is supposed to have been seen by many visitors to the garden. Although Eleanor of Toledo was famously demanding, Vasari tells us it was Duke Cosimo himself, spurred on no doubt by his successful garden at Castello (see page 127), who wanted to adorn Brunelleschi's unfinished palazzo with 'gardens, groves, fountains, fishponds and other suchlike things'.

There was a natural amphitheatre behind the palace, created when stone for its building was quarried. This may have prompted Baccio Bandinelli's reaction when he was asked in 1551 to design a fountain for the new garden: 'It seems to me that this field which I have seen has been so well placed by nature that I have seen no other like it.' The architect chosen for the transformation was Niccolò Tribolo, who had already been working on Castello for over a decade. In 1550 he laid out his design for the axial development of the garden, with blocks of trees planted on the hills surrounding the natural hollow which would later become the amphitheatre. The axis led from the *cortile* (courtyard) up the hill to the rectangular basin visible in Utens's 1599 lunette, which collected water brought by the aqueduct of Arcetri to irrigate the garden. The Vasca del Forcone (Forcone Basin) replaced it in the eighteenth century. A large, white marble Fountain of Oceanus was planned for the area of level ground behind the palace, a dramatic focal point against the dark backdrop of evergreen trees. It was while on a journey that same year to select a block of granite for the basin of the fountain that Tribolo caught a fever and died. With Castello still in progress as well as any number of other projects including tableaux, triumphal arches, engineering works and even firework displays, he may have been exhausted by the pace of work demanded of him by Cosimo. The Fountain of Oceanus was eventually sculpted by Giambologna. Recorded as standing in the amphitheatre in 1577, it was moved in the seventeenth century to the centre of the Vasca dell'Isola (Island Pond). It is now part of the collection of the Museo del Bargello, while an early twentieth-century replacement stands on the island.

Tribolo's design would be executed by a number of other artists, including Bartolomeo Ammanati, who extended the wings of the palace to echo the contours of the horseshoe-shaped valley, creating a link between building and landscape. In this theatrical space, many extravagant masques and spectacles would be performed. In 1589 Duke Cosimo's younger son, the future Ferdinando I de'Medici, married Catherine de'Medici's granddaughter Christine of Lorraine. In a lavish entertainment put on for the aristocratic guests, the courtyard at the Pitti Palace was flooded for a mock sea battle between Turks and Christian galleons. Fire-eating dragons added to the effect.

Neither Tribolo nor Ammanati took architectural advantage of the shape of the splendid natural arena behind the palace, a missed opportunity which Georgina Masson, comparing the Boboli to Villa d'Este (1550) and Vignola's design at Caprarola (1559), attributed to extraordinary Tuscan conservatism.

It was not until 1630–34 under Duke Ferdinando II de' Medici that the green amphitheatre became a stone theatre, with tiers of seats installed for spectators by the grand-ducal architect Giulio Parigi. In the summer of 1637 an equestrian ballet was performed for the wedding of Ferdinando II de' Medici and the granddaughter of the Duke of Urbino. Henry James, visiting the Pitti Palace in 1874, imagined the 'generations of Medici [who] have stood at these closed windows, embroidered and brocaded according to their period, and held *fêtes champêtres* and floral games on the greensward'.

Parigi also carved out the second main axis of the garden leading east–west to the Vasca dell'Isola. It is approached by Il Viottolone, a long avenue of cypress, the planting of which began in 1612. The avenue is lined with statues of the classical and Renaissance periods, some of them placed here after the sixteenth-century dispersal of Cardinal della Valle's famed antique sculpture collection. The antiquarian William Beckford greatly admired the Boboli's 'white statues of fauns and sylvans . . . glimmering among the broad masses of shade and dusky alleys'. Behind the Cypress Avenue stretches the old *ragnaia*, crossed by 'dusky ilex-walks' and still the haunt of owls by night. The drinking troughs which hunters left out for the birds form the theme of the 1620 Fountain of the Mostaccini, a long, cascading water chain which flows downhill beside a path.

The Viottolone leads to the baroque fantasy of Parigi's 1618 Piazzale dell'Isolotto. In its centre, a balustraded island, contained by a moat and supposedly based on the Maritime Theatre at Hadrian's Villa in Tivoli, is laid out as a lemon garden with fruit trees. Perennials are planted in the box-edged beds and antique roses have been replanted on the island. Access is guarded by paired sandstone columns topped by marble goats, a Medici symbol. From the safety of the island stone figures of *putti* once mischievously shot arrows across the water. Among the famous statues, Andromeda sits on a rock, her feet in chains, while Perseus gallops across the water to her rescue. Tribolo's massive granite basin supports a copy of his giant Oceanus, incongruous in its monumentality among the light-hearted, seventeenth-century bucolic figures of hunters and peasants. The granite block for the basin, discovered on the island of Elba, was 6 metres/20 feet wide and had to be dragged into Florence by twenty-five pairs of oxen.

Duke Cosimo and Eleanor of Toledo had always intended the Boboli Gardens to house some of their collection of rare and exotic plants. Saffron crocuses were grown here and the royal couple planted rows of asparagus beds. Eleanor also grew the prized dwarf fruit trees, which gave aristocratic ladies the dainty pleasure of picking fruit 'without danger of dirtying their skirts'. This advantage was alluded to in a book published in 1589. The sublimely

situated Giardino del Cavaliere (Knight's Garden), with its view over the hills of Florence, was remodelled by Giulio Parigi in 1612 to accommodate rare species. It now holds a box parterre with roses and peonies. In 1785 Grand Duke Pietro Leopoldo of Lorraine dismantled the former menagerie housing a collection of rare animals to build the fine rococo *limonaia*, intended as a hothouse for the lemon trees of the Isolotto. A garden was created in front of it which, since the *limonaia*'s restoration, has been attractively reconstituted. The box parterre is filled with potted citrus, roses and summer perennials. Cacti in pots line the front. The *limonaia*'s wall is topped by statues. Alongside the second-century white marble Muses, note a curious seventeenth-century figure, *The Bagpiper*. The beautiful gates are decorated with rope-effect wrought-ironwork and pineapple finials.

Among the Boboli's grottoes, the most fantastical is the Grotto Grande. A modification of a building by Vasari, who was responsible for the columned façade, it was transformed into a grotto between 1585 and 1587 by Bernardo Buontalenti, the sculptor, architect and inventor, for his patron, Francesco I de' Medici. Francesco had a passion for stones and minerals, and for him Buontalenti conceived a veritable cabinet of marvels. Its three rooms are a showcase for Florence's many different skills and include frescoes, sculpture, mosaics and bas-reliefs modelled in *spugna*. Stalactites hang down and the walls are covered with corals, shells, enamelled glass, haematite and quartz. The Grotto is also an encounter between art and science. In an era obsessed with magic and alchemy, its theme, inspired by a fable in Ovid's *Metamorphoses*, was that of metamorphosis brought about by the cleansing and regenerating effect of water, the precursor of cosmic creation. Water seeped continuously through pipes in the walls of the Grotto and the ceiling vault is said to have held a crystal bowl in which fish swam. Michelangelo's unfinished *Prisoners*, seemingly struggling to free themselves from the stone, were placed by Buontalenti in corners of the Grotto. They have been replaced by copies; the originals are in the Accademia. The beautiful frescoes by Bernardino Poccetti portray the natural world with portraits of exotic beasts and pastoral scenes.

The Madama Grotto, commissioned by Duchess Eleanor and built between 1553 and 1555, is the oldest in the garden. Its façade, covered with stalactites from the Valdimarina area, is decorated with the Toledo coat of arms. Inside, the Grotto is covered with *spugna* and more stalactites. The sculptures of animals emerging from the walls are by Giovanni di Paolo Fancelli and Baccio Bandinelli.

Above, from left Statues in niches decorate the amphitheatre; *Monumental Head* by Igor Mitoraj; statues from different periods are scattered throughout the garden.

Giardino Bardini

There have been seven centuries of gardening on this steep hill rising from the River Arno to the Forte di Belvedere within Florence's medieval city walls. A garden is first mentioned here in 1309 in an inventory of the Palazzo Mozzi. The palace is described as having 'a large loggia and a garden behind . . . and adjacent house with orchard and lawn, and walled land behind the house'. Hitherto fabulously rich – as Florence's Papal Treasurers they could afford not only a garden and loggia but also 'a stove and a hot room for sweating' – the Mozzi had suffered a collapse of their trading company in 1303. This was the start of a series of financial voltes-face in which the Mozzi sold and bought back their ancestral home over the next 600 years.

This first small walled garden was surrounded by terraced orchards, whose survival through the fifteenth and sixteenth centuries is charted in two views of the city in the Firenze com'era Museum. In the seventeenth and eighteenth centuries the garden was divided, with the Mozzi managing to hold on to the larger, eastern section. On the western side, the Manadori family built themselves a villa, admired even in the mid-seventeenth century for its soaring views over Florence. By the late 1700s Mozzi fortunes were riding high once more. The architect Gaspero Maria Paoletti was engaged to restore the palace, along with Villa Medici, Fiesole, which in 1781 the Mozzi had inherited. This architect probably also contributed to the late baroque embellishment of the central staircase, which already divided the garden. The next significant date was 1815, when Luigi le Blanc began the transformation of the land around Casa Manadori. He created an Anglo-Chinese garden, laid out an English wood, and built a rustic grotto in the

Above A lunette of the garden in the style of Giusto Utens was painted in 2005.
Below, left The restored baroque flowering staircase.
Below, centre A stone lion gazes down on the garden.
Below, right Pomona, goddess of orchards and gardens, dressed in eighteenth-century peasant costume.

fashionable romantic style. All this the Mozzi were able to buy back in 1839. They now owned a garden combining three different elements, just as it does today: ancient terraced orchards, eighteenth-century baroque features and a nineteenth-century romantic park.

The antiquarian Stefano Bardini, after whom the garden is named, bought the whole property in 1913, and demolished the walled garden to make a carriage drive connecting the two houses. More importantly, he created the panoramic Belvedere Terrace, enlarging the two eighteenth-century Kaffeehaus pavilions and linking them with sandstone pillars from Pistoia. Urns and Venetian statues complete the grand effect, as you look down and marvel at one of the very finest views of Florence. By the end of the century, all this was in ruins, the orchard terraces abandoned, the baroque staircase crumbling and overgrown. When restoration began in the year 2000, the aim was not only to reinstate this lost past but also to create a new and beautiful garden with important botanical collections.

The baroque flowering staircase has been brought back to life, the fragments of mosaic decorating its walls reassembled, the fountain basins repaired. Herbaceous borders now frame the sloping, grassy terraces; colourful ribbons of iris line the steps. In the spring border hostas mingle with soft yellow euphorbia, with *Heuchera* 'Palace Purple' adding a deeper note. In summer, a tall display neatly alternating broad and narrow foliage combines yellow foxgloves with the light blues of agapanthus, next to a subtle china-blue wash of *Campanula persicifolia* 'Chettle Charm'. *Liriope spicata* 'Gin-ryu' and *Brunnera macrophylla* 'Langtrees' add their contrastingly shaped, silver-variegated leaves. At the foot of one flight of the baroque staircase, the guardians of the garden sprawl haughtily beside the steps. These statues of Pomona, goddess of orchards and gardens, and Vertumnus, god of seasons and plant growth, are dressed not as Roman divinities but in eighteenth-century peasant costumes.

To the left of the garden, a zigzag path winding up to the Belvedere Terrace through orchards planted with old varieties of fruit trees was an eighteenth-century walk. At the bottom it has been edged with old varieties of cream and apricot roses; the view unfolds over a low box hedge on the left. The stone-tiered open-air theatre is modern, based perhaps on the contours of an ancient quarry. Halfway up is the Belvedere Circle, one of the original resting places, where centuries-old holm oaks have been clipped to form a shady bower. A nineteenth-century bench, painted with botanic motifs, faces a wisteria-draped tunnel, underplanted with the hydrangea collection. Sixty varieties grow here, including the dramatic rust-red lacecap *Hydrangea serrata* 'Beni'. As you climb up this refreshingly shady walkway, the city walls climb above you.

The Bardini Garden was restored by the Fondazione Parchi Monumentali Bardini e Peyron with the support of Ente Cassa di Risparmio di Firenze. It has been aptly described by Mariachiara Pozzana, who advised on it and has written about it, as a garden full of light and flowers. Placed as it is between Forte di Belvedere and San Miniato, it once again occupies one of the best viewpoints in Florence. A lunette of the garden in the style of Giusto Utens was painted in 2005.

Giardino Torrigiani

Hidden away behind high walls near the magnificent and public Boboli Gardens (see page 104) is a secluded and romantic private park. At 7 hectares/17 acres, it is one of the largest privately owned gardens within the city walls and belongs to the Torrigiani family, whose ancestors have held land here in this part of the Oltrarno since the sixteenth century. The park, which began as an orchard purchased by Raffaello Torrigiani in 1531, has had a prolific and fruitful gardening history. By 1824 it was famous enough to merit a descriptive guide, which commended its garden of citrus and flowers, its aviary and the stream, spanned by a magnificent bridge.

Giardino Torrigiani was extended at the beginning of the nineteenth century by Marchese Pietro Torrigiani, who took down Florentine houses and rebuilt them elsewhere to create space for his extensive, English-style romantic park. His chosen advisor in 1813 was a cultivated Frenchman, Luigi de Cambray Digny, who was not only an architect but, like Torrigiani himself, a Freemason. In 1819 another architect, Gaetano Baccani, took over. He was responsible for the park's dominant, neo-gothic tower, sited on a mound near the massive, sixteenth-century Medicean walls which run through the garden: together, they create an ideal picturesque, gothic landscape. Baccani could not resist romanticizing the scene even further by adding his own battlements to the walls.

With its scenic winding paths, groves of trees, little hills and valleys where deer were intended to graze, the park is remarkable in itself as a romantic landscape. But it also harbours an intriguing air of mystery created by its association with nineteenth-century Freemasonry. Carved columns delineate a symbolic itinerary, and statues and architectural curiosities represent secret Masonic themes. A dedication to research and a spirit of enquiry is still a hallmark of the Torrigiani Garden. The tower itself was built as an observatory and also housed a library and a collection of astronomical instruments.

The garden is divided between the Torrigiani and the Torrigiani Malaspina families, and you may be shown around by members of either. The entrance gate on the Torrigiani side leads in from Via del Campuccio into what was once the core of the garden, symbolized by a simple box parterre set in a large circular lawn. The original Italian Garden would have been square. Around the lawn are placed urns, framed by a cloudburst of apricot roses. Wild Mediterranean rosemary grows here, brought in from the Tuscan island of Capraia, where the late Marchese Torrigiani's wife had her home. Without the winds that in Capraia keep it pinned to the rocky island soil, the rosemary here grows tall and luxuriant and gives off a strong lemon scent. Statues of the Four Seasons stand on the cross-axes of the parterre, and in the middle is a massive sculptural group – *Seneca Pointing the Way to the Young Pietro Torrigiani* – by the nineteenth-century sculptor Pio Fedi. The late marchese considered this neoclassical sculpture, erected by his great-great grandfather, too large and out of proportion to the rest of the composition, but it is there to stay.

The path through the garden winds past magnificent trees, including centuries-old beech, *Magnolia grandiflora*, cedars of Lebanon, an Atlas cedar and American oaks. In the autumn, golden-yellow and conker-brown horse-chestnut leaves mingle with yellow and orange plane trees and the acid yellow of limes, the majestic trees reflecting the richness of this garden in the nineteenth century. In 1839 an inventory was published,

listing more than 13,000 plants grown in Giardino Torrigiani, with another 5,500 planted in vases and urns.

On a hill in the *bosco*, its dark vegetation symbolizing the theme of Night and Death, is one of these urns, its bowl entwined with a serpent to represent Pharmacy. Pietro Torrigiani is supposed to have erected it in honour of his doctor after being treated successfully for an illness. Also symbolic of the dark theme is a grotto built to represent an ossuary and reached by a path lined with Egyptian-style herms.

The Torrigiani Garden also contains some of the eye-catchers and follies found in English picturesque landscapes, intended to add interest and depth even to small-scale landscape views such as there are here. An aviary (now closed) is designed as a *tempietto*; there is a stream with a bridge, a romantic 'ruin', a hermitage and chinoiserie, here represented by a Chinese balance. The Casino, now lived in by the marchese's daughter, was used by gymnasts exercising in the park. In the background, adding their own romance to the garden, are the towering, sixteenth-century city walls, built during the war against Siena and now peaceably covered with ivy and flowering capers.

Because the garden is divided within the family, the division is notional rather than physical, delineated by mowing stripes on the grass. By the original entrance in Via dei Serragli is a sphinx with two nineteenth-century tablets advising visitors on Rules of Behaviour. 'Dogs are not allowed,' they read, 'nor are horses and carriages. Do not touch the flowers, plants or minerals. No games allowed without special permission. Walk only on the paths.' The rules were not observed by the occupying British troops who, during the Second World War, shot the hand off the

important baroque statue group of Diana and Actaeon. Bullet holes are still visible on the drapery.

The Torrigiani Malaspina branch of the family live in an eighteenth-century villa on this side of the garden. The Temple of Arcadia here, a symbol of the ideal of pastoral life, refers to the fact that this is the 'light' side of the garden, as opposed to the 'dark' theme of the other side. Vieri Torrigiani Malaspina, an agriculturalist, has founded a plant nursery here, and restored the antique greenhouses on the same spot where in 1716 the distinguished botanist Pier Antonio Michele founded the first botanical society in Italy.

Even the Torrigiani family find their 7-hectare/17-acre park in the heart of the city 'almost unbelievable' in its greenness and tranquillity. Coming from Rome, as members of the family often do, they 'treat it like coming to the country'.

Opposite Gaetano Baccani's nineteenth-century neo-gothic tower (*above*), sited near the sixteenth-century Medicean walls (*below*).
Above, left and centre The reconstituted Italian Garden.
Above, right Statues in the garden follow a symbolic itinerary representing secret Masonic themes.

Giardino di Palazzo Corsini al Prato FLORENCE, TUSCANY

The broad expanse of Via il Prato is testament to the great open *prato* (meadow) that once covered this area. As early as Dante's time, the Prato d'Ognissanti had been used by the citizens of Florence to exercise, hold markets and watch horse races. In 1590 Alessandro Acciaiuoli bought a large tract of land in the Prato, near the city walls, to build a *casino*, surrounded by parkland, where he could indulge his passion for botany and gardening.

Bernardo Buontalenti, architect to the Medici, was given the commission but financial pressures caused difficulties and thirty years later in 1621 the Acciaiuoli property was sold to Filippo di Lorenzo Corsini, whose family still owns it today.

Filippo had bought himself 'a large house begun and not finished, with a garden and a *ragnaia*'. He entrusted the completion of the house and its garden to the Florentine architect and sculptor Gherardo Silvani. Silvani laid out the Italian Garden; his design for a late Renaissance town garden is still unchanged to this day.

The villa on the Prato with its large garden (extended by Silvani) and airy loggia (1625–8) was originally a summer house for the Corsini

family. However, between 1834 and 1836 it was enlarged and became the permanent residence of Neri Corsini, Marchese di Laiatico and his wife, Eleonora.

The sober and imposing façade of the palace on Via il Prato completely conceals the delightful and exceptionally well preserved garden that lies behind it. From the loggia, a central avenue stretches the whole length of the garden, its perspective further lengthened by a double line of statues in descending height, which gives the avenue an illusion of greater distance. The statues, dating from the second century AD, include the deities Ceres, Diana and Bacchus, and were part of the collection of antiquities belonging to the long-lived bibliophile and art collector Cardinal Neri Corsini (1685–1770), nephew of Pope Clement XII. An array of classical inscriptions, also acquired by the cardinal, covers the loggia walls.

The core of the garden consists of a box parterre with clipped, geometrically shaped beds. These are filled with a soft planting scheme by landscape designer Oliva di Collobiano of stachys, teucrium, lavender and santolina, enlivened by peonies and pink roses. The long rectangular

Left A view across the parterre, with its lemon pots and Roman statues, to the arcaded seventeenth-century loggia.
Below A shield emblazoned with the Corsini coat of arms rests against one of the many statues in the garden.
Right *Acanthus mollis* carpets the shadier areas of the garden.

beds which line the central avenue are studded with lemons in terracotta pots; lavender spills over the low box hedging. The precious Impruneta pots are moved one by one in a small wheelbarrow to the safety of a *limonaia* each winter. A century-old colony of tortoises has the run of the parterre.

To each side of the parterre, winding paths lead off into *boschetti* planted in the nineteenth-century romantic style. Statues stand under holm oaks and the architectural leaves of acanthus carpet the ground. The *boschetti*, a cool and shady retreat in the heat of the day, are lit up by fireflies on summer nights. One of the *boschetti* may have been created out of the original *ragnaia*.

At the end of the garden, twin *limonaie* containing antique gardening tools face each other across the central path. Here, the composition is more relaxed, with little lawns and bushy white oleanders with loquat and cherries under a canopy of great lime trees. A box-edged bed near an entrance gate in the enclosing wall contains a luminous combination of *Hydrangea quercifolia* and *H. arborescens* 'Annabelle'.

By the left-hand *limonaia*, a path bordered by irises and pink peonies leads on into another garden where pomegranates and quinces, along with the exotically beautiful and hardy pineapple guava (*Feijoa sellowiana*), encircle a lawn centred on a round pool with a fountain. A simple iron gate in the garden wall offers a glimpse of the unexpected glory of Giardino Corsini al Prato: the vast, secret meadow, in the heart of Florence, which gives the palace its name.

Villa Capponi

High up on a steep road at Arcetri, yet ten minutes from the Ponte Vecchio and within earshot of the Duomo's great bell, Villa Capponi's intimate, jewel-like garden descends the hill in three terraces behind vase-topped, scalloped walls. Most un-Tuscan in their rococo light-heartedness, these walls were described in Shepherd and Jellicoe's 1925 survey of Italian Renaissance gardens as 'wall-tops so bubbling with fun that they chase away the cares of all who come'.

Visitors have always loved this exquisite but homely little garden, and successive owners have cherished it ever since Gino Capponi bought himself a small house here on the Pian dei Giullari hillside in 1572. Though no proof survives, it is believed that he may have built the unusual walls and, besides aggrandizing the house, laid out the lush grass avenue or bowling green alongside it – a space for his family to play games, take exercise and gather together on holidays, just as Alberti advised when extolling the benefits of villa life during the Renaissance. Villa Gamberaia (see page 122) also has a bowling green.

Nowadays the view straight ahead from this lawn is blocked by a cypress hedge – a deliberate ploy to enable the garden to reveal its secret places gradually. Standing sentinel in one corner is 'the mother of the garden', a cypress that is 200 years old. Other trees have been positioned to screen out less beautiful parts of the Florence skyline, leaving views of the cupola and Forte di Belvedere to dominate.

Guarding the entrance to the Lemon Garden are two haughty terracotta gryphons. The same scalloped walls here mean that this too may be a survivor of the original late Renaissance layout. Inside the parterre the planting is in blocks of blue (myosotis followed by

Above The Secret Garden.
Below The garden façade of Villa Capponi.

ageratum), which the present owners feel combines especially well with box.

The Capponi clung to their villa right up until 1882, when it was sold to Mrs Harry Warren Scott, a connection of the Duke of Portland, grandmother of Queen Elizabeth The Queen Mother and kindly 'Aunt Louise' to her niece, Lady Ottoline Morrell. Mrs Scott too made her mark on Villa Capponi, adding two loggias, one with *pietra serena* columns salvaged from an old Florentine market. Directly beneath the loggia terrace, 4.5 metres/15 feet down and largely hidden from view, is the cloistered Secret Garden, its sun-warmed walls a haven on sunny winter days. Once entered only by means of an underground passage from the house, it is now reached easily by a staircase built by Mrs Scott. For Maria Teresa Benedetti of the family who currently own and look after Villa Capponi, the Secret Garden is a happy and numinous place. The colours are light and airy: on the walls, white and yellow Banksian roses mingle with plumbago, citrus and the 'Mermaid' rose. In the centre, dahlias and pink lychnis form a soft carpet. Visible through a window, appropriately for this contemplative space, is the austere outline of the Certosa of Florence.

More steps lead down to the Fountain Garden, added in the 1860s by Mrs Scott. Here, Maria Teresa Benedetti has simplified the 'fussy, English style', creating the restrained and monumental Giardino d'Inverno (Winter Garden). Pots of pale blue plumbago replace the orange trees killed off in the hard winter of 1985; happily, after four or five years, the mandarin arch recovered.

In 1929 the villa's new American owners engaged Cecil Pinsent to build them a swimming pool lower down the slope, where the garden blends into olive groves and the countryside. Such a sensitive site drew on Pinsent's ability to 'listen to the landscape' in each commission – here by enclosing the pool within discreet cypress hedges, thus extending the harmonious interplay between closed and open spaces which is at the heart of Villa Capponi.

The garden has inspired many imitations, not least Garsington in Oxfordshire, English home of Ottoline Morrell. Ottoline had twice taken refuge with Aunt Louise, once as a girl with typhoid, and later after a disappointed love affair with Axel Munthe of San Michele (see page 223), and Villa Capponi's beauty and romance had, by her own admission, sunk into her soul. 'I drank then of the elixir of Italy – I drank so deeply of it that it has never left me.' When she came to lay out her famous garden at Garsington, it was Villa Capponi's confining box hedges and panoramic open terraces that Ottoline had in mind.

Above, left A terracotta lion rests amidst clipped box on the edge of the Lemon Garden.
Above, right The Winter Garden, redesigned by Maria Teresa Benedetti.

Giardino dell'Iris

Hidden away in a corner of busy Piazzale Michelangelo is the entrance to one of the gems of Florence: its lovely Iris Garden. In May, when the prestigious International Iris Competition takes place, the hillsides below the famous square are a tapestry of jewel-like colours.

Despite the roped-off beds, where you can watch judges making notes on new hybrids sent in from all over the world, this is first and foremost an idyllic country garden. The irises grow not in regimented rows but in gentle drifts under ancient olive trees. 'We wanted to keep it rustic, like a simple Tuscan plot,' says Valeria Roselli, a guide and member of the Italian Iris Society.

The Medici began the cultivation of *Iris pallida* in the Chianti region, where little else would flourish. While the men worked in the vineyards and olive groves, women and children were left to clean the rhizomes: orris root was a highly prized element in perfumery. *Iris* 'Florentina', now rare, once grew in profusion on the walls of Florence. The flower gave rise to the city's emblem: the so-called Florentine 'lily' is actually an iris.

The Iris Garden was created by a redoubtable group of Florentine ladies in 1954, with the support of the local authorities. The ladies ran the garden at their own expense, lending their gardeners and donating the plants. Their influence can still be seen in the 1950s roses which survive in the garden, many of them red to remind growers that a truly red iris is the iris grower's holy grail.

Each year's entries have had three years of growth in the garden in order to reach their peak. They then join all the earlier iris hybrid collections, kept here since 1957 as though in a living museum. Each new iris is the result of fashions that come and go, driven by the fickle desires of the market. A 1938 iris, 'Snow Flurry', was the first iris with pronounced ruffling and is the mother of all the frilly irises around. Valeria cites with approval a US grower who specializes in horns and flounces: 'His white iris is airy – like a ballerina.' On the other hand, a bronze and white iris of 2008 is dismissed: 'It may look like an orchid but it hasn't got an outstanding personality.'

'An iris', according to the judges, 'should be a candelabra, not a stick, with at least seven buds on each stalk, opening in a gradual way from the top.' Most important is the branching and durability of the flowers, with the colour accounting for only 10 points out of 100.

Nevertheless, colours are hotly contested, with amethyst the current favourite, exhibited in shades ranging from a deep velvety purple – the colour of the local Fiorentina football team – to Plicata irises in white with a lavender frill. Scents vary also. 'Iris can smell of pineapple, lemon, even of cat's litter, as well as the true delightful iris smell,' observes Valeria.

There is a small historic collection in the garden, at the foot of the slope, with irises beautiful in their simplicity. Intense yellow *Iris ensata* and the later-flowering Japanese *I. ensata* have colonized the lake.

To encourage flower growth, all the irises are fed with potassium. The clay soil is enriched with nitrogen and rested by the cultivation of beans. In this much-cherished garden the only unwelcome visitors are porcupines, who relish the rhizomes like truffles.

Right, above A Plicata iris.
Right, below Drifts of iris amidst the ancient olive trees.

Villa Le Balze

In 1911 an American philosopher, Charles Augustus Strong, bought the only piece of land he could find in Fiesole. He wanted to build a villa near I Tatti, home of his Harvard friend Bernard Berenson, and chose Berenson's architects, the partnership of Cecil Pinsent and Geoffrey Scott. But the site that Strong had plumped for was by no means ideal – long, narrow, perched midway down a vertiginous hill. As the present-day Curator of Le Balze observed, it needed all Cecil Pinsent's skill in architecture and landscape design to avoid the anxious feeling of hanging on to a cliff, which itself overhangs eternity.

Pinsent's solution to this topographical challenge was a longitudinal garden with the villa in the centre. Two parallel horizontal axes run past either side of the house. A series of formal, enclosed garden rooms open into each other. Statues, niches and other eye-catchers as well as openings in the walls create an impression of long views and perspectives. This, and the way the garden's boundaries blend gently into the surrounding countryside, helps disguise the narrowness of the site.

Pinsent was, according to Sir Geoffrey Jellicoe, who walked the hills of Fiesole with him in 1923, a 'maestro at placing buildings in the landscape'. He was also deft at managing the needs and personalities of his illustrious and often very demanding clients. At Le Balze the garden has an austere character. The mood is quiet and discreet, the planting subdued. Each individual garden enclosure has a rather cloistered feel – peaceful and inward looking. The restraint of the garden is Pinsent's response to his scholarly client's sober personality and ordered, contemplative life.

The entrance to Le Balze halfway up a steep hill was, as Pinsent left it, an unassuming door in the wall. Now there is a gate, and with it a tantalizing glimpse of the cool, green world beyond.

In his plan for Le Balze, Pinsent was able to follow Alberti's principle that villas and gardens should be placed on hillsides to catch health-giving breezes and frame vistas with 'a delicacy of gardens'. In the first of Le Balze's garden rooms, an arched cypress hedge frames picture-postcard views across to the domes and rooftops of Florence, which seem close enough to touch. The green arches are a comparatively recent innovation by the curator. Research then showed that Pinsent had had exactly the same idea, only he had achieved his effect by training orange trees. But what was once Strong's Orange Garden fell victim to the extreme winter weather. In these Fiesole hills, the temperature can drop to minus 10 degrees Centigrade (it can rise to 40 degrees in summer).

The heart of Le Balze is the formal Winter Garden underneath Pinsent's graceful loggia. Evergreen, scented *Trachelospermum jasminoides* cloaks the loggia wall. Lemon trees in pots enliven the formality. On the other side of the villa, another formal garden, monastically simple in colour and design, is overlooked by Strong's library. His desk was raised on a plinth, enabling him to contemplate his garden while he wrote. One hopes that the sight gave him joy. Pinsent's progress in the garden was notably slow, and Strong's time at Le Balze all too short. He died young, his peaceful life marred by financial anxieties.

Above, left The Winter Garden under Cecil Pinsent's graceful loggia.
Above, right Cypresses provide strong vertical accents in the garden.

In one part of the garden, Pinsent let himself run riot. The exuberantly decorated fountain grotto was constructed by Pinsent of *pietra spugna* and pebble mosaic in late Renaissance style. It houses Venus and the sea god Triton astride a dolphin. Look closely and you will see a medallion containing Pinsent's portrait. A double stone staircase leads up from the fountain to a path and on to a high loggia. From here, there is a bird's-eye view of the whole garden. It is more architecture than horticulture – a sequence of geometric 'rooms' with 'windows' framing views and clipped topiary and architectural items serving as punctuation points.

Pinsent's achievement was to let such formality fade out gradually into the natural landscape beyond. One axis comes to a gentle halt in a grove of ilex trees. The other becomes a path, bordered with plane trees and Florentine iris, and bordering a cultivated hillside. Here wild flowers carpet the ground, lilacs bloom, and acer and cotinus splash crimson against the grey-green olives.

Le Balze was occupied by German forces during the Second World War. Much damage was done. By happy coincidence, it was Cecil Pinsent, commissioned into the Allied Army to advise on the loss of Italian works of art, who helped put it right.

In 1979, according to Charles Strong's wishes, the villa was given to Georgetown University. It is much enjoyed by the students, beautifully cared for by the staff and quite obviously loved.

Below, left The garden unfolds in a series of 'rooms'.
Below, right A figure in Pinsent's fountain grotto.

Villa La Pietra

Left Villa La Pietra, on the top terrace, separated from the garden by a stone balustrade lined with statues, looks down the dominant central axis of the garden.

La Pietra is named after the first milestone on the road from Florence to Bologna, and is set back at the end of a 0.8-kilometre/½-mile-long cypress *viale*. It appears entirely seventeenth century, but neither house nor garden is as it seems. The original house, a typical four-square Renaissance country villa, received a new façade in the seventeenth century when a stately baroque exterior was grafted on to the fifteenth-century building like an architectural second skin.

As for La Pietra's formal Italian Garden, the nineteenth-century passion for 'English' landscaping swept it away. It remained an undistinguished mêlée of lawns dotted with trees and shrubberies until Arthur Acton, a leading figure in the turn-of-the-century Anglo-Florentine community, decided to recreate here the ideal Tuscan garden. La Pietra's reconstructed formal garden was planned 'as he imagined it might have been'. It is a Florentine garden, but one conceived by an Edwardian Englishman 'with all the creative ingenuity', his son observed later, 'of a Cinquecento architect'. In fact, debate continues as to whether an amateur like Arthur could have designed and managed such a large scheme on his own. Whatever the answer, his was certainly the guiding spirit.

In the fourteenth century the estate belonged to the Macinghi family. They sold it to the Sassetti, who were to become rich as a result of Francesco Sassetti's position in the Medici bank. In 1468 Francesco retreated here to enjoy *villeggiatura* in his newly built country house with his ten children. A

civilized man, he collected manuscripts and commissioned artists, notably Ghirlandaio, who painted the frescoes in S. Trinita's Sassetti Chapel. Francesco can still be seen kneeling there in his capacity as proud donor.

In fact it was the seventeenth-century Capponi who rebuilt and redecorated La Pietra. On the garden front, the cardinal's hat of Luigi Capponi, the papal librarian, presides over his family's coat of arms.

For five years the Actons were tenants at La Pietra. Arthur's wife, Hortense, was able to buy it from a branch of the Capponi in 1908 with the aid of her American family's banking fortune. Riches became Arthur. He had, as Bernard Berenson observed, 'a flair for good things'. The family collection included over 5,000 objects ranging in date from Etruscan times to the twentieth century. The garden, with some 180 statues, was planned according to Renaissance principles as an architectural extension of the house. It was also to be an open-air gallery, a further showcase for the collection. Among the thousands of books amassed by the Actons, there were surprisingly few on gardens. The family viewed their garden as a backdrop to their house and their art.

A fresco inside the villa shows La Pietra in the mid-eighteenth century, its dirty white façade – a colour scheme later superseded by the tawny yellow now so typically Florentine – abutted by two walled gardens. Of these one survives, the original walled *pomario*, still encircled by its urn-topped, *rocaille*-encrusted walls and still containing four pear trees,

each more than 200 years old. Its airy *limonaia* still gives shelter to over a hundred lemon and orange trees. Irises and violets and climbing yellow roses bloom against the walls.

It was on the steep slope on the eastern side of the villa that Arthur Acton began his twenty-year project, a reimagined Renaissance garden. Drawing its inspiration from sixteenth-century Florentine gardens, his plan was a series of broad, stepped terraces in the Tuscan style. On the top terrace, the villa is separated from the garden by a stone balustrade set with statues. Steps lead down to the first terrace. The view is straight downhill along the dominant central axis of the garden.

The Actons sketched out the main axes for the garden on a 1908 survey they had commissioned of the parkland. They then put their plan into action with considerable speed. It was a strongly linear concept, but this is a garden that is anything but austere. The two broad terraces – known as the *prima vasca* and *secondo vasca* after the fountain basins at their centre – are laid out with box hedging in a simple geometric style. But on either side of the central terraces lie a series of romantic *stanze di verzura* (garden rooms). Views open up to the surrounding countryside; statues emerge, half-hidden, from the greenery. There is a theatrical play of light and shade. Indeed, sunlight and shade, urns and fountains, vistas and glades – all have been carefully positioned and distributed, along with the busts, balustrades, architectural fragments and statues from Roman times to the nineteenth century which adorn this garden. Between the two *vasche* terraces is a flight of steps that is said to be the only built element to have survived from the original Italian Garden. The *secondo vasca* ends theatrically in a peristyle pergola of Corinthian columns set in front of a wall of greenery, which separates it from the olive groves beyond.

At this point, as Nick Dakin-Elliot, the garden curator at La Pietra, points out, the Actons were not enormously rich. They searched for and bought architectural fragments for their garden, which they then successfully cobbled together: rills purchased from the Boboli; the columns for the pergola in the *secondo vasca*, fortuitous twentieth-century finds. Some of the arches and columns in the garden are even made out concrete – *pietra finta*. The statues are placed for aesthetic effect, not, as in a Renaissance garden, to reinforce the iconography. The result is a highly individualistic, theatrical garden – almost, as many have commented, 'like a stage set'.

The long *prato ovale*, where five species of wild orchid grow, is an example of this quixotic theatricality. Here, in the bowl of a carefully placed urn, the distant cupola of Florence's Duomo appears to be sitting like an egg in its eggcup.

Perhaps the most brilliant of all La Pietra's visual caprices is the stunning *teatrino* (Green Theatre) with its box ball 'footlights' and playful eighteenth-century Venetian statues, supposedly by Francesco Bonazza, some of whom seem to be offering fruit, flowers and even a drink to the audience. While these statues are eighteenth century, rescued from villas in the Veneto, many others in the garden are less refined nineteenth-century copies. The theatre was a focus of entertaining at La Pietra. Many amateur theatricals were held here, with Serge Diaghilev and Brigitte Bardot among the professionals who performed over the years.

In 1962 on his mother's death, the Actons' son, the historian and connoisseur Harold Acton, took over as master of La Pietra. Although he had lived away for many years, his childhood home was imprinted on him. His memoirs recall the peaches on *rocaille* walls, the fireflies on June nights, the olives like 'silvery smoke' in the valleys. Away at boarding school in England, he drew cypresses 'on every available sheet of paper'.

Harold Acton had come home to La Pietra after the war in which his younger brother had died, leaving his parents devastated. After this blow, the creative energy went out of La Pietra; the garden ossified. Even when he took over, Harold Acton saw himself first and foremost as a custodian, the keeper of his parents' creation. Along with Bernard Berenson, Acton became one of Florence's living monuments; La Pietra turned into a place of pilgrimage for visitors. To live in such a place, Acton once observed, makes heavy claims, especially on a writer. But he believed that we all have our garden to cultivate – and La Pietra was his own 'earthly Paradise'.

Harold Acton died in 1994, leaving the villa and its contents and estate to New York University, his family having had connections with NYU. The university has poured money and expertise into the garden's restoration, taking its cue from archive photographs of its 1930s heyday. Zinnias and cannas have been replanted on the *prima vasca*, and vases and statues have been placed in their original positions under the watchful eyes of two brothers who have worked at La Pietra for over half a century. The younger of the two gardeners, both now in their seventies, still works in the *pomario*, growing the vegetables that Il Barone liked.

It has taken ten years for the university to repair and restore the statuary at La Pietra, a job once entrusted to one man who spent three months gluing broken limbs back together and cleaning off the moss. This has been a tactful restoration: wherever possible, mossy stonework and bumpy pebble mosaics have been preserved and original planting has been saved. La Pietra has lost none of its unique magic.

Opposite, above Stanze di verzura (garden rooms) lead off the central terraces. A columned arch is glimpsed at the end.
Opposite, below The Lemon Garden and *limonaia*; and, set among the box, a musician, one of the many statues in the garden.
Above, left Part of a walled *pomario* with its *rocaille*-encrusted walls.
Above, right The *teatrino* (Green Theatre).

Villa Peyron al Bosco di Fontelucente

FLORENCE, TUSCANY

This green and tranquil place, a combination of formal Italian Garden, forest and lake, owes its existence to the ancient woodland spring of Fontelucente. Water from this spring powers the twenty-nine fountains that spurt and spray throughout the garden: if its dark and mysterious woods are the soul of Villa Peyron, the fountains are its playful spirit.

The Italian Garden is at the back of the spare stone villa: it faces south and descends the hill in formal terraces. Along one side is a dark bulwark of trees, and in front, framed by pencil-thin cypresses, is a sublime view of Florence. When Paolo Peyron, the creator of the garden, came to live here in the 1930s, his first act was 'to make a hole in the woods, to open the view to the landscape'. His aim, he said, was to create a stage, with the city of Florence as a backdrop. The cypresses help to telescope the view, adding even more theatricality.

First to live here in these green hills were the Etruscans. A Renaissance villa was then built, probably over Etruscan remains. This was radically remodelled when Angelo Peyron, scion of a successful textile-manufacturing dynasty, bought the property in 1914. Of his four children, it was Paolo who would inherit the villa and its 50 hectares/124 acres of forest, olive groves and arable land. It was his connoisseur's eye that was behind the restoration and extension of the formal garden. He created the lake, positioned statues and fountains, and opened up woodland paths.

Above A view up the sloping formal Italian Garden, edged by undulating waves of scalloped box.
Below The Cloister Garden with its small stone chapel and adjoining cloister.

Left One of the parterres lined with
Venetian statues and urns.
Below Piazzale Riccardo Muti,
honouring the conductor and the
Muse of Music.

Working to no overall plan and without professional advice, he developed Villa Peyron bit by bit.

The main axis of the garden is the raised central walkway that runs off-centre to the villa, bordering the parterre. Venetian statues, rescued in the nick of time from doomed villas in the Veneto, separate the upper and lower parterres and enhance the woods and garden. The raised walkway, which offers a pleasing, overall view of the garden, follows the route of the original carriage drive as it appears in an eighteenth-century engraving of the villa. Edged by undulating waves of scalloped box, this ramp continues downhill to a balustraded fishpool, where puff-cheeked cherubs ride dolphins, blow conch shells or hold up beakers to drink. Beyond this fishpond, once the swimming pool but reclaimed by Paolo Peyron, is the central feature of the garden, its soaring bird's-eye view over the roofline of Florence.

Nothing is allowed to jar with the natural surroundings at Villa Peyron. Deer, boars and badgers roam the surrounding woods. The garden is a tapestry of different greens, from the dark shapes of cypress and cedar to the lighter greens of wisteria and box. Statuary and fountains are placed so as to appear an integral part of the garden. The planting is simple and repetitive – oleanders, wisteria, lavender, roses and sweet-smelling osmanthus. This is a very restful garden, composed of the elements that Geoffrey Jellicoe considered to be the essence of all Italian gardens – 'evergreens, stonework and water'.

On the other side of the walkway from the parterre is the intimate Cloister Garden, centred on a small stone chapel with adjoining cloister. Behind, in a change of scale and style, a magnificent double staircase sweeps down towards the lake. Cypresses flank this staircase and statues of shepherds and shepherdesses give it a romantically bucolic air. By the lake is the grassy amphitheatre of Piazzale Riccardo Muti, where statues of musicians and dancing Terpsichores honour the Muse of music, as well as

the famous conductor. Across the lake, fields of olive trees stretch, silvery grey, into the distance.

There is a delightful woodland walk at Villa Peyron, peopled with statues and scented by wild honeysuckle and *Viburnum tinus*. Since Paolo Peyron's death, the garden has been beautifully maintained by the Fondazione Parchi Monumentali Bardini e Peyron, which restored Giardino Bardini (see page 106) and has been supported since 1998 by Ente Cassa di Risparmio di Firenze. The Florence-based Garden and Landscape Design School has its headquarters in Villa Peyron. Lessons are also held at Villa Bardini and at other chosen Tuscan gardens.

Giardini di Villa Gamberaia

FLORENCE, TUSCANY

Edith Wharton, that connoisseur of Italian gardens, adored Gamberaia, calling it 'probably the most perfect example of the art of producing a great effect on a small scale'. Besides its exceptional water parterre, it has all the features of a classic Italian Renaissance garden – grotto, nymphaeum, *bosco*, *limonaia* and a cypress avenue – and, next to the house, linking the various elements of the garden, a long and stately grass walk or bowling green, used for ball games and other exercise. Yet the whole garden, perched on a hill and encircled by its stone retaining wall, amounts to only 1.4 hectares/3½ acres. It is this, as much as its beauty, that appeals to visitors. Gamberaia is on a scale we can all relate to, planned and nurtured by people not especially rich but of moderate means. Indeed, its first owner that we know about was a stonemason, Matteo Gambarelli. The core of his fifteenth-century holding can still be seen in the house, adjoining the *limonaia*.

Gamberaia, literally 'place of the crayfish', is documented as early as 1398, when it belonged to a nearby Benedictine convent, close to ponds and streams where *gamberi* (crayfish) were caught. A century later, Matteo Gambarelli, the stonemason owner, watched his two sons grow up to become well-known Renaissance architects and sculptors. For some time, the whole family must have prospered, but by the end of the sixteenth century they were obliged to sell the property, and it was the Lapi family who built Gamberaia as we know it today.

In 1900, as Janet Ross relates, a discovery was made in the garden: a broken shield with the inscription 'Zenobius Lapius erexit ac fundavit'. This was the foundation stone laid by Zenobi Lapi, a Florentine merchant who in 1610 began building the house and laying out the gardens. His nephews inherited the villa but one died before he could enjoy the fruits of his legacy. The other, Andrea di Cosimo Lapi, lived at Gamberaia and lavished money on it for fifty-nine years.

Andrea is supposed to have loved water and fountains. We know that he purchased several springs near by, along with the right to pipe water over his neighbours' land. In 1636 a lawsuit was taken out against him by a neighbour whose water he is supposed to have diverted. An early inventory of the 1620s mentions various areas of the garden, including what may have been the bowling green. Such was Andrea's passion for Gamberaia that on his death in 1688 he was heavily in debt, with consequences for his heirs. The villa had to be remortgaged to pay off the creditors.

Above Villa Gamberaia seen across the shimmering water-filled parterre.

In 1717 Gamberaia passed to the aristocratic Capponi family. It was a Capponi, a connoisseur with a passion for antiquities, who probably improved the garden into something near its present form. A mid-1700s engraving by Zocchi shows the cypress avenue maturing, the *bosco* half-grown, statues in place and tall trees (many of which still stand) along the bowling green. Apart from the water parterre, the basic layout of the garden is recognizably what we see today, a survival that Edith Wharton ascribed to its 'obscure fate': gardens with rich owners were not so lucky.

Gamberaia was also fortunate to have a succession of owners with taste. It was an inspired idea to take a traditional box-lined parterre and fill it not with flowers but with stone-lined pools of water. The result, said one admirer, is 'like some shimmering flower-strewn Persian carpet'. We can see just this effect today: the pink standard roses and terracotta urns and statues (note the delightful statues of dogs) glow against their evergreen backdrop and the grey of stone and water. At the end, a semicircular pool framed by a cypress arcade preserves part of the elliptical form of the rabbit island that once terminated the eighteenth-century parterre.

It was one of Gamberaia's more exotic owners, the Romanian Princess Ghika, sister of the Queen of Serbia, who, at the turn of the twentieth century, put in place the Water Garden, with the help of Martino Porcinai, father of the famous modernist landscape designer Pietro Porcinai. In her day, the princess was a celebrated beauty, but she preferred a retiring, contemplative life, her only interests, so her neighbour Bernard Berenson claimed, being herself and her garden. Iris Origo recalled visiting Gamberaia, hoping to catch sight of its reclusive owner, but saw (if at all) only 'a veiled figure at an upper window'. Other visitors, too, tell us that she left the house only in the early morning hours to inspect the garden, or for solitary midnight strolls along the cypress avenue.

Gamberaia has been famous for a long time: it has been held by many as the perfect example of garden architecture. From the grassy terrace directly outside the villa, the view soars across the Arno valley all the way to the domes and slender spires of Florence. Walk the length of the bowling green, a *tapis vert* 183 metres/600 feet long alongside the house: at one end there is the nymphaeum, at the other a statue of Diana silhouetted against olive groves and what must be one of the most breathtaking views in all Tuscany. On the cross-axis lies a secluded *gabinetto rustico*, described by Harold Acton as an 'open-air boudoir'. Its high walls are decorated with shells, stalactites, rusticated stonework and smiling terracotta statues in niches; its wrought-iron gates bear the emblem of the Florentine lily. Four flights of balustraded steps lead up to the shady *bosco* on one side, the Lemon Garden on the other. The venerable collection of citrus trees still overwinters in the *limonaia*. Once upon a time, too, there were *giochi d'acqua*, ready to catch out and soak unwary visitors who paused at the sandstone fountain. The controls are still there, in a room underneath a stairway.

For all its current perfection, Gamberaia's villa and garden were badly damaged by the fire set by retreating German troops who had occupied the villa during the Second World War. Both found a saviour in Dott. Marcello Marchi, who used old maps and engravings to restore the garden over six years, beginning in 1954. Since 1994, his son-in-law, Dott. Luigi Zalum, has been a devoted custodian of the villa, of which he has been co-owner since 1978, and has carried on the work of restoration and renovation.

Right, above Pink roses and terracotta statues of dogs surround the pools. In the distance, olive groves climb up the hillside.
Right, below A large umbrella pine shades the grassy terrace outside the villa.

Villa I Tatti

Above A severe green parterre lines either side of the mosaiced central staircase.

By 1900 one-sixth of Florence's population were English-speaking expatriates, refugees 'from the land of fog and the land of haste'. Living on the hills around the city and restoring the crumbling villas on their slopes, they were in need of an architect who could reproduce for them classic Renaissance formality or the grandeur and flourish of the Baroque. During his forty successful years of designing for the expatriate community, Cecil Pinsent was their man.

Pinsent was first introduced to the art historian and critic Bernard Berenson and his wife, Mary, in 1907, when they had already owned I Tatti, their villa at Settignano in the hills outside Florence, for two years. He did not make an impression. 'We have had a young architect named Cecil Pinsent . . . staying here,' wrote Mary. 'He seems nice but not very exciting.' But Pinsent returned, in the company of Geoffrey Scott, formerly Berenson's secretary, for whom Mary Berenson nursed a secret *tendresse*. A Pinsent–Scott partnership in design and architecture, helping with the renovations she planned at I Tatti, was her best way of keeping Scott near by. 'The Artichokes', as she called them, were in business. For the next two years they were to live virtually on site.

Pinsent was only twenty-five when he received this, his first and most significant commission. The challenge facing him was considerable for such a novice. The relatively modest sixteenth-century house – 'a library with rooms attached', Bernard Berenson famously called it – stood on steeply sloping ground about mid-way down the hill. Directly in front of the villa was a sloping Lemon Garden, enclosed to the south by a *limonaia* where, as Kenneth Clark recalled, Mr Berenson sat and talked to his guests after luncheon. Pinsent was to make use of this *limonaia* as a screen to hide the unfolding terraces of the Italian Garden below, so that they appeared to the unsuspecting visitor as a surprise – a baroque device which had the advantage of effectively creating two enclosed garden rooms. In the Lemon Garden (now the Enclosed Garden and full of spring and summer colour), beds surrounding persimmon trees were installed to satisfy Mary Berenson's love of flowers. Urns, recognizably of Pinsent's design, crown the *limonaia*'s roof, while through its centre runs the main axis of the garden.

So steep was the hillside at Settignano that at the top of the Italian (or Green) Garden, Pinsent engineered a double staircase to lessen the gradient. He used the curve this formed for a small pool, above which stands a statue of the Virgin. Bernard Berenson himself seems to have been responsible for the winsome statuettes of a puppy and a kitten bearing baskets of fruit which perch near by. On each descending terrace, a pair of narrow, symmetrical parterres balances the strong central axis of the descending steps. Clipped holm oaks and cypresses form the boundaries to the garden, while grass and box topiary add to the severely green effect.

As you descend the central steps, the Green Garden's decorative details emerge. The pattern of the parterres is visible and, though statues are used sparingly, the staircase is decorated delightfully with rectangles of *ciottolato* (mosaic pebblework). At the very bottom of the garden are two elegantly formed reflecting pools. Alongside the Italian Garden, the majestic cypress avenue is cleverly tapered to increase the effect of its length.

Kenneth Clark maintained that Bernard Berenson disliked Pinsent's 'imitation Baroque garden', while others have theorized that Mary Berenson's interference gave rise to conflicting egos at I Tatti. Renaissance in detail, in principle Pinsent's scheme for the Italian Garden reflects his youth and is perhaps lacking in scale. Harold Acton considered its 'dainty precision' more English than Florentine. And, returning to I Tatti after the Second World War,

Pinsent himself reconsidered the proportions of his terraces, wishing he had made them wider.

More likeable is Pinsent's intimate, enclosed Giardino Pensile (Hanging Garden) to the west of the villa. His scalloped, urn-topped neo-baroque walls set off a restrained, grey-green parterre composed of blocks of clipped lavender, enclosed by box. Swags of wisteria clothe the walls and the garden, where scholars still stroll today, has a serene, meditative atmosphere. Berenson often wandered along the paths of Settignano and seems to have preferred the natural areas of the garden – its olive groves, the open wildflower meadow and the holm oak wood.

Bernard Berenson died in 1959, leaving his beloved villa and its collections to Harvard University. They maintain it as a centre for Italian Renaissance studies. Bernard and Mary are both buried in the chapel at I Tatti.

Villa della Petraia

A short distance from Castello (see page 127) and worth visiting at the same time is another Medici property, Villa della Petraia. The Medici emblem with its famous *palle* (balls) is emblazoned over the front entrance. A high tower is all that remains of the ancient keep which, in 1364, withstood a siege by Pisan troops and mercenaries led by the famously bloodthirsty *condottiere* Sir John Hawkwood. In the fifteenth century the property belonged to the Strozzi family, rivals of the Medici, from whom it was confiscated. It was then owned by the Salutati, one of whom was manager of the Medici bank. Villa della Petraia was eventually bought in 1544 by Cosimo I de' Medici, who gave it in 1568 to his fifth son, Ferdinando de' Medici, a generous patron and able administrator who laid out the Villa Medici gardens in Rome (see page 196). A cardinal at the tender age of fifteen, Ferdinando in 1587 succeeded his older brother as Grand Duke of Tuscany and set about transforming the 'gentleman's house' at Petraia into a grander, princely residence.

Giusto Utens recorded the garden made by Ferdinando and his architects – possibly Bernardo Buontalenti, and later Raffaello Pagni – in a lunette, one of the series *Ville Medici*, which Utens painted for Duke Ferdinando's favourite summer residence, Villa di Artimino, between 1599 and 1602. Within enclosing walls, three levels of scenic terraces looked out over Florence and across the Arno valley to the Carrara mountains, a testament to the amount of earth that had to be moved in this 'stony' place. The Renaissance poet Ariosto is supposed to have written lines in praise of the view from Petraia, while standing on its terrace:

To see the hills with villas sprinkled o'er
Would make one think that, even as flowers and trees,
Here earth all towers in rich abundance bore.

A copy of the Utens lunette hangs at Villa Petraia. While it cannot be taken as conclusive evidence – Utens tended to paint aspirations rather than what he saw before him – it does show a garden of everyday simplicity which, despite the abundance of water in these hills, lacked the fountains and statues which so magnificently adorned Castello. On the upper terraces, simple, square compartments were lined, probably, with the dwarf fruit trees so highly prized in Renaissance gardens.

In 1864, during the Risorgimento, Florence was adopted as the temporary capital of Italy. Petraia became the royal residence of Vittorio Emanuele II of Savoy and his morganatic second wife, Rosa Vercellana,

Right, above A box-edged parterre filled with flowers replaces the former Medici fruit orchard.
Right, below The long *vasca* used to store water for the garden.

Countess of Mirafiore. During their time here, the eastern upper terrace was transformed with aviaries built to house Vittorio Emanuele's collection of rare birds. Curving flower beds in nineteenth-century style were designed to surround the famous fountain on which stood Giambologna's figure representing Venus or possibly Florence. Part of an iconographical theme glorifying the Medici at Castello, the fountain was moved to Petraia in the eighteenth century. The nineteenth-century scheme favoured by the Savoy royal couple has been restored, using elliptically shaped beds outlined with terracotta shells. A plaster copy of Giambologna's Venus presides; the graceful original can be seen inside the villa.

Although Duke Ferdinando's son, Don Lorenzo de' Medici, commissioned magnificent frescoes to celebrate his family, painted by Volterrano under the loggias of the courtyard in 1637–46, in the garden only one feature remains from the original Medici scheme. This is the long *vasca*, used to store water for the garden, on the middle terrace. To one side, a recreated flower garden containing bulbs – tulips, fritillaries and hyacinths – has been planted.

In the lunette by Utens, the lowest terrace is seen as an elaborately designed Medici fruit orchard. Within two identical squares, the fruit trees grew, sheltered by circular pergolas of evergreens. The space was further divided into quadrants by intersecting paths. The orchard has been replaced by a box-edged parterre filled with flowers, centred on a fountain surrounded by circular box hedging.

A charming relic at Villa della Petraia is the platform in an ancient ilex tree where Vittorio Emanuele would picnic with his bride. One of the leaders of the turn-of-the-century Anglo-Florentine community, Janet Ross, recalled huge ilex trees and 'a rustic staircase [which] twines round the trunk of the largest of these ... leading up to a platform among the branches, where Victor Emmanuel used to dine'. The King's view of 'villa-crowned' hills is now sadly altered.

G.F. Watts painted a view of Petraia. The painting hangs in the Watts Gallery, south of Guildford, in England.

Right, above A copy of Giambologna's *Venus*, moved from Castello. The original is in the villa.
Right, below The long *vasca*, still a cool, refreshing sight on the middle terrace, is the only feature to remain from the original Medici scheme.

Villa Medicea di Castello

Castello was one of the first of the Medici properties. In 1477 Lorenzo and Giovanni di Pierfrancesco de' Medici, great nephews of Cosimo the Elder, bought a fortified building here from the della Stufa family, which included a thirteenth-century tower. Lorenzo, from a cadet branch of the Medici, was a knowledgeable patron of art. It was for him that Botticelli painted the *Primavera*, which with *The Birth of Venus* hung at Castello until both were moved to the Uffizi.

Lorenzo di Pierfrancesco undertook a rebuilding of Castello, adding ground-floor rooms with a courtyard, loggia and stables. On his death, the villa passed to his nephew, the warlike *condottiere* Giovanni dalle Bande Nere. His son Cosimo (1519–74), the future Cosimo I, Grand Duke of Tuscany, spent part of his boyhood here and retained an affection for Castello that was to last a lifetime.

Cosimo was only seventeen when he succeeded his murdered predecessor, Alessandro de' Medici. His first year was an exacting one, as he fought off the Florentine aristocrats who sought to influence him and faced down a military threat from dissident republicans. Having come through 'the trials he had in the first year of his princeship,' Vasari tells us, Cosimo 'began to take some leisure and particularly to frequent the villa di Castello'.

No sooner had Cosimo become Duke of Florence in 1537 than he began to redesign his favourite residence. This was a time of deep unease between the citizenry and their would-be rulers. Duke Alessandro de' Medici – tyrannical and corrupt – had been assassinated; Cosimo himself, his ruthless effectiveness still not widely recognized, seemed as yet young and untried. His garden would serve as propaganda, portraying him, through its magnificence and celebratory iconography, as the ensurer of Florence's peace and the source of future prosperity. Flattering allegorical representations would serve to extol and elevate his princely virtues. The humanist and scholar Benedetto Varchi, who was given the task of inventing all this adulatory symbolism, was to convey, among other messages, the idea that the Medici ruled their territory like a fruitful garden, and to demonstrate, through landscaping, grottoes and aqueducts, Cosimo's authority over land and water.

Castello has been called the perfect example of the classic Italian garden. It remains an exceptionally well-preserved example of a Tuscan garden which looked back to the principles laid down by the fifteenth-century Renaissance polymath Leon Battista Alberti. 'Before the entrance,' Alberti advised, 'let there be ample space for carriages and equestrian exercise . . . In the grottoes of caves the ancients used to make a crust of rough and rocky material . . . let water flow from divers places where it is least expected . . . Let the alleys end with fruit trees and evergreens and enclose that part which is sheltered from the wind with box hedges . . .' All of these precepts were followed at Castello, and Cosimo himself would still be able to recognize his garden. Pivotal was the iconographical programme of fountains and statues devised to celebrate Cosimo by Varchi.

The garden was laid out in 1538 on the sloping ground behind the villa to the design of architect Niccolò Tribolo (1500–50). It was a vast and elaborate concept, involving earth moving and the channelling of water by aqueduct from nearby springs. Vasari described its position: '. . . the midday sun searches it out and bathes it with all its rays . . . and it stands so high that it commands a view not only of the whole palace but also of the plain . . .' The layout was geometrical: a central axis ran the length of the

garden up to the retaining wall and the ilex wood beyond. Three stepped terraces, linked by avenues and stairs, were divided by hedges and lines of trees into sixteen garden compartments. To each side of the main garden, two *giardini segreti* contained, on one side, a tree house, and on the other, according to Vasari, 'strange and medicinal herbs'. Water was at the heart of the garden. 'A man is not powerful until he is as powerful by sea as by land,' opined Duke Cosimo, ordering the galleys that would eventually go into battle with the Christian forces against the Turks at Lepanto in 1571. Water flowed through the garden, supposedly from the Apennines, represented by Bartolomeo Ammanati's colossal bronze figure of Appennino, added later in 1563, which dominates the upper garden from the centre of a pool inside the *bosco*. Clasping his arms across his torso, as water streams down his long hair and into his beard, this naked depiction of a shivering man represents the mountains from which flow the rivers that irrigate Tuscany.

Above The garden holds one of the most important collections of potted citrus in the world, including *bizzarie*.

From the pool in the *bosco*, water flowed into the Grotto of the Flood, sprinkling from its elaborately decorated ceiling, flowing into its massive, carved marble basins and springing up in jets from the pebble mosaic floor. This was possibly a reference to Duke Cosimo's generosity in piping clean water from his aqueducts to public fountains, or perhaps a metaphor for his success in cleansing Florence from the evils of its past. The grotto shelters an enchanting menagerie of life-size, sculpted animals, made from coloured stone and adorned with real antlers, horns and tusks. Designed originally by Tribolo, although the grotto was probably completed by Vasari, they were chosen not for their charm but to celebrate the life and history of the Medici. Thus the giraffe is said to recall a sultan's exotic gift to Lorenzo the Magnificent in 1487, while the humble goat may represent the sign of Capricorn, Cosimo's emblem. The unicorn, with its magical power to purify water with its horn, alluded to the duke himself.

Set along the central axis were two stately fountains, planned by Tribolo, who also sculpted their marble bases. Nearest the villa stood Ammanati's great bronze group of Hercules and Antaeus, an allusion to Cosimo's victory over Florence's republicans, as well as his power over Earth (Anteus was the son of the Earth). Higher up the slope and surrounded by the ring of cypress trees visible in the 1598–9 lunette by Giusto Utens, Giambologna's graceful figure of Venus (Florence) wringing out her hair wetted by the waters of the Arno and the Mugnone rose from a white marble basin. Of these two statues, both central to the Castello garden, one is under restoration and the other was moved in the eighteenth century to the neighbouring Medici villa of Petraia (see page 125).

Within the evergreen circle, Tribolo installed *giochi d'acqua* under the paving stones. These, with the spray from the fountain, helped chill the

stifling summer air. Duke Cosimo, as he became afflicted with ill health, would retreat inside the circle, where stone seating around the fountain tempted the family to linger in the cool. In 1544 he spent a pleasurable hour there with his children, watching as the court dwarf attempted to trap songbirds in a boxwood hedge. Sadly, the ring of trees was cut down when the fountain was moved. Edith Wharton was one who mourned the resulting 'sun-scorched expanse'.

Castello remained a Medici property until 1743. The last but one Grand Duke of Tuscany, Cosimo III, cultivated there the Indian jasmine known as 'Mugherino del Granduca', given to him in 1688 by the King of Portugal. In the eighteenth century, under the House of Savoy, much was lost or swept away. Today Castello belongs to the state: under its care, the famous Medici citrus collection has been reinstated. One of the most important collections of potted citrus in the world, it now comprises 500 trees, some descended from Medici cultivars. It also contains *bizzarie* (strange and rare grafted hybrid varieties). The collection had a narrow escape during the freezing winter of 1985, when only the head gardener's prompt action in lighting warming fires at night in the *limonaia* saved it. Within Castello's box compartments, peonies and antique roses in gentle colours mingle companionably with lavender, cistus, gaura, agapanthus and teuchrium alongside bulbs and herbs. Jasmines flourish in pots, and plumbago, roses, vines and citrus, with an underskirt of irises, line the walls – a replacement for Vasari's much-admired espaliered pomegranates and bitter oranges. The great pots of citrus and trained dwarf varieties lining the paths call to mind the Medici grandees who once walked here.

Above Ammanati's colossal bronze figure of Appennino.
Left The Grotto of the Flood, with its enchanting menagerie of life-sized sculpted animals with real antlers, horns and tusks.

Villa Guicciardini Corsi Salviati FLORENCE, TUSCANY

Unlike most Tuscan villas, this one stands in flat terrain, facing on to a busy suburban road. Its dramatic roofline, with statues silhouetted against the sky, is visible from far off, towering above the urban sprawl. Somehow, the approach through such ordinary surroundings does not dampen the sense of expectation one feels on arrival at the villa's front door, even though the walled garden remains out of sight, still concealed behind the long façade.

In 1502 Jacopo Corsi bought an estate here 'with Master's Abode and Worker's House'. A sixteenth-century fresco inside the villa shows this to have been a fairly typical Tuscan house, with a simple garden containing a fountain, and grass divided by paths into squares. During the family's long tenure, the garden was to be altered several times, as successive generations of Corsi put their stamp on it. It was in the mid-eighteenth century that the garden took on much of the appearance it has today, when it was remodelled into the baroque style fashionable at that time. The back of the building became the front façade and the connection with the Arno valley, located south of the estate, lost some of its importance.

A 1740 engraving by Zocchi recorded this radical transformation. The façade of the villa was transformed into a graceful baroque outline, its roof

lined with balustrades and decked with statues, pinnacles and urns. Two balustraded belvedere towers anchor the building. The aviary attached to the villa in the seventeenth century was turned into a large open loggia, looking out on to a circular pool with fountain jets. This charming loggia, now filled with plants, is frescoed with birds overflying classical ruins.

Beside the round pool was a rectangular basin (once the seventeenth-century fishpond), decorated with statues of the Four Seasons. This canal-like basin is choked with waterlilies today; clouds of erigeron grow where water once cascaded from stone masks into clear, sparkling water. The long basin lines up with a narrow eighteenth-century canal on the other side of wrought-iron gates: the ornamental gates are clearly pictured in the seventeenth-century print. The canal, which ended in a fountain, was once enlivened by water jets and small cascades.

Zocchi's engraving shows the rectangular garden enclosed by walls lined with statues, just as it appears today. These lively statues of peasants, dogs

Above The walled garden is lined with statues of peasants, dogs and classical figures as shown in Zocchi's 1740 engraving.

and classical figures still look down on us from their pillars. The diamond-shaped beds of the ornamental parterre, with their elaborate geometric patterns, indicate a composition that in its intricacy and interest may have been meant to compensate for the lack of views.

In the nineteenth century the garden was inevitably romanticized, its *bosco* provided with mounds, a miniature lake and a sham castle. Later in the century the villa became known for its collection of rare and exotic plants. Palm trees towered over the parterre; two new hothouses provided shelter for succulents. Rarities were grown – rare carnations, the double ranunculus *roselline di Firenze* and the jasmine 'Mugherino del Granduca', introduced at Castello by Cosimo III (see page 128). By the time Marchese Giulio Guicciardini Corsi Salviati came to inherit the estate in 1907, the garden was a melange of different generations' taste and conflicting garden styles.

That the marchese approached the restoration of the garden with great sensitivity can be appreciated from the monograph he wrote about his daunting task: 'I took warning from the mania that possesses some people for redoing our villas and gardens too much and, in their desire to bring them back to one period, depriving them of the traces left by the passage of time that give them a human and living character.' Choosing to restore as much of the eighteenth-century character as possible, he removed the exotics in their hothouses and reinstated the lemon trees, fountains and diamond-shaped parterres. A labyrinth was added (based on the one at Hampton Court), and a delightful Green Theatre based on the eighteenth-century Heckentheater (Hedge Theatre) at Schloss Mirabell in Salzburg. Green 'wings' of box show up a statue of Apollo, god of music and poetry, presiding at the back of the stage. The box Prompter's or Conductor's Box is sunk in a pit facing the theatre.

The garden at Villa Giucciardini Corsi Salviati is an unexpected haven in the midst of busy suburbs. Still owned by the family, it now houses the University of Michigan's summer programme.

Above Attached to the house is an open loggia frescoed with birds flying over classical ruins.
Left The Green Theatre, based on the eighteenth-century *Heckentheater* (Hedge Theatre) at Schloss Mirabell in Salzburg. Apollo, god of music and poetry, presides.

Poggio Torselli

Located near Machiavelli's Albergaccio, this elegant eighteenth-century country house with a fifteenth-century core looks out over its own olive groves and vineyards on to a classic Tuscan landscape, with the cupola of Brunelleschi's dome visible on clear days across the valley. Once known as the 'Queen of Villas', the estate was recorded in land registers as early as 1427. It has belonged through the centuries to some of Florence's most distinguished families – the Corsini, Strozzi, Capponi, Antinori and Orlandini del Beccuto, in whose ownership it remained until 1722. In the 1690s the Orlandini renovated the villa and probably also put in the western entrance road, now the cypress avenue, and laid out the Italian Gardens on two stepped terraces on the villa's eastern side.

The present owners bought Poggio Torselli in 1990 and immediately embarked on a four-year project of meticulous conservation. The old cypress *viale*, its severity lightened by underplantings of pink roses and blue ceratostigma, leads up to the villa's serene, cream-stuccoed, western façade, crowned by a gable on which stand statues of the Four Seasons. This theme of the seasons can be found on frescoes inside the villa, and is echoed in the replanted Italian Garden on the eastern aspect. To the north, park-like grounds of clipped evergreens paired with glimmering white roses give out on to a stone terrace built against the house wall. A belvedere offers a view which swoops down over the silvery haze of olive-clad hillsides, all the way to Florence.

The south-western flank of the villa is guarded by another line of regimented cypress along the side drive, their dark mass a frame for white 'Iceberg' roses, erigeron and potted white hydrangeas. A statue of Bacchus presides. Against the villa walls are propped antique Etruscan burial urns – the San Casciano Hills were an Etruscan stronghold. Near by is a nineteenth-century carriage room with equestrian mounting block: together, they reflect the centuries of human habitation on this site.

In the restoration and replanting of Poggio Torselli's gardens, the owners managed to combine artistry with scholarship. The Italian Garden has little of the sobriety and restraint seen in classic Tuscan gardens: season by season, it is a riot of exuberant colour. Each year, the owners create a plan and devise a colour scheme to take the garden through the seasons; each year it changes at least twice. The most beautiful months are said to be April and May, when the tulips are in bloom, dwarfed by stately crown imperial fritillaries, and the spikes of *Hyacinthus orientalis* appear through a mist of myosotis. In summer, the beds are a vibrant mix of skilfully chosen plants. Some, like the dwarf fruit trees and aromatic herbs, were common to eighteenth-century gardens. Others, like the violet-blue *Salvia farinacea* 'Evolution', are up-to-date varieties. *Nicotiana sylvestris* anchors the beds; lilies mingle with roses. Among the potpourri of pinks, peonies, and dwarf dahlias, asters, tall cannas, abutilon and *Verbena bonariensis* arch and sway. Around the fountain, a deep salmon-pink variety of *Lobelia × speciosa* grows with dainty pink and white erigeron and the showy giant *Hibiscus palustris*. At the end, overlooking the valley, a stone table sits invitingly under a shady arbour. Just below, under the olive trees, is an enchanting ornamental vegetable garden, recreated in the late 1990s. All the Tuscan staples are here – beans, artichokes, corn, fennel, tomatoes, asparagus – all decoratively displayed, and mixed with love-in-the-mist, poppies and cornflowers.

Top The Italian Garden on the eastern side of the villa.
Bottom Behind the fountain sits a stone table under a shady arbour. Just below the retaining wall, under the olive trees, is the decorative vegetable garden.

Towards the *limonaia*, where swallows nest and centuries-old citrus trees shelter during winter, herbs grow in pots among more flamboyant planting. Scarlet and burgundy *Lobelia cardinalis* 'Queen Victoria' vies with violet-blue *Verbena hastata*. *Anagallis* 'Skylover' adds its own azure blue to the mix.

Underpinning the display is a careful approach to conservation, inspired by the owners and their scholarly advisor, the landscape architect Dr Ada V. Segre. She researched the historical planting schemes, partly eighteenth century and partly early twentieth century; the present layout dates back to 1925. Signor Gianfranco Luzzetti, one of the owners, designed the swimming pool and the lower-terrace Olive Garden under the restored *orto*. Signor Luzzetti specifically wished to preserve the topography of the original flower beds and the stonework of the terracing. The most striking original feature of the garden is the early eighteenth-century open-air canal, which was used to water the raised beds along the wall and, thanks to recent repairs, still works. The canal has little bowls at set distances: cold water running from the water tank warms up in the bowls before overflowing to the beds.

At the back of the house, Japanese anemones rise through a frilly skirt of *Acanthus mollis*, and dusky pink verbena grows alongside vivid blue salvia. Around the swimming pool, the olives have been retained and underplanted with iris, cistus, rosemary and lavender, with roses twining up the olive trees. Cypress and umbrella pines mark the perimeter of the garden, as it blends into the agricultural estate (which produces olive oil and wine of great quality).

Supremely well run, Poggio Torselli nevertheless retains a tranquil, unhurried feel that befits its age.

Above Geraniums spill over the wall, above a border with seasonal planting.
Right The ancient cypress *viale*.

Vignamaggio

This sublime, pink-washed Renaissance country house sits on a hill in the midst of its own estate in the heart of classic Chianti countryside, near the Vecchia Chiantigiana, the old Chianti road. In 2004 the estate celebrated 600 years of wine-making: in the early 1400s there was already mention of 'wine placed in barrels at Vignamaggio'. The robust simplicity of the main house dates it, too, back to the fifteenth century. In the 1600s the Gherardi bought it, adding a wing and leaving the villa exactly as it looks today. 'Listen,' wrote an entranced visitor in 1659, 'I am a countryman and would like you to know what corner of the earth under this sky makes me feel so blessed. The place is called, after the vines of Bacchus and the most flowering month of the year, "Vignamaggio". It is surrounded on all sides by the most beautiful grapevines, and the pervading spirit of spring in this place merits this name. It is the villa of the Gherardis . . .'

Before the Gherardi the owners of the estate had been the Gherardini and it was during their tenure that Leonardo da Vinci is supposed to have stayed at Vignamaggio before he left Tuscany for Milan in 1506. The Gherardini had a daughter, Lisa, born in 1479, and married at fifteen to a prosperous widower, Francesco del Giocondo. 'For Francesco del Giocondo Leonardo undertook to execute the portrait of his wife, Mona Lisa,' writes Vasari in his *Life* of the 'marvellous and divinely inspired Leonardo', leading successive art historians to speculate that Lisa Gherardini of Vignamaggio did indeed sit for the most famous portrait ever painted. Whether Leonardo painted her at Vignamaggio we do not know, for the Gherardini also owned a Florence town house near Santa Trinità. Leonardo's biographer Charles Nicholl thinks that on balance Vasari was right, and that Giocondo did commission the portrait of his wife, the young mother and well-to-do Florentine housewife, in around 1503. In 2003 the Louvre celebrated the painting's 500th birthday.

At the side of the house, two mossy and venerable statues of a lion and a dog share the timeless view from the terrace over vineyards and olive groves, scattered hamlets and cypress-fringed hills. In front, the Renaissance purity of the villa is echoed by the simplicity of the grass and box parterre, its cushiony globes of box a counterfoil to the line of soaring cypresses near by. Great pots of citrus line up in front of the house, while jars spilling with plumbago and jasmine dot the grass and gravel. Winsome terracotta statues of the Four Seasons, entwined with roses, mark the central path to another part of the garden.

It was the Counts Sanminiatelli in the 1930s who successfully re-imagined and redesigned a Renaissance garden, respecting the horizontal line of eight 100-year-old cypress trees as a natural division. Beyond here on the right lies the sunken Fountain Garden, reached by a sloping pebbled ramp planted with banks of hypericum on either side. Box hedges enclose the fountain and box topiary mounds rise in the middle of simple grass plats divided by gravel paths. At the end, through a dark green arched cypress arcade, can be glimpsed the silvery grey of olives.

Right, above Vignamaggio – the pink-washed Renaissance country house behind the box parterre.
Right, below The Fountain Garden, used as a setting for Kenneth Branagh's film of *Much Ado About Nothing*.

On the other side of the central path, box curves in *broderie* shapes around holm oaks pruned into massive cones. Both these gardens are familiar from Kenneth Branagh's film of *Much Ado About Nothing* in which Vignamaggio stood in for Messina, and Benedick and Beatrice, Claudio and Hero danced, schemed and sparred among the topiary domes and cypress walks.

At the end of the cypress avenue a terracotta urn stands on a marble base. Two piers, once part of the original gates to Vignamaggio, lead to a stone path bordered by rosemary and overlooking the valley. A cypress *viale* leads all the way to the wood: it was the poet Bino Sanminiatelli's wish to link the house and woods with a cypress-lined path.

Sig. Gianni Nunziante, who now lives here, has carried out a great deal of research and restoration. Vignamaggio has never looked lovelier, and while one half of the building is private, the other half is now open as a hotel. Guided tours and lunches with olive oil and wine tastings can be arranged. 'It takes rather a long time,' says Sandro, who organizes them, 'because everyone enjoys it so much.'

Above Winsome terracotta statues of the Four Seasons, entwined with roses.

Giardino di Bibbiani

The austerely beautiful villa, a property of the Frescobaldi family, was left by Anastasia Frescobaldi to her son Cosimo Ridolfi in 1809. Ridolfi was asked by his mother to 'render pleasant this estate of Bibbiani which she loved, how much she could not say, as a paternal keepsake'. After burying her in the chapel here, Cosimo Ridolfi, who was to become a famous agronomist and professor of agriculture in Pisa, set about creating this important 20-hectare/50-acre botanical park around his much-loved family home. In 1843 he published a catalogue of the plants cultivated at Bibbiani, many of them exotics from other climate zones. Ridolfi was passionately committed to Bibbiani, finding in its care 'a pastime that is both delightful and instructive . . . My dearest studies seem even sweeter to me amid the impenetrable brush that I am transforming into flowering woods.'

He planted his botanical park in the natural style fashionable at the time with spreading lawns and romantic, winding paths. Among his introductions were eucalyptus, which reached Europe around 1840, and the American giants *Sequoia sempervirens* and *Sequoiadendron giganteum* in

1845. *Hovenia dulcis*, one of the oldest trees in the park, came to Bibbiani in 1829. Among the many araucarias, a new species was identified, grown from a seed sent to Ridolfi, and subsequently named *A. ridolfiana* in his honour. Ridolfi had 400 varieties of camellia: only four or five survive, but the original porcelain labels remain. Of the many significant examples of *Pinus*, a gigantic 200-year-old *P. pinea* is of unparalleled size and beauty. A towering 25-metre/82-foot Caucasian fir (*Abies nordmanniana*) is one of the present owner's favourites. Majestic lime trees frame a meadow behind the house, where an eighteenth-century sham ruin, the romantic Bad Man's Arch, marks the former entrance to the villa from the River Arno. In past centuries, visitors from Florence would land at a small harbour built out into the river and from there make their way to Bibbiani.

In 1903 the Bibbiani estate was sold to Baron Raimondo Franchetti, who expanded the collection, planting *Pinus nigra* and *P. sylvestris* on one side of the main drive, with alternating *Sequoia sempervirens* and the incense cedar (*Calocedrus decurrens*) on the other. Originally planted too

close together, some of these trees have failed to thrive, leaving gaps in Franchetti's scheme. At the bottom of the drive, the first great tree to appear is a pecan, *Carya illoinensis*. Local firemen cut the dead branches off the big pines and two great *Washingtonia filifera* every four to five years. The owners repay them with an equal amount of wine.

In 1937 Bibbiani came into the ownership of the del Gratta family from Pisa. It is now beautifully cared for by part of that family, Pier Lorenzo and Donatella Marchiafava. They have retained the collecting tradition and restored Bibbiani after the damage to its great trees caused by bombing during the Second World War. In 1991 a new catalogue was created with the help of the University of Florence. Since then Pier Lorenzo has concentrated on expanding the collection of exotic conifers. In particular, he studies the genus *Pinus*, each year adding new species: *P. coulteri*, the big-cone pine; *P. nigra* subsp. *laricio*; *P. palustris*, one of seven species of longleaf pines; and *P. aristata*, the Rocky Mountain bristlecone pine. This high-altitude pine, often found growing at the tree line, is rare in Europe. To find the ideal, free-draining substratum for it, Pier Lorenzo mixed earth with the sand used for cleaning marble walls. From his flourishing nursery, Pier Lorenzo takes his pines to exhibit at shows, and is in touch with botanical gardens as well as the head gardeners at Isola Bella and La Mortola (pages 21 and 76).

Nearer the house is a formal garden in typical Italian style, and a green theatre in box, bay and cypress, made at the end of the nineteenth century. But the real privilege of a visit to Bibbiani is to wander in awe through its great park, pondering the mystery of its mighty trees. There are four different itineraries to choose from.

L'Apparita

This supremely simple yet sophisticated garden, a 1960s masterpiece by the landscape architect Pietro Porcinai, mirrors the Tuscan countryside that surrounds it, creating a setting of uninterrupted harmony. There are no roads or fences. The approach road was moved, so as to be hidden from the house, and the car park sunk to conceal the sight of any cars. The unbroken views range over the rolling Tuscan landscape all the way to Siena, which floats in the distance like a hilltop city in a Renaissance painting.

The villa's architecture is unusual. A simple building with the rustic feel of a farmhouse, the villa is made remarkable by a classically designed, strikingly elegant loggia in the shape of two tiers of four rounded arches. This loggia has an austere beauty and purity of line that has led to it being attributed to the master, Baldassare Peruzzi, himself. Loggias were a familiar device in Renaissance architecture, creating an airy yet sheltered observation point from which to admire the surroundings. As has often been pointed out, Peruzzi could not have designed all the buildings associated with him. Nevertheless, he was in Siena after the Sack of Rome in 1527. There is a suggestion that this beautiful loggia might have stood alone as a rural pleasure pavilion, and that the house was added to it later.

The garden was made over the years 1966–70 for Don Giovanni Guiso, a connoisseur and theatre-lover. Its central feature is a delightful contemporary Green Theatre, designed by Porcinai as an amphitheatre, with benches set out on a grassy hillside, sloping down to the central stage. Like Greek amphitheatres, Porcinai's elegantly refined theatre has as its backdrop a breathtaking view, as on the distant horizon Siena's spires and cupolas hover above its circular grass stage. Not much is allowed to detract from this sublime, natural arena. Hedges of laurel and pomegranate form the 'wings'; five small pillars support classical vases encircling the stage; at the top of the slope two more urns paired with two cypresses stand alongside a 'ruined' wall. The wall bears one of the many inscriptions – words by

Tasso and Baudelaire – that are scattered around the garden. The Green Theatre was inaugurated with a classical concert in 1969 and has been used regularly for concerts and poetry readings ever since.

In an outbuilding Don Giovanni created a second theatre with an eighteenth-century backdrop, found in another Tuscan villa. This now houses some of his collection of antique miniature theatres, formed over many years.

L'Apparita was recently inherited by Don Giovanni's nephew, Don Paolo Guiso, who brings the same generous, hospitable spirit to this exceptional place. The villa has been called 'la più bella casa rurale del mondo' (the most beautiful rural house in the world).

Above An inscription commemorating the inauguration of the garden.
Left The contemporary Green Theatre, designed by Pietro Porcinai.

Badia a Coltibuono

The gardens at Badia a Coltibuono, a former medieval abbey, take much of their peaceful spirit from what was once the monks' *hortus conclusus*, sheltering in the lee of the great abbey church of Vallombrosa. Its high stone tower is visible above the surrounding fir and chestnut woods.

Lorenza de' Medici, the Italian cookery writer, came to Badia a Coltibuono on her marriage and found a perfectly preserved medieval settlement with a house backing on to the ancient church. The sixteenth-century frescoed refectory of the abbey is still in daily use as a family sitting room; the coat of arms on the ceiling is said to show a monk with a planting dibble. The frescoed walls display the life of St Lawrence, who roasted to death on a gridiron and ended up as the patron saint of chefs. The grill emblem crops up elsewhere in the house, for example over the front door, providing a suitable motif for the famous cookery school started by Lorenza de' Medici and now run by her son. Pupils at the school live in here, and overnight guests can stay in the surprisingly large monastic cells. From the windows there is a view of distant mountains floating in a blue haze, while in the foreground white cattle graze in a

field bordered by cedars and pines. Wood pigeons coo and the centuries of peace here are palpable.

Francesco di Moncino, who was the abbot in 1427, wrote a description of the garden which mentioned 'a kitchen-garden cum pergola', with grapes for eating but not for wine. As the Vallombrosa monks were known for their bibulousness, this led Lorenza de' Medici to conclude that the wily abbot was deliberately underestimating his abbey's wealth. The medieval poet Folgore da San Gimignano was more effusive, describing 'very broad paths, all straight as arrows and covered by pergolas of vines'. 'Arbors of oranges citrons persimmons lemons and all other tasty fruits' lined the paths, and such strong scents wafted through the garden that 'they seemed to be in the midst of all the spicery that ever grew in the Orient'.

Who better to care for this monastic *orto* than Lorenza de' Medici, who has replanted the garden with sensitivity and skill. She inherited the basic layout from a 1907 redesign by her husband's family, the Stucchi, who have lived here since 1846. Inevitably, she has had to weave in some nineteenth- and twentieth-century elements, such as the great *Magnolia grandiflora* beside the early twentieth-century Italian-style box parterre laid out in front of the house. Research done by the family suggests that this was once the site of a garden of medicinal plants grown for the infirmary. Now, the fresh green rectangles of box act as a calm foil to the riot of Virginia creeper, Banksian roses, campsis and plumbago which cover the house and romp along its balustrade.

Tours start in the central courtyard, where swallows swoop and dive past walls covered in trachelospermum. Lavender brims from pots and *Hydrangea anomala* subsp. *petiolaris* thrives in a huge oil jar. On either side of the front door are potted olive trees. The entrance to the garden leads down a ramp straight to a vine-covered pergola with, underneath, rows of 'Annabelle' hydrangeas, their flower heads lime green in the shade. Green grapes hang down from the vines; white Japanese anemones froth in the background. The effect is breathtaking – like being under cool, green water.

There is an appealingly domestic quality to this garden, which harks back to the simplicity and self-sufficiency of its monastic history. Its large rectangular space still bears traces of the outline of the ancient *pomario*. It has been divided into sections by vine-covered pergolas in an echo of its past. One section is planted with roses and peonies, with a pergola shaded by Banksian roses. Herbs and fruit bushes grow under the vines. In another, a productive vegetable garden is surrounded by aromatic herbs, planted, as the monks planted them, to ward off insects. Towards the woods and hills the garden simplifies into simple grass squares.

There are original touches everywhere. On the terrace under the magnolia, a favourite seating area is surrounded by pots of different scented thymes, which then march two by two up the steps to a higher terrace. Up here behind another vine-covered pergola underplanted with roses is another simple parterre enclosing pots of lemons in orderly sequence.

This is a garden for all seasons. In early summer sweet-smelling Banksian roses and wisteria combine to create what Lorenza de' Medici describes as a typical nineteenth-century colour scheme of lilac and yellow. Later, huge billowing banks of lavender attract fluttering white butterflies. On July evenings the great white heads of the 'Annabelle' hydrangeas gleam in the twilight. Later, Virginia creeper turns the house a fiery red.

Badia a Coltibuono has its own mountain spring, which supplies the house and fountains and makes the garden possible. Olives, vineyards and garden are all organically farmed. The estate is run now by Lorenza's children: Guido in the school and Paolo in the restaurant. The eldest, Emanuela, keeps up the monastic tradition by ensuring that this ancient abbey in the Chianti hills remains open to everyone.

Opposite, above A frescoed coat of arms inside the abbey, showing a monk with a planting dibble.
Opposite, below The Italian-style box parterre, laid out in the early twentieth century on what may have been the site of a medieval garden of medicinal plants.
Below Rows of *Hydrangea arborescens* 'Annabelle' stretch the length of the vine-covered pergola.

Castello di Brolio

The magnificent fortress of Brolio commands a breathtaking view over a timeless Tuscan panorama of hills and fields studded with cypress and pine and embroidered with olive groves and vineyards. It is a landscape seemingly unchanged since Ambrogio Lorenzetti painted his frescoes of it in nearby Siena, whose rosy-red towers are hazily visible from Brolio on the far horizon.

Lorenzetti has been placed at the very start of Western landscape art. But by the time he was painting in the 1300s, the castle at Brolio had stood for 300 years and the Ricasoli family who live here had already been associated with wine for two centuries.

Brolio held a strategic position on the border of the medieval territories of Florence and Siena, whose support for two opposing powers – Florence for the papacy and Siena for the Holy Roman Empire – locked them in bitter rivalry. Despite being within sight of Siena, Brolio served as the southernmost outpost of Florence. 'When Brolio growls,' the saying went, 'all Siena trembles.'

Bloody battles were fought all over this area of southern Chianti until the Medici grand duchy united the cities of Tuscany. Brolio's massive fifteenth-century stone battlements, supposedly built by the military architect-engineer Giuliano da Sangallo, now look down peaceably on a parterre with lemons and antique roses. On the panoramic south terrace, with its shade-giving lime, holm oak and stachyurus, the impressive buttresses against the castle walls are purely decorative, planted in box. And the castle itself, despite its ancient origins and warlike past, was transformed in the nineteenth century by the architect Pietro Marchetti into a neo-gothic, red brick fairytale, complete with turrets, balconies and mullioned lancet windows. The Ricasoli responsible for this crenellated gothic fantasy was Bettino, hero of the Risorgimento, who in 1866 succeeded Cavour as Prime Minister of Italy. In the nineteenth century, too, exotics were introduced in the woods: sequoia, Himalayan cedars, cedars of Lebanon, Sabineana pines – youngsters all, compared to Brolio's venerable cypress avenue. There are paths through these woods, some leading downhill to the Ricasolis' attractive, modern *osteria*, serving Tuscan food and wines from the estate. Above the castle entrance is a charming *bosco pensile* with a strawberry tree (*Arbutus unedo*).

But the glory of Brolio is its view. It is still possible to walk the ramparts and admire it, across 485 hectares/1,200 acres of unspoilt agricultural estate: to the south, the towers of Siena and the bulk of Monte Amiata; to the far west, the ancient hills of Volterra; to the north, the green slopes of Radda in Chianti. In the foreground is the ultra-modern Brolio winery, famous for its Chianti Classico. In the 1950s the Ricasoli brand was sold to Seagram's and the wines necessarily became more commercial. It was Barone Francesco Ricasoli who in 1993 bought back his birthright and, with the help of the local neighbourhood, started again, replanting the vineyards and restoring the good name of Ricasoli.

Right, above The neo-gothic red brick Castello di Brolio, with its turrets and mullioned lancet windows.
Right, below Beneath the ramparts lies a peaceful grassy parterre, which has lemon trees and roses during the summer months.

Castello di Celsa

The rugged mass of medieval Celsa dominates the wooded ridge on which it stands. A mile or so further along, cut out of the hillside, can be seen the 200 steep steps leading up to the *romitorio* (hermitage) at Cetinale (see page 150), the great garden restored and enlarged by the late Lord Lambton.

The thirteenth-century castle has seen tumultuous events, including a sacking by Austrian–Spanish troops in 1554. After the Celsi, it was owned by the Chigi family and, latterly, the Aldobrandini, who restored the garden and inserted their coat of arms into the parterre.

Celsa is known, however, for its association with Baldassare Peruzzi, the versatile, Sienese-born, Renaissance architect and painter. He was responsible for the harmonious yet austere circular brick chapel, exemplifying what Harold Acton praised as his 'extreme purity of proportion and perspective'. Peruzzi probably also designed the walled, parterred terrace in front of the castle, which ends now in a balustraded demi-lunar pool, with an unspoilt view to the towers and turrets of Siena. *Broderie* containing the Aldobrandini arms has replaced the original linear Renaissance parterre.

During the Baroque period the castle was to be transformed into a more elegant villa, with a triple arched screen, surmounted by a balustrade, closing off the courtyard to form an impressive entrance. Acton considered this graceful screen to harmonize so well with Peruzzi's work here that he questioned whether it might be by Peruzzi himself, rather than a later addition. In fact, the screen, as a drawing shows, was one small part of a plan for a huge baroque palace, the rest of which was never implemented. Much later the castle was given a neo-gothic makeover.

Also dating to the Baroque period, the *bosco*, some distance from the house, was once dotted with small buildings. One that remains – a pavilion for hunters – still retains its beautiful frescoed ceiling. The balustraded fishpond with its reclining river gods was restored by Prince Aldobrandini after the Second World War. A seventeenth-century drawing still held in the castle shows the trees around the fishpond clipped like stage wings. The monumental cypress avenue leading up to the fishpond is 1920s Italian Revival and an effective replacement for the nineteenth-century rose arches which were there before.

In the early nineteenth century, when Celsa was one of many Chigi villas, it was visited by the scholar Joseph Forsyth, who found it even more neglected than Cetinale. He blamed the indolent and city-loving Sienese nobility, who were not interested in the joys of nature or improving their estates, but 'loiter round the villa just as they loiter round the town'. During the autumn *villeggiatura*, a 'swarm of bachelors' would tour the family's country villas, 'the uncles and brothers of the heir inherit[ing] ... a right to board and lodging in every house belonging to the family'.

As late as 1925 photographs show the garden in a sad state of decline. Today, thanks to Prince Aldobrandini and his descendants, helped by the input of former garden advisor Alessandro Tombelli, Celsa is well cared for again.

Above, left The walled parterre in front of the castle, with Baldassare Peruzzi's Renaissance circular brick chapel.
Above, right The cypress *viale* is 1920s Italian Revival.

Villa di Geggiano

Geggiano is an untouched rococo gem, a joyous confection of baroque fantasy and prettiness, miraculously unchanged today. 'The house', says its present owner, Count Andrea Boscu Bianchi Bandinelli, who came back from Rome to live here, 'does have a joyful feel – the joy of summer holidays in the country. And it was made for a young couple in love, who lived a long and happy life here.'

These two, Anton Domenico Bianchi Bandinelli and Cecilia Chigi-Zondadari, married in 1768, thus bringing together two important Sienese families. Geggiano had come to the Bandinelli as a dowry 250 years earlier and, except for the addition of a few rooms, had not changed much since. A simple rustic retreat in the Chianti foothills, it was not considered elegant enough for a fashionable young couple, who looked beyond the borders of Tuscany to the best of European style. Over the next years the plain four-square house was transformed with a riot of *toile de Jouy* and eighteenth-century Parisian wallpapers, and furnished with delicately painted Venetian furniture, copied from originals by Sienese craftsmen. It was also turned back to front, with the addition of an elegant stuccoed and shuttered façade.

The newly resplendent villa looked across a *piazzone* enclosed by scalloped walls of rosy-red Sienese brick to its own Green Theatre. Here, a raised semicircle of grass acts as stage, and from two flanking brick arches Comedy and Tragedy, sculpted by the Maltese sculptor Bosio, look down from their niches. The graceful pediments are crumbling now, but still visible are the legs of the figures who once held aloft the Bandinelli and Chigi coats of arms. This stage, with its wings of clipped cypress and laurel, behind which actors could move about unseen, has been in use ever since Alfieri rehearsed his casts here in the eighteenth century. Concerts now take the place of plays. At the back of this graceful little theatre, a solitary tall cypress makes a dramatic focal point.

For anyone standing in the *piazzone*, the height of the surrounding walls is exactly judged to afford them a view of the skyline. This conceit, Count Andrea thinks, was not the device of an architect but suggested by Anton and Cecilia themselves. The vases that once topped the wall's twelve gate piers have largely disappeared. However, the mould that formed them has been found and will be put to use again. Sadly, the *grotteschi* of monkeys are too costly to replace.

Above Villa di Geggiano, overlooking the *piazzone*.
Below, left to right One of two brick arches flanking the Green Theatre, which has been reproduced on a painted chair inside the villa; and one of the monkey *grotteschi*, perched on a pillar.

To the west, the gates lead to a simple *orto pomario*, a kitchen garden but based on a formal garden structure. In the centre is a pergola of table grapes from which tunnels covered in vines and roses radiate outwards. Zinnias, peonies and *Rosa* 'Mutabilis' add colour to the garden. *Rosa* Iceberg, donated by enthusiastic visitors, climbs a tree. Trachelospermum grown over an arch frames a picture-book view of distant Siena. At the back of this charming country garden is a *cisterna*, originally a *peschiera* full of carp. 'The carp ate the mosquito larvae,' says Count Andrea, 'and then the owners ate the carp.' The *cisterna*'s typical eighteenth-century demi-lunar shape suggests it was probably designed when the house was modified.

Geggiano is approached through a double cypress avenue, planted as part of the original landscape design and ending in a *rond-point* in box, scalloped to echo the *piazzone*'s scalloped brick walls. The venerable holm oak avenue leading to the gates was once a *ragnaia* when birding – netting tiny songbirds in nets strung across avenues of trees – was the most popular and widespread form of hunting. Villas Gori and Castello were among other villas boasting their own *ragnaias*. Inside Geggiano a tempera painting of the seasons by itinerant Austrian artist Ignazio Moder shows women birding by trying to trap birds in their capacious skirts.

Geggiano's extraordinary survival – the paintwork is fresh; even the furniture is arranged as it was in the eighteenth-century inventory – owes much to its breezy hilltop site and lack of heating. As this was a summer house, there are no chimneys. Nineteenth-century 'improvements' were avoided through lack of money.

In the early twentieth century the owner, Ranuccio Bianchi Bandinelli, was an archaeologist, art historian and friend of Bernard Berenson. He saved the house from destruction by the Nazis by flourishing a letter signed by Field Marshal Kesselring. The letter had been meant for another villa, but Ranuccio used it to protect Geggiano, claiming moreover that

Goethe, not Alfieri, had used the Green Theatre to stage a play. Ever since, Goethe has been known as the patron saint of the house.

Ranuccio, 'The Red Count', was a card-carrying Communist who in 1950 gave away 80 per cent of the vineyards and twenty farm houses to his 'share-cropping' farmers to form a co-operative which is still active today. Count Andrea and his brother Count Alessandro are now renting and buying back the vineyards and re-establishing their label. Records show that the estate's Chianti wine was exported to London as far back as 1725.

To preserve Geggiano, the two brothers work together, Andrea from his computer, Alessandro from his tractor in the vineyards. This unique place is in good hands.

Above Vases and monkey *grotteschi* top the piazzone walls. Through the gateway at the end of the *orto pomario* is a view of distant Siena.
Left The *orto pomario*.

Il Bosco della Ragnaia

Si non qui, dove? (If not here, where?) is the motto of this decidedly mysterious and enigmatic contemporary garden, which sprang up in 1995 when American artist Sheppard Craige bought 9 hectares/22 acres of neglected woodland near San Giovanni d'Asso in the midst of some of the most perfect landscape in all of Tuscany. Sheppard's project began straightforwardly enough. He chose a wood because he wanted to garden in the shade, and he chose this wood because it was an ancient *ragnaia*, once used for netting birds, whose magnificent and venerable holm oaks had become choked in a jungle of encroaching undergrowth. Local youths were co-opted to clear the tangle of creepers and brambles that had long obscured the trees.

From this, the garden developed organically. There was no plan, besides Sheppard's strong desire to abandon canvas and paints to work physically and directly with landscape. There had even been a feeling sometimes, he says, that the *bosco* was waiting for him. And 'one day I showed up.'

As an American living in Italy, Sheppard had visited the classical Italian gardens and admired the simplicity of their construction – 'stone, water, gravel and leafy evergreens'. By working within this tradition, with similar materials, the same attention to symmetry, and strong horizontal and vertical lines, he hoped to achieve a landscape as thought-provoking as the great Renaissance gardens, but in a modern idiom. His Garden of Ideas, he says, is less influenced by Renaissance themes and preoccupations than by the literary frame of reference of the English eighteenth century. Part philosophy, part Zen, part literary construct, part classical allusions, the *bosco* also owes much to the questioning, questing, contemporary gardens of Charles Jencks and Ian Hamilton Finlay. Pan, that sprite of Nature, and Vertumnus, the Etruscan god of the changing seasons, also have a voice in the woods.

The entry to the *bosco* is deliberately triumphal, to give the visitor a sense of arrival and welcome. Almost immediately, one of the recurring themes of the garden, Time, marks its passage with the Hill of the Painted Posts, on whose summit four stones bear the enigmatic inscriptions 'Never', 'Often', 'Sometimes', 'Always'. It is odd, thinks Sheppard, to see these words used together, and odder still to see them carved in stone. Further on, a travertine table with a curved base is lit by windows of light cut out of the tree canopy. It is, at first glance, an unexpected and arresting sight. On another level these spots of sunlight in the *bosco*'s gloom act as a metaphor for the other theme of this garden, which is certainty versus uncertainty, knowing and not knowing. Meanwhile the table, says Sheppard, is 'waiting for something'.

The *bosco* has a playful spirit and likes to surprise its visitors with optical illusions. The Great Circle, with its splendid evergreen oak, reveals itself at close quarters to be an oval. From the Observatory platform, the long central axis of the garden is visible. Steps lead down to the Fountain of Good Sense. Based on the famous fountains of antiquity, it nevertheless does not claim to heal the sick or predict the future. It merely offers good sense, the first test of which, says Sheppard, is not to drink its water.

The garden on the valley floor is a play on the classic Italian garden. In its parterre, the motif of a slanted square enclosed within a rectangle came from a Roman mosaic at Fishbourne. in England. Alongside the cubes of

Above Sheppard has placed two yellow columns in the garden, inscribed '*Dunque*' (Therefore) and '*Invece*' (On the Other Hand).
Left The garden on the villa's floor is a play on the classic Italian Garden.

box are woodland plants – hypericum, epimedium, *Cornus alba* 'Sibirica', pulmonaria. In spring, the woods are carpeted with vinca, hellebores and wild garlic. The Dutch field maple (*Acer campestre* 'Elsrijk') makes a lacy pattern against the holm oaks.

A straight path lined with pots getting progressively smaller refers to the Renaissance discovery of perspective. An inscription on the Altar of Doubt – *Que sais-je?* (What do I know?) – is dedicated to the sceptic Montaigne. Sheppard has created a do-it-yourself oracle, and an ivy circle to stand as the centre of the universe – a riposte, he says, to those who claim the universe has no centre.

Sheppard is an admirer of Louis XIV, and his garden has been cultivated on a kingly scale. On a slope outside the *bosco* is a striking formal landscape covering the whole hillside. Composed mainly of cypress and holm oak, this is gardening in the grand manner; yet the garden, whose starting point was two trees already growing there, is sited deliberately in the middle of nowhere. Such mystery and unlikeliness only add to the beauty and impact of this magic hill. It is to Sheppard Craige's great satisfaction that while 'tourists jump out of their cars on the opposite hill and take pictures of it . . . they don't know what it is.'

La Foce

This celebrated and beautiful garden is the result of a partnership between an Anglo-American writer who loved English flowers and yearned for 'a pretty house and garden', and an English architect living in Florence who designed in a sympathetic Italianate style. That they were the oldest of friends added to the happiness of the collaboration. As the current owner of La Foce, Benedetta Origo, has said, this is 'a garden in Italy, gardened in an Italian way but created by an Englishwoman'.

It was not an auspicious start. Iris Origo's words about the wild surroundings that would become her home have become justifiably famous, as have her two classic memoirs, *Images and Shadows* and *War in Val d'Orcia*. The Val d'Orcia forms the rugged background to this story – a 'lunar landscape', wrote Iris Origo, 'treeless and shrubless but for some tufts of broom . . . on that autumn evening it had the bleakness of the desert'. This was 1924 and she was describing her first sight of the *crete senesi*, an inhospitable landscape consisting of low hummocks of eroded clay – grey, bleached and somehow inhuman. To the west, the looming bulk of an extinct volcano, Monte Amiata, dominated the barren valley. The villa itself, a former rustic inn, stood on a bare, windswept ridge amongst crumbling farm buildings. These were the unpromising beginnings to what in less than twenty years would become a mature garden of great beauty, set in a fertile valley of vineyards, wheat fields, woods and olive groves. 'Through sheer effort of will,' commented Iris's friend Bernard Berenson, 'a land which seemed entirely barren has been made to flower.'

It was the architect Cecil Pinsent's genius to take this demanding site and humanize it into the sort of trim, Florentine garden that recalled Iris Origo's own childhood. Both Pinsent and his clients, Marchese Antonio and Marchesa Iris Origo, shared a love of order and geometry. As fast as Pinsent provided La Foce with its enclosed gardens, its walkways and parterres, Iris Origo clothed them with her favourite flowers and flowering shrubs. In the first cold winter of 1925, when the pit for the fountain was being dug, she was already planting roses. At the same time, Pinsent's vision linked the emerging garden to the untamed landscape beyond by framing it in carefully chosen vistas from viewpoints throughout the garden. Peter Curzon, a landscape architect who advises on La Foce, puts it like this: 'The landscape enhances the sophistication of the garden, and the hedges underline the beauty of the landscape beyond.' In fact, it was Antonio Origo who came up with the idea of the cypress-lined 'Cinquecento' road, which zigzags up the opposing hill to a group of farmhouses which Pinsent designed. This famously picturesque road, which is now portrayed on postcards as an iconic symbol of Tuscany, can be observed from various areas of the garden, especially from the path to the woods.

While Antonio Origo worked throughout the 1920s and 1930s to restore the estate, Iris Origo and Cecil Pinsent started La Foce's garden. Iris had spent her childhood at the Villa Medici in Fiesole while Cecil Pinsent was making alterations to its garden for her mother, Lady Sybil Cutting. Marooned as a solitary, only child in this nucleus of Anglo-Florentine society, Iris professed herself bored in her youth by 'so much culture' and endless 'talk about Florentine coffers and garden plans'. Only later, when confronted by the need to restore her own house and the necessity to make a garden, did she discover a suppressed knowledge which came to her aid.

La Foce's garden was made in four phases between 1927 and 1939 and follows the historic tradition of gardens in Italy, in that its garden rooms and

Top The garden façade gives out on to a series of interlocking garden rooms.
Bottom Cecil Pinsent's Lower Garden, overlooking the distinctive *crete sinesi* and Antonio Origo's famous cypress-lined 'Cinquecento' road.

terraces are laid out on differing levels, according to the natural rise and fall of the land. The first garden to be made was the Fountain Garden in front of Pinsent's new wing for the house, which he enclosed with bay hedges and a high brick wall to create a sheltered, domestic space. The fountain – one of the first built features that Pinsent installed – was symbolic of the Origos' efforts to bring water to this barren land. This area has always been the heart of the garden at La Foce, with tea taken inside a monumental bay grotto containing one of Pinsent's elegant, curved, baroque-influenced stone seats.

The Lemon Garden, started in 1933, is sheltered by walls topped with lichen-encrusted travertine vases made from Pinsent's own drawings. Pinsent designed nearly all the stone elements in the garden with his inimitable blend of historicism and modernity, and using travertine, which he and Iris Origo preferred for its rough, rustic appearance. The layout here is consciously Tuscan with thick box hedging and potted lemon trees standing on plinths within the parterres. Iris then made beds around the edges, now planted with roses, clematis and honeysuckle, with pomegranates basking in the sun by the south-facing wall. Slightly to the left of the main axis of the Lemon Garden, Monte Amiata looks down over La Foce from its commanding height, over a landscape that is now a World Heritage Site.

One of the sights of La Foce in May is the wisteria pergola, first planted in 1924 and reached from the Lemon Garden by a travertine staircase. A solid bank of purple blossom, it curves sinuously around the contour of the hill, disappearing around the corner to meet the path to La Foce's shady woods. Behind the pergola there was a rose garden with geometrically shaped, stone-edged beds, which Iris Origo filled with her favourite roses in a scheme of deep red (R. 'Charles Mallerin') fading into pink (R. **Handel**) and then a combination of pink and yellow (R. **Peace**). When Benedetta Origo took over from her parents, the roses needed to be replaced. The decision was made to replant with perennials in a subtle mix of blue and grey; lavender, artemisia, perovskia and santolina now billow out over the travertine borders.

The very last part of Cecil Pinsent's design for La Foce, the Lower Garden, was completed in 1939 on the eve of war. This intensely green garden is best admired from the terrace at the end of the Lemon Garden, from which a double staircase leads down. Wedge-shaped box parterres point towards an octagonal pool; its clear water reflects a classic Italian view of grey stone, clipped evergreens and sky. A statue of a Caucasian man carrying gardening tools on his shoulder adorns the back of a curved travertine seat, one of

Pinsent's designs. Garden historian John Dixon Hunt recently identified this figure, which dominates the lowest area of the garden, as the pair to the statue of a Moor bearing a cornucopia on his back, which stands at the top of the cypress *allée*, the garden's highest point. The two statues may once have adorned gateposts outside a grand Tuscan villa. The view from the seat in the Lower Garden looks back across the pool at an elegant grotto inserted by Pinsent into the Lemon Garden's retaining wall.

If the Fountain Garden is the heart of La Foce, its soul resides in the chapel that Pinsent built in the woods after the death from meningitis of Gianni, the Origos' eight-year-old son. The cemetery, where Iris and Antonio were also later buried, is reached from the garden by a woodland path. This woodland garden Iris planted with shrubs and ornamental trees, finding solace in her gardening.

Iris's memoir, *War in Val d'Orcia*, paints a vivid picture of La Foce during the war. The villa was shelled, and Pinsent's gracious terraces given over to machine-gun trenches. Afterwards, the ground was left pitted with shell holes and, for a time, rendered dangerous by mines.

When Marchesa Origo died in 1988, her daughter Benedetta took over at La Foce. Under her care, the garden, still very much a living garden, continued to evolve at a gentle pace. Nine years after her mother's death, Benedetta opened the garden to the public. She is helped by the curatorial assistance of Peter Curzon, an English landscape architect based in Italy. For Peter, the reason La Foce is so much loved is clear: 'I think what makes La Foce so unusual is that it is unpretentious. It was made for pleasure and not to impress. That is what makes it so special.'

Below, left The 1933 Lemon Garden, enclosed by walls topped with Pinsent's own travertine vases.
Below, right One of Pinsent's baroque-inspired stone seats.

Valle Pinciole

This beautiful garden manages to be both intimate and yet on a grand scale. An intricately layered composition of outdoor garden rooms, it blends seamlessly into the soft Cetona countryside. By turns formal and informal, it takes its shape from the terracing carved long ago out of the hillside for growing vines. The garden looks both inwards into its own intimate spaces and outwards on to the surrounding landscape of misty valleys and small, rounded hills. The ancient town of Cetona perches on a nearby hilltop: an arched window, put in by owner Federico Forquet, frames it like a Utens lunette.

Federico Forquet and Matteo Spinola acquired the house in the early 1970s and created this paradise over almost forty years. Both had an eye for beauty, Federico Forquet as a designer and Matteo Spinola as a plantsman and naturalist. Their garden, having evolved so slowly, reveals its secrets gradually, around each corner of a bay hedge, each turn in a tufa path, each step from light into vine-trellised shade. Throughout the garden, luxuriant planting contrasts with simpler, more serene areas intended to rest the eye and calm the senses. Everywhere drifts of plants echo each other harmoniously in a masterly display of subtle planting.

This is a hillside garden, its entrance high up the hill near a studio set in an olive grove. Yellow roses and bronze iris encircle the olives. A woodland path bordered with ferns, euphorbias and hellebores leads past the studio down the slope. Further down, in the sunlight, the path is edged with a cushion of pale pink roses, and then double borders of rosemary with lavender, pale pink cistus and contrasting lime euphorbia. On the left, the view opens out over olive groves, wheat fields and cypress-studded hills.

Another path turns right at a statue collared by deep purple berberis. This purple is picked up and echoed by a cotinus and then by purple-black iris in front of a pergola of white wisteria.

The main path runs downhill into the series of hedged outdoor rooms that are at the heart of the garden. In the gentle, countrified style that fits so well with the rural setting, the tufa paths are not geometrically aligned. In one enclosure, a charming pavilion looks out over fruit trees; in another, a simple grass lawn contained by bay hedges faces a classic Tuscan view. Federico Forquet plans to remove the intervening border to create a ha-ha, bringing the country into the garden. Elsewhere, he has cut down one cypress in an *allée* –

'I could not be here when it was done: I could not bear it,' he says – to open a window on to the landscape.

At its centre, near the house, the garden opens out on to a large, grassed open space. On the horizon, silhouetted against the hill and marking the territory, is the stand of massed cypresses that was one of Matteo's first plantings. Around the sides of the lawn runs a box hedge crisply edged with tufa; pyramids of box delineate the openings to paths. The planting is of English country favourites in gentle hues – white and soft silvery pink aquilegias, clear blue *Allium caeruleum* and iris; silvery artemisia; tiny white *Deutzia* 'Nikko'; white tradescantia; and the opalescent, ruffled petals of delicate *Rosa* 'Fimbriata'. In the centre of the grass stands an arbour clothed in roses and wisteria, its base banked up with rosemary.

In this garden of English country flowers there are two deliberate *hommages* to the classic Italian garden. The Lemon Garden in a courtyard near the house is laid out with interlocking blocks of box to a design suggested by Russell Page. A frequent visitor to the house, he dispensed advice, as he often did while staying with friends. The mellow tufa paths and edgings, which provide the unobtrusive backbone to the garden, were Page's proposal.

The oldest part of the garden is on the slope below the house. A central path leads under a pomegranate arch towards a terracotta statue, through another series of garden rooms. The formality here is unaffectedly rustic, with green architecture, the result of clipping and topiarizing the plants. A witty touch is the collection of spherical topiary – balls of yew, thuja, myrtle, laurel, pittosporum and *Myrsine africana* huddled, as if about to roll downhill, behind a wattle fence. Further down, a round-pillared, brick pergola pays tribute to one erected in the same style at the Medici Villa del Trebbio, which was rebuilt in the fifteenth century for Cosimo the Elder by Michelozzo Michelozzi. In his lunette, Giusto Utens pictured the result.

This complex and ambitious garden was the creation of two cultivated, energetic and talented owners, who, despite success in their own professions, did not discover gardening until the chance purchase of a packet of seeds. From these seeds Valle Pinciole grew over four decades into the many-roomed paradise it is today. It was a labour of love, as Federico Forquet makes clear: 'I put my heart into this garden.'

Far left The stand of cypress silhouetted against the hills was one of Matteo Spinola's first plantings.
Left A trellised pergola shades a tufa path.
Right, top The central arbour clothed in roses and wisteria, with rosemary planted around the base.
Right, centre The Lemon Garden laid out in a courtyard at the side of the house, with a design of interlocking box suggested by Russell Page.
Right, bottom A collection of spherical topiary – balls of yew, thuja, myrtle, laurel, pittosporum and *Myrsine africana* – behind a wattle fence.

Giardini di Villa Cetinale

The drive to Cetinale winds past agricultural buildings and the old *granaio*. No longer is there a splendid view of the villa, as was the case with the original entrance leading off the old Siena road. In fact, this approach through a huddle of farm buildings suits the domestic scale of the building. Elegant and harmonious though Carlo Fontana's seventeenth-century baroque transformation of a modest Tuscan farmhouse undoubtedly was, Cetinale was never a showplace: rather, it was a working farm which served as a bucolic retreat from the intrigues and pressures of Rome.

Fontana was commissioned to aggrandize the villa in 1676 by Flavio Chigi, the art-loving nephew of the Chigi pope, Alexander VII. The architect had already worked on projects for the Chigi family in Rome. Flavio Chigi, created a cardinal in 1657 at the young age of twenty-six, was one of the last such cardinal-nephews to be raised to his rank through what came to be known as nepotism, a word derived from the Italian *nipote*, meaning nephew. At Cetinale, Fontana added the grand double staircase and marble portal over what was then the main entrance on the northern front. He decorated both façades of the villa with 'florid escutcheons' – papal mitres, a cardinal's hat and the Chigi coat of arms. More to the point, where before there had been only farmland he created a magnificent baroque garden.

Edith Wharton visited Cetinale during her tours of Italian villas and gardens in the 1880s and immediately fell for its position in the midst of woods, olive groves and cornfields. She thought Fontana wise to 'profit by the natural advantage of the great forest of oak and ilex . . . and to realize that only the broadest and simplest lines would be in harmony

with so noble a background'. Fontana, once a draughtsman for Bernini, used the ilex-covered hill to create a spectacular single axis of dramatic length. It is almost 5 kilometres/3 miles in a straight line through fields and woods from Giuseppe Mazzuoli's colossus of Hercules, through the villa and beyond it up the 200 steps of the Scala Santa to the Romitorio (Hermitage). 'This effect of distance and grandeur', wrote Edith Wharton, 'is produced at small cost and in the simplest manner . . .' Admiring it, Harold Acton recalled a mathematician who once told him that 'there was nothing more beautiful than a straight line.'

Villa Cetinale is now entered from the south, through a crisply charming, walled Lemon Garden, with a rose-covered *limonaia* and the family chapel to one side. Statues of spring and summer by the baroque sculptor Giuseppe Mazzuoli preside over low box hedges studded with round box domes, behind which stand citrus trees in large terracotta pots. Beyond, on the northern side of the villa, Fontana's axis continues down a long, grassy avenue through the faded brick piers that marked the original approach to the villa. Topped by busts and obelisks, the piers curve inwards, serving to enclose and focus the perspective further. The walk terminates in an unusual semicircular, open-air theatre, from where the steps of the Scala Santa begin their steep climb. Announcing the entrance to the theatre and gazing back haughtily at the villa is a bust of Napoleon, who supposedly came to Cetinale in 1811. The bust was rescued from a thicket of ivy, which may have prevented it from being stolen like the other busts that once encircled the theatre's walls.

Up the hill rise the mysterious oak woods where, for twenty years in the late seventeenth and early eighteenth centuries, the Palio was staged.

Among the trees is a frescoed archway, the entrance to the Thebaid (Holy Wood). Scattered with statues of saints by Mazzuoli and containing seven votive chapels dimly frescoed with religious scenes, the sacred grove is said to allude to the Egyptian desert, home to many early Christian hermits. Joseph Forsyth, an early nineteenth-century visitor to these woods, wrote that Cetinale 'owes its rise and celebrity to the remorse of an amorous cardinal who, to appease the ghost of a murdered rival, transformed a gloomy plantation of cypress into a penitential Thebais, and acted there all the austerities of an Egyptian hermit'. It may be that this is a penitential wood in which Cardinal Chigi wished to express remorse and atone for a crime. However, Lord Lambton, the saviour and restorer of Cetinale, considered this as, first and foremost, a pleasure garden with additional holy elements. If the Latin inscription to be found on a garden wall was his, the cardinal does not sound like a humbled man: 'Whoever you are who approach, that which may seem horrible to you is pleasing to me. If you like it, stay; if it bores you, go away. It's all the same to me.'

The Romitorio, towering over the Scala Santa, is large enough to make an impact from 5 kilometres/3 miles away. It is decorated with a giant cross, a sign beckoning onlookers to a life of prayer and meditation as they ascend closer to God. The Romitorio, visibly dominating the landscape from so far off, also serves the function of theatrical backdrop.

In 1977 when Lord Lambton took over Cetinale, the garden was overgrown, the Romitorio vandalized, the brick walls cracked and loosened by tree roots and ivy. He embarked on a thirty-year programme of restoration, still ongoing under the stewardship of his son. With his companion, Claire Ward, he extended the flower garden begun in the early twentieth century by the English mother of a Chigi owner. The English gardener's gift for intimacy is on display here. Iron hoops, discovered abandoned and rusting in the undergrowth, have been re-instated to carry a collection of climbing roses. A blue and yellow border – ceanothus, rosemary, agapanthus, senecio – basks against a sunny wall. The famously gnarled and ancient wisteria creates a haze of purple during the early summer. Dark pink peonies, irises, lilies and familiar English perennials weave a rich tapestry against a formal Italian structure of ilex tunnels and clipped box enclosures. One garden room contains a modern classical forest of yew cones; another, an orchard with cypresses and yew surrounded by fruit trees planted in squares and circles according to Renaissance patterns. In the immaculately kept *orto*, sweet peas, tulips and lavender grow alongside the vegetables.

On the olive terraces beneath the now-restored clock tower is a wildflower meadow sprinkled with daffodils, tulips and grape hyacinths, followed in summer by poppies and self-seeded blue geraniums. In 1977, when he bought the villa from the Chigi, it was this natural meadow that appealed to Lord Lambton as much as Carlo Fontana's baroque splendour.

Lord Lambton's son Ned inherited Cetinale in early 2007. He is now putting his own stamp on the garden, including expanding the *orto*.

Opposite The family chapel in the walled Lemon Garden in front of Villa Cetinale.
Right, above Potted clipped box adds formality to a curving path.
Right, below A view beyond the garden into the forest of oak and ilex.

La Porrona

La Porrona's owner, Pino Brusone, was the director-general of one of Italy's most famous and dynamic fashion houses. In search of a country refuge which would offer a different, more holistic way of life, he decided to look for a farm rather than a villa. It was a long search but eventually he found La Porrona, a large estate near Montisi in Tuscany, which sits on its hill like a ship on the high seas. A former fortified farmhouse, it still retains its rifle holes (now glassed in) and arrow slits; its spacious, elegant, terracotta-tiled ground floor was originally used to house sheep and pigs.

La Porrona commands views that roll out over the Tuscan countryside, crossing vineyards and olive groves, copse-dotted hills and valleys lined with fields, all the way to Siena. To the west is a ruined castle; to the south, the view stretches right to the foot of Mount Amiata. With such an unspoiled rural backdrop, the garden was to be laid out not so much as a garden but as what its designer Peter Curzon calls 'an enhanced agricultural landscape'. It had to 'keep true to the atmosphere of the place while using many of the conceits of landscape gardening'; it was a difficult balancing act.

As you pass through the outer gate, the first view is of the house sitting above on its hill, surrounded by descending terraces carved out of the olive groves. The climb up to the house is through an olive grove among banks of lavender, rosemary and 'Sea Foam' roses. At the top of the steps, a vista opens to the left down a wide grassy avenue bordered by massed *Rosa* × *odorata* ' Mutabilis', *R.* 'Sally Holmes' and country hedgerow plants such as may, broom and dogwood. Clumps of cypresses stand alongside, framing the magnificent views. At the far end is the garden's *pièce de résistance*, a rustic, thatched dovecote, perched on

gnarled branches, like a tree-house. Behind it is a curved wooden bench, echoed by a curved evergreen hedge.

To the right, the grass avenue passes in front of the house, swathed in white wisteria with *Rosa* 'Mermaid', white *R. banksiae* var. *banksiae* and *R. bracteata*, and past the gate to the outer courtyard, now hedged with bay and attractively planted with iris, clary (*Salvia sclarea*) and other different salvias. Opposite is the charming *orto*, contained within a rustic wattle fence and shaded by pomegranate trees. The top level contains vegetables for the house; lower down is a cutting garden, crisply edged with santolina. The *orto* stands at a cross-axis of the garden, a path bordered by mulberry trees which march across the outer courtyard towards the distant fields; at the end, two cairns mark the descent into the valley where the lake, dug to provide water for the garden, lies peacefully amongst a grove of trees.

Much thought has gone into La Porrona's garden to enable it to blend seamlessly into the countryside. Softly billowing banks of lavender, rosemary, germander, caryopteris and phlomis, chosen to attract butterflies, echo the contours of the surrounding, gently sloping fields. There is a sophisticated naturalism at work here, as in the pergola garden set with painted blue buckets containing clumps of lavender. Beyond the garden fence is an amphitheatre of gently sloping fields where cattle, horses and a donkey graze in an idyllic rural landscape.

Above, left Billowing banks of lavender, rosemary and caryopteris echo the contours of the surrounding, gently sloping landscape.
Above, right A rustic pergola set with buckets of lavender.

Far from the house, set amongst olive groves, is the swimming pool, which was raised with a rustic stone wall to provide 180-degree views over the unfolding, timeless Tuscan landscape. Near by, crowning the top of a small hill, is laid out an ancient *ragnaia* of holm oaks: still surrounded by bits of its encircling stone wall, it contains a stone refuge for hunters dating back to the early nineteenth century. It has recently been restored by Pino Brusone.

La Porrona may be a rural dream come true but it takes hard work to husband the wine, olive oil and fruit, to milk the cows, make cheese and collect honey from the hives. Even to maintain the balance of this subtly beautiful, understated country garden requires constant attention and a discerning eye. The reward is an idyllic home surrounded on all sides by some of the most beautiful views in all of Tuscany.

Above, left The planting is cleverly aligned to open up views.
Above, right A thatched dovecote stands at one end of the garden.

Il Giardino di Orlando

SIENA, TUSCANY

'The moon rises as the sun sets,' says Sarah Sesti of the 360-degree view from her ridge over the Montalcino vineyards. In 1975 the Sesti family bought an abandoned *casa colonica* with a chapel next to a ruined thirteenth-century tower. Restoration started with the house and the outhouses; now they are about to begin work on the tower. In the meantime, her husband, Giuseppe Sesti, an astronomer, taught himself wine-making and now produces organic Brunello di Montalcino to an award-winning standard.

The straight and regimented lines of vines all around her influenced Sarah when it came to designing Orlando's Garden, in memory of her son. 'I wanted looseness – not a manicured look. And I wanted wild flowers, because the vineyards took all the hayfields.' With the help of her eldest son, Cosimo, an architect, two 'O' shapes were carved out, joined by steps. Sarah planted the first with a ring of olive trees in the centre of mown grass. At the far end is a formal pool at the edge of which stands a marble replica of the beautiful wing of the 190 BC Greek sculpture the Nike of Samothrace.

Designer, plantsman and friend Michael Ward helped Sarah with the planting. The aim was 'gardening in the air'. Sarah wanted 'movement, a light, airy feel, plants moving with the wind'. Gentle terracing links this garden to a second O of clover. Valerian, alliums, cardoons, bronze fennel and rosemary line the steps. A fig tree overhangs the space, and a head sculpted by Emily Young from *marmo giallo di Siena* presides.

In the clay soil the phormiums have reached 1.75 metres/6 feet, despite facing north in a relatively sunless position. Euphorbia, senecio – all the dry plants flourish, floating in a sea of waving calamagrostis, brought from France by Michael. Low-growing, purple-flowered *Origanum* 'Herrenhausen' accompanies *Tulbaghia violacea*. Pale pink *Phlomis italica*, foxgloves and cascading *Rosa* 'Albéric Barbier' add their soft tones to this serene and peaceful spot.

Above and below, left Two 'O's – for Orlando – are linked by steps and framed by naturalistic planting.
Below, centre A replica of the wing of the Nike of Samothrace, carved by two students at the Accademia di Scultura at Carrara, under the supervision of Sarah's friend Professor Piergiorgio Balocchi.
Below, right Emily Young's head, sculpted from *marmo giallo di Siena*.

Il Giardino Corsini: Orto Botanico della Casa Bianca

This distinguished nineteenth-century botanical park is in mid-restoration, which could mean, hopes its owner Don Alessandro dei Principi Corsini, that English visitors will enjoy it all the more. 'The English love to see gardens in the process of being restored, whereas Italians like it all finished.' Alessandro speaks perfect English and is happy to host and guide parties through the garden. When they arrived to live on the Casa Bianca estate in 1982, the Corsini found a house which, as the German wartime HQ, had suffered a direct hit by Allied bombers in 1943. Thirty more bombs had fallen in the park, whose trees were also scarred by gunfire and shrapnel during the Second World War.

After the war, La Casa Bianca was first abandoned and then used by the family as a summer house, with its overgrown garden largely ignored. The part of the property owned until recently by Alessandro's aunt had been deliberately left untouched in an attempt to return it to the wild. This, then, was the 'jungle of local and exotic vegetation' that faced the Corsini in 1982. Most daunting of all was the discovery that nearly all the plant inventory, including labels identifying the unusual and exotic species planted in the nineteenth century, had been vandalized, lost or destroyed. Of the 1,800 ceramic plant labels made by the porcelain manufacturer Ginori in Florence in the 1860s and 1870s, only 300 could be found. This made it more difficult when the time came to draw up an inventory of the hundreds of plants in the garden that had managed to survive war and neglect.

The arboretum's setting is superb, on a steep hill overlooking the picturesque, natural harbour of Porto Ercole, with two sixteenth-century fortresses, built by the Spanish, guarding each flank. Glimpses of Porto Ercole Bay, curved around a glittering, blue sea, appear and disappear through the trees. Very little documentation survives on the building of this important botanic garden: it was the creation of Baron General Vincenzo Ricasoli, younger brother of Bettino Ricasoli of Castello di Brolio (see page 140), who succeeded Count Cavour as second Prime Minister of the new Italian Republic. General Vincenzo Ricasoli led a contingent of the Savoy cavalry, who were allies of the British, French and Ottoman forces, into battle against the Russians in the Crimean War.

Vincenzo was friendly with Thomas Hanbury at La Mortola (see page 76). His garden at Porto Ercole was founded in 1867, the same year that Hanbury bought his rugged promontory near the French–Italian border and determined to turn it into a haven for acclimatizing exotic plants. Ricasoli needed all his determination to realize his dream. His first challenge was terracing the precipitous hillsides, for which he hired recently liberated Russian prisoners. The Russians built the steps and sturdy dry-stone walls with granite from the island of Giglio. Ricasoli's second challenge, poor soil, was solved by bringing in earth from the chestnut woods of Genoa and Umbria. He also developed a system for rinsing large quantities of local seaweed and then using it as mulch.

Right, above A nineteenth-century plant label.
Right, below Rough-hewn steps connect the eight terraces.

After only eight years, the botanist general had trialled 536 plant species, including 52 different eucalyptus. His agents roamed the world in search of seeds and plants to send back speedily by steamship. By 1888, 1,866 species had been imported, of which as many as 1,500 survived the winters. They came from the Americas, the Middle East, South Africa and Australia, as well as the East and West Indies. By 1885, Ricasoli had the pleasure of seeing his botanic garden described as 'the most important park for the acclimatisation of plants in Italy and Europe'.

When he took over, Alessandro Corsini began to clear the jungle of undergrowth and restore the nineteenth-century infrastructure, damaged by tree roots and marauding wild boar. To identify the exotic plants, Kew came to his rescue. Their experts on tropical plants worked with others from the universities of Pisa and Florence. The arboretum now holds over 1,350 trees and shrubs, including important collections of palms and eucalyptus. In this garden are some of the first washingtonia to be planted in Europe, as well as two rare nannorrhops palms, one 140 years old, which, unusually for Europe, bloom and fruit regularly. The first *Phoenix sylvestris* to be planted in Europe is also recorded here.

The park is now a delightful place to walk, its eight rocky terraces criss-crossed by rough-hewn steps and traversed by meandering paths. Around the concert area – Alessandro hosts a music festival each summer – an immense brachychiton from Australia puts on a spectacular show of red flowers, which fall to cover the ground in a flame-coloured carpet. A camphor tree stands in the clearing, along with a sterculia, also known as the tropical chestnut; near by is an Australian black paperbark (*Melaleuca lanceolata*). Towards the entrance cluster the more delicate trees, including a specimen of the giant *Agathis australis*, a species tall enough to rival the Californian sequoias. A stone bench invites visitors to linger in the shade of an Aleppo pine (*P. halepensis*).

Colour is brought to the garden by such tropical beauties as bougainvillea, oleander, plumbago, jacaranda and hibiscus. They flower against a backdrop of all the different shades of green, from grey-green casuarina and eucalyptus, to the dark bottle-green of cedar and araucaria. Underneath the tree canopy, yuccas, cordylines and agaves form a spiky undergrowth.

Puccini, a family friend who often summered here, would compose in the garden, where he was once interrupted by Alessandro's father, Cino, then aged twelve. 'He rode by on his bicycle and saw the old man in a straw hat with lots of papers, writing. When my father asked him what he was doing, the old man replied with one word: "Turandot", to which young Cino answered, "What a great name for my boat." '

Above, left Palms shade the garden's paths.
Above, right The dry-stone walls of granite from the island of Giglio were built after the Crimean War, by recently liberated Russian prisoners.

La Ferriera

Perhaps only the daughter of a famous nurseryman could have taken on an arid hilltop in southern Tuscany and faced down bitter winter winds and blinding summer heat to create out of such desolate surroundings this lushly romantic plantsman's garden. The Maremma has traditionally been a poor region battling its climate, not a place for frivolities. Yet this did not deter Contessa Giuppi Pietromarchi and her husband, Antonello, when they bought their home, a former hunting lodge, on impulse, in one afternoon. Over forty years of gardening artistry have gone into making this intensely personal and poetic place. Contessa Pietromarchi gardens with keen practical intelligence and a painterly eye.

What she inherited here was minimal. The former owners, in an attempt to shield themselves from the intense summer glare, had planted four rows of *Pinus pinea* on the slope in front of the house. To the left an olive grove was another legacy. Olive, pine and cypress are the beloved trinity of the Tuscan landscape. The Pietromarchi set out not only to preserve them but to make a garden that blended in with the countryside.

Years of careful pruning have coaxed the pines into airy, arching shapes, their branches criss-crossing high above like intricate medieval vaulting. Beneath is an emerald grass carpet, achieved by years of work and experimentation with both the soil – a mix of volcanic soil and gravel – and seed for shady sites. Feeding is done every month, watering every night. Off to the side, the blooms of *Hydrangea quercifolia* **Snow Queen** and *H.q.* 'Harmony' gleam palely in what one admirer called 'the delicious gloom'. It is, says Giuppi with some satisfaction, 'like a green cathedral with windows opening on to the sea'.

Straight ahead, steps lead down to a lawn studded with trees planted by the Pietromarchi in a former sheep meadow. Here, roses make their appearance: 'Bobbie James' clambers up a cypress; soft pink, sweet-smelling 'Follette' and silvery-pink 'Madame Pierre Oger' light up a corner. Giuppi grows few English roses by choice, finding them too heavy with a tendency to collapse in the heat, whereas the China roses thrive. A collection of Banksian roses includes the covetable pure white 'Purezza', also found in the collection of the Roseto Botanico Carlo Fineschi. Bred by an Italian, Quinto Mansuino, in 1961, this vigorous, repeat-flowering form, one of the few Western hybrids of the Banksian rose, can bloom for a month at La Ferriera. When the Banksians finish, *Rosa* 'Félicité Perpétue' takes over.

Through a gate framed by obelisks is Giuppi's pavilion studio, housing her remarkable collection of gardening books. It is reached by a path through one the garden's most romantic areas: a forest of datura, fronted by agapanthus and backed by climbing jasmine and the sun-loving English shrub rose 'Sally Holmes'.

With its pale, soft hues and sympathetic planting, this is a garden in harmony with surrounding nature. Giuppi has kept the olive grove

Above, left A sculpture stands in a shady corner of this poetic Maremma garden.
Above, right Roses flower prolifically among the olive trees.

but transformed it into a grove of enchantment, encircling the trees with silver collars of artemisia, ballota and lavender, a cool foil to the warm tones of old roses growing through their branches. The damask rose 'Leda' displays its dramatic deep pink buds and pure white flowers. 'Souvenir de Saint Anne's' and 'Perle d'Or' flower gracefully in the heat. 'La Mortola', recently planted, 'Alchymist' and 'Buff Beauty' set off the blue-green olive leaves. Coppery-pink-centred 'Paul Transon' and creamy, frilled 'Lamarque' create a much-loved duet.

A tree-house made from cork bark marks the descent to the lower garden, where a row of oleander, backed by eucalyptus, faces a hedge of *Rosa* 'Complicata'. Contrasting with the oleander is the ivory and cream Italian-bred Floribunda **Sans Souci**.

Giuppi, a reluctant swimming-pool owner, has made her pool look like a *vasca* and surrounded it with carefully positioned boulders dug up during its excavation and now covered in lavender and artemisia. A fence around the pool is clothed by the little crimson rambler rose 'Rose-Marie Viaud'. At the back, where the garden meets the fields, is a show-stopping border, creative planting at its very best, with sinuous lines of *Stipa tenuissima*, bronze fennel and the black lilyturf *Ophiopogon planiscapus* 'Nigrescens', enhanced by the recent addition of *Sambucus nigra*.

In July the highlight of this garden is the magical blue glade Giuppi has created of agapanthus under olive trees. Near by, *Hibiscus syriacus* 'Oiseau Bleu', *Hebe* 'Midsummer Beauty' and the anise sage (*Salvia guaranitica*) flower in a blue haze.

Tucked away to one side are two small garden 'rooms', one an exotic garden with plants Giuppi has collected on her travels. A musa arches over a curved bench, and in July the petals of the Jerusalem thorn (*Parkinsonia aculeata*) turn this garden into a yellow bower.

Nearer the house *Rosa* 'Pierre de Ronsard' climbs up a tree while 'La Mortola' and different Banksians cover the lower terrace in a froth of white. 'Albéric Barbier' romps down some steps alongside David Austin's **Winchester Cathedral**. The showy blooms of *Romneya coulteri* are set off by the sculptural form of *Melianthus major* – just one more example of this remarkable gardener's inspired planting.

Below Boulders found on site have been imaginatively placed and softened with lavender and artemisia.

LE MARCHE

The gently rolling hills of the Marche stretch from the Adriatic coast to the eastern flanks of the Apennine mountain chain. Until quite recently this quiet agricultural region dotted with small towns built of rosy Marche brick retained a virtually unchanged rural landscape. It is for this reason, as the association Le Marche Segrete points out, that the region still retains a wealth of historic gardens. Its relative isolation meant that change came slowly to the Marche, sparing its gardens from the whims of fashion and enabling its rich artistic heritage to survive. Under Federico da Montefeltro, its duke from 1444 to 1482, the city of Urbino was a hub of Renaissance art and culture and contributed two of the greatest artists to work in Renaissance Rome – Raphael and Bramante.

The dramatic mountain range of the Monti Sibillini in the south-west of the region has been made into a huge natural park divided between the Marche and Umbria. It includes one of the most spectacular sights of the region in spring – the incomparable Piano Grande. 1,250 metres/4,000 feet above sea level, this vast, treeless plateau is carpeted in May and June with wild tulips, crocuses, narcissi, grape hyacinths, poppies and rare orchids and fritillaries. This abundant flowering is known as the Fioritura.

Villa Giardino Buonaccorsi

This exuberant garden is an almost complete survival from the eighteenth century. Always known simply as the Villa Giardino Buonaccorsi, it was commissioned by the family of that name. They were grand enough to send several cardinals to the Vatican and own a splendid palace in Macerata. The palace was designed by Contini, a pupil of Vanvitelli, and another pupil, Andrea Vici, probably designed Giardino Buonaccorsi.

Time has stood still in this enchanted place; to visit the garden is to be transported back to another century. Jokes, curiosities and eighteenth-century high spirits abound. Giardino Buonaccorsi is a relic from another age.

The house, part of which is seventeenth century, stands on a small hill inland from the sea. The garden is laid out to the south-east of the villa, sheltering in its lee from the north wind. Five sunny terraces, linked by stairways, descend the hill. Each enjoys a lovely view across the gently rolling Marche countryside. From the topmost terrace, near the house, the sea is just visible. On this level also is the chapel, still consecrated, its entrance framed by a 200-year-old cypress arch.

In the villa there hangs an engraving – reproduced in Georgina Masson's book on Italian gardens – which shows figures in eighteenth-century dress in the foreground. In the background is Giardino Buonaccorsi, almost exactly as it appears today. Perhaps the most miraculous survival in the garden is the layout of the parterres. Stone-edged beds in geometrical shapes like stars and hexagons radiate outwards from their central obelisks. The pattern dates back seventy-odd years to the seventeenth century – revealing evidence of the provincialism and backwardness of Marche garden design at the time.

This is a garden known for the splendour of its statues. There are 105 of them, mostly from the Venetian workshop of Orazio Marinali. Guarding the vicinity of the house is a handsome pair of hunting dogs. On the second terrace, strutting along a dividing wall, is the line of jaunty, carousing dwarfs who give it its name – Viale di Nanni-masquerado. Elsewhere, shepherds, gods and goddesses, Roman emperors and figures in classical drapery bring to the garden the sense of life and movement that is the essence of the baroque.

Giardino Buonaccorsi is that rare thing, a real Italian flower garden, preserved in perfect order by its devoted head gardener and custodian, Signor Machellari. Nothing is bought in. With the help of two pensioners, 6,000 plants are grown from seeds and cuttings and planted out twice

a year. Signor Machellari is in his garden at six each morning ready for four hours of watering. He plans the beds in rotation, favouring zinnias, pansies, salvia, godetia, marigolds and geraniums in sock-it-to-'em colours. His father, the gardener here before him for forty-four years, comes in often to watch and advise.

Narrower than the top two terraces is the third terrace, the Avenue of the Emperors, whose likenesses, sober, upright and redolent of all the Roman virtues, line the walk leading to the statue of Flora under a broken-pediment arch. So different is the style of these figures that it has been suggested that they are survivors from an earlier Renaissance garden. In the eighteenth century, possibly to humanize them, the Caesars were encased in niches of evergreen. These are now lost. So, too, are the chairs that once flanked Marinali's Flora. If you sat on one, the arms came down to imprison you while water spurted and you were drenched. Two other *giochi d'acqua* survive, one near by, at the foot of the steps to the ivy tunnel.

On the lowest level is a wide, grass path along which, until her death in 1970, the elderly Contessa Buonaccorsi would stroll under an umbrella

in the heat. The delightful *teatro* is dedicated to Pan, the guardian of the garden. His figure, dressed as a huntsman in painted green coat, stands in the middle. In the niches are painted wooden automatons including a harlequin and a Turk, originally worked by bellows.

The garden's most effective joke is reserved for the Grotto, where there is a magnificent eighteenth-century devil, horned and with a tongue lolling from side to side. He pops out from his concealed hiding place to taunt two figures of friars, and to surprise the visitors.

Page 159 The baroque garden of Villa Sgariglia.
Opposite, far left Giochi d'acqua, surviving from the eighteenth century, at the foot of the ivy tunnel.
Above, centre The garden holds 105 statues, mostly from the Venetian workshop of Orazio Marinali.
Above, right One of the carousing dwarfs in the Viale di Nanni-masquerado.

Giardino Sgariglia

Behind the serene brick villa by the eighteenth-century architect Giosafatti is an intimate courtyard garden of the same date. To emerge from the house into this courtyard is like walking on to a theatre stage, enclosed by terraced tiers of rosy Marche brick planted with espaliered citrus and adorned with potted lemons, obelisks and busts. They look down on the space beneath like so many spectators from the gods.

It was Giuseppe Giosafatti, from a family of sculptors and architects, who eventually brought the baroque style of Gianlorenzo Bernini from Rome to the far-flung Marche. Arriving here late, its effect was muted and restrained: Giosafatti's own buildings are noted for their sober and stately distinction.

Here, in a joyous burst of theatricality, he let himself go. Villa Sgariglia's garden is a minor masterpiece of esoteric baroque flourishes. At the back, stepped and scalloped walls hold in their curved embrace a lotus-shaped pool. Above it, a coat of arms surmounts a central arch, and two Roman busts preside. Four arches of pebble mosaic, topped by busts, hold urns – another device of the Baroque. The garden's statuary, says Giulia Panichi Pignatelli of Le Marche Segrete, was originally chosen by Giosafatti 'to contrast the *hortus conclusus*, man's ordered world, against the chaos of nature outside the walls and beating against the gates'.

Behind the pool is a nymphaeum with cool, arcaded rooms and, at the side through iron-barred windows, a bucolic view over fields and woods. Beyond the walled courtyard, the garden has no boundaries, blending imperceptibly into the woods and wheat fields. Near here is the mouth of a tunnel, an ancient underground escape route. This, and the circular watchtower in the corner of the garden wall, remain as testament to distant battles fought over this part of the Marche. The Saracens, too, attacked the coast at a time when this site was a Dominican convent.

The sea is visible from the top terrace's brick-walled walk, where mandarins grow in the ground, surviving winter with the help of the area's benevolent microclimate. (The lemons, however, need protection and are trained up against the walls inside iron fruit cages.) To walk on these upper levels surrounded by the scent of lemons while looking down on this exquisite little garden is a delight.

Behind the curved back wall plumbago spills out in a blue cloud against the pink brickwork, and visible through one of the arches, an urn-topped column stands alongside a stately palm. A rosemary walk leads past a wheat field curved like a natural amphitheatre, overlooked by a hillside dotted with vines and olives. There are two brick *vasche* here, which water the garden, one dating back to the sixteenth century, the other a circular basin fed by seven wells. The path leads up the hill to the woods to the house where the gardeners sleep. Domenico, the head gardener, a former farmer, has worked for the family here for fifty years.

On the other side of the house, through a rose garden, is a gate leading up into the woods. Brick steps climb the hill, shaded by ancient cypresses and flanked by mysterious and symbolic stone sculptures: crouching lions and lichen-covered pine cones, blurred by time and half-visible in the shadows.

Above The intimate courtyard garden, enclosed by terraced tiers of rosy Marche brick planted with espaliered citrus and dotted with potted lemon trees
Left Brick steps shaded by ancient cypresses and flanked by two symbolic sculptures of crouching lions climb the hill into the woods.

Borgo Storico Seghetti Panichi

Planted four square on a knoll with views over the Tronto valley to the distant Sibilline Mountains, and with the blue Adriatic far beyond, the palazzo's lofty, austere façade recalls the medieval castle that once stood here. The tower – all that remains – was incorporated into what became an aristocratic summer residence. The house was bought by the present owner Giulia Panichi Pignatelli's great-grandfather in the early 1800s, but it was not until 1875 that the garden was laid out to the design of the great German botanist and landscape architect Ludwig Winter.

Winter faced the challenge of a bare, rocky hilltop, which he proceeded to shape into gentle mounds and slopes, encircled by white gravel winding paths, a Winter trademark. Princess Pignatelli still marvels at the skilfulness of his design – the mapping of curves and vistas, the gradient of the flower beds, and the underground watering system he put in, still in perfect working order today – all minutely calculated without the aid of a computer. A new, gently curving carriage drive followed the contours of the hillside, each turn carefully planned to give arriving guests the best possible views over the estate. To aid Winter's landscaping, a constant train of labouring ox carts carried fresh earth from the Tronto riverbanks to deposit on the bare, windswept summit.

In making the garden, Winter had on his side a copious supply of water and, as he delightedly discovered, a microclimate in the Tronto valley similar to the one on the Ligurian coast. Here he had been head gardener for the Hanbury brothers at La Mortola in Ventimiglia (see page 76), where his love for exotic plants and interesting new species had been given full rein. With Winter's favoured palms and exotics able to grow here in the Tronto valley in open ground, Borgo Seghetti Panichi would become 'a displaced landscape', a French-Ligurian romantic garden in the midst of the Marche.

Winter's hand is evident immediately with a majestic palm, *Jubaea chilensis*, at the start of the drive – a signal, Princess Pignatelli thinks, which said, 'Welcome, you are entering Ludwig Winter's garden.' Near by is *Phoenix canariensis*, with the fan palm (*Chamaerops humilis*) and the windmill palm (*Trachycarpus fortunei*). *Cycas revoluta*, the Japanese cycad, has grown to monumental size.

Winter's signature plant was *Washingtonia filifera*, grown usually in a triptych; he admired it for being the most generous of trees. His stately threesome still stand together here, monoliths in a lawn of emerald green. Their trunks have scars caused by frost: Winter dared to plant palms outside when other nineteenth-century gardeners kept them cautiously immured in greenhouses. To protect them from the cutting east wind, he used a particularly Italian device, a sweet bay (*Laurus nobilis*) tunnel.

If spectacle was Winter's first intent, his second was to assail the senses with scent. To the side of the house, *Magnolia grandiflora* flowers scent the whole area with their fragrance.

At the back, to the north, is the most charmingly romantic part of the garden, where Winter created a miniature oriental landscape, reflecting the Chinese influence prevalent towards the end of the nineteenth century. A rustic bridge made of vine branches spans a pool overhung with yellow *Styphnolobium japonicum* 'Pendulum' (syn. *Sophora japonica* 'Pendula'), one of the few imported into Europe at that time. Winter's majestic palm trees are reflected in the still waters, and the fan-shaped leaves of *Ginkgo biloba* add to the oriental mood. 'No one would be surprised', Princess Pignatelli

observes, 'if they saw a pensive, gentle Japanese girl with a pretty painted sunshade walk by.'

In the middle of the pool a statue of Venus with Cupid presides among sheets of blue agapanthus, whose stately heads and slim stems, redolent of palm trees, Winter preferred to most other flowers. As a rule, he considered flower colours too intrusive in the green symphony he wished to create. Blue and white, in iris and roses, were tolerable, but in general Winter inclined towards mass and monumentality rather than colour. The exception was his love for the fiery hues of autumn: in November the park is set alight by the amber glow of *Ginkgo biloba* leaves and the smouldering red of *Taxodium distichum*, while plane, beech and chestnut trees blaze russet and orange against a dark background of holm oaks.

Winter, as he often did, created a *pensatorio* – a place for thinking and dreaming – in this garden. Hidden to one side are two stone seats backed by enfolding hedges of bay laurel. On the southern sunny side of the house, he put in terracing more suited to the steep hills of Liguria, where he had gardened before, than to the spacious, rolling Marche countryside. Land is plentiful here and terraces not needed. On the terracing is a box-hedged herb garden with oranges and lemons – again, typical of Liguria – relishing the microclimate by flourishing in the ground. Bay trees contained in circles of brick provide height among the basil, oregano, parsley and sage.

Giulia Panichi Pignatelli and her talented daughter Stefania have restored this terracing with the care and respect they have shown to all of Winter's garden. Courageously, they have taken the decision to open up views, felling a row of mature limes (a twentieth-century addition) which were blocking vistas of the valley. Their aim, Stefania says, of which Winter surely would approve, is 'to achieve leaf contrast, wherever possible, in front of rigorous architecture'. Where the limes once grew, the Mexican blue palm (*Bratiea armata*) now stands, cleverly sited in front of Himalayan cedars.

Giulia and Stefania have spent time studying the therapeutic effects of plants, in particular the electromagnetic fields they can release, which are said to be beneficial to the human body. Two years of research have resulted in the first bioenergetically mapped historic garden of Italy. Today, visitors to the castle can find peace and well-being in these special bioenergetic areas of the park. A range of organic skincare products is made with the oils and plant essences found in this harmonious place.

Giulia and Stefania also run the association Le Marche Segrete, a conservation body founded in 1996 by the owners of some of the Marche's most important villas and gardens.

Page 163 The villa reflected in the lake at dusk.
Right, above A rustic bridge made of vine branches spans a pool overhung with yellow *Styphnolobium japonicum* 'Pendulum' and bordered by agapanthus.
Below The family chapel overlooks the Marche countryside.

UMBRIA

Umbria, one of Italy's smallest regions, is bordered by its larger and more illustrious neighbour Tuscany to the west, by Le Marche to the east, and by Lazio to the south. Often known as 'the green heart of Italy', it is the only Italian region with neither a coastline nor a common border with another country. Hilly and wooded, its valleys studded with castles and watchtowers and covered with lush chestnut forests, Umbria retains a medieval character and many traces of the Etruscan civilization: some of the most important finds have been collected together in the National Archaeological Museum of Umbria.

Umbria contains some of Italy's most iconic towns, including Todi, Gubbio, Orvieto, Perugia and Assisi. Yet its smaller, medieval towns – Montefalco, perched on its ridge, Bevagna with its delightful medieval square – are among its most accessible treasures. Benozzo Gozzoli's frescoes in Montefalco show Bevagna, where St Francis preached to the birds, on the plain, and Assisi hovering in the distance – much the same view as can be seen from Montefalco nowadays.

Lake Trasimeno, one of Italy's largest lakes, is famous as the site where Hannibal ambushed and annihilated the Roman army in 217 BC. Near Norcia, and surrounded by the rugged peaks of the Sibillini mountain range, is the Piano Grande – a vast plain which in spring is carpeted with wild flowers.

Il Giadorto

Daniela Fè d'Ostiani's garden is high up on a hill overlooking Lake Trasimeno and its islands. Huge tubs overflowing with *Rosa* 'Blanc Double de Coubert' greet you as you enter, but here the white rugosa rose is crammed in with feathery bronze fennel – a magical combination, typical of Daniela's skill for pairing plants.

Made from scratch and developed over the past thirty years, the garden descends the hill in a series of gentle terracing. Each new level had to be dug out of the steep and stony hillside, something difficult to imagine now that it is mature and billowing with an exuberant medley of plants. In this natural country garden, each season has its planting scheme, and everywhere Daniela's love for roses, and for English herbaceous plants, is visible.

A new decorative herb and vegetable garden has been made round a pergola covered with the thornless apricot rose 'Crépuscule'. The planting here is relaxed, and in early summer ablaze with flowers of yellow, orange and red, muted by the grey plants Daniela uses everywhere 'to calm the garden down'. Golden hops swathe an arch; red *fagioli* beans climb a trellis; elsewhere, golden solidago and coreopsis mingle with poppies, kniphofia and yellow iris. In late summer the colours darken into blues and mauves, with asters, dark dahlias and the castor oil plant (*Ricinus communis*). The *orto* has been featured in a book, *Horti Felici*, by the landscape architect and writer about gardens Paolo Pejrone, who, early in his career, was a pupil of Russell Page.

A green grove enfolds the house, its trees hung with Banksian roses. At the front, in the first part of the garden to be made, is a terrace where *Carex pendula* sprouts from crevices. The green *Rosa × odorata* 'Viridiflora' flourishes here, along with mounds of euphorbia, ceonothus and a huge thirty-year-old cotinus. Stately *Dahlia imperialis*, safely housed in a pot, is moved inside in November. The border opposite is filled with white and yellow roses: 'Phyllis Bide', 'Moonlight' and the darker-centred 'Cloth of Gold'.

Page 165 A tranquil corner of Il Giadorto.
Above, left Paeonia × lemoinei 'Chromatella'.
Above, right The trees are swathed with Banksian roses.
Right Kolkwitzia amabilis 'Pink Cloud' and *Rosa* 'Dainty Bess' in combination.

At the back of the house the garden unfolds in a series of flowering glades, to one side a border of blues and yellows, centred on the distant view of the *orto* and *Rosa* 'Crépuscule'. A dramatic tree peony (possibly *Paeonia* × *lemonei* 'Chromatella') anchors the palette, its deep tone echoed by the copper-coloured Italian tea rose 'Clementina Carbonieri'. The theme is then lightened by the creamy apricot geum 'Lionel Thomas' and by the buttery-yellow roses 'Rêve d'Or' and 'Graham Thomas'. Deep blue iris, aquilegia, geraniums and a luxuriant clump of *Scilla peruviana* complete the planting.

On the other side of this terrace, the beautiful, clear-pink, single-cupped blooms of *Rosa* 'Anemone' garland an apple tree. Bourbon roses are partnered by *R.* 'Penelope', and the compact, pale pink China rose 'Irène Watts' emerges from a colourful display of pink cistus, purple alliums and magenta *Gladiolus communis* subsp. *byzantinus*. In the shelter of a shady wall are *Macleaya cordata*, hostas, oak-leaved hydrangeas and, a favourite of Daniela's, *Hydrangea arborescens* 'Annabelle'.

Down some steps is another, sunnier glade, shaded in part by a loquat tree (*Eriobotrya japonica*) and by *Ceanothus* 'Concha' overhanging the grass. Delicate, silvery-pink *Kolkwitzia amabilis* 'Pink Cloud' and *Rosa* 'Dainty Bess' make an artful combination. Other roses, all picked to flower in June, Daniela has deliberately planted in pairs. Arching white *R.* 'Nevada' grows with *R.* 'Marguerite Hilling'; the fleshy, pale pink blossoms of the Bourbon rose 'Souvenir de la Malmaison' accompany single, elegant

R. 'Complicata'. To partner pink China roses like lilac-pink 'Le Vésuve' she favours bronze iris.

When Daniela runs out of space for roses, she uses trees as hosts. *Rosa mulliganii*, *R.* 'Cécile Brünner' and the Wichurana rambler *R.* 'May Queen' all flourish aloft. The enormous canopy of salmon-pink 'Lady Waterlow' encompasses several tree-tops. Along the path to the wood the tones deepen with berberis and *Buddleja alternifolia* accompanying *Rosa glauca* and the deep crimson, yellow-stamened rose 'La Belle Sultane'. Crimson-mauve 'Souvenir de la Bataille de Marengo' (the "Old Spanish Rose") grows near by. In spring the woodland garden is full of daffodils and crocus, and *Hyacinthoides hispanica* among lamium.

Towards the back of the garden, behind the well, steps lead down to an Italian Garden. At the top a tamarisk grows near another kolkwitzia and a Judas tree, each chosen to flower in succession. The scheme in the Italian garden is yellow and grey, anchored by cardoons and teucrium balls. At the end of an *allée*, *Euphorbia characias* makes a statement in a huge pot. Lower down, blue and white are added to the colour scheme with roses, including 'Sea Foam' and the double white 'Madame Hardy' lasting, Daniela says, till Christmas. The potager is trim and decorative with santolina-edged compartments where lettuces and onions grow in neat circles. Standard 'Sea Foam' roses have an underskirt of parsley, and marguerite daisies make a charming hedge.

Left The potager, with clipped santolina and box.

Giardino all'Italiano di Villa Aureli PERUGIA, UMBRIA

Villa Aureli is a small gem, the country home of a cultivated and artistic eighteenth-century Perugian nobleman, little changed and much cherished by the present owner.

Sperello Aureli's charming embellishment of what had been a plain early sixteenth-century villa reflects the playful and gracious spirit of his age. Villa Aureli has a unique and pleasing eighteenth-century atmosphere. Inside it is a riot of *trompe l'oeil*, lacquering, marquetry and chinoiserie. The painted furniture still remains *in situ* matching the walls, delicately painted in rococo or neoclassical style. During the Second World War when the villa was occupied by successive waves of foreign troops, the furniture survived behind a false wall in an upstairs room where it had been hidden by the gardener.

Outside the villa is the harmonious Italian Garden, complete with eighteenth-century Orangery, and a mellow brick containing wall punctuated by piers topped with balls and obelisks. Arches and pediments, windows and swept-up walls all contribute to the broken silhouette typically associated with the Baroque.

The garden still retains much of the layout visible in a nineteenth-century plan, with lemon trees in each box-edged compartment and two matching fountains, although only one is present. Nearest the entrance, the box enclosures are filled with massive blocks of yew: formerly spherical, these were transformed into cubes. Near by is an iris garden, and a delightful viewing tower overlooking fields sloping up to a gentle ridge with umbrella pines on the horizon. The encroaching suburbs of Perugia seem very far away. The current owner (also Sperello but Alighieri – he

Left, above A majolica bench rests under a brick arch.
Left, below The soaring arched roof of the eighteenth-century Orangery.

Left The Italian Garden, contained by
a mellow brick wall punctuated by
piers topped with balls and obelisks.
Below A latticed window made
of the semicircular tiles known as
ciambelloni.

is descended from Dante) says that the villa has a typically Italian setting:
'The architecture of the house, then the connection between house and
garden, then the connection with the wider park and landscape.'

Much of the box planted by the first Sperello also survives, as do some
of the pots for the ancient lemon trees. In the past, sixteen men were
needed to lift these pots on to frames and manoeuvre them into place.
Now a tractor manages it.

The three huge limes shading the house are a nineteenth-century
addition. Originally four, these great trees were heartily disliked by
the present count's mother during her suzerainty. When one lime
unexpectedly died, family lore decreed that her hostility had killed it.

The *bosco* also figures in the nineteenth-century plan, showing winding
paths curving around laurel enclosures. A straight central path now cuts
through the *bosco* and leads to a niche in the brick outside wall. On either
side, cut into the wall, are latticed windows. This lattice pattern, made
up of semicircular tiles known as *ciambelloni*, dates back to Roman times:
similar examples have been found in Pompeii. The wooden moulds in
which the tiles were made still lie somewhere in the villa grounds, along
with Roman amphorae and Etruscan burial urns.

The Orangery (as it has always been known, despite housing mostly
lemon trees) is frescoed with painted creepers and sheaves of corn against
an overall background of trellis work. The soaring arched roof, like an
inverted boat, is similar to that of the *limonaia* at Villa di Montefreddo in
nearby Bagnaia. In the past, an extensive water system drained water from
the roofs into an underground channel, which ran through the Orangery
into a fountain and then into the basin (now used as a swimming pool)
directly underneath the terrace. Grand gates in the terrace wall open
into an *allée* which, mysteriously, seems to lead nowhere. Another *allée*,
across the road on the axis of the entrance front, is given over to use by
villagers. It, too, goes nowhere in particular and may have been purely a
landscaping device.

The current Count Sperello, an astrophysicist, is as attached to this
unique historical survival as were his ancestors.

Orto e Giardino di Barbanera

Just outside Spello and looking up at the walled medieval town on the slopes of Monte Subasio is a new garden and *orto*, which has been created in the grounds of an old silk factory. The green-shuttered eighteenth-century building has medieval origins and was also used as a tobacco-drying site before being abandoned for four decades. The owners of Editoriale Campi, a 100-year-old family firm, then moved in and restored the building with great style, creating offices for the publishing company and an airy white loft in which to live.

Editoriale Campi publish *Barbanera*, the most famous almanac in Italy, now 250 years old. Legend tells us that the original Barbanera was a hermit in the Apennines who sallied forth to give advice to a neighbouring farmer. A stamp issued in 2012 shows Barbanera's portrait from the first eponymous almanac, published in Foligno in 1762; in the background alongside the sun and moon are silhouettes of farmers with oxen ploughing the fields. Many modern Italians would not be without *Barbanera* even today but use it not to seek advice for their crops but to play the lottery.

The owners have carried their sense of style into the two new gardens they have made in front of and behind the house. Simplicity, authenticity and understatement were their watchwords, and they chose as their designer the English landscape architect Peter Curzon

Below, left The original back gates lead into the *giardino*, divided into four seasonal gardens by lavender-lined paths.
Below, right In the *giardino*, light filters through the central pergola, covered in ten different grape varieties.

– assisted by Anne Hanley, an English garden expert who lives in Umbria. Peter Curzon had designed La Porrona (see page 152), a Tuscan country garden which manages to blend effortlessly into the surrounding rural landscape. He instantly understood what was wanted here and has tried to evoke the traditions of the almanac as well as the spirit of the place.

Because this was a silk factory, ninety-seven new mulberry trees (the mulberry being the tree on which silkworms feed) have been planted, along with quinces and medlars. The fruit orchard has been retained and expanded, with the trees expertly pruned back to the best of health.

Almanacs traditionally gave advice on *ortos*, and the *orto* here has pride of place. It is designed so that visitors have to walk through it on their way into the building. The lucky employees are encouraged to pick what they want as they make their way home. Simply laid out and enclosed by hedges, the *orto* is circular with gravel paths. A mix of vegetables, fruit and old-fashioned flowers, it is at its best in July, when the beds overflow with lush fecundity, and cosmos, calendula, dahlias and zinnias blaze with colour among the rocket, lettuce, broad beans and towering maize. The pergolas, copied from an iron vine pergola found on site, are weighed down with grapes, pears and kiwis as well as roses and honeysuckle. Five different kinds of *fagioli* grow and five different courgettes. In the heat of the sun, ornamental tanks containing lotus flowers give a cooling glimpse of water.

Behind the house, near an avenue of ancient limes, the original back gates lead into the *giardino*, which is divided into four seasonal gardens by lavender-lined paths. In the rose garden, long-blooming *R. mutabilis* mingles with the delightfully scented Bourbon rose 'Louise Odier' and the pretty, scalloped-petalled rose 'Baron Girod de l'Ain'. Iris, lavender and, later, perovskia complement the roses. The central pergola is covered with ten different grape varieties, including the oval-shaped 'Pizzutello', a grape noticed by Pliny as having the appearance of an olive. Across the path in the herb garden, wild strawberries have naturalized under an olive tree. The shade garden gleams with the lime-white heads of *Hydrangea aborescens* 'Annabelle' alongside *H. quercifolia* 'Snowflake'. Eleagnus and escallonia which grow nearby will be trimmed in waves as a foil to the luxuriant hydrangeas. A limestone tank, possibly Turkish in origin, holds water in the pomegranate garden.

The Fondazione Barbanera 1762 holds an archive well worth visiting with the garden, and easily accessible by appointment. It holds 6,000 historic almanacs from around the world, the earliest dating back to the fifteenth century. A searcher is employed to scour Europe's flea markets for long-lost almanacs to augment this vast and fascinating collection. In the spirit of the collection, the Barbanera website gives traditional advice on the monthly cultivation and care of fruit and flowers, but still finds a place for biodynamic gardening governed by the phases of the moon.

Above left A limestone tank provides a cooling glimpse of water. *Hydrangea aborescens* 'Annabelle' grows alongside.
Above right In the *orto*, zinnias and brightly coloured annuals splash colour among the fruit and vegetables.
Below Home is Where the Heart Is (Pliny the Elder).

Santa Maria in Portella

This is a garden full of rare and exquisite roses. Owner Helga Brichet is a world expert, regularly invited by the Chinese to lecture in China on Chinese roses. Her great love, however, is *Rosa gigantea*, the rampant wild rose with blooms as big as magnolia blossoms, first spotted in the 1880s by amateur botanists and Raj stalwarts Sir George Watt and Sir Henry Collett in India and Burma respectively. Graham Stuart Thomas called *R. gigantea* 'the Empress of wild roses'; the common name is the Manipur wild tea rose. From 1903 the first hybrids appeared, among them 'Belle Portugaise', created by the French Director of the Lisbon Botanical Gardens. This rose, *R. gigantea* crossed with the Tea rose 'Souvenir de Madame Léonie Viennot', is now flourishing in Helga's garden.

'*Gigantea* roses', says Helga, 'have oomph. This plant is only seven years old and already she has created a huge canopy.' Too vigorous for a mature olive tree to shoulder, the rose has had to be propped up on each side by four bamboo poles, creating an arbour big enough to stand under, roofed by luxuriant, shell pink blossom. Near by, similarly supported, is the rose 'Belle Blanca', a white mutation of 'Belle Portugaise', with an enchanting display of large, open-faced ivory blooms. Beyond them, overlooking vineyards, is an entire grassy slope of olives, each circled by lavender, each hosting a different *R. gigantea* hybrid, the naturalness of the setting a perfect backdrop for these vigorous, semi-wild roses.

The hybrids, despite being so floriferous, do not usually reflower, except as second-generation bush roses, such as the fragrant, repeat-flowering, saffron-yellow 'Squatter's Dream'. Named after a racehorse, this was bred in 1923 by the Australian *R. gigantea* enthusiast Alister Clark, who lived a long and happy life down under, nurturing his passions for fox-hunting and breeding roses and narcissi. His 1915 rose 'Jessie Clark' is here, a 6-metre/20-foot climber with scented rose-pink flowers, named after his niece. Alister Clark, who lived till 1949, kept a notebook in which he recorded all his *R. gigantea* crossings. Towards the end of his life, he left this notebook out in his garden overnight: rain fell, washing away the only record of a lifetime of distinguished rose breeding.

The Clark roses that have come down to us are now collected in Helga's garden. Cuttings of them have been taken by John Hook, who

runs the nursery La Roseraie du Desert in south-west France. The species *R. gigantea* and many hybrids are for sale there. Except for the French hybrid 'Emmanuella de Mouchy', which manages to grow outside Paris at L'Haÿ-les-Roses, these roses thrive only in a hot, dry climate.

The most beautiful, perhaps, of all Helga's *gigantea* roses is an Indian hybrid bred in a hill station and rightly named 'Amber Cloud'. From a froth of pale saffron foliage, the flowers emerge, at first small and coppery, and then getting bigger and paler. The effect of the petals is translucent, as though you are looking into amber. Among a group of Indian-bred roses elsewhere is the beautiful *R. gigantea* hybrid 'Manipur Magic'. Crossed with 'Rêve d'Or', it has creamy flowers with a pale lemon centre.

A tunnel next to the *gigantea* roses is covered with *R.* 'Veilchenblau', *Clematis jackmanii* and *R.* 'La Mortola', and planned to flower later. Opposite, the back wall of the fifteenth-century stone chapel (frescoed inside) is clothed with white-pink *R.* 'Adélaïde d'Orléans' and *R.* 'Félicité Perpétue', part of Helga's new collection of Hybrid Sempervirens.

Opposite Gigantea roses cascade over olive trees against a backdrop of cypresses.
Above A peacock roams the garden.

Judas trees and *Ginkgo biloba* are among the many trees which Helga and her husband, André, have planted since they first came here from Rome in 1973. Clouds and trails of *R. banksiae* spiral up into these trees. This rose is known in China as the Seven-Mile Rose because its scent is said to waft for seven miles. As well as *R. banksiae* var. *normalis*, Helga has all the *banksiae* cultivars: Mansuino's double white 'Purezza', double yellow 'Lutea', small white *R. banksiae* var. *banksiae* and the sublime single yellow *R. banksiae* 'Lutescens'. She also has 'Di Castello', a cross between *R. banksiae* 'Lutescens' and 'Lamarque', its creamy, double flowers hailed by Charles Quest-Ritson, author of *Climbing Roses of the World*, as perhaps the prettiest all the Banksian roses. Its smell he described memorably as a mix of tea and violets. Also present is the *R. banksiae* × *R. gigantea* cross found by Martyn Rix in a garden on the French Côte d'Azur.

The section of Chinese roses borders a field. Here, appropriately, grows the Lijang rose, so strong and vigorous, despite its soft pink beauty, that it is used in China to divide up fields. Here, too, crimson *R.* × *odorata* Sanguinea Group and deep velvety-red *R.* 'Cramoisi Supérieur Grimpant' glow lustrously against the silvery-grey leaves of olive trees, and 'Fortune's Five Colour', a rose imported into Europe during the period of the Opium Wars, displays its pale pink, cerise-striped blossoms.

On her frequent visits to China, Helga is keen to rediscover old varieties. One rose – deep pink with a yellow centre – she found in a cemetery. A part of her garden is dedicated to *R.* × *odorata* 'Mutabilis' and her children, including a rose from Bermuda, 'Bermuda's Yellow Mutabilis'.

Along the drive is the Noisette area, where pink and apricot roses climb the dark green cypress trees. Near by, a twenty-year-old specimen of the deep yellow Noisette 'Rêve d'Or' cascades over an ancient mulberry tree, a relic of the time each small farm had silkworms and merchants would tour the country, collecting the cocoons. By the front door is climbing 'Papa Gontier', its cerise, yellow-centred flowers splashing colour against the stone.

As befits a past President of the World Federation of Rose Societies and its Conservation Committee, Helga has a rose named after her, as does her husband, André. At Santa Maria she has not only a unique collection of Chinese and hybrid *gigantea* roses but a garden which is a singular delight, where peacocks wander freely against a backdrop of rolling Umbrian countryside.

Left Roses create canopies among the trees.

LAZIO

The history of gardens in Lazio is chiefly the history of Renaissance Rome, where the gardens of Ancient Rome were recreated and redesigned by Renaissance architects. It is also the history of the Renaissance cardinals, who used Rome's splendid history for their own personal glory, commissioning iconographical designs for their gardens which melded the classical past with vaunting displays of family pride. Layer upon layer of terraces, grottoes, statues and fountains testified to this desire to impress. Lazio's gardens are, moreover, the result of their terrain. Montaigne, visiting Roman gardens in 1581, admired their 'singular beauty . . . and here I learnt to what extent art is aided by a hilly, steep and irregular site, for they derive advantages from this which cannot be matched in our level gardens, and they make the most skilful use of this variety in the terrain.'

The Renaissance garden architects were following the precepts of Leon Battista Alberti (1404–1472), who was himself influenced by the architectural writings of Vitruvius, the Roman author whose book on architecture is the only major work on the subject to survive from classical antiquity. Pliny the Younger's newly rediscovered letters about his garden were equally influential in Renaissance garden design, emphasizing, as they did, the importance of views, the interconnection between villa and garden, and the joy to be had from skilful topiary.

Castello Ruspoli-Vignanello

Page 175 Bonomelli's parterre at
Castel Gandolfo.
Left The parterre of Castello
Ruspoli-Vignanello picks out
the initials of the seventeenth-
century owners.

Castello Ruspoli, in the village of Vignanello, boasts the best-preserved Renaissance parterre to survive anywhere in Italy. It is planted – so as to be seen from above – directly under the windows of the Ruspoli family's imposing fortress in the Cimini Hills. This stronghold, originally a fortified monastery, was transformed in the 1530s, probably by Antonio da Sangallo the Younger, into a vast Renaissance palace. It was to house Sforza Ercole Marescotti and his new bride, Ortensia Farnese, who had received it as a wedding gift from the Farnese Pope Paul III.

Ortensia was the first in a line of strong women at Vignanello. Legend states that, having killed her husband with a poker, she went on to take over Sforza's estates and erase his coat of arms from the family crest. This story may be borne out by the fact that her next two husbands also met violent deaths.

According to some sources, Ortensia's grandson, Marcantonio Marescotti, inherited her hot temper, dying, probably at the hands of an enemy, in around 1608. His wife, Ottavia, also seems to have left her mark on Vignanello, but in an altogether more peaceable fashion. The daughter of Vicino Orsini of Bomarzo (see page 178), she might well have had an interest in gardens, and everything conspires to suggest that it was she who was responsible for the parterre. A marble slate under the family crest at the entrance to garden states that it was finsihed in 1611 and is dedicated to the counts of Vignanello and Pararrano, Galeazzo and Sforza, who were Ottavia's sons.

Remarkably, despite Castello Ruspoli's position on a hillside, the garden has none of the terracing and water channelling that would be expected. Instead, a flat plateau was created for the garden by moving earth; this was then linked to the palace by a drawbridge over the moat, and surrounded for privacy by a protective brick wall. The pattern of the parterre, divided into twelve rectangular compartments, is exactly as it was laid out 400 years ago, although originally clipped herbs might have been used instead of box, and the compartments filled with some of the colourful new plants then arriving from the 'Indies'.

The parterre picks out Ottavia's initials in a double O in one compartment, as well as those of her two sons, Sforza and Galeazzo, intertwined in another. The fact that Marcantonio's initials are not included dates the parterre to the years between his murder in c. 1608 and Sforza's coming-of-age in 1618, thus making it indisputably Ottavia's creation. Sforza's marriage to a rich Ruspoli heiress brought the castle into the Ruspoli family. An eighteenth-century Ruspoli, Francesco, friend and patron to Handel, added his initials, FR, in one of the front box compartments. To enjoy its full effect, the parterre must be viewed as intended, from above. This is allowed on Sundays from Easter to the end of October or for groups larger than twenty by appointment.

The taller hedging is a mix of *Myrtus communis* subsp. *tarentina*, viburnum and laurel. The inner hedges are of box, beautifully maintained by Santino, Castello Ruspoli's legendary gardener for thirty years. Santino attributes the health of these hedges to the fact that they are planted on a bank of earth, heaped high enough for light and air to circulate. They are cut twice a year, and Santino is well known for using a knife shaped like a scythe. Another idiosyncrasy is the habit of planting garlic and onions in the pots containing Vignanello's precious lemons, specimens of which are placed around the parterre: this is done to prevent leaf curl. Santino also weeds the immaculate parterre by hand.

Just outside the gates to the park is Vignanello's old Column of Justice. It stood once in the main piazza, where offenders were manacled to it for

punishment. To one side, on a narrow terrace is a *giardino segreto*, with another, this time early twentieth-century, parterre, designed by the great-grandmother of the present owners, Maria Anita Lante della Rovere, who grew up in the Villa Lante in Bagnaia (see page 182).

The present chatelaine of Vignanello, Princess Claudia Ruspoli, has shown herself to be as protective of this special place as her ancestors, having secured EU funds to restore the parterre and thus saved this historic garden for posterity.

Above A pavilion stands in a corner of the garden.

Sacro Bosco di Bomarzo

VITERBO, LAZIO

Left One of the fantastic monsters who inhabit the park: a dragon attacked by lions.

Bomarzo – now that you can no longer visit it 'by the pale moonlight' as Sir Walter Scott advised – is best seen in the misty depths of autumn or winter. Then the park is empty of the chattering schoolchildren who migrate there each summer. Seen in the half-light of a drear winter's day, the stone monsters in Bomarzo's woods regain some of their intended air of mystery and menace.

Bomarzo was a medieval fortress, converted like other strongholds in the Cimini Hills into a more elegant and fashionable Renaissance villa. The *castello* can still be seen high on a cliff, looming over the valley a quarter of a mile below, while the park, laid out in that valley, is just visible from the north-facing apartments of the castle. Bomarzo's park, the *sacro bosco* (sacred grove), was laid out under the direction of a sixteenth-century papal soldier, Vicino Orsini, who, having hung up his sword, hired sculptors and labourers to bring his strange vision of a landscape of eccentricities and monsters into being.

We can only surmise about the inspiration behind Bomarzo, but it seems likely that, having inherited these wild and rocky slopes for his park, Orsini was influenced by what he found there – in particular, the huge natural outcrops of stone. At vast expense, these were sculpted over the years into a cast of extraordinary *grotteschi* – grappling giants, an enormous tortoise with a figure on its back, a monstrous gaping mouth, fantastic creatures, some animal, some barely human. A wood – the *sacro bosco* – referred to in numerous inscriptions found in the park was then planted to set the scene, like a backdrop in a theatre. In this disturbing setting, the monstrous beasts appear to be about to leave their shadowy world and walk out into ours down the precipitous slopes of the Cimini Hills.

It is hard to conceive that Bomarzo is 13 kilometres/8 miles from and roughly contemporary with Villa Lante, so far removed is it in spirit, so

entirely opposed to the ideals of harmony, symmetry and proportion which governed the Renaissance. Yet that Orsini gloried in his own originality is evident from inscriptions anticipating the wonder of visitors at 'so many marvels' – marvels that surpassed, he says, even those of the ancient world. Orsini's own voice is recognizable everywhere in the park in the shape of such incised inscriptions. Elsewhere, he praises his creation, 'which resembles itself and nothing else'.

Orsini worked on the *sacro bosco* until his death in 1584, adding to his stone menagerie. Although well connected – his wife was a Farnese, cousin to Cardinal Alessandro Farnese at Caprarola – he was never prominent himself, or powerful. Nevertheless, to set himself against the times as he did, laughing, some said, in the face of the Renaissance, Orsini must have been a singularly self-confident and robustly individual character. During his lifetime, visitors flocked to view the *teatri e mausolei* he had created. Only after his death did interest wither.

Visitors originally entered the Parco dei Mostri by a bridge over a rivulet on the lowest of three levels. The current entrance is further upstream, but it still makes sense to make your way down to start at the bottom level. Here we come across some of the most photographed monuments in the park. The gigantic tortoise carrying the figure of Fame on its back would have been instantly recognizable to sixteenth-century visitors as representing *festine lente* (make haste slowly). The relevance of Pegasus further on is more obscure. It may be that Orsini was taking aim at one of his contemporaries, Ippolito d'Este, whose own statue of Pegasus with the Muses was meant to confirm his status as an artistic patron. The leaning house, too, may have been built with mockery in mind. The conundrum that when you stand inside it is the outside that appears to be tilting may in fact be questioning Renaissance ideas of perspective. Or possibly we are being told a morality

Left A colossal female statue bearing a vase, said to represent the snare of lust. *Below* The terrifying Mouth of Hell, which acts as an echo chamber.

tale about the deviousness of the world outside.

On the second level, a colossal female statue bearing a vase has been said to represent the snare of lust. At the end of the long terrace walk, another female figure, this time recumbent and reclining with a river god beside a pool, may stand for unrequited love. The jury is still out on the meaning of the elephant.

Of all the monuments in the park, possibly the most terrifying is the Mouth of Hell, the more so because it was built as an echo chamber to pick up and amplify sound. It is said that to speak inside the Mouth is to make yourself heard anywhere in the park.

We know so little of Orsini's real intentions at Bomarzo that the symbolism of his creations has naturally been the focus of fierce debate. Bomarzo has been variously described as a pagan underworld, an exploration of the dark forces of life, and as the converse, the documenting of man's journey through earthly snares to the temple of divine love. The monsters have been the subject of legend for centuries. As late as 1980 an exorcism was performed on a specially procured altar set up in the wood. What is certain is that when Salvador Dali visited Bomarzo in 1949, the valley was choked with undergrowth, the statues hidden or felled like those of 'Ozymandias'.

Three years later the restoration began.

Palazzo Farnese di Caprarola VITERBO, LAZIO

The great pentagon-shaped villa was built on the foundations of a fortress designed around 1520 by Baldassare Peruzzi and the military architect Antonio da Sangallo the Younger. Surviving drawings by Peruzzi clearly show its defensive bastions, intended to contribute with the other Farnese fortresses of Ronciglione, Nepi and Borghetto to the defence of Farnese lands. Through shifting alliances, prudent marriages and opportunistic purchases, the Farnese had managed to extend their domain through Lazio, and controlled its main communication arteries right up to the gates of Rome. The first Cardinal Alessandro Farnese planned to build this great fortress on the easily defended ridge of Caprarola, a territory he had bought in 1504 and where he had created for himself a hunting reserve.

With his accession to the papal throne as Pope Paul III in 1534, work on the Caprarola fortress was abandoned. In 1559 a project by the architect Jacopo Barozzi da Vignola envisaged a Renaissance palace rising from the foundations as a different but equally potent symbol of Farnese power.

Vignola was working to a commission from another Alessandro Farnese (1520–89), Pope Paul III's grandson. A cardinal at the age of fourteen, by eighteen he was Vatican Secretary of State. Clever, diplomatic and

sociable, the Great Cardinal, as he became, was a prominent patron of the arts. Extremely rich, he amassed collections of gems, books, pictures and antiquities and, fond of architecture, was said to suffer from the so-called 'stone disease'. At first unconvinced about Caprarola as a site – he would have preferred the more civilized setting of Frascati – he ended up saying that three works had perfectly succeeded and captured his heart. These were the Palace of Caprarola, his beloved daughter Clelia and Vignola's Church of the Gesù, where the cardinal planned to be buried. His tomb lies before the high altar there.

Perhaps the most ambitious of these works was Caprarola, for which the cardinal engaged the best artists of the age. However, the planning was Vignola's, to whom the credit goes for this masterpiece of 'restrained majesty'. Vasari, visiting in 1568, lamented that 'the place can be little

Above, left The water staircase of entwined dolphins rises to Giacomo del Duca's Casino del Piacere (Lodge of Pleasure).
Above, right The closely clipped box parterre of the Secret Garden to one side of the Casino.

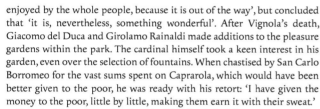

enjoyed by the whole people, because it is out of the way', but concluded that 'it is, nevertheless, something wonderful'. After Vignola's death, Giacomo del Duca and Girolamo Rainaldi made additions to the pleasure gardens within the park. The cardinal himself took a keen interest in his garden, even over the selection of fountains. When chastised by San Carlo Borromeo for the vast sums spent on Caprarola, which would have been better given to the poor, he was ready with his retort: 'I have given the money to the poor, little by little, making them earn it with their sweat.'

Georgina Masson has pointed out that Vignola wisely did not attempt a garden that rivalled the palace's magnificent scale. Instead, the gardens at Caprarola are a princely and private retreat, an escape from the pomp and ceremony of the Church in Rome. Two *giardini segreti* devised by Vignola are placed behind the villa, each facing the side of the pentagon which housed the cardinal's summer or winter rooms. The design of fountains and parterres could thus be enjoyed by the cardinal and his guests from the windows of the palazzo. A wooden bridge, spanning the moat, connects each garden to the building at the *piano nobile* level, heightening the effect of grand outdoor rooms. Both gardens are square; fruit and flowers once filled the Summer Garden's parterre. In the Winter Garden, a central avenue leads to the Fountain of the Rain. Michel de Montaigne, who visited this grotto in 1580, wrote that 'water showering out into a small lake, gives to the eye a close imitation of the fall of real rain'.

From here, a path leads through woods of chestnut, pine and larch, echoing the Groves of the Ancients, to the secluded delights of the upper garden, well away from the splendours of the palace. Here, crowning a small hill, sits Giacomo del Duca's Casino del Piacere (Lodge of Pleasure), the very private retreat of a humane and cultivated sixteenth-century Prince of the Church. At the bottom of the hill, in an open sunlit clearing, the round Fountain of the Lily faces uphill towards the water staircase. It is composed of entwined dolphins, a talisman for a safe and blessed journey across the sea or to another, immortal world. At the top of the water staircase giant statues representing the Rivers Tiber and Arno dominate the perspective, spilling water from cornucopias into the great *bicchiere* (drinking vessel). This enormous urn is set into a basin, from the rim of which spout further jets. In the Secret Garden to the side of the Casino, twenty-eight caryatids

sculpted by Pietro Bernini, father of Gian Lorenzo Bernini, preside on the low wall that encloses the closely clipped box parterre. Male and female, and sculpted in humorous, grotesque style, they balance on their heads tall baskets. These were a reference to Ancient Greek *canephori*, Athenian maidens whose duty it was to carry baskets on their heads in solemn procession – a reference the cardinal's guests, at home with classical antiquity, would have been expected to understand. In a charming touch, the caryatids at the corner of the square face each other and hold hands.

The cardinal particularly enjoyed dining in the cool portico of his beloved Casino, looking down on the play of water from the many murmuring fountains. The disapproving San Carlo Borromeo, after having visited the garden, is said to have wondered: 'What will it be like in Heaven?'

Above, left Giant statues representing the Rivers Arno and Tiber spill water from cornucopias into the great *bicchiere* (drinking vessel).
Above, right Three of the twenty-eight caryatids sculpted by Pietro Bernini.

Villa Lante

Villa Lante, a garden with no main building but two small symmetrical *casini*, has come down to us largely unchanged in structure since its main layout was completed by the end of the sixteenth century. It has been admired for 500 years as the perfect example of a Renaissance garden. Montaigne, visiting in 1581, thought the fountains surpassed those at Pratolino and Villa d'Este. Sacheverell Sitwell, a twentieth-century visitor, called Villa Lante 'as much a work of art as any poem, painting, piece of music'. For Edith Wharton, it possessed a unique kind of 'garden-magic'.

This masterpiece of Italian Renaissance garden design has long been attributed to Jacopo Barozzi, known as Vignola; there is documented evidence of a site survey he conducted. His successor Giacomo del Duca has also been mentioned, and Tommaso Ghinucci, planner of the fountains and waterworks at the Villa d'Este in Tivoli, is thought to have contributed to the garden at Villa Lante. Authorship remains a much-debated question.

Certainly, the garden's first owner, the rich and refined Cardinal Gambara (Bishop of Viterbo 1566–88), loved it so much that he resisted repeated attempts by the papacy to wrest it from him. Yet Villa Lante was never a palace such as Cardinal Farnese's Caprarola. Nor was its aim a virtuoso display of erudition, as at Cardinal d'Este's garden at Tivoli. These two cardinals were Gambara's contemporaries and friends. They were laying out their gardens as Cardinal Gambara, not many miles away, contemplated his.

Some years before Vignola had drawn up plans for Caprarola in which he explored his fascination with proportion and perspective. Now in 1566 his design for Lante – along a single central axis following the natural slope of the site from north to south – was a hymn to symmetry. But in its modest scale it differed completely from the other cardinals' villas. What Gambara had wanted, and what Vignola gave him, was not a place for entertainment and display but a private retreat, an intimate summer residence, a place of *delitie* (delights).

What Vignola found at Bagnaia, a small town perched on a volcanic ridge, famous since Roman times for its mineral water, was a steep, sloping site where a fifteenth-century cardinal – Villa Lante is the tale of four cardinals – had built himself a simple hunting lodge and an early sixteenth-century cardinal had fenced off a park for game. This became the *barco* (park), a sylvan frame for Vignola's garden architecture and an allegorical representation of the 'wilderness', the primitive state of innocence from which man emerges and triumphs over nature with the aid of reason in a new golden age of civilization.

Built into the hill in a series of tiered terraces, the entire rectangular layout can be seen from the original entrance at the bottom of the slope. But the garden is best 'read' – to the sixteenth-century observer it would have been a narrative – by starting at the top.

Here, the current curator observes, 'formality meets the forest.' The water, in an allusion to its natural origins, bubbles out from rocks within a mossy grotto. From now on it will be controlled as it descends: corralled into the Fountain of the Dolphins (its water jokes still in play), and channelled through the incomparable *cordonata* or water staircase, whose stone volutes, moulded in the shape of crayfish limbs, pay graceful tribute to Cardinal Gambara, the crayfish (or *gambero*) being his emblem.

Right, above The *cordonata* (water staircase), its stone volutes moulded in the shape of crayfish legs, descends through the terraces.
Right, below The Fountain of the Giants.

Between the magnificent Fountain of the Giants (the Rivers Arno and Tiber symbolizing friendship between the Medici and the papacy) and the sparkling Fountain of the Lamps, which dominate the two middle terraces, the water glides quietly along a runnel cut into the mottled stone surface of the Cardinal's Table. In this water channel, the cardinal cooled his wine when dining outdoors, much as Pliny the Younger describes Roman diners cooling trays of food in the first century AD.

At Villa Lante the focus is the garden. Cardinal Gambara's house, designed in the form of symmetrical twin *palazzine*, is an elegant but understated component of Vignola's scheme. 'The house, small but clean, is pleasing,' said Montaigne. In fact, Cardinal Gambara had to make do with just one *palazzina*, having been stung into stopping works by criticism from San Carlo Borromeo. ('Monsignor, you would have done better to construct a convent for nuns with the monies you have wasted on building this place.')

It was the fourth cardinal at Villa Lante, Cardinal Montalto, owner of the villa from 1590 to 1623, who completed the second pavilion, faithfully carrying out Vignola's plan. With its leafy canopy of great plane trees and the background murmur of falling water, it must have been an entrancing place to live. The twentieth-century planting of hydrangeas, azaleas and camellias is an intrusive distraction from the architecture.

The garden gains in elegance and formality as it descends. The water finally comes to rest in the Fontana dei Mori on a circular balustraded island within a square pool – such geometrical interplay symbolizing the final triumph of the human intellect over Nature, a concept Vignola had begun to explore at Caprarola.

Where there was once a simple pyramid of water, Cardinal Montalto substituted the superb Fountain of the Moors, with its four youths holding aloft the Montalto crest: they were christened 'Moors' simply because of their construction in darkened *peperino* stone.

The surrounding box and yew parterre was once trellis-fenced and held fruit and flowers. Now, patterns of *broderie* are a legacy of a French member of the Lante family.

The Lante held possession of the villa until 1932, presiding over a period of gradual decay. In 1911 an American lady writer staying at the villa was scandalized to find Duke Antonio Lante using the frescoed loggia of Palazzina Montalto as his garage. Now the property of the Region of Lazio, the garden is a well maintained conservation success story.

At the current entrance, the Fountain of Pegasus is the sole survivor of the once numerous fountains of the park. In spring, the park offers a walk amidst woodland with splendid carpets of cyclamen. Remnants of a chestnut orchard, with ancient trees, can still be seen.

Above Between the Fountain of the Giants and the Fountain of the Lamps the water glides along a runnel cut into the mottled stone surface of the Cardinal's Table. Wine was cooled in this water channel.
Left Twin *palazzine* flank a box *parterre de broderie*.

Giardino del Castello Orsini di Vasanello VITERBO, LAZIO

The massive-walled Orsini castle, begun in 1285, casts a forbidding shadow over Vasanello's central square. Yet inside, this grim fortress reveals itself to be an unexpectedly delightful and feminine retreat, its intimate rooms and wooden ceilings all colourfully frescoed. During the fifteenth century the castle was the country home of three of the most famous women of the Renaissance, whose spirit lives on here. All three were connected to the charismatic Cardinal Rodrigo Borgia, who in 1492 was elected Pope Alexander VI. Giulia Farnese ('Giulia the Fair'), wife of the unprepossessing owner of Vasanello, was Rodrigo's mistress. He established her in a palace next to the Vatican, where she lived with his natural daughter, Lucrezia Borgia. The third member of the trio was Giulia's own stepmother-in-law, the ambitious Adriana de Mila, who saw a chance in this arrangement to promote her diffident, squint-eyed stepson, Orsino Orsini, Giulia's husband. A Spaniard and cultivated, Adriana was also the Pope's cousin, and she was granted guardianship of young Lucrezia.

Despite her riches and beauty, Giulia seems to have been a sweet-natured and home-loving young woman, whose long absences from Rome taking care of Vasanello exasperated her papal lover. She remembered the people of Vasanello in her will, leaving especial provision for unmarried women. Her magnificent wardrobe was tactfully divided up between her nieces.

Giulia's daughter Laura was a more homespun character, described as 'rustic' by contemporary chroniclers. Her name is incised three times in the stone of Vasanello: once near her window, once outside the door to her apartments and once in the lintel above her chamber. With Laura's marriage to a della Rovere, Vasanello went out of the Orsini family. Later it was owned by the Colonna and the Barberini, and then, from the early 1900s, the Misciattelli.

Donna Elena Misciattelli, an archaeologist, has been restoring the castle for seven years, having started with the garden 'to refresh me and to give me strength for the rest'. What she inherited was a tangle of brambles

where poppies bloomed on waste ground. To create her medieval garden, she travelled widely – for example, to the Monks' Herb Garden at Winchester Cathedral – and studied sources such as the famous list of plants in the eighth-century *Capitulare de Villis* of Charlemagne. Boccaccio provided further inspiration, as did medieval books of hours.

Steep tufa steps lead down to the *hortus*, sited in the lee of the ancient castle wall, which is pockmarked with Etruscan tombs. Capers flower in the wall: Elena starts them off by inserting the seed into a fig and pushing this fig, the caper's nourishment, into a crevice. A turf seat under sweetly scented jasmine is typically medieval.

The soil here is poor and stony, but in raised hurdle beds pumpkins thrive; hollowed-out pumpkins were used as bottles. A persimmon tree (from Elena's grandmother's time) is girdled with myosotis. All the other trees – pears, prunus, white mulberry – were common in the Middle Ages, including the apple 'Rosa Romano', an ancient cultivar grown in Pompeii. In the vegetable garden there are cabbages and *cavalo nero*. The last beds hold plants used for dyeing. A pergola of white currants and apples, lined with a box hedge, comes from an illustration in a book of hours.

The *hortus conclusus*, centred on a white marble fountain, pays tribute to Boccaccio, while echoing the medieval idea of a paradise garden. From the central white fountain run four paths, representing the four rivers of paradise. White roses and deep red (Damask) roses symbolize the grace of Christ and the blood of the martyrs. The garden is scented by

bergamot, *Citrus × aurantium* (Sour Orange Group) 'Bouquet', brought back by the Crusaders. Donna Elena has designed a pergola like those pictured in medieval manuscripts, underplanted with wild strawberries and entwined with roses and grapes – all the different varieties that grow in Lazio.

Donna Elena's design for the *herbularius* (herb garden) is based on parts of a map of AD 795 from the Benedictine Abbey of St Gallen in Switzerland. One bed contains umbellifers; another, cooking herbs. There are helenium and Jupiter's beard (*Anthyllis barba-jovis*) to stave off colds; a bed of melissa, marigolds and hollyhocks for treatment of the skin. The garden includes stachys, catmint and pinks, which provided calming tinctures; poisons (hellebores, digitalis, anemone and pulsatilla), which were used as medieval anaesthetics; astilbe, which worked like aspirin to bring down fevers; and horseradish, mint and rue, considered good for the digestion. Many of the seeds used here came from the Cluny Museum.

In medieval monasteries the *pomarium* (fruit orchard) was also used as the monks' graveyard. Here, old varieties of fruit trees have been planted. At the end of the garden, the Labyrinth, like those also seen in books of hours, was based on a design drawn to symbolize the castle in a new brochure. Going away, Donna Elena gave the brochure to her gardener's son, with the joking suggestion 'Copy that!' When she came back, he had.

Palazzo Patrizi

Palazzo Patrizi, near the volcanic lake of Bracciano north of Rome, is also known by its historic name of Castel Giuliano. Its surroundings have been inhabited since Etruscan times. Deep in its mysterious woods and hidden behind lush drifts of acanthus and curtains of ivy, Etruscan tombs are carved out of the side of the hill. Roman ruins, too, are scattered over this evocative landscape, along with an ancient iron works, all evidence of its long human habitation.

In the Middle Ages this was a stronghold of the Venturini family, Roman patricians. In the years that followed, the land was divided and parcelled out as dowries to other great families – the Chigi, Massimo and Orsini among them. After 1546 all these parcels were bought up and joined together again in one great estate by Giovanni Patrizi and his descendants, one of whom, Patrizio Patrizi, was granted a marquisate in 1635 by the Chigi pope, Alexander VII. So the Patrizi palace, with its rose and creeper-covered walls, is a largely seventeenth- and eighteenth-century building added on to a much older nucleus.

Castel Giuliano commands a strategic hill at the foot of the volcanic

Tolfa Mountains. Ancient paths used by hunters in search of boar criss-cross the wooded slopes; the hills are covered with sweet chestnut and Mediterranean flora such as oak and pine. In this antique and unchanged landscape, to make a garden with the qualities to blend in required an innate historic and artistic sensibility. Marchesa Umberta Patrizi, who with her husband restored the castle and its park after decades of neglect, rose magnificently to the challenge.

Roses are the marchesa's passion. Castel Giuliano is now one of the most important private rose gardens in Italy, a riot of scent and colour with hundreds of old roses crowding the borders and scrambling luxuriantly over the palace walls. The approach is naturalistic and harmonious with shrubs, herbs and perennials orchestrated to take up the theme when the roses bow out. The composition, though relaxed and informal, is underpinned by her immense knowledge of plants.

From the grassy courtyard, lawns slope gently away into the shadows cast by magnificent umbrella pines and cedars. To one side, the differing blues of teuchrium, rue, campanula and pale ceanothus flower with

white spiraea, silver elaeagnus and graceful *Exochorda* × *macrantha* 'The Bride'. Further on, against a stone wall, the creamy shades of the English roses **Winchester Cathedral** and **Saint Cecilia** combine with the floribunda 'Apricot Nectar', growing among the tall spires of apricot-coloured foxgloves.

In an enclosed courtyard garden, crimson is trimmed with grey like a major-general's coat, as the red roses 'Wilhelm' and **Benvenuto** glow against *Stachys byzantina*. The deep purple clematis 'The President' adds a dusky note, and white foxgloves and the snowy blooms of *Hydrangea quercifolia* gleam in contrast.

On the very left of the garden is the butterfly garden, where steps lead down a sunny slope planted with tumbling roses, banks of cistus, oleander, pink oenothera and aromatic herbs. The effect is of sweet disorder and, in places, of a naturally flowering hillside. Fragrant shrubs attract the butterflies which hover overhead.

Almost English in its romantic profusion, Palazzo Patrizi's garden is a country garden of a kind rarely found in Italy. Swifts wheel and dive around the roofs of the old buildings. There are views out to the green hills and the heady scent of roses in the sunlight. In the cool of the woods, the ground is strewn with giant pine cones.

The Rose Festival held in early May attracts the best nurseries and rose-growers from throughout Italy. The palazzo's gardens are open to the public and the marchesa's prized roses are at their peak.

Opposite Box domes in the courtyard garden.
Above, left *Rosa* 'Paul's Scarlet Climber'.
Above, right Acanthus surrounds the entrance to an Etruscan tomb in the woods.

Il Palazzo del Quirinale

The palace was home to popes, and then kings, and is now the residence of the President of the Italian Republic. It sits astride the Quirinal Hill, described by John Evelyn as 'most excellent for ayre and prospect'. The cool air on the summit had attracted refugees from the humidity and stench of the narrow streets round the Tiber since Roman times. Part of the mosaic floor of a villa has been found in the Quirinale gardens, along with many other Roman remains.

From the 1550s Cardinal Ippolito d'Este rented a small villa here belonging to the Neapolitan Carafa family, while his own monumental project at Tivoli was being developed. As late as 1580 Michel de Montaigne, who had visited Monte Cavallo, as the hill was also known, was describing the gardens there belonging to Cardinal d'Este as some of the most beautiful in Rome. Such a fine hilltop retreat seems to have attracted papal attention. Both Pius IV (who was a Carafa) and Gregory XIII, who was in search of a papal retreat away from the low-lying and unhealthy Vatican, seem to have spent summers enjoying the health-giving breezes and 'perfectly pure air' of the Quirinale. However, it was not until the papacy of Sixtus V (1585–90) – who with his architect Domenico Fontana carried out an extensive public works programme in Rome – that the villa came to the Holy See and the Quirinale estate became an official papal residence. This was to last until 1870 and the birth of the Kingdom of Italy.

Successive popes put their stamp on the huge palace, employing the best craftsmen and most favoured architects of the day. Domenico Fontana was responsible for the spacious Piazza del Quirinale and for erecting there the massive antique marble statues of the horse tamers (representing Castor and Pollux), which are traditionally said to have adorned the Baths of Constantine. Fontana was followed in time by Carlo Maderno and later still by Gian Lorenzo Bernini. The hydraulic Organ Fountain, 'refreshed with water music', said John Evelyn, is set in a grotto below the palazzo and visible from the terrace where popes have traditionally taken the air. It is generally attributed to Maderno.

In 1644 John Evelyn visited the palace again and 'now saw the garden more exactly'. He observed high hedges of myrtle 'above a man's height; others of laurel, oranges, nay, of ivy and juniper'. He also admired a 'vast, entire antique porphyry' basin from which flowed 'a plentiful cascade', and a grotto roofed with rich mosaic work. Evelyn considered the garden 'one of the most magnificent and pleasant in Rome. I am told the gardener is annually allowed 2000 *scudi* for the keeping of it.'

The 1683 engravings by G. Falda show a geometric layout of around sixty square parterres. Avenues of cypress dissect the parterre, and garden rooms, some of them thickly planted, are visible. This rectilinear plan survived almost unchanged until the nineteenth century, when a broad central avenue, dominated by a fountain, divided the garden. Today, in the Italian Garden, the box and laurel hedges have grown to create *allées* of dappled shade, opening out into enclosed, gravelled *salotti* (salons), where whispered conversations took place and musicians played. Stone benches line the walks, and statues, many from the collection of the Cibo family, depict artisans, satirical images and figures from the *commedia*

Left Giochi d'acqua surprise the unwary visitor.

Left The Palm Avenue contains some of Il Quirinale's renowned collection of palms and cycads.

dell'arte. The American writer Charles Platt, visiting the garden in the 1880s, admired the wonderful effect obtained by 'courts connected by long alleys, . . . with the doorways and arches apparently carved in the dense green . . . To one who doubts the advantage of straight lines in gardening, the extreme beauty of the perspective in the Quirinal would teach much.'

The Palm Avenue contains some of the Quirinale's renowned collection of palms and cycads, many of them hundreds of years old. Forty-three species of palms grow here, some dating back to the eighteenth century. Unfortunately, during the snowy winter of 1985, several had to be replaced. Of the cycad collection, one of the most important in Europe, virtually all the plants are female: the sole male, distinguishable by its slender, torpedo-shaped cone, is near the end of the avenue on the left.

The English Garden was the favoured recreation area of the Savoy royal family, who exercised their horses in the still visible manège, while the Savoy princes played tennis under the 300-year-old plane tree, one of the oldest in Italy. In this part of the garden, shaded by towering palms and pines, are displayed the numerous Roman sarcophagi found on site.

In front of the handsome, white, eighteenth-century Kaffeehaus, its roof lined with classical busts, is a pool containing a white marble statue group from the royal gardens at Caserta (see page 216). Colourful bedding surrounds the pool and, among the magnolias, araucarias, palms and pines, marble statues on pedestals are liberally placed around.

After many centuries of rich and powerful owners, all of whom were determined to leave their mark, the garden, not surprisingly, lacks coherence. An open-air museum reflecting the tastes of successive popes, it is dotted with busts and statues, overflowing with fountains, and brimful

of urns, including vases emblazoned with the coat of arms of Savoy. An arboretum of specimen trees contains many presented from abroad, including an olive given to the President of Italy by Yasser Arafat.

Above Palms cast magical shadows along the avenue.
Below, left Among the statues is a white marble group from the royal gardens of Caserta.
Below, right Busts and statues reflecting the tastes of successive popes line the paths in this open-air museum.

Giardini Vaticani

To visit the Vatican Gardens, it used to be necessary to proffer a letter of introduction from a cardinal, which was then inspected and stamped by the Vatican major-domo. Nowadays, guided tours are organized by the Vatican City Information Office for Pilgrims and Tourists. The Vatican's massive, bulwarked walls conceal 23 hectares/57 acres of green space, covering nearly all of the hill behind the Vatican Palace and the Basilica of St Peter. This cultivated hillside has provided a retreat and a place of exercise and meditation for popes since the Middle Ages. Yet only an inviting glimpse of the umbrella pines rising above the Vatican's high walls hints at the garden's presence.

In the ninth century, after a Saracen attack in which gold and silver was looted from the basilica, Pope Leo IV enclosed the undefended church with his Leonine walls. However, it was not until 1279 that the Orsini pope, Nicholas III, a Roman aristocrat, adopted the Vatican as his permanent residence. Having settled here, he planted an orchard and a lawn and enclosed this cultivated area with walls – later swept away. Nicholas III's successor, Pope Nicholas IV, added a garden of simples (medicinal herbs) to the *orto*. There is still a kitchen garden here, worked by Carmelite nuns and providing vegetables, salads and herbs for the Pope's table.

The libertine pope, inappropriately named Innocent VIII (1484–92), retreated from the Vatican to a private villa he built on top of the Vatican Hill. Its name, Villa Belvedere, was a tribute to its sweeping views. Among Innocent's cardinals was the formidable Giuliano della

Rovere, described even then as 'Pope and more than Pope'. In 1503 he would be elected to the papacy and earn the sobriquet Il Papa Terribile or the Warrior Pope.

Warlike and forceful though Julius II undoubtedly was, his name resounds through history as a sponsor of the arts, instigator of the Sistine Chapel, friend to Michelangelo, supporter of Raphael and, in the Vatican Gardens, far-seeing patron to Bramante. Under Julius's patronage, Rome experienced a flurry of magnificent projects, including the great scheme to rebuild St Peter's. The city was to be re-established in direct succession to the Roman Empire and as the centre of the Christian world.

Donato Bramante, Julius's preferred architect, came from near Urbino and initially trained as a painter. Vasari tells us that, having come to Rome in 1499, he spent the next years working 'in solitude and contemplation, examining and measuring the Roman ruins in and around the city'. This familiarity with classical form would bear fruit in Bramante's 1504 design for the Cortile del Belvedere (Belvedere Court). The court was to be a private pleasure garden commissioned by Pope Julius to house his classical sculpture collection, as well as to link the Vatican Palace to Innocent VIII's hilltop Belvedere villa. The *Apollo Belvedere*, now in the Vatican Museum, stood here, as did the magnificent

Above It is said that that Michelangelo designed the mighty dome of St Peter's to be seen from the Vatican's gardens.

classical marble *Laocoön and his Sons*. A giant bronze pine cone and two bronze peacocks from Emperor Hadrian's garden still adorn the steps of the Belvedere villa. At a time when garden design was little advanced from the flat medieval *hortus conclusus*, Bramante's scheme, with its strong central axis and changes in height achieved by ramps and staircases linking terraces, evoked the symmetry, proportion and scale of classical architecture. Moreover, it found a new and innovative style within it. On a difficult and uneven site, he introduced the depth and perspective then being seen in Renaissance painting, and achieved a unity of concept that would reverberate across Europe, influencing garden architecture for centuries to come. The Belvedere Court was the first and most influential of Rome's High Renaissance gardens, and stands out as a milestone in the history and development of gardens. Its perspective was destroyed when Sixtus V built the Vatican Library over part of it. Some of it can be seen, sadly diminished and used as a car park, during a visit to the Vatican Museums.

It is said that Michelangelo designed his mighty dome of St Peter's to be seen from the Vatican's gardens. Suspended like a great lantern against the sky, it soars over the green, tree-studded lawns, dominating the skyline and bringing unity to the gardens' eclectic mix of styles, objects and periods. Within their walled confines, the Vatican Gardens have seen individual gardens started, buildings and fountains added, and constant alterations made over centuries of different popes. The faithful have added to the mix: there is a Chinese pavilion presented by Chinese Catholics and a copy of the Grotto of Lourdes, a gift from the French. A fragment of the Berlin Wall is here, as is a gnarled and ancient olive, a transplant from Gethsemane. A rose garden and an Italian garden, laid out in the curving *broderie* of the French style, sit alongside an English garden and a 1.75 hectare/4 acre wood. There is even a piece of the Polish mountainside where Pope John Paul II loved to climb. Jutting up from the Leonine wall is the ninth-century Tower of St John, which Pope John XXIII restored as a peaceful retreat in which to work: it is now used as lodging for important guests. In front of the administrative building, the Governor's Palace, the reigning pope's arms are laid out in a parterre of brilliantly hued bedding.

Among the many fountains is the baroque Fontana dell'Aquilone (Fountain of the Eagle), the gift of the Borghese Pope Paul V (1605–21)

to celebrate his restoration of Trajan's aqueduct bringing water from Lake Bracciano to Rome. Thirty water jets spout from its mossy surface and from the mouths of Borghese dragons, while waterfalls pour cascades of sparkling water down the tufa rocks. An eagle – another reference to the Borghese arms – perches, wings proudly outstretched, on top.

The jewel of the gardens is Villa Pia, the exquisite Renaissance garden retreat built by the humanist Pope Pius IV, who in its decoration brought classical iconography and imagery into the service of his faith. Pope Pius's casino was completed by Pirro Ligorio between 1560 and 1562. Ligorio, who had already masterminded the garden at Villa d'Este (see page 201) for Cardinal Ippolito d'Este, was an erudite and enthusiastic antiquarian, who supervised the excavation of Hadrian's Villa and was the author of a famous map of ancient Rome. The casino complex consisted of two pavilions, one an open-sided loggia, connected by a graceful oval courtyard with a fine marble patterned floor. Pools and the sound of water surround the loggia. Against its exterior wall, in the sunken, eighteenth-century piazza where tour groups stand and marvel, the goddess Cybele presides in a niche above the water, in a scene reminiscent of the nymphaeum-pavilions of ancient Rome. Flanking the statue of Cybele are brightly coloured mosaics illustrating fish, fruit and fowl, entwined in sinuously curving branches of leaves. The mosaics are not original and were probably done by the Vatican School of Mosaics during a restoration of the nineteenth century. An engraving by G. Falda dated 1683 shows parterres in star shapes radiating out from the casino; these have long disappeared.

Pius IV, a gregarious and open-minded pontiff, held scholarly discussions in the casino with the intellectuals of the day, his close advisor Cardinal Carlo Borromeo among them. Ligorio's Villa Pia remains the earliest and perhaps the most beautiful example of a garden pavilion. It was swiftly emulated, first by Cardinal Alessandro Farnese at Caprarola (see page 180) and then by many other garden architects.

Above, left The Italian Garden, laid out in curving *broderie* in the French style.
Above, right Mosaics decorate the Renaissance garden pavilion built by Pope Pius IV.

Villa Giulia

The Villa Giulia, or Villa di Papa Giulio, a sober Renaissance edifice now suffering the indignity of facing on to a busy road, was once the centre of a large papal estate with famous gardens and extensive vineyards stretching down to the Tiber. A private landing stage awaited the papal parties who sailed expectantly up river from the Vatican in flower-decked boats. A long *allée* led them to the villa.

In 1552 Pope Julius III had begun to transform the country property he had inherited into a pleasure pavilion designed for lavish papal entertaining. His villa's position just outside the city walls made it ideally suited for days spent in luxurious ease with favoured guests, or evening banquets with dancers and lute-playing minstrels. The threat of malaria may have made it unwise to linger longer there.

As a result Villa Giulia is not the substantial country house it would appear: in fact, it is not much more than a façade, fronting the graceful horseshoe-shaped colonnade that encircles its first courtyard. These colonnaded arms in turn link up with the porticoed screen dividing the courtyard from the famous nymphaeum beyond. A masterly interplay of spaces, the casino is also a supreme example of the interlocking between house and garden which characterized the Renaissance villa.

Pope Julius not only had a musical ear – he brought Palestrina to Rome and made him his Maestro di Capella – he was also a renowned connoisseur, who came to be remembered far more gratefully by art lovers than by theologians or church historians. Among his favourite architects was Jacopo Barozzi da Vignola, who had worked for François I at Fontainebleau and would a few years later be responsible for Caprarola (see page 180). John Shepherd and Geoffrey Jellicoe, whose masterful study of *Italian Renaissance Gardens* was first published in 1925, considered that Vignola stood alone – for his freshness, his grace, and his combination of superb technique with a shrewd understanding of human nature.

He may well have needed this quality when it came to Villa Giulia. Pope Julius, who was not above offering direct and knowledgeable advice himself, had assembled a galaxy of talent: four of the pre-eminent architects of the day. Vignola worked alongside the Florentine Bartolomeo Ammanati, while Vasari, in his *Lives of the Artists*, gave himself the major credit; Michelangelo was on hand with yet more guidance.

The result is a masterpiece of small-scale grandeur, from the frescoed, vaulted colonnade abutting the refined Mannerist screen to the theatrical semicircular nymphaeum, the heart of the villa complex. Like the Roman sunken gardens on which it was based, the nymphaeum, with its refreshing fountain, cool, ferny recesses and reclining river gods, was intended as a refuge for alfresco dining out of the heat of the Roman sun. On its floor, an exquisite classical mosaic depicting a squid and a sea satyr continues the watery theme. Sir George Sitwell, an Edwardian visitor to the villa, imagined dining 'in a watery saloon, surrounded by running streams and bubbling fountains . . . part mossy cave, part treasury of sculpture, part house, and yet part garden as well'.

The villa now houses the National Etruscan Museum. There is a simple modern garden alongside it.

Right Vignola and Vasari worked on the Villa Giulia with guidance from Michelangelo.

Villa Madama

Villa Madama's period of glory was brief, but its influence was far-reaching. On the wooded slopes of Monte Mario, Cardinal Guilio de' Medici, illegitimate son of the murdered Giuliano, set out to build a palace – 'the best and most beautiful that could be desired', Vasari tells us.

The setting was superb, sited beside a spring and with views across the *campagna* to the Tiber. The architect was no other than Raphael, gifted, like his Renaissance contemporaries, in several disciplines. Yet both the house and the project were fated. Villa Madama (its name comes from Margherita, illegitimate daughter of the Emperor Charles V) remains, in Edith Wharton's words, 'Raphael's unfinished masterpiece'.

The drawings now in the Uffizi envisaged a four-square villa built around a great open courtyard. From here, four exits were to lead to different areas of the garden: on one side there was to be a loggia giving on to a series of terraced gardens; on another, an amphitheatre which was to be dug out of the hill. With the living accommodation squeezed to the sides, this, with its linked courts and loggias, was to be a garden house to entertain in, albeit one of a vast size. And if the scale was that of Rome, the rural setting and views were redolent of Florence. Young Giulio, after his father's death, had been taken into the household of Lorenzo, his uncle. He must have whiled away his youthful summers at various Medicean villas in the Tuscan hills.

Of Raphael's glorious scheme only a wing remains. The curved brick wall built as part of the great round courtyard now serves as the villa's semicircular façade. In 1518 Raphael had entrusted the execution of his plans to Antonio Sangallo's family, aided by the artists Giulio Romano and Giovanni da Udine. When Raphael died unexpectedly in 1520, aged only thirty-seven, the two painters quarrelled – 'like madmen', we are told. Costs rose as the hillside site proved unstable. Then in 1527 came the Sack of Rome at the hands of Charles V's unpaid, mutinous Spanish mercenaries. The cardinal, now Pope Clement VII, watched helplessly from his refuge in Castel Sant'Angelo as smoke from his burning villa rose above the slopes of Monte Mario. Later he tried rebuilding but his heart was not in it. Of the glittering array of brilliant and talented young men who had dined at his table off gold plate, many had perished in the slaughter.

When Goethe visited Villa Madama, he enjoyed it as a picturesque ruin. Henry James thought it hauntingly melancholy, 'the shabbiest farmhouse with . . . dunghills on the old parterres'. Now, with the benefit of a partial restoration (guided by the Sangallos' drawings), the terraced hillside unfolds in a series of airy, green outdoor rooms, hanging dizzyingly over the stupendous view.

Leading out from the exquisitely frescoed loggia, the Giardino della Fontana is planted with a simple green parterre. Baccio Bandinelli's muscled sculpted giants guard the pedimented arch to the next garden. They are rare survivors of the looting in the Second World War: possibly they were too heavy to move. But the garden gets its name from Giovanni da Udine's celebrated Elephant Fountain, designed to commemorate Annone, the Indian elephant brought to Rome from Goa by a Portuguese ambassador in 1514. The animal lived first of all in the Belvedere Court and became a pet at the papal court. It took part in processions and was a favourite with the Roman crowds. When the elephant died after two years in the Eternal City, it was with a grieving pope by its side.

With Villa Madama, Raphael had consciously set out to rival the descriptions of villas in antiquity and Vitruvius' prescriptions for the best villa sites. The Romans too had thought nothing of vast landscaping projects, of turning hillsides into terraced gardens to take advantage of fine views. In the early sixteenth century Raphael was shown the rediscovered letter Pliny the Younger had written about his Tuscan garden. It described a 'hippodrome garden', a miniature version of the Hippodrome in Rome, the sort of playful conceit that Romans loved.

Pliny described the 'cool shadow' of the sheltering cypress trees contrasting with the 'open sunshine' of the inner circuits. He talked of grass lawns and box clipped into shape. He might have been admiring the peaceful green Hippodrome Garden at the Villa Madama today. Here, marble bowls of white tracheleospermum light up the dark cypress backdrop. On the right, the spires and cupolas of Rome appear and disappear through arches cut in the hedge.

Villa Madama's legacy was of a garden where indoors and outdoors met, where horizontal terraces cut into the hillside created a series of panoramic garden rooms. Villa Imperiale at Pesaro is one of the gardens that bear its imprint.

Now run by the Italian Foreign Ministry, Villa Madama is a retreat for visiting heads of state.

Opposite Looking out from the frescoed loggia across the simple green parterre of the Giardino della Fontana. Baccio Bandinelli's sculpted giants guard the pedimented arch into the next garden.
Above left Giovanni da Udine's Elephant Fountain.

Villa Medici

Villa Medici is the home of the Académie de France in Rome. Founded in 1666 by Louis XIV, the academy was moved to Villa Medici in 1803 by Napoleon. Its aim was to give young French artists an opportunity to study great works from the Renaissance or antiquity. The tradition continues today but includes students from other disciplines. 'I should . . . wish', wrote Henry James after his visit in January 1873, 'that one didn't have to be a Frenchman to come and live and dream and work at the Académie de France . . .' Villa Medici he considered 'perhaps on the whole the most enchanting place in Rome'.

Silhouetted against the Pincian Hill, Villa Medici is one of the landmarks of Rome. The Pincian Hill was recognized in Roman times as the Collis Hortulorum (Hill of Gardens), the most famous of these being the lavish garden of the late Republican historian Sallust. Sallust designed his gardens with architectural terracing and a domed nymphaeum, built over a natural spring, and paid for them with the spoils of a governorship in Africa. To the delight of eighteenth-century Grand Tourists, who were as interested in the classical landscape beneath their feet as they were in horticulture, Villa Medici incorporated part of Sallust's ancient pleasure garden.

Two other sixteenth-century cardinals owned the villa before Cardinal Ferdinando de' Medici bought it in 1576, by which time it had been enlarged and considerable sums had been spent beautifying the grounds and ensuring a water supply. Ferdinando, a cardinal at fifteen, was a voracious collector of antiquities; he wished his garden to provide a backdrop for his sculptures and other classical finds. As the garden writer Kirk Johnson has pointed out, Villa Medici was known more for its antiquities and its view over Rome than for the design of its gardens.

Shortly after acquiring the villa, the cardinal called on Bartolomeo Ammanati for advice. Within a few years the garden façade had been richly ornamented with classical friezes and reliefs. John Evelyn visited in 1644 and admired 'the whole of the outside of the *facciata* . . . encrusted with antique and rare basso-relievos and statues'. This style of decoration led to it being considered the most lavishly ornate villa in High Renaissance Rome.

In 1578 Cardinal de' Medici had bought Cardinal della Valle's sculpture collection, the most famous in Rome, which had been put together before the collection of antiquities had become a competitive pastime among the elite. In the centre of the cardinal's new loggia stood Giambologna's statue of Mercury; outside, against a side wall at the end of a walk, was the famous classical ensemble of Niobe and her children. Dug up in 1583, it was immediately purchased by the cardinal. This group of statues, described by Pliny the Elder as once decorating the Temple of Apollo Sosianus, now merits a special room in the Uffizi. The famous Medici Venus was part of the villa's collection too, until 1677, when Pope Innocent XI's concern about its indecency led to its being moved permanently to Florence. It was the French neo-classical painter Ingres, Director of the Académie from 1835 to 1840, who took it upon himself to commission copies of some of these missing works, helping to restore Villa Medici's garden façade to its former, richly ornate appearance. The cardinal also acquired an Egyptian obelisk, which had belonged to Rameses II. This, too, was taken to Florence and re-erected in the Boboli Gardens. It was replaced at Villa Medici by a nineteenth-century copy.

A 1614 engraving by J. Larus affords an early glimpse of the design of the garden, with its spacious courtyard balancing the villa, its wide central walk and its geometrical parterres. The garden was laid out according to a mathematical square grid, explains Giorgio Galletti, the landscape architect and expert on Medicean gardens who oversaw the restoration. This solution tallies with Cardinal Ferdinando's known fondness for cartography and mathematics. The geometrically aligned beds adjoining the courtyard housed a rare apothecary's garden of simples (medicinal herbs) and scented flowers: the green garden that replaced this is a nineteenth-century interpretation. In the *bosco*, prior to the restoration, overgrown hedges of viburnum, ilex and bay masked the shape of the original low parterre, and the herms that once stood here were obscured by untamed vegetation. Yet in Ferdinando's garden, this *bosco* was a carefully maintained, productive space: a bountiful *orto* can clearly be seen in the 1614 engraving.

Above The garden behind the villa is laid out according to a mathematical grid. The obelisk in the centre is a nineteenth-century copy of an Egyptian obelisk once owned by Rameses II.
Below A fresco decorates Ferdinando's private pavilion.

To the east of the parterre is a wall set with niches, supporting an upper *bosco* with views over the parterre and lower garden. A shady walk through leafy undergrowth of box and acanthus keeps pace on the right with a vista of the spires and cupolas of Rome. This was the 'little dusky forest of evergreen oaks,' so admired by Henry James, with its 'dim light as of a fabled, haunted place . . . At the end of the wood is a steep, circular mound, up which the short trees scramble . . . with a long mossy staircase climbing up to a belvedere.' John Evelyn, visiting Villa Medici for the second time in 1644, had described 'a mount planted with cypresses, representing a fortress'. This man-made hill or *montagnola* was built over the remains of a nymphaeum, once part of the Horti Aciliorum, a famous second-century garden on the Pincian Hill. Its remains could still be seen, according to John Dixon Hunt, until the late sixteenth century.

Today, the mount, which suffered greatly from erosion, has been restored and planted with holm oaks. Giorgio Galletti explains, 'You can prune holm oaks very successfully; we did not want to plant big trees.' The *montagnola*'s

spiral paths, which no doubt appealed to Ferdinando's love of geometry, have been replaced. Two herms stand guard at the foot of the steep steps.

The 1683 view of Villa Medici by G. Falda refers to this mount as a 'Mausoleo circondato di Cipressi'. One theory has linked it to the Mausoleum of Augustus near by, which was converted into a garden by the Soderini family, with trees growing on its slopes, as at Villa Medici. On the garden façade of Ferdinando's villa were placed garlands from the Ara Pacis, possibly symbolizing another link between the Medici and Augustus. In a further classical allusion, the *montagnola* may refer to Mount Parnassus, home to the Muses and source of learning and inspiration: this allegory was a fruitful one in Renaissance gardens. However, Giorgio Galletti warns that 'too much symbolism can be attached to a feature which was in itself very practical: the *montagnola* was also used for hunting birds.'

Ferdinando had a private retreat in the garden, which enabled him to enter and leave the grounds unobserved. In the north-east section and overlooking the Aurelian Wall, this little pavilion has been dated to 1576. However, its superb frescoes of the same date by Jacopo Zucchi were only rediscovered in 1985, concealed under a coat of whitewash. Zucchi's pergola of animals is based on Konrad von Gesner's *Historia animalium*, first published in 1551, which set out to make an inventory of all the animals known in the Renaissance; Gesner was thereafter known as 'the German Pliny'. Giorgio Galletti points out that there is nothing religious in the frescoes: the symbolism of Aurora rising could mean that this was a lovers' trysting place. Velázquez, who visited Villa Medici during the summer of 1630 because it had 'most excellent antique statues for him to copy', painted two landscape views of the pavilion, one, famously, with washing hanging out. This has given it its name, the Velázquez Loggia or Pavilion.

Studios for the *pensionnaires* were scattered throughout the garden and housed Boucher, Watteau and Fragonard as well as Bizet, Debussy and Berlioz. Manet, David and Degas all failed to become scholars, as did Ravel, despite trying five times. Balthus, like Ingres, served as Director of the Académie.

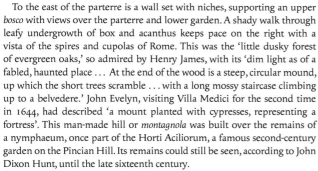

Above, left This steep circular mound – or *montagnola* – with a long mossy staircase climbing up to a belvedere, is built over the remains of a Roman nymphaeum.
Above, right Parnassus with attendant Muses and the winged horse Pegasus.
Left Jacopo Zucchi's fresco of a pergola with perching animals and birds.

Villa Wolkonsky

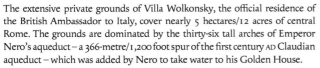

The extensive private grounds of Villa Wolkonsky, the official residence of the British Ambassador to Italy, cover nearly 5 hectares/12 acres of central Rome. The grounds are dominated by the thirty-six tall arches of Emperor Nero's aqueduct – a 366-metre/1,200 foot spur of the first century AD Claudian aqueduct – which was added by Nero to take water to his Golden House.

The garden's framework is provided by the aqueduct and by a towering canopy of magnificent trees. Underneath, in the thick undergrowth of acanthus, Roman capitals and bas-relief fragments lie scattered around. Marble hands, faces and chunks of Roman statuary stud the aqueduct's neat brickwork and resurrected Roman columns play host to showers of climbing roses.

This eclectic garden blends classical antiquity with English formality in the shape of garden rooms edged by formal hedging. And somewhere, among the luxuriantly tumbling roses, in the deep, cool grottoes and along the shady woodland walks, the romantic, free spirit of Princess Zenaide Wolkonsky, creator of the garden, still mysteriously survives.

Until 1830, when Princess Zenaide bought the plot of land here known as the Vigna Falcone, the area remained open countryside, given over to vineyards and pasture. A map of 1676 by G. Falda shows a few villas scattered sparsely over the Equiline Hill, while a modest house is lodged in one of the aqueduct bays. Princess Zenaide's views stretched across the timeless Roman *campagna* with its lines of aqueducts to the far-off Sabine and Alban Hills. Here, she would build her villa. 'What bliss', she had written, 'to be streaming towards Italy, to leave behind the cold winds . . . the sluggish nature of the north!'

Princess Zenaide came from a distinguished Russian family; her father was an ambassador in the service of Catherine the Great. She was born in 1789, a year of turbulence which seemed to be reflected in her impulsive, emotional and headstrong nature. Gifted, musical and beautiful, she became the mistress of the young Tsar Alexander I. Having converted to Catholicism, in her later years she became zealously religious, giving away money and even her clothes to help the poor. A biography of her by Maria Fairweather, herself an ambassador's wife who lived in Villa Wolkonsky, relates that she died of a chill in her seventies in 1862, having given her warm petticoat to a beggar woman she saw suffering in the winter cold.

Princess Wolkonsky repaired the crumbling aqueduct and in 1830 commissioned a Roman architect, Giovanni Azzurri, to build her a small summer villa, vaguely Renaissance in style, which fitted under three of the aqueduct arches. To her drawing room came visiting celebrities including Walter Scott, Stendhal and Donizetti. Gogol, a close friend, would lie for hours on her terrace on top of the aqueduct, contemplating the blue heavens as he plotted his novel *Dead Souls*.

Princess Wolkonsky laid out the garden with a romantic profusion of roses, her favourite flowers. An Allée des Memoires and an Allée des Morts commemorated in busts and stone tablets, and with inscriptions on ancient marbles, those she had loved, from Tsar Alexander to beloved household pets.

Zenaide's son, Alexander Wolkonsky, excavated some of the Roman tombs in the wooded, northern area of the property. The most famous, Claudio Vitale's family tomb, commemorates by inscription two architects, father and son, who may have worked on the aqueduct close by. Through Alexander Wolkonsky, Zenaide's property descended to the Campanari family, whose frequent sales of land enabled them to build a new, much grander house to the south of the original villa in 1890.

In 1922 the whole property was sold and the main villa enlarged to become the splendid residence of the German Ambassador. In 1947 the British took over, and during the next ten years restored Nero's aqueduct. Today, the garden is an orchestrated medley of scent and colour, beginning in early spring with camellias, hellebores, crocuses and daffodils, followed by mimosa and flowering cherries and then by the roses, peonies and cistus of summer. Among the garden's formal enclosures different rooms include a vegetable and cutting garden with sweet peas for the ambassador's table.

At the end of a path at the far end of the garden is a reconstructed *tempietto* with five columns and a conical roof. It shelters a white marble copy of a torso of Venus, donated by a former ambassador.

Above, left Emperor Nero's aqueduct runs through the grounds of Villa Wolkonsky.
Above, right Fragments of Roman statuary lie scattered in the thick undergrowth.

San Liberato

'I feel Russell Page on my shoulder,' says Claudio Palermo, the current custodian of the gardens at San Liberato.

From the lake shore road, the drive to San Liberato loops uphill. The planting, naturalistic at first, turns into an avenue with olives, oleander and banks of rosemary. You come to a halt in a little square in front of the pillared Romanesque church, sole survivor of what was once a Roman market town. Page smothered its fourth-century walls with pink valerian and climbing roses. In the courtyard, among the potted olive trees, stands a 260-year-old fig. Under an aged cypress, the lid of a Roman sarcophagus serves as a bench. Over the hedge in the distance sparkles Lake Bracciano, a volcanic crater lake. From this centuries-old and sacred place, Russell Page drew the inspiration for his garden.

His client was a discerning one. Count Sanminiatelli, a noted art historian, had sited his new house away from the church, higher up on a ledge in a natural amphitheatre hewn out of the chestnut woods. In this, he was following the precepts of the great Vignola, architect of Caprarola and Villa Giulia, who cautioned against building on top of a hill.

Having finished his 'simple' country house, Donato Sanminiatelli wanted a 'garden-park', integrated into the landscape. Searching for a

landscape designer of the right sensitivity, he came across the work of Russell Page. In 1964 Page paid his first visit to view the job. Tall and commanding – 'awe-inspiring', Contessa Sanminiatelli thought him – it was by no means certain that he would take it on. But he was instantly won over by San Liberato – by its tranquillity, its layers of history, the space it afforded him to plant in a grand style. The mineral-rich volcanic soil – 'something radioactive in the soil', Page called it – enabled the great trees he loved to grow at a stupendous rate. Returning fifteen years later, he found that the 1-metre/39-inch tulip tree (*Liriodendron tulipifera*) he had planted in 1964 was already 20 metres/66 feet tall.

Russell Page began near the church, where he created a *hortus conclusus* under two olive trees. A wash of mostly soft blues and greys – hebe, caryopteris, *Melianthus major*, ballota – gives it a monastic feel.

Two paths of stone taken from a Roman road lead across the grass down the main vista (framed by trees Page planted) in the direction of the lake. This lawn the Saniminiatelli had already created, levelling it out and

Above, left Russell Page created a *hortus conclusus* under two olive trees.
Above, right A shady path lined with bergenia.

building a maintaining wall. Beneath the wall, Page made a cutting rose garden for Maria Sanminiatelli – one of her expressed wishes, along with 'antique roses [and] a lane where my daughters, still little girls . . . could one day wander with their fiancés'.

In the beds Page planted around the lawn, Contessa Sanminiatelli's old roses clamber up olive trees. Low walls and steps of the local volcanic stone divide up the beds and add to the monastic ambience. The beds are edged with *Geranium × oxonianum* 'Wargrave Pink', *Iris germanica*, agapanthus, white and blue. Erigeron and campanula spill out of crevices. Stately *Crinum × powellii* peers through a gauzy veil of *Gaura lindheimeri*.

Further into the parkland are Russell Page's favourite bean-shaped beds, 'slightly curved', as he liked them, 'with a hump in the middle'. The whites and pinks of summer-flowering shrubs give way to the golds and russets of autumn. *Cercidiphyllum japonicum* is here, with *Parrotia persica* and *Amelanchier canadensis*.

With so many colourful deciduous trees, Page anchored the garden by planting a big conifer every 25 metres/82 feet. There is a magnolia grove and a cherry orchard. In the woodland garden, primulas and *Anemone blanda* are followed by camellias, azaleas, hydrangeas and kalmia – all flourishing in the acid soil. Conditions, however, are not easy. There is no frost in winter but in summer temperatures reach 40 degrees Centigrade. Yet Signor Palermo does not water much – 'You encourage fungi' – preferring to mulch with organic compost.

Page designed the ethereally romantic Viale Bianco especially for the Sanminiatelli women. Having worked closely with keen botanist Donato

Sanminiatelli, Page continued, after Donato's death in 1979, to advise and encourage his widow. They became firm friends, meeting, Maria Sanminiatelli remembers, in Rome to scour the ecclesiastical outfitters for Page's favoured purple socks.

In 1990 San Liberato was opened up to the public. It now hosts weddings and events to pay for the maintenance of the garden. While Russell Page's spirit still reigns here, and many of his notes for the garden survive, new projects including an Upper Arboretum and a Medici Fruit Garden keep San Liberato very much alive.

Above Gaura lindheimeri and *Crinum × powellii* grow in profusion.
Left Part of the garden's collection of palms and tree ferns.

Villa d'Este a Tivoli

The son of Alfonso I, 3rd Duke of Ferrara, and Lucrezia Borgia, Cardinal Ippolito d'Este was among the richest cardinals in Rome. As a younger son, going into the Church had been an inevitability for him. By the age of ten, he was titular Archbishop of Milan; at twenty-seven he was the family envoy to the court of François I of France. The French king, who looked on him as an adviser and a protégé, added to Ippolito's wealth by granting him rich abbeys. On his return from France, nothing seemed to stand between the cardinal – still only twenty-nine – and the papacy.

That he did not succeed in his great desire has been attributed to fear of his already ample power and of his overweening ambition. In 1550, Julius III, for whom Ippolito had voted in the papal conclave, offered him the governorship of Tivoli as compensation. At forty, the cardinal found himself removed from Rome, taking up residence in the ancient convent of St Mary Major. Immediately, he began the transformation of the convent into a palatial villa, a demonstration of his wealth and administrative skills as well, perhaps, as a salve to his frustrated ambitions.

A keen collector of antiquities, Ippolito would have appreciated the classical resonance of the Tiburtine landscape, where both Catullus and Horace had owned country villas, and where, in the second century AD, Hadrian had built his palatial imperial residence. The cardinal now instructed the antiquarian and archaeologist Pirro Ligorio to survey and excavate Hadrian's Villa. Later on, Ligorio would become superintendent of ancient monuments to Popes Paul IV and Pius IV. For now, his unearthing of mosaics and marbles from the classical site gave Cardinal Ippolito an unrivalled opportunity to enrich his collection. When Ligorio undertook the design of the garden at Villa d'Este in 1560, it would be intended as a frame for many of these marbles, and also informed by his study of Hadrian's Villa.

The garden was to be constructed on the steep hillside below the site of the monastery. It was intended to be entered from the bottom of the hill, where its full extent could awe visitors making the long climb up to the villa at the top. On each ascending terrace was a cross-view, providing the opportunity to display cleverly engineered and spectacular feats of water. Water, used extravagantly and scientifically, was the medium of the garden, the means by which its complex mix of iconography, allegory, family history, learning and personal glorification could be expressed. The garden was an example of a much-enjoyed Renaissance conundrum: the idea of nature tamed and sculpted into a man-made vision of beauty, which then, teasingly, set out to imitate nature.

The logistics involved in order to bring this about were immense. Much of Tivoli was destroyed; great rocks were excavated and moved, and earth was brought in to create the terraces. An aqueduct was built and when this proved inadequate, a tributary of the River Aniene was diverted and channelled. The cardinal shared some of the costs with the townspeople, who at least gained clean drinking water in their fountains. However, at some point the citizens of Tivoli revolted and the cardinal was prevented from further expropriations of property within the city walls. While in France, the cardinal had seen the latest hydraulic machines for powering waterworks. At his villa, French engineers such as Luc le Clerc worked alongside home-grown experts such as Tommaso Ghinucci and the experienced Roman fountain-builder Curzio Maccarone. Another Frenchman, Claude Venard, was responsible, with le Clerc, for the famous Organ Fountain. Such was their ingenuity that 12.25-metre/40-foot jets of water were operated through natural pressure, while all the fountains in the garden could work simultaneously without the benefit of a pump. There is one now.

A principal iconographical theme of the garden is the link between the d'Este family and Hercules – from whom, both literally and metaphorically through his association with strength and power, the d'Este claimed to trace their lineage. Hercules, giant-sized, was portrayed in the Fountain of the Dragons placed at the main axis of the garden, where his statue stood in a niche under the double staircase. The fountain depicted the eleventh

Above, left A sphinx sits in front of the Avenue of the Hundred Fountains.
Above, right The Fountain of Tivoli (also known as the Oval Fountain).

labour of Hercules in which he had to steal the golden apples guarded by the hundred-headed dragon Ladus. In his poems, the cardinal's friend Marc Antoine Muret, a French humanist and one of the best Latin prose stylists of the Renaissance, revealed much about the symbolism of the garden. 'The apples that Hercules won from the sleeping dragon', he wrote, 'Hippolyte now possesses. In memory of this, he desired these gardens to be dedicated to the donor of the gift.'

Apples of the Hesperides also appear in the Fountain of the Owl. John Evelyn, visiting a century later, was delighted with both fountains. He appreciated the dragons 'casting out large streams of water with great noise . . . In another garden is a noble aviary, the birds artificial, and singing till an owl appears, on which they suddenly change their notes.' The Fountain of the Owl must have been one of the wonders of the garden, its water-automated birds chirping their hearts out on delicate copper branches until interrupted by the hooting of the owl. The golden apples can be seen on the pilasters, entwined with vines.

The elaborate baroque portico, guarded by gigantic herms, which protects the Organ Fountain, dates from 1611 and was the intervention of Cardinal Alessandro d'Este. The fountain itself, begun in 1568, used water rushing into a cavity to propel air from the organ pipes. The idea was based on descriptions given by the first-century BC architect and engineer Vitruvius. The water organ has been restored and once again plays its surprisingly harmonious music.

The Fountain of the Organ stands behind the spectacular Neptune Fountain, with its giant statue of Neptune presiding behind a curtain of water in a niche. In 1661 Bernini designed the central cascade but the fountain that we see today is the result of additional powerful jets of water added in 1927. The roaring water shoots up and cascades down in a silvery haze in which hangs an ever-present rainbow.

The most romantic part of the garden is the murmuring wall of the Avenue of the Hundred Fountains, running between the Tivoli Fountain and the Fountain of the Rometta, and half-shaded by light filtered through overhanging trees. At 130 metres/426 feet long, the fountain avenue took the cardinal's men five years to construct between 1565 and 1570. In three tiers, jets spurt upwards and fall into three narrow canals, symbolizing the three local rivers, the Albuneo, Erculaneo and Aniene. The top level is ornamented with miniature stone boats and the d'Este fleur-de-lis and eagles. Above the central canal, terracotta bas-reliefs inspired by Ovid's *Metamorphoses* once alluded to the garden's theme of transmutation. Neglected, they have crumbled into ruin behind a covering of moss and maidenhair ferns. In a display of humour and ingenuity which has never failed to delight the public, water shoots out of the mouths of zoomorphic masks.

The Fountain of Tivoli (Oval Fountain) and the Fountain of the Rometta represent the dichotomy of Rome and Tivoli in the garden. The natural beauty of Tivoli, symbolized by the fountain representing its great waterfall, is balanced, at the other end of the avenue, by the artificial beauty of the monuments of Rome. A horse stands for Tivoli; a lion for its rival, Rome. The cardinal may have been recalling the sentiments of Horace: 'When in Rome, I love Tivoli, fickle as I am; when at Tivoli, I love Rome.' Nevertheless, the Rometta Fountain has a decided poignancy in that it is a reminder of Ippolito's thwarted ambition. Pirro Ligorio designed for him a semicircular landscape of the city of Rome, its temples, palaces and seats of power reproduced in miniature over seven little hills. This had to be the cardinal's consolation prize.

In Ippolito's time, any colour in the garden would have come from the coloured marbles he appropriated – blue, green and purest white marble from North Africa. Nowadays the Italian state, which owns and runs the garden, has added modern planting. Pale pink roses tumble out of pots; old roses cover the walls in a gentle mix of creams and whites. Zantedeschia surrounds some of the pools and santolina is clipped into neat, geometric blocks. In the courtyard of the Fountain of the Egg, fruit trees, pots of agapanthus and irises grow with hostas and rounds of box. It is all carefully orchestrated and manages not to be distracting.

Above, left The elaborate and intriguing Avenue of the Hundred Fountains.
Above, right Water pours from the many bosoms of Diana of Ephesus, a sixteenth-century copy of a classical statue.

Parco Villa Gregoriana

This famous, ancient landscape with its rocks, caves, streams, foaming waterfalls and plunging, tree-covered slopes has been enjoyed since Roman times. Horace dreamed of spending a peaceful old age here, gazing across at the temples of Sibyl and Vesta – which survive to this day, still clinging to the brink of a precipitous cliff. A seventeenth-century engraving by G. Volpi imagines the poet's view.

A first-century Roman and father of a consul, Manlius Vopiscus, built his sprawling villa here amidst 'the ancient sacred woods'. The Roman poet Papinius Statius described it admiringly in AD 92, purring over its coloured marbles, gilded architraves, rare and precious objects, and fountains in every room. The ruins of this ancient building, crumbled into the dust of centuries, are the closest Gregoriana has to a villa.

In the eighteenth century, the 'terrible beauty' of the River Aniene gorge and waterfalls made it a place to visit on the Grand Tour. Adventurous young travellers let themselves down on ropes to peer into the mysterious grottoes; others, not so intrepid, amused themselves picnicking on the acropolis within the 'round and lovely' first century BC Temple of Vesta.

Such a profoundly romantic scene was bound to influence eighteenth-century artists and writers. 'High upon that steep, the Sibyl's mouldering Temple', Wordsworth described it. Landscape gardeners, too, adopted the template, with many an eighteenth-century picturesque landscape gaining a dramatically sited temple.

The Middle Ages saw watermills hard at work in the gorge, with vineyards planted on the eastern slopes. The mills were fed by channels that Tivoli's inhabitants, from Roman times on, had burrowed out of the fragile calcareous rock in an attempt to divert the water where it was needed, and to protect their town from flooding. The danger from unpredictable flash floods was a real one, given Tivoli's location on the rim of an unstable cliff at the very point where the Aniene plummeted into the ravine, carrying water from the mountains to join the River Tiber. Pliny the Younger described such a disaster in AD 105, when the flood 'split open the hills', bearing away houses, ploughs, even herds of oxen, in the torrent.

In 1809 Napoleon's Governor of Rome, General Miollis, excavated the gallery cut through the rock which bears his name, creating a tunnelled walk, lit by openings from which to admire the views. This opened up access to Villa Gregoriana's 'romantic crater'.

Miollis's intervention came shortly before another disastrous flood in 1826, when, once again, many inhabitants of Tivoli perished. However, this time the tragedy prompted intervention by the Pope himself. Pope Gregory XVI, a dyed-in-the-wool conservative who banned railways within the Papal States, was nevertheless an enthusiast for architecture. He co-opted French engineers to transform the gorge in 1835. By digging a capacious new tunnel through the mountain, they diverted the waters to create the majestic sight of the 180 metre/590 foot drop of the Great Cascade, which pours its thunderous torrents over the lip of the cliff well away from Tivoli.

Right, above The Temple of Vesta, dating from the first century BC, is perched on the brink of the steep cliff.
Right, below A waterfall cascades over the rocks as it rushes through the gorge.

For his time, Pope Gregory's ideas on this at least seem radical. They included not only taming the river but creating a Tiburtine landscape park out of this wild and rocky place. Its steeply sloping paths skirted crags, disappeared into tunnels and linked the grottoes, enabling the public to enjoy, with a shiver, what a nineteenth-century guide to Tivoli called 'this terrible yet delightful place'.

When Fondo per L'Ambiente Italiano (FAI) rediscovered it in 2002, Pope Gregory's landscape park was forgotten and neglected, its clear streams contaminated and malodorous, its rocks blackened by pollution, its paths blocked by landslides and choked by weeds. Pope Gregory's 'gentle and strong trees' – cypress, pine and box – were dead or swept away. From the bottom of the ravine, FAI took out five tons of rubbish. Crashed cars, ancient washing machines and discarded fridges were brought up by divers and floated away down the river for disposal. Climbers secured by ropes set to work to scrub the rocks by hand. The project took five years of research and eighteen months of hard labour. Public subscription targeted certain works; the rest of the money came from the bank Unicredit and the Province of Rome. With the help of FAI's stalwart membership, a disaster was transformed into a destination.

FAI's next project is to replace the 'lovely evergreens' with which the far-seeing pope adorned his park, taking care, as with a cypress wood marking a burial ground, 'to give the impression that they had grown there spontaneously'. It will have the benefit of records preserved in the Vatican, which pinpoint the original location of every tree.

Top A tunnelled walk lit by openings enables the visitor to enjoy what a nineteenth-century guide called 'this terrible yet delightful place'.
Bottom Rocky steps link the steep and winding paths which run throughout these restored 'ancient sacred woods'.

Parco di Villa Belvedere Aldobrandini

Frascati, or in classical times Tusculum, home to Cicero and Lucullus, witnessed an explosion of house building from around 1550 to 1620. John Raymond, a mid-seventeenth-century English visitor, counted ten cardinals with country homes there, taking advantage of the fresher air and magnificent views across the *campagna* to Rome. The Frascati villas soon became a tourist attraction, and were pictured in contemporary engravings.

Of them, Villa Aldobrandini was by far the best known. It was set in the most dominant position, as befitted its owner, Cardinal Pietro Aldobrandini, nephew of the Aldobrandini pope, Clement VIII. This pope had an affection for Frascati, which did much to turn it into the fashionable resort it became. As pope, Clement VIII was unable to buy the villa for himself, and he therefore gifted it to his nephew with funds from the Reverenda Camera Apostolica, the central board of finance in the papal administrative system. Cardinal Pietro then paid out of his own pocket for the renovations to both the villa and his garden.

One of the cardinal's first steps was to buy the neighbouring estate: 'That both from the front and from the sides, from the south and from the east, there be no one who commands or looks into my property; on the contrary that from all places I be the higher as I am now.'

In 1598 Giacomo della Porta, pupil of Vignola, began to enlarge the existing modest villa. He died in Rome in 1602 before his plan – a unified scheme for an imposing palace set off by a dramatic garden cutting a dash on the hill behind – could be carried out. The architect Carlo Maderno took over and, in all its essential details, followed della Porta's design. The towering villa, anchored to its magnificent setting by wide terraces and huge curving ramps, was intended to speak of papal glory and Aldobrandini power: the cardinal was also Secretary of State for the Vatican. No matter that this commanding structure was only two rooms deep and more of a summer pavilion than a permanent residence; its distant views and vast horizons were meant to call to mind the long reach of the See of Rome.

The scheme for the garden was ambitious, and work on it continued till 1620. To help engineer the innovative waterworks, Maderno drafted in both his uncle, Giovanni Fontana, and the curator of the fountains at the Villa d'Este, Orazio Olivieri. So keen was the cardinal to eclipse his clerical and princely rivals that a draughtsman was despatched to sketch features from Villa Lante, Villa d'Este and Pratolino.

The result, rising up the hillside, was an extraordinarily fine water garden and one that differed from previous Renaissance gardens with their harmonious, interlinked terraces, Arcadian aspirations and sense of individual discovery and enjoyment. Here, the garden was at the back: the best and most dramatic view of it was from the cardinal's own first-floor window. It all pointed to a new way of thinking, in which one man's power and authority visibly dominated his surroundings. To impress their contemporaries further, Maderno devised for the cardinal an array of water displays, tricks, novelties and surprises, some of them borrowed from other gardens. Geoffrey Jellicoe considered Aldobrandini as welding 'all other gardens into practically one scheme'. Edith Wharton was quick to recognize the first flamboyant stirrings of the baroque style.

By 1604, with most of the fountains already built, the problem for this new garden in the bone-dry landscape of Frascati was one of water supply.

Among the splendid villas of the papal nobility, there was by now urgent competition for sufficient water. In 1601, Cardinal Aldobrandini seems to have appropriated a spring that fed into the Altemps family property. Altercations ensued until an official act of purchase – to which Clement VIII is said to have contributed – resulted in the building of an aqueduct over 8 kilometres/5 miles long. By 1605 the cardinal's aqueduct was flowing with water to supply his garden.

Even now, with its pools empty and most of its fountains stilled, the central feature of the garden is still the great semicircular water theatre. Carved out of the hill behind the villa, it was considered by Edith Wharton to be too close to the house. She found no sympathetic correlation between the two very different architectural styles: the first consciously classical, echoing Vignola's nymphaeum at Villa Giulia in Rome (see page 193), the

Above Part of the great semicircular baroque water theatre behind the villa.

second, thought Wharton, curious and fantastical – more like Strawberry Hill gothic than seventeenth-century Italian. Others, though, have seized upon such differences as part of the drama and tension of the baroque.

If today it has a melancholy air, let us imagine the water garden as it was when John Evelyn 'tooke coach' there in May 1645. Through a narrow cleft in the steeply wooded hillside, the water cannoned down in a series of rills and falls. It dashed down water staircases; it swirled in garlands down the mosaiced sides of the Pillars of Hercules. It disappeared and then re-emerged in the water theatre to envelop in mist mighty Atlas (representing Pope Clement) shouldering the world. In the stifling heat of a Roman summer, it must have been a spellbinding sight. Refreshing too: because of the quantity of water jokes, John Raymond reported that visitors like him 'must looke to goe away wet to the skinne'.

And there was more. In a room off the theatre, Evelyn famously described 'an artificial grot wherein are . . . all sorts of singing birds, moving and chirping by force of the water'. In a room full of such wonders, Evelyn seems to have enjoyed the noises most, writing of a monster 'making a terrible roaring' and the 'fury of raine, wind and Thunder'. Of all these marvellous water-driven automata nothing remains.

Villa Aldobrandini was damaged badly in the Second World War and has yet to see a full recovery. Relatively unvisited, it is a peaceful place to stroll, amongst the 'speckled mystery' of its great plane trees, planted in an allusion to the plane groves of the ancients. Just off the path through the woods of chestnut and oak leers a giant stone mouth, said to represent the entrance to Hades. It still has the ability to frighten unwary walkers.

Left Among the chestnuts and oaks leers a giant stone mouth, said to represent the entrance to Hades.

Giardini di Castel Gandolfo

Left Bonomelli's twentieth-century parterres overlook the Latium plain.

Since classical times the hot and weary citizens of Rome have escaped the sweltering city summer for the breezy Alban Hills, where Castel Gandolfo stands on the edge of a volcanic crater lake. In the first century AD the luxury-loving Emperor Domitian built a magnificent summer palace here between the lake and the Tyrrhenian Sea. Domitian's architect, the gifted Rabirius, who designed the Emperor's other splendid palace on the Palatine Hill, graded the slope to accommodate this colossal mansion on three levels. The highest level was the domain of the palace servants and housed vast water tanks storing spring water brought to the palace by three aqueducts. Parts of these aqueducts survive 2,000 years later, still carrying fresh water to Castel Gandolfo.

On the middle level stood the imperial palace itself, built of Orvieto stone and precious marbles from far-flung quarries throughout the Empire. Rabirius's architectural preference was for exceptional ceiling heights and innovative light effects. The insecure emperor added mirrors throughout his palaces in order to watch his own back. The summer palace was protected by a high wall set with four nymphaea. This walk, the Viale dei Ninfei, is now one of the central axes of the garden.

On the lowest level the still-intact *cryptoporticus*, a huge tunnel, was used by well-fed Romans to walk off their gargantuan meals. A hippodrome and an extensive park completed Domitian's palace, which he loved so much that he lived in it for most of the year.

Domitian's pleasure palace was abandoned after his death, though Hadrian roughed it here for a time while his own grand villa at Tivoli

was being completed. Gradually, through the centuries, the palace was ransacked, some of the most precious marbles making their way back to Orvieto, where they embellish the cathedral.

No records exist until the twelfth century, when the Gandolfi built the massive four-square fortress commanding the hill, and thus gave the village its name. The Savelli, a powerful clan who could boast two popes as kinsmen, held on to this castle for three centuries, finally ceding it to the Church in 1596 in payment of a debt.

It was the Barberini Pope Urban VIII in 1626 who first used it as his summer residence, considering this the healthiest spot in the Alban Hills. He added gardens, employing the baroque architect Carlo Moderno for his renovations. Near by, Taddeo Barberini, the Pope's nephew, built his own Villa Barberini on part of the terraced site of Domitian's palace. Later, this too was acquired by the Church, along with another villa, Villa Cybo, and its extensive gardens.

When in 1929 Emilio Bonomelli began to restore the garden at the request of the Pope, he did so according to classic Italian principles, while respecting the layout and levels of the Roman palace. On the topmost level of the garden is preserved a Roman theatre: fragments of painted stucco show theatregoers standing watching a play. Ancient trees dot the park-like grounds, including an 800-year-old holm oak marking the entrance to a *piazzale* with nineteenth-century herms of the emperors. To walk along the Viale dei Ninfei leading off it, between two massive Barberini vases, is to walk under Domitian's great wall. Holm oaks grow on top and to the right, ancient umbrella pines offer shade. Four Roman nymphaea still bear holes meant for aqueduct pipes. At the end, where the path curves, stairs in neat Roman brickwork lead to what was once Domitian's private doorway. The main entrance to the imperial palace is now a charming garden, where hostas, vinca, *Hydrangea quercifolia*, azaleas and woodland geraniums romp under the shade of holm oaks. Near by, wild flowers, poppies and honeysuckle have colonized Domitian's walls, and a statue of the Virgin now has pride of place in what once was the very heart of Imperial Rome.

Bonomelli's magnificent twentieth-century parterre laid out on the terrace one level down is best seen from above, where its intricate geometric pattern, imitating the ceilings of Roman basilicas, can be admired, ablaze with annuals. A rectangular pool creates width; cypresses and umbrella pines frame a view over the Latium plain. At the end of the 300-metre/985-foot-long central path a dark wall of cypresses sets off a huge statue in white marble. All four hundred cypresses in the garden are still cut by hand with a sickle.

Halfway along, a second parterre is skilfully arranged to seem a continuation of the first, its thinness and extra length disguised by a more robust pattern designed around fountains. To the right the walls of Domitian's *cryptoporticus*, said to be the longest to survive from antiquity, are softened with falling roses. Inside its cavernous interior, local villagers took refuge for three months during the worst bombardments of 1945. A cross now stands on an altar here, where the Emperor and his guests once promenaded.

The Lemon Garden, more than any other, incorporates the Roman ruins, with citrus planted in earth in what were once the palace rooms. Melissa, salvia, fennel, rosemary – all the dry-loving herbs curtain the ancient walls, while erigeron dances between crevices in the brickwork.

An imposing stairway leads to the garden's lowest level, where the design becomes noticeably more austere. In the Piazza Quadrata, a Roman equestrian statue, a precious find dug up in the hippodrome, stands alone surrounded by walls of clipped evergreen arched like ancient aqueducts. In the spacious Garden of Mirrors, square lily pools mirroring the sky are cut severely into an exquisitely kept lawn. Only the *giardino inglese* around the corner seems oddly out of place, its romantic hillside covered with flowering shrubs and roses.

The opulent scale, perfection and astonishing grandeur of this garden is still imperial, even today. Nine gardeners tend to every horticultural detail. Beyond the garden, olive groves, vineyards and the pontifical farm supply the Pope's table as well as the religious communities within his estate. Much work is done to prepare for the Pope's annual recess, starting in July. Pope John Paul II, who particularly loved Castel Gandolfo, would often stay here until the end of September, taking evening walks, praying and meditating in his favourite spot, finding peace among the greenness.

Right, top The intricate geometrical pattern of Bonomelli's parterre imitates the ceilings of Roman basilicas.
Right, centre The Lemon Garden, incorporating the Roman ruins, is planted with herbs and rock plants.
Right, below A clipped magnolia stands at the centre of the *parterre de broderie*.

Giardini della Landriana

Fifty years ago this beautiful 10-hectare/25-acre garden was a dusty, barren wasteland, swept by salt-laden winds and home to nothing except a few straggling pines. Even to till the soil was dangerous: nearby Anzio meant a risk of uncovering buried mines. This was the abandoned farm that in 1956 Marchesa Lavinia Taverna bought on a whim at auction.

It had two things in its favour. One was its undulating landscape. The other was Lavinia Taverna herself, a self-taught, gifted amateur who disliked the formality and 'parched brightness' of the classic Italian garden, and set out to create a gentler, more romantic vision. Landriana, with its thirty-two different garden 'rooms' and tapestry of English cottage-garden plants, carries echoes of Sissinghurst and Hidcote.

It did not begin like this. Lavinia Taverna was from the start a keen-eyed plant collector with a tendency to order plants in lorryloads, but she plonked them, as she was the first to admit, with little artistry 'here and there'. It took Russell Page to look at the collection of plants that was Landriana in 1968 and say to the marchesa: 'Let's make a garden.'

Page, introduced to Lavinia Taverna by Donato Sanminiatelli of San Liberato, was, first of all, a friend. Deep in conversation, he toured the property with the marchesa, and out of such walks ideas were born. Such slow beginnings suited the designer, who aimed to create a garden at ease with itself and with its setting. Good bones were a necessity, as were contrasts between defining lines (paths and hedges) and open space. Russell, said the marchesa, carried his ideal proportions in his head. At no stage did he offer, or she request, a master plan. He would sit and reflect, in fierce concentration, on his folding stool; and then get up and, with a

practised eye, peg out the next border, or path, or garden room.

Page did do drawings for his two main garden rooms, the Orange and Olive Gardens. The former he planned as a rose garden. Lavinia Taverna replanted it as a citrus garden almost by chance: the nursery she used had some mature orange trees. A witty take on the usual formal Italian garden, it is also a masterly play on size. Large globes of standard bitter orange trees (*Citrus × aurantium* Sour Orange Group) contrast with neat ground-hugging

Left The Orange Garden, where large globes of standard bitter orange trees (*Citrus × aurantium* Sour Orange Group) contrast with neat ground-hugging domes of *Myrsine africana*.

domes of *Myrsine africana* (used here because it is darker than box). *Acer platanoides* 'Globosum' adds height. Cheerful yellow creeping Jenny (*Lysimachia nummularia* 'Aurea') acts as ground cover.

Pages's plan can be traced in the straight line leading down the central axis of the Orange Garden, across the Cypress Avenue (lined with pots of pale pink roses), through the Olive Garden and into his famous White Walk. A majestic cork oak announces the entrance to the Olive Garden. Here, a palette of soft yellows, greys and mauves – bronze fennel, *Artemisia abrotanum*, *Allium rosenbachianum*, *Sisyrinchium striatum* 'Aunt May', *Verbena bonariensis*, *Rosa* Limelight – complements the silvery backdrop of the venerable olive trees.

During his second visit, Page designed the romantic Viale Bianco (White Walk). Alongside tufa steps cascade some of Landriana's 300 different roses – *R.* 'Sea Foam', *R.* 'Penelope', *R.* 'Madame Alfred Carrière'. The effect is opalescent pearl-pink rather than stark white, with *Salvia sclarea* var. *turkestanica*, *Gaura lindheimeri*, *Lavandula stoechas* and a froth of erigeron adding warmth to the pallor. In full sun, and sheltered by tall bay hedges, *Romneya coulteri* and *Carpenteria californica* are thriving.

In the Magnolia Garden is a very special tree, *Magnolia delavayi*, which was brought back from China by a French missionary. The Italian Garden – an intricate, interlacing pattern of squares and rectangles – is softened by the use of purple *Verbena peruviana* as ground cover. In the quirky Jasmine Garden, pyramids of jasmine, surrounded by black mondo grass (*Ophiopogon planiscapus* 'Nigrescens'), stand in a thyme lawn against a stepped bay hedge.

Russell Page envisaged the wide grassy paths in the Valley of Old Roses, but the inspired planting is the marchesa's own. Silver-tinged *Elaeagnus* × *ebbingei*, lavender, pinks, catmint and thyme give a blueish hue to the beds of massed old roses. (Always plant close together, said Russell Page: 'Plants keep each other company and grow more quickly.')

In another valley, drifts of multi-coloured *Rosa* × *odorata* 'Mutabilis' grow amongst convallaria and domes of myrtle. The rosary tree (*Melia azedarach*) gives shade. Here, in this formerly treeless landscape, the trees – umbrella pines, cypress, carobs, white poplars – anchor the garden.

When Page designed it, the Grey Border was near the house. It has been moved to near the exit, but the effect he wanted – planting like waves coming in to shore – is still detectable. The Blue Garden is the marchesa's masterpiece: a vast, grassy rectangle bordered by olive trees and, underneath, seraphic drifts of blue – agapanthus, salvias, ceratostigma, *Hibiscus syriacus* 'Oiseau Bleu', and the blue daisy *Felicia bergeriana* as ground cover.

Above The Olive Garden, with plants in a soft palette of colours – bronze fennel, alliums, artemesias, sisyrinchiums, *Verbena bonariensis* and *Rosa* 'Limelight'.
Left In the Valley of the Roses, drifts of old roses grow among silvery elaeagnus, lavender, catmint and thyme.

Il Giardino di Ninfa

'There is something unearthly about Ninfa which possesses and absorbs every sense.' So wrote the nineteenth-century writer and Italophile Augustus Hare, contemplating this, the most evocative of all gardens, romantically sited amidst the silent ruins of a medieval town. 'The only inhabitants are the roses and lilies and all the thousands of flowers which grow so abundantly in the deserted streets, where honeysuckle and jessamine fling their garlands through the windows of every house, and where the altars of the churches are thrones for flame-coloured valerian.'

Hare was writing in 1874 of the wilderness that had spread its protective green cloak over the razed buildings of Ninfa ever since the town's brutal and bloody sacking in 1381. Untouched by man, the houses had become 'green mounds' of vegetation. Ivy climbed the church bell towers and banks of nettles blocked the streets. Ninfa remained isolated, marooned in the lonely, brigand-plagued Pontine marshes. It was not rebuilt, perhaps through a fear of malaria, but more likely because of its indefensible position on the flat at the foot of the Lepini Mountains. Pliny had written of the temple for nymphs here, which had bequeathed the place its name, but for centuries thereafter this once-prosperous town remained abandoned, its ruins a mute witness to terrible events. When a garden did come to be made among the ruins almost half a century after Augustus Hare, spades dug into the earth to plant roses or fruit trees would meet resistance from 'an amazing quantity of human bones'.

Efforts had been made to revive the enclosed garden next to the castle, which the Caetani, owners of the estate since 1298, used occasionally over the centuries. In the seventeenth century, Duke Francesco Caetani, Viceroy of Sicily and 'no less good at governing flowers than men', planted tulips there and bred a recently rediscovered Caetani lemon.

But the story of the garden at Ninfa is the story of three generations of Caetani, the last of their 1,000-year line. Ninfa is their legacy. Its romantic English spirit, redolent of Nymans or Sissinghurst, owes much to an nineteenth-century English Caetani bride: Ada, wife of Onorato Caetani, Duke of Sermoneta. Ada was a spirited woman, fond of hunting and climbing, who liked nothing better than to take her children and guests on adventurous picnics among Ninfa's mysterious ruins. As she picnicked, Ada would plant rose cuttings she had brought with her against the tumbledown walls. The garden historian Charles Quest-Ritson, who has identified many of the roses at Ninfa, thinks that old examples of *R. laevigata*, *R. bracteata* and *R.* 'Follette' may well date back to this time.

If Ninfa began, as some people say, as a kind of game, in time it became a passion. Ada's son Prince Gelasio Caetani (1877–1934) was a practical man, an engineer. He cleared undergrowth, stabilized ruins, restored the town hall for his own house and marked out the garden's structure by planting trees. The great cypresses which give Ninfa its backbone are his: they march along what was once the main street of the medieval town. The holm oaks, *Magnolia grandiflora* and massive black walnut (*Juglans nigra*) were all planted by Gelasio. Meanwhile, Ada was planting roses – 'Kiftsgate', 'Mermaid', 'Buff Beauty' and the Banksian rose. Together, says Lauro Marchetti, Ninfa's quiet-spoken director, Ada and Gelasio were responsible for the genius of the place: its unique, transient, indefinable beauty.

Right Cypresses and umbrella pines are planted throughout the wild garden, while roses of 200 different species cover the tumbledown walls of the ruined medieval town.

Roffredo, Gelasio's brother, came to Ninfa with his American wife Marguerite Chapin in 1934, their young son Camillo having inherited. 'Roffredo was a pianist who also composed,' Lauro explains. 'He was a godchild of Liszt. He was not a botanist but he loved playing with water in the garden. By placing stones in the water, he created different sounds. He imagined Ninfa as a song.' To do this, Roffredo diverted water from the lake into numerous rivulets and channels. Marguerite's contribution was to plant dogwood, flowering cherries, crab apples and magnolias in Ninfa's unique natural style. One of the garden's great sights, a ditch turned white by a river of zantedeschia, was planted under their joint stewardship. Shortly before Roffredo died in 1961, a visitor noted that the abandoned town had become a garden.

The guiding spirit at Ninfa is an artistic one. This Lauro attributes to Lelia Caetani, who inherited the estate from her parents after her brother Camillo was killed in the Second World War. 'You can see that Lelia was a painter if you look around the garden. Today, if we have to plant, we look at Lelia's paintings for inspiration.'

The garden is approached down a drive lined with *Rosa roxburghii* 'Plena'. It is one of approximately two hundred species of roses at Ninfa. They rampage over house walls, festoon church towers, cascade through the branches of trees and tumble over the fallen stones, luxuriating in the cool, damp microclimate created by Ninfa's river. The river is the heart of the garden, drifting lazily past giant clumps of *Gunnera manicata* and

towering umbrella pines, slipping soundlessly under a Roman bridge hung with purple wisteria. Busy little streams meander off in different directions, chuckling through groves of silver birch, past virginal clumps of arum lilies. At the foot of the ruined houses, ferns and *Acanthus mollis* cluster protectively, the domestic scale of the buildings adding poignancy to their melancholy beauty.

Groves of flowering cherries are followed by glossy white magnolias and waves of purple-blue paulownias. Lilac-flowered *Melia azedarach* harmonizes with dusty pink tamarisk and the purple leaf plum (*Prunus cerasifera* 'Nigra'). A ribbon of purple lavender unwinds along the base of a wall. Elsewhere, a lavender-lined path leads across the garden towards the church of San Biagio on its mound. Around the ruined church is Lelia's rock garden, where she ventured almost daily armed with sunhat and wicker basket. A patchwork of valerian, erigeron, alyssum and aquilegia, scattered with California poppies, it basks in the sun. A grass path leads up to a shady seat, sheltered by the rose-covered church walls. This is perhaps the garden's most tranquil spot, overlooking the prunus valley, and with the majestic backdrop of the Lepini Mountains visible through a protective gauntlet of cypresses. At the boundary of the garden near the town walls, the impression is that of the Roman *campagna* with lofty ruins set among cypresses and stone pines.

Lelia and her English husband, Hubert Howard, shared an enduring commitment to Ninfa and, being childless, took care to safeguard its future. Botanical archives were put in order and a foundation set up to preserve and protect the garden. Esme Howard, Hubert's nephew, is a member of the Roffredo Caetani Foundation's General Council. He also founded and now advises the International Friends of Ninfa (UK), a lively association that recently helped restore Lelia's rock garden.

The young Lauro Marchetti was guided and educated to ensure the continuity of the garden. Steeped in Lelia's ways, he is the guardian of a rare and fragile artistic sensibility. The challenges facing the garden are immense. Ninfa is open for a limited number of days each year for its own protection. Nevertheless, 50,000 visitors a year come to see it, most between April and June. More hard landscaping, to protect fragile borders and lawns, has recently been carried out in the local tufa – a typically sensitive Ninfa solution. Projects outside the walls, such as a 81-hectare/200-acre wetland reserve, should also help to take pressure off this irreplaceable garden.

Above Ivy cloaks a stone arch.
Left The river is at the heart of the garden.

Il Giardino di Torrecchia Vecchia LATINA LAZIO

Left The ruins of the medieval castle and village, abandoned for around 800 years, are the backdrop for an impressionist planting scheme, mainly in green and white.

The long drive up to Torrecchia unfurls along a nut avenue and then through meadows of wild flowers, backed by misty hills. The view opens out on to sunlit fields sprinkled with cornflowers, poppies and daisies, and then closes in again as the road travels through dark and mysterious woods. Huge trees loom overhead, bringing a sense of the valley closing in. At the end is a stone archway, and then the villa, once a seventeenth-century granary, surrounded by the thirteenth-century ruins of a castle and its surrounding village. Stuart Barfoot, the talented and artistic English head gardener who ran the gardens at Torrecchia Vecchia for ten years, remembers his first impression of them as of 'a sort of eighteenth-century Arcadia'.

In 1992 Prince Carlo Caracciolo, founder of the newspaper *La Repubblica* and brother of the well-known Italian gardening guru Marella Agnelli, bought, with his wife Violante, this 600-hectare/1,482-acre estate in the rolling, wooded hills of southern Lazio. It came with a hilltop of medieval ruins, abandoned for around 800 years, possibly because of malaria or after an earthquake. As the Caracciolo began to stabilize the crumbling walls and clear them of ivy, they discovered Roman remains.

All this warned them to tread lightly. Advice was sought from Lauro Marchetti, director of Ninfa (see page 211), the poetic and naturalistic garden that had been created around another medieval settlement down on the plain. For the wild, romantic garden she planned for herself within Torrecchia's ancient, girdling walls, Violante Caracciolo decided that she needed an Englishman's eye.

At the 1994 Chelsea Flower Show she met Dan Pearson, the English landscape designer known for his gentle, impressionistic planting and sensitivity to landscape. Together, they decided on the ethos of the garden. It was to be mainly green and white with a touch of blue and pink – nothing overly sophisticated; a garden blurring at the edges into the countryside, and looking as if it could, at any moment, return to nature.

With 1.75 hectares/4 acres of gardens, ensuring a water supply was a priority. Lauro Marchetti had already sunk a borehole. Water was pumped from it into the stream that flows through the garden to join a newly made lake. Streams of blue and white *Iris japonica* pour like rivulets downhill towards this lake, where the cherry *Prunus pendula* 'Pendula Rosea' leans over to caress the water with its branches. At the top, where the water emerges, snowy white zantedeschia lights up the huge leaves of gunnera.

The Caracciolo had started planting around the ruins even before Dan Pearson arrived, putting in white wisteria, passiflora and white Banksian roses, which grew to tremendous heights in a few summers. Now, *Podranea ricasoliana*, too, scales the ancient walls, along with tracheleospermum and white solanum. Around the ruined castle, white hydrangeas bloom at the base of the walls. Banks of wild *Impatiens balfourii*, its seeds collected by Stuart Barfoot in the mountains, soften the rugged stone. Inside the castle walls is a discreet swimming pool, from which patches of sky can be glimpsed through the broken tracery of the windows. At the back of the castle, wild white roses clamber up cypress trees and white nicotiana spreads like a skirt at their feet.

The villa's front courtyard is sheltered by a square of venerable pomegranate trees, successfully transplanted here despite their great age. In front of the guest quarters is another courtyard where pots of Madonna lilies, pale blue hydrangeas, citrus, daisies and erigeron flower. To the side of the villa, deep blue clematis is set off by an explosion of white *Rosa* 'Madame Alfred Carrière', which Dan Pearson has used repeatedly throughout the garden.

Ahead, a camomile path leads through a meadow of wild flowers. Down the slope, two beds outlined with box balls are filled with pale blue delphiniums and glowing apricot *R*. **Sans Souci**. This newly planted part of the garden has more than a hint of Englishness about it. Primulas, peonies, aquilegia, hostas and apricot foxgloves mingle in a soft-hued palette and, as an experiment, blue Himalayan poppies have been planted. To the left is a swooping view over a valley where long-horned Maremma cattle graze.

Once the garden's structure was in place, with a series of outdoor rooms and secluded retreats in which to take refuge from the intense Italian heat, Dan Pearson brought in Stuart Barfoot to run the garden. To maintain Torrecchia's unique and delicate atmosphere of sweet disorder hovering on just the right side of wildness was a supreme balancing act. Stuart took to it immediately, relishing 'the power of nature in the garden, and the feeling that man's presence and influence is only temporary here'. He brought his own artistry to Torrecchia, starting a magnolia collection and establishing his own wildflower seed mix of larkspur, nigella and *Salvia sclarea* to scatter. He introduced more bulbs, including white wild cyclamen and the aptly named *Narcissus poeticus*. In the shade of the old cemetery hostas, foxgloves and Candelabra primulas shelter beside *Hydrangea involucrata* 'Yoraku-Tama', introduced by Stuart. Much of the appeal of Torrecchia comes from small, tenderly maintained, secret corners such as this, which contrast with the grand sweeps of planting.

By the ruined wall and the tower which mark the ancient entrance to Torrecchia, towering banks of heavenly blue *Salvia uliginosa* spill across the grassy path. Opposite, huge swathes of white Banksia roses flower in profusion.

Carlo Caracciolo's favourite spot to relax after a week in Rome was the enchanting pool garden, made by Dan Pearson in the ruined chapel. In the central water tank lotus and water lilies grow, surrounded by self-sown poppies, huge *Salvia turkestanica*, pale blue larkspur and white valerian, billowing airily amongst the more formal potted lemons. Alliums sprout up by the score in spring. Through the ruined windows, with wild flowers growing in crevices on their sills, are views of the lush Lazio countryside.

A grassy lawn separates two June-to-September borders. In shades of blue and white, these contain *Romneya coulteri*, ceanothus, plumbago and oleander among drifts of nigella and agapanthus. Nearer the house, under a catalpa tree and a holm oak, datura grows happily with white hydrangeas, white foxgloves and Japanese anemones in the shade. A cascade provides the gentle sound of falling water and, to the side of the house, a magnificent wisteria showers its long white racemes over the terrace.

Stuart Barfoot created a charming *orto* for the prince in response to his request for an area of more colour. In shades of deep crimson and soft apricot, it contains within its picket fence the single-flowered rose 'Mrs Oakley Fisher', penstemons, dahlias, *Allium sphaerocephalon* and single black opium poppies, lightened by the continually flowering David Austin roses **Golden Celebration** and **Jude the Obscure**. Against the walls behind, soft yellow jasmine, honeysuckle and the huge rambler rose 'Follette' echo the theme.

Violante Caracciolo died four years after Dan Pearson began to plan the garden. The prince lived on to see his davidias flower, dying in December 2008. His son, Carlo Revelli Caracciolo, now cherishes Torrecchia Vecchia.

Stuart Barfoot looks back on his time at Torrecchia as a life-changing experience, during which he learned to garden in tune with the natural landscape. *Selvatico-curato* is his name for the delicate task of maintaining the harmony between wild nature and control. At Torrecchia, romantic naturalism and a fresh simplicity combine with an intuitive respect for the spirit of place.

Above A window in the ruined chapel, now the pool garden, looks out over the landscape.
Left The pool garden, where lotus and water lilies grow surrounded by self-sown poppies, *Salvia turkestanica*, pale blue larkspur and white valerian.

CAMPANIA

Campania was the summer retreat of choice for rich Romans, who built vast porticoed and colonnaded villas with sea views over the Bay of Naples. The Emperor Tiberius is supposed to have owned twelve villas here dotted among the islands and along the coast. His Villa Jovis, which occupies one of the highest points on the island of Capri, can still be seen, with its terraced gardens and grottoes. At Pompeii and Herculaneum, Roman town gardens can be studied, having been preserved for posterity under a layer of ash. A fresco from the House of the Golden Bracelet in Pompeii gives the impression of standing on the edge of one of these Roman gardens. It includes plants such as *Viburnum tinus*, oleander, roses, *Arbutus unedo*, iris, the opium poppy, ivy and the hart's tongue fern, growing in the shade of an oriental plane. Other frescoes of Roman villas show urns and statues, architectural trelliswork, walkways and pavilions, and tufa stone and mosaiced niches for fountains. Formal symmetrical gardens were laid out in front of these Roman houses. A fresco from a villa at Stabiae, near the Bay of Naples, shows a waterside villa with a high belvedere or viewing tower. All this has come down to us through the fulcrum of the Renaissance. The influence of Roman garden design has been felt for nearly 2,000 years.

The Bourbons ruled the Kingdom of the Two Sicilies from 1735 until 1860. The vast royal gardens at Caserta, commissioned by the kingdom's first Bourbon ruler, Carlo III of Spain, reflect the French influence of le Nôtre and were intended to emulate the gardens at Versailles.

Parco della Reggia di Caserta e Giardino Inglese

Page 215 The Avenue of Ombrellini in the Giardini dei Duchi Guevara di Bovino. *Left* Paolo Persico's tableau of Diana and Actaeon in white Carrara marble sits among mossy rocks at the foot of the cascade. *Opposite* The English Garden, laid out for Queen Maria Carolina in 1782, is an example of the eighteenth-century passion for English landscaping.

The great royal gardens at Caserta stretch for 3 kilometres/2 miles behind the vast palace begun in 1751 by Carlo III of Spain, first Bourbon ruler of the Kingdom of the Two Sicilies. Carlo was the son of the Spanish king Philip V and of Elisabetta Farnese. The Caserta gardens, designed by Luigi Vanvitelli in the French manner and intended to emulate the gardens at Versailles, reveal the influence of André le Nôtre but, in their imaginative corralling of water and use of iconography, also reflect characteristics of Carlo's Italian heritage. We know, for example, that he had visited and no doubt admired the gardens at Villa d'Este. As the great-grandson of Louis XIV he had also been a guest at Versailles.

At Caserta, an aqueduct, the Ponte Maddaloni, brought water from Monte Taburno, 34 kilometres/21 miles away, to the royal gardens. Six hillsides were blasted during the nine years of its construction between 1753 and 1762, and three viaducts built to bear its weight. Having reached the brow of Monte Briano, the hill behind Caserta, the water poured 15 metres/50 feet down a rocky water staircase as it made its way down to join the 3-kilometre/2-mile-long stretch of water flowing across the plain between Monte Briano and the palace.

Carlo III, an accomplished huntsman, would often ride out from Naples into the woods of Caserta. Naples, ruled by viceroys for 200 years, did not offer sufficient grandeur for a king and was vulnerable to attack by sea. He thus decided to commission a new capital 30 kilometres/19 miles to the north of Naples in the then tiny village of Caserta. In 1756 Luigi Vanvitelli published sixteen engravings, the *Dichiarazione dei disegni del Real Palazzo di Caserta*. Behind the palace was to be a vast, grandiose *broderie* parterre, laid out with plants and curlicues of coloured pebbles. Central fountains boasted

of Caserta's supply of fresh spring water, which was to be transported by canal to the streets of Naples. The sprawling palace was at the heart of a new ideal city with spacious piazzas and wide avenues laid out to a geometrical plan. Aligned on the centre of the façade was the Via Appia, the Roman road linking Caserta and Naples, a self-conscious allusion to the mantle of Rome falling on Carlo III's reign. When the King saw the scheme, he was reportedly filled with emotion 'fit to tear his heart from his breast'.

Little of Vanvitelli's great plan was ever realized and Carlo never slept a night at the Reggia, his new palace. In 1759 he abdicated to become King of Spain, handing over his Italian possessions to his eight-year-old son, Ferdinand. Vanvitelli, engrossed in building the palace, did not turn his attention to the garden until the water had arrived by aqueduct in the 1760s. It was not until 1769 that he took up work on the garden once more, only to die four years later in 1773. Carlo Vanvitelli now took up the reins from his father. He simplified as well as aggrandized the plan, in a scheme that recalled French landscape design, installing the wide watercourse which runs three straight kilometres/2 miles from the *reggia* across the plain to the foot of the Briano Hills. Clipped hedges border the canal, backed by groves of trees. A narrow ribbon of grass – Vanvitelli seeded turf in the royal cowsheds – runs alongside the water.

The iconography of the garden unfolds in a series of basins and fountains, decked with statues in snowy white Carrara marble, distributed along the length of the canal. The water flows discreetly underground from each set-piece statuary group to the next. At the furthest end, among the mossy rocks at the foot of the cascade, Paolo Persico's lively tableau of Diana and Actaeon is frozen at the moment when Actaeon, bewitched by Diana, is turning into a stag. Antlers are bursting from his head, while Diana gazes at him from the safety of her own island with a delicate expression of sadness and resignation. Her nymphs clutch their breasts and hold their heads in perturbation and Actaeon's hounds cluster round him, baying with alarm. The tableau is a reference to both Carlo III and Ferdinand's love of hunting. Carlo III is supposed to have hunted daily to ward off a hereditary tendency to melancholy. The following group, sculpted by Gaetano Salomone in 1780, also has a hunting theme, as Venus and her nymphs say farewell to Adonis, who is destined to be gored to death by a wild boar. The boar can be seen waiting expectantly among the many representations of wild animals.

The water, disappearing once again, re-emerges in Gaetano Salomone's 1783 Fountain of Ceres. The goddess is enthroned, accompanied by nymphs and river gods and with the emblem of Sicily held aloft by a *putto* at her side. The Fountain of Juno, across the Bridge of Hercules, was to have marked the climactic point of the watercourse. The work of several sculptors, it was to have contained a large group of statues portraying in white Carrara marble Juno with Aeolus, the keeper of the winds. The Palace of the Winds is here, represented by an arched, rusticated bridge over which pours a sparkling cascade. Winged figures depicting the winds tumble hither and thither on the rocks alongside. The group was never completed, although Vanvitelli's model in wood survives. Worth noticing are the statues of slaves placed on the balustrades of the stairways: these have been said to allude to Muslim slaves captured in the Mediterranean and used in the building of the Reggia.

The relative modesty of the Fountain of the Dolphins may be the result of the straitened finances that prevented the completion of the Fountain of Juno. The Fountain of Margherita is even simpler, with only a basket of flowers.

It has been said that Carlo Vanvitelli's grand vision, while spectacular viewed from the air, is less convincing for the tired individual on foot. Searching hopefully for the end of the garden 3 kilometres/2 miles away, he or she finds it inevitably obscured in a haze of distance. More accessible is the charming *giardino inglese*, laid out for Queen Maria Carolina in 1782, an example of the passion for English landscaping which swept away so many classically inspired gardens in the eighteenth century. 'At present, Anglomania rules my plantomania,' wrote Catherine the Great to Voltaire. Queen Maria Carolina, Ferdinand's wife, too, became swept up in this trend in which art became the study and imitation of nature. Maria Carolina was persuaded into her new enthusiasm by the urging of Sir William Hamilton, the British Envoy to the court at Naples. As the sister of Marie Antoinette, she may have also wanted to compete with the gardens of the Petit Trianon.

Work on the English Garden began in 1782 under the supervision of a botanist brought out from England, John Andrew Graefer, who created one of the first and finest landscaped gardens in Italy. At 23 hectares/57 acres within its encircling wall, the garden is laid out as a park with grassy slopes, sinuously winding paths, lakes, sham ruins, sculptures and magnificent trees. Graefer's love of botany was mirrored by the Queen's enthusiasm for exotic plants: the first camellia in Italy was grown here and dedicated to Maria Carolina. Graefer obtained plants from Australia, China and Japan, and Sir Joseph Banks contributed seeds collected on Captain Cook's first great voyage on the *Endeavour*. King Ferdinand interfered by suggesting a labyrinth, 'where he might lose his courtiers'.

Three-hundred-year-old tulip (*Liriodendron tulipifera*) and camphor (*Cinnamomum camphora*) trees tower above the garden; there are groves

of paulownia and glades of palms. Eucalyptus, *Ginkgo biloba* and different pines were acclimatized with catalpa, cedar, magnolia, myrtles, and trees and shrubs from all over the world. Birdsong and the sounds of trickling water accompany a walk around the garden, the water flowing into a lake where a ruined temple, designed by Carlo Vanvitelli, is upheld by columns from Pompeii, where Sir William Hamilton organized the first proper excavations. Near the lodge where Graefer lived is the working hub of the garden, with the greenhouses where this ardent gardener potted up his samples. A sunken, shaded area holds ferns in pots, and massed camellias grow in a grove near an orangery. The original collection of antique camellias, like the rose garden, was sadly lost.

In 1997 a freak wind badly damaged the English Garden. Restoration was undertaken using the first catalogue listing its botanical species, which was compiled in 1803 by Graefer's son. The English Garden restoration team also hopes to resurrect Maria Carolina's vegetable garden. Sir William Hamilton considered the melons grown there the best he had ever tasted.

Giardino dei Duchi Guevara di Bovino

The Duke Guevara di Bovino was a friend of Sir William Hamilton. Ambassador Hamilton was, from 1764 to 1800, the British Envoy to the court at Naples; more famously, he was the doting, compliant husband of the notorious Emma, who was to cuckold him publicly with Admiral Nelson. Here in this garden, Emma is supposed to have performed her 'Attitudes', watched by her much older husband and an admiring crowd. Draped in shawls to simulate classical dress, she struck poses in imitation of the attitudes pictured on Greek vases. Her audience, many of them Grand Tourists who had come to view the new excavations at Pompeii, competed to guess at the poses and display their classical knowledge. In the spring of 1787 an enthralled Goethe, who came two nights in a row, described this one-woman show as like 'nothing you ever saw before in your life', and noted 'the old lord' visibly idolizing 22-year-old Emma. To show her off, Hamilton constructed a backdrop for her consisting of a tall, coffin-like box, black inside, with a gilt frame. In the 1940s a wardrobe belonging to Emma Hamilton was sold in an auction in Rome as having come from the palace here.

Anna Maria Suardo Guevara, Duchess of Bovino, created her garden at Recale in the early 1780s, when, like other Neapolitan courtiers, the family moved near Caserta to attend the Bourbon King Ferdinand IV and Queen Maria Carolina. While her husband hunted with King Ferdinand – a bloody affair involving the royal army, bands of peasants and 400 hunting dogs

– the duchess indulged her passion for gardening. In 1781 the King gave her the perfect present: water for her garden, channelled in brick conduits straight from the aqueduct of Caserta's royal palace.

The entrance to the garden leads through the courtyard of the pink-washed villa, along an avenue of agapanthus and through a massive yew arch. On the right the graceful domed tower is of eighteenth-century origin, built as a viewing tower as well as for water storage. On the left, the sunken path was used to bring horses up from the stables, out of sight of fastidious ducal eyes, to the courtyard where carriages awaited. Straight ahead, a gravelled path lined with box and *Cycas revoluta* ends in a pretty arched pavilion, its walls frescoed by Filippo Pascale, who worked alongside Vanvitelli on the magnificent library ceiling at the royal palace. Here stand massive and ancient trees – cedar, *Magnolia grandiflora* and, most magnificent of all, a camphor tree. In the acid soil, camellias flower, including the rare *Camellia japonica* 'Atroviolacea'.

The Italian Garden, created in 1770, centres on the delightful Avenue of Ombrellini, with benches made of stone from Vesuvius, on which the duke and duchess could rest in the shade of box trained into umbrella shapes. There were box elbow rests and, from behind the benches, servants offered the perambulating nobles tea and coffee in the fashion of the day. Tea, served by pretty girls, was all the rage: Emma Hamilton herself was a 'blender',

with one of the first collections of teapots among her prize possessions.

In her palace grounds at Caserta, Queen Maria Carolina vied with her sister Queen Marie Antoinette by creating an English Garden far bigger than the Jardin Anglais at the Petit Trianon. Sir William Hamilton advised her, and the whole extravagant scheme, involving a lake, a small waterfall, a valley and almost a million exotic plants, sparked off a passion for botany among the court nobles, who bought cycas (Maria Carolina's favourite plant) and washingtonia palms from the Queen's greenhouses by the score. All through Caserta, cycads still flourish on modest balconies and in tiny urban plots.

The English Garden inspired here, as it did in many other places, a new romantic and naturalistic style of gardening. Pruning was out and nature reigned uncontained. At Recale the duchess's new wood was a wood of life, not a *ragnaia* for hunting. Shady paths still wind around the oaks and holm oaks, underplanted with ruscus. Here and there, *Cycas revoluta* in pots gives an exotic feel.

An iron *berceau* marks a visible change of taste from the eighteenth to the nineteenth century, when a passion for flowers developed: roses were planted and thousands of agapanthus once bordered the paths. Twenty years ago, as part of the restoration, agapanthus was reintroduced into the garden. Now they do so well that the owners sell the surplus bulbs. Near by, an avenue of coral trees (*Erythrina crista-galli*) splashes scarlet against the blue.

The last Duchess of Bovino gifted the palace to the Porfidia family in 1939. They planted an *orto*: photographs show statues incongruously placed among beds of tomato plants. But the outline of the original garden remained tantalizingly clear, and the Porfidia eventually called in architect Nicola Tartaglione for advice. To him, to Maurizio Stocchetti and to others of his conservation group, goes the credit for restoring and now running this remarkable survival: the private pleasance of an eighteenth-century Neapolitan noble at the Bourbon court.

Above Waterlilies flourish in a pool in the corner of the garden.
Below The Avenue of Ombrellini shaded by box trained into umbrella shapes. The benches are made of stone from Vesuvius with backs and armrests of box.

Opposite, far left A gravelled path lined with box and *Cycas revoluta* leads to an arched pavilion.
Opposite, left *Cycas revoluta* grows in circles of box.

Il Chiostro di Santa Chiara NAPLES, CAMPANIA

This enchanting cloister garden was commissioned in 1783 by the abbess of a rich, aristocratic religious community. Domenico Antonio Vaccaro (who had already landscaped Palazzo Tarsia) was chosen to create a garden suitable for 'the decorum of noble ladies'. A clay surface was specified so that 'walking and running would be comfortable and much more delightful'.

Vaccaro's masterstroke was to use Neapolitan majolica tiles to decorate the seventy-two octagonal pillars, benches and fountain basins in the garden. The palette is of citrus colours to echo the citrus trees and herbs planted in the four parterres, as well as blue and green for the sky and the grass. The pillars show vine shoots, citrus and other fruits such as bananas and figs. Their wooden covering, lost in the 1800s, has been partially replaced.

The tiles (from the workshop of Donato and Giuseppe Massa) covering the backs of the seats show rural pastimes rather than devotional themes. Among the country folk making merry, there is only one notionally religious scene: a Clare nun feeding cats against the background of the monastery. Such exuberance seems far from devotional, but these eighteenth-century nuns used the garden to stage concerts, plays and even balls for the Neapolitan court.

The cloister walls were frescoed in the first half of the seventeenth century. The Franciscan monastic complex also houses a museum and a collection of eighteenth-century Christmas cribs.

Above Many of the majolica tiles show rural scenes.
Below Tiles in a yellow, blue and green palette decorate the seventy-two octagonal pillars and benches.

La Mortella

In 1949 the English composer William Walton and his young Argentinean wife Susana drove down to Ischia in a Bentley, intending to find some peace far from the pressures of London, where he could compose. Intending to stay six months, they never left. Susana Walton died here at La Mortella – the place of myrtles – in March 2010, surrounded by the remarkable, exotic garden she had created with the advice of the great landscape designer Russell Page. He is included in the inscription on Sir William Walton's memorial, William's Rock – a pyramid-shaped stone boulder, placed on the side of the hill overlooking the Bay of Forio and the blue Tyrrhenian Sea. Such was Sir William's admiration for Russell Page that when he appeared on BBC Radio 4's *Desert Island Discs*, Page's *The Education of a Gardener* was his chosen book.

The parched, sun-baked gully in which the Waltons decided to live and make a garden had many such lava boulders strewn along its rocky floor. Laurence Olivier, for whom Walton wrote the music for the film *Henry V*, dismissed the site as 'a stone quarry'. Barren and waterless, it was nevertheless in a hollow overhung by cliffs and thus shielded from the worst of the winter storms. Its fertile, black volcanic soil was the result of a lava stream from nearby Mount Epomeo, Ischia's highest mountain. While her husband composed, Susana Walton spent her first years breaking boulders and shifting rocks while excavating the precious soil from underneath a hard crust of lava.

Above, left The path forming the central axis of the garden is bordered by lush banks of *Zantedeschia aethiopica*.
Above, right Sir William Walton's memorial rock – a pyramid-shaped stone boulder overlooking the Bay of Forio and the blue Tyrrhenian Sea.

In 1956 Russell Page came to La Mortella and, inspired by the dramatic terrain, drew up what Lady Walton called 'a handsome plan'. This plan, dictated by the gully's shape, ran as a basic straight line as far as it could along the valley floor until turning sharply to make an L shape. Page recommended that the house should be tucked under the cliff 6 metres/20 feet or so above the gully, where three enormous boulders seemed to him to have been placed 'in a spatial relationship that might have been set out by a Zen master in Kyoto'. He advised that the other large boulders should be kept free of vegetation, thus enhancing the drama of the site.

Despite Page's warnings of the hard work that lay ahead, the Waltons began their garden in a state of 'blissful ignorance'. Page's instructions, written out in three days, were enough to keep Lady Walton busy for ten years. They included the advice 'Never plant one, plant a hundred', and to plant very young trees which would be able to withstand the winter gales. It was his recommendation to terrace the hillside following the contours of the slope, a feat of dry-stone walling that would take seven years to complete. When it was finished, Susana Walton softened the hillside – 'bristling with stone' – by planting South African bulbs such as agapanthus, freesias and ixia.

Russell Page, to whom leaf contrasts, shape and texture were as important as flowers, envisaged a restrained and harmonious garden, a place of serenity where Walton's music could be heard. He took his cue from the cliffs, hung with arbutus, pistachios, bay and evergreen oaks, as well as the *macchia* of broom, cistus, euphorbia, Jerusalem sage and wild myrtle. He devised a scheme that included desert stalwarts like aloes, agaves and yuccas with Mediterranean, Californian and Australian shrubs, lightened by aromatic, silver-leaved ground cover. The new plants were sheltered from the fierce sun under roofs of straw matting. Despite water delivered by the lorry load, they faced a struggle to survive.

It was twelve years later when Page returned for a second visit to find that the house had been built and that water had arrived on tap, conducted from Naples to Ischia by pipes laid underneath the sea. Page was able to re-work his original plan, adding a series of fountain jets – 'like exclamation marks', said Susana Walton – along the original straight axis of the garden. Page's predilection for the serene straight lines, rills, fountains and contemplative enclosed gardens of Islam is evident at La Mortella in the geometry he imposed on this dramatic natural setting. Theatrical and exotic planting now followed, thriving in the newly humid conditions. A lush grove of tree ferns, a serendipitous addition to the garden, had begun in 1964 with three plants sent back in a shoebox from William Walton's Antipodean tour. This success had changed the direction of the garden. So, too, did Russell Page's reaction to the modest fountain Sir William had built among the giant lava boulders: 'Pee-pee de chat', he called it.

Page's own, more ambitious design began with an egg-shaped pool with soaring water jet, placed near the volcanic rocks at the foot of the house. Here, the sacred lotus (*Nelumbo nucifera*) grows, while around the linked series of pools and fountains presses a jungly vegetation of yuccas, aloes, cycads and the arching bracts of the Mexican blue fan palm (*Brahea armata*). Susana Walton retained a special love for the cycads, growing when dinosaurs still walked the earth. The silk floss tree (*Chorisia speciosa*) served as a reminder of her Argentinean homeland. She had first picked a seedpod off a tree in Buenos Aires by standing on the roof of a taxi taking her to a performance of William Walton's music.

La Mortella's garden holds a themed and controlled lushness, with layer upon layer of carefully devised texture, just as Russell Page would have wished. Tender, tropical plants jostle each other in jungly profusion, sending out brilliantly hued flowers and bracts, the colour of exotic parrots. Groves of flowering hibiscus and abutilon mingle with banana palms, huge strelitzias, jacarandas and daturas as big as trees. A ground cover of luxuriant begonias, orange clivias and an exotic medley of fuchsias is offset by the black grass *Ophiopogon planiscapus* 'Nigrescens', and by a huge variety of ferns. *Woodwardia radicans*, a rooting fern from the Canary Islands, covers the valley. Around the pools cluster hostas and zantedeschia, papyrus and gunnera, with hydrangeas leaning forward to enjoy the moisture. The dramatic Chilean bromeliad *Puya berteroana* stands out with its 1.75-metre/6-foot metallic-blue flower spike.

Russell Page, Lady Walton once said in a radio interview, had a feel for the poetry of space. Where she just wanted to plant trees, he concentrated on how they would let the light through and the effect of sun filtered through foliage. The effect, of sunlight slatted through palms, can be seen especially where a rill, redolent of the Alhambra, flows to meet the octagonal fountain. Page designed this fountain in 1983 for William Walton's eightieth birthday.

The most dramatic plant in the Valley Garden is the giant *Victoria amazonica* waterlily, housed in the colourful Victoria House. Here, too, grow orchids, bromeliads and the Philippine jade vine (*Strongylodon macrobotrys*), with its vivid emerald flowers. Frogs croak among the huge, architectural leaves of the water lily and iridescent tropical creepers hang down.

Lady Walton began to develop the Hill Garden after her husband's death in 1983. Despite the rocky terraces, the olives and the umbrella pines, she has imported a slightly eastern feel, spiced with whimsy and symbolism. A tea house brought back from Bangkok accompanies the Crocodile Pool

stocked with Nile water lilies. The Temple of the Sun with bas-reliefs of Apollo by the sculptor Simon Verity is echoed in the nymphaeum, where Verity's Aphrodite reclines on a rock inside the grotto. Overlooking the sea and built into the rock face is a spectacular Greek theatre, where youth orchestras perform each summer.

Susana Walton turned La Mortella into a tribute to her late husband's life and music, setting up two charities, the Italian Fondazione William Walton e La Mortella and the British William Walton and La Mortella Trust, to promote his music and take care of the gardens. Dr Alessandra Vinciguerra, director of the gardens, has introduced a collection of more than 120 species of aloes. A quercetum – a arboretum of quercuses from hot regions of the world – has been planted, and Chinese hybrid roses suitable for the region have been added. Two concert seasons are held each year along with master classes and summer schools for young musicians. This is Sir William's memorial. The garden, lush, theatrical, intense and created and cared for by Susana, is hers.

Above Exotic ground cover of clivias, ferns and begonias.
Below The giant *Victoria amazonica* water lily is housed in the colourful Victoria House.

Villa San Michele

Left The whitewashed walls of the villa provide a backdrop for a collection of curiosities and antiques. *Below* The wisteria-covered pergola shades a cliff-top walk.

You approach the house sideways like a crab, having negotiated a narrow street winding up between the souvenir shops from the main square. Before you know it, you are alongside it, cricking your neck to crane upwards at its white façade. The view beckons you on, so follow it. Instead of entering the house, continue on past its ivy-clad walls and make your way down a shaded walk until you emerge into the sunlight to be rewarded with a dizzying, glittering panorama of the Bay of Naples. You look straight across the water at Vesuvius; turn the other way and you look down over Capri harbour. Lift your eyes once more and there on the opposing crag are the ruins of Emperor Tiberius's once-mighty Villa Jovis. From here from AD 27 to 37 the Roman Empire was ruled.

Tiberius built twelve palaces on Capri, one of them on this very spot. Beyond the ancient gateway, which marks the end of the short cliff walk, are the Phoenician Steps, said to date from Imperial Rome. Until the road was built in the 1870s, these steps carved out of the rock were the only link between Anacapri and the rest of the island.

Back in 1876 when Dr Axel Munthe first came to San Michele, he did so by climbing these 777 steps. What he found here – besides the incomparable position – was a ruined chapel and a simple farmer's dwelling. The farmer, immortalized in Axel Munthe's world-famous book *The Story of San Michele*, was scraping a living tending his figs and vines. The ground he worked was hard and stony, littered with columns, capitals, chunks of marble and limbs of statues. Some of the ruins the farmer incorporated into his house; other pieces he chucked into the Bay of Naples. The remains were known to the locals as *roba di Timberio* (Tiberius's stuff).

It was twenty years between Munthe's first visit to Capri and the laying of the foundation stone of his new Villa San Michele. In the meantime he had made his medical reputation, becoming physician to Queen Victoria of Sweden. The villa, built to his direction by local farmers, was idiosyncratic and small. He was, in any case, less interested in it than in the loggias, pergolas and terraces he built around it. 'Light, light, light' was what he wanted, and the ability to watch the sea and the sky. 'Nothing superfluous, nothing unbeautiful . . . The soul', he wrote, 'needs more space than the body.'

Today you enter Axel Munthe's garden through his house and both are kept beautifully in a manicured style by a Swedish foundation. From the sculpture loggia with its views out to sea, a wisteria-covered pergola shades a cliff-top walk. On one side is clipped ivy; on the other, clivias,

backed by hydrangeas, iris, ferns and agapanthus. It is gentle, seasonal planting, immaculately maintained. At the end of the pergola the planting becomes more natural with *Quercus ilex*, herbs and acanthus.

Here was one of Queen Victoria's favourite spots and here her dogs are buried. Narrow steps lead to the upper garden past a fragment of an imperial villa, excavated by Munthe. He found a black and white mosaic floor with a vine-leaf border and walls frescoed with dancing nymphs.

Behind the chapel, on the parapet, a 3,000-year-old granite sphinx looks out to sea. Straight downhill from the chapel marches a cypress walk. This was planted by Munthe on a moonlit night over a hundred years ago, using cuttings from the Villa d'Este. The trees are underplanted with ivy and ferns, and to satisfy Munthe's desire for running water, a rivulet was created to flow alongside.

The garden is lush, green and secluded away from the cliff top, full of wonderful curiosities and antiquities. A papyrus grows in a Roman sarcophagus. The Cosmati table, so Munthe said, was rescued from some washerwomen in a village near Palermo. The wide variety of plants ranges from a Swedish birch, rare so far south, to a banana tree. Spring colour comes from tulips, tree peonies and, against one wall, a serpentine planting of forget-me-nots – a flowing wave of blue. A garden pavilion, the bamboo-roofed Olivetum, holds an exhibition on Capri's flora and fauna to the delightful accompaniment of birdsong.

This magical place has over the past hundred years hosted many admiring visitors, among them Henry James, who thought it 'a creation of the most fantastic beauty, poetry and inutility that I have ever seen'. It is still unmissable today, but its fame has spread and by mid-morning it can become busy with tour buses. To enjoy San Michele in peace as it is meant to be enjoyed, it is essential to get there early.

Below, left A 3,000-year-old granite sphinx looks out to sea.
Below, right The entrance to the garden is through the sculpture loggia.

Villa Cimbrone

In 1904 a romantically inclined Englishman visiting Ravello on a Grand Tour did what so many of his countrymen have done since: he bought himself a house in Italy. Lord Grimthorpe, a rich banker, is supposed to have paid the Amici family a purchase price of 100 lire. What he received in return was priceless. Besides the tumbledown farmhouse, its wood, its vineyard and its walnut trees, Grimthorpe now owned the tip of a rocky spur jutting out 304 metres/1,000 feet above the Tyrrhenian Sea, which gave him what is generally considered the most dramatic of all views of the Mediterranean.

He would spend twelve years constructing a house and garden worthy of the site, dying in 1917, just after its completion. To help him, he chose not an architect but a local man, Nicolo Mansi from Ravello, a tailor some said, but a well-travelled one: he met Lord Grimthorpe in England. Together they built the part-gothic, part-Venetian and part-Moorish (in homage to Villa Rufolo) mansion with its fantastical turrets, battlements and cloisters.

The garden was equally eclectic, constructed piecemeal in stages with no overall plan. Decidedly unclassical, capricious and eccentric, it reflected one man's extravagant tastes, and that man, as it has been observed, could only have been an Englishman.

Somehow this lush and curious landscape works, with its mix of extraordinary vistas, lawns dotted with yuccas and palms, English borders, dappled woodland paths and colourful parterre gardens laid out like a series of exotic nineteenth-century rooms. Classical mingles with Moorish in a singular blend of styles and centuries, while Lord Grimthorpe's favourite quotations – admonishing or comforting but always faintly melancholy – are scattered around.

The only plan initially was to run a long straight *viale* through the centre of the garden up to the tip of the spur. A line of *Pinus pinea* was planted to reinforce the division between the garden's two halves: the open east side, overhanging the sea, and the wooded west, overlooking the mountains. These towering trees now form a giant canopy.

Top The Belvedere Terrace, a vertiginous platform lined with eighteenth-century busts with their backs to the sea.

Left and below Flights of steps link the terraces and paths that meander around the garden.

All the way down this central Viale dell'Immenso, the promise of the sublime view lures you on. At its end under the graceful arched roof of the Temple of Ceres, the central figure of the goddess stands on a round plinth outlined against shafts of sunlight. Beyond her at last is the Belvedere Terrace, constructed in 1911–13, a vertiginous platform suspended in an infinity of sea and sky. The breathtaking vista is disregarded only by the row of eighteenth-century busts lined up with their backs to the sea. Opposite them, seats invite you to linger.

Just below the terrace is a bar, with a small balcony jutting over the steep drop. Ahead are boulder-strewn slopes covered in wild broom and rosemary; to the left, the rocky inlets of the coast disappearing into a far-off haze; to the right, a Saracen tower and then, over a crag, Amalfi. A meandering path leads away from the sea and round the promontory. Here the planting is more natural to blend with the inland view of mountain valleys and olive groves. Ilex, arbutus and eucalyptus shade *Cyclamen hederifolium*; drifts of blue winter-blooming *Iris unguicularis* are among many wild flowers that have naturalized here.

At intervals along the route Mansi placed statues and pavilions, including, at the end of a cypress *allée*, the round Temple of Bacchus, sited over Lord Grimthorpe's ashes. Horace's evocative words praising love of hearth and home are etched into the frieze.

Down below in a hillside cave known as Eve's Grotto, a white marble nymph rests on a bed of leaves. D.H. Lawrence, a guest at Cimbrone in spring 1927, found her ' too ... pale, altogether too demure after her fall'. He then proceeded to entertain his fellow guests by covering 'Eve' with earth until she was mud-coloured from head to toe. The next day, the gardeners rescued her and she was white again.

Nearer to the house the strangely hybrid Moorish pavilion, surrounded by antiquities, real and copied, is supposed to have been Lord Grimthorpe's favourite spot for taking tea. During his life and after his death illustrious guests flocked to the villa, including Wagner, Virginia Woolf, Winston Churchill and Greta Garbo. Next door, in La Rondinaia, a cliff-top eyrie hewn out of the rock by Grimthorpe's daughter, Gore Vidal famously lived and wrote for forty years.

Villa Rufolo

Boccaccio, writing in 1349 after his exile from Florence, gives a description of the Amalfi coast which could appear in a tourist guide today: 'The coast of Amalfi overlooks the sea and is dotted with villages, gardens and fountains, and inhabited by very rich men . . . among the villages is one called Ravello, which, like today, was inhabited by men of great wealth . . . the richest of them all was called Landolfo Rufolo.'

Boccacio, extraordinarily enough, was looking back – a century or more – to the time of the Rufolo, merchant princes and owners of a fleet of ships, who used them to import luxury goods from the East. In 1266 Matteo Rufolo became banker to Charles of Anjou, the Angevin King, who was ruler of Naples but whose crown the Rufolo held in pawn.

From the outside, thirteenth-century Palazzo Rufolo with its high wall and two towers has the appearance of a medieval fortress. Inside, it was probably very different, a place of beauty and repose, with a medieval pleasure garden of which one important fragment remains. Palazzo Rufolo's charming garden loggia, with its arches open to the sea breeze, was probably designed as an alfresco dining room where the Rufolo could entertain their illustrious clients.

The Saracens were still attacking the Amalfi coast as late as the sixteenth century and Palazzo Rufolo is a mix of Moorish and Romanesque architecture, which is typical of Ravello. As a result, many nineteenth-century visitors thought the palace's gardens 'exotic', 'Norman' or 'Saracenic', and did not recognize them as conventional and very proper Victoriana.

In 1851 Francis Neville Reid, a diplomat and amateur archaeologist, bought the ruined palazzo and decided to restore it. For the house he determined on historical accuracy with respect for

Left A giant umbrella pine frames the famous view from the terrace, over twin domes, out into the Gulf of Salerno.

the original fabric, and so engaged Michele Ruggiero, superintendent of the excavations at Pompeii. For some reason this scrupulousness did not extend to the garden. This was laid out in terraces to take advantage of the dramatic setting high above the sea, but the terraces themselves he made into parterres of technicolored Victorian bedding.

Somehow it works: the pots of bright geraniums perched on ledges, the yuccas, aucuba, pansies, marigolds and fuchsias, the cordylines like small trees. Each level is designed to be seen from above against the backdrop of the incomparably beautiful Gulf of Salerno. Perhaps only nineteenth-century bravura could compete.

There are peaceful areas to which you can retire from this assault to the senses. On the middle level an oleander walk offers seats and, to one side, framed against the distant mountains, the sight of a fine example of *Cercis siliquastrum*. On the bottom terrace a pergola covered with *Rosa banksiae* at each end provides shade and simple seating. In the more informal part of the garden, dominated by a huge cypress, palms and umbrella pines frame the famous view over twin domes out into the Gulf, a photograph seen on a hundred travel brochures. The Victorian creator of the garden, Neville Reid, went on to found a school for gardeners which is still active today.

Such a heady mix of history and natural beauty must have captivated Wagner when he visited the garden in May 1880. Rufolo was the inspiration for the enchanted garden of Klingsor in one of his last operas, *Parsifal*. Now every June to October Villa Rufolo hosts a festival which includes classical and jazz concerts, a cinema festival and contemporary art and design exhibitions. The concerts are held in the garden. Wagner is often on the programme.

Above Parterres of brightly coloured Victorian bedding fill this terrace with pansies, marigolds, fuchsias and yuccas. Pots of bright geraniums perch on ledges.

PUGLIA

Puglia makes up the heel of Italy. Famous for its acres of vineyards and legions of huge, gnarled and ancient olive trees, its stone-walled fields also produce grain, tomatoes and peppers, pistachios, speciality vegetables and melons, all of which end up in the abundant Pugliese cuisine. The region produces 70 per cent of Italy's olive oil.

With its history of seafarers, invaders and conquerors, Puglia's coastline bristles with watchtowers and fortresses built to fend off Saracens and marauding pirates. Even the farmhouses (*masserie*) are fortified, with towers and massive stone walls to deter invaders. Along the coast, the great castles built by the Emperor Frederick II of Swabia include the unique thirteenth-century, octagonal Castel del Monte, a blend of Islamic, North European gothic and antique classical architecture. In Puglia's towns, the central streets, arranged like Arab *kasbahs*, are a legacy of invasion, as are the Norman cathedrals. The cathedral at Lecce, built of malleable sandstone, is an ornate and fantastical example of Lecce baroque.

Puglia's weather, with temperatures of up to 40 degrees Celsius in summer, favours drought-resistant plants. The region is home to one of the world's great cactus collections. Each year, over one May weekend, the capital, Lecce, opens its courtyards in a festival – Lecce Cortili Aperti – a chance to see inside the hidden gardens of the city's historic private palaces.

La Cutura

The name 'La Cutura' refers to rocks, and this unique cactus garden is dramatically set off by its rocky setting. A former quarry within the 15 hectare/37 acre grounds even holds a secret garden, sheltering rare and tender plants. The eighteenth-century former *masseria* was turned into a botanical garden thirty-five years ago by Dr Salvatore Cezzi, now one of the world's great authorities on cacti. Dr Cezzi was drawn to these plants, known to the Italians as *piante grasse*, by a passion inherited from his Spanish grandmother, who taught him that cacti display a personality unique among plants. His botanical park, an important scientific resource, is one of the two or three finest collections of cacti in Europe, fascinating as much for the surreal strangeness of the plants as for its remarkable variety. Beautifully choreographed, it has a charming, relaxed atmosphere – it is the garden of someone who loves all kinds of plants. Twice a year Dr Cezzi travels to the deserts of South America in search of new cacti to add to the 3,500 specimens from all over the world already held here.

From the entrance courtyard, the first garden to be reached is the Rock Garden, an artistically arranged display of agaves, aloes, yucca and opuntia, some 6 metres/20 feet high, corralled within stone-edged beds. Architectural plants such as *Yucca elephantipes* and a magnificent *Y. rostrata* add height alongside the dramatic rosettes of *Dasylirion serratifolium*, whose tufts at the end of thin, razor-sharp leaves give this spiky plant an ethereal appearance. The blue agave (*A. tequilana*, from which tequila is made) grows here, along with the fresh, green spikes of *A. ferox*. Visitors, says Salvatore Cezzi, are fascinated by the night-blooming cactus, cereus, its fragrant white flowers among the largest in the cactus family. Another favourite is Gruson's cactus (*Echinocactus grusonii*), named after the plant collector Hermann Gruson, and growing in a neat, spherical ball.

From the Rock Garden, you can glimpse a corner of the giant greenhouses. They are the centrepiece of the garden, holding 2,000 cacti and other plants from Mexico, Africa and the deserts of South America. A twenty-year-old crested form of myrtillocactus dominates one corner of a greenhouse, along with a magnificent saguaro cactus, state flower of Arizona and symbol of the American Southwest. This is also known as the desert tank because of its ability to expand to hold water. The distorted shapes and monstrous knobbles, bumps and whorls of the crested or monstrose cacti have a strange beauty, despite being deformations of nature. They are much prized by collectors. In the South American area there are Peruvian cacti which change colour when the sun's rays strike them. From Mexico comes a plant called *Cephalocereus senilis*, "Old Man of Mexico", so called, Dr Cezzi says, because of its small white beard. From Brazil, the rose cactus (*Pereskia grandifolia*) is an unusual, shrub-like cactus growing 3–6 metres/10–20 feet tall. Its pretty, pink, rose-like flowers have been used to make necklaces for dancers.

There is a collection of old roses at La Cutura with more than a hundred varieties. In the Italian Garden, medicinal plants like sorrel, yarrow, valerian and liquorice grow in profusion, contained in geometric beds. Four arches of sweetly scented *Pittosporum tobira* lead out on each side of this garden, while philadelphus and cotinus peek over the hedge.

Dr Cezzi's prized Secret Garden is reached through a pine forest. Steps cut in the rock lead down to the old tufa quarry, its walls hung with curtains of yellow *Gelsemium sempervirens*. Here, two greenhouses shelter tender, subtropical plants – orchids, gardenias, mimosa, fragrant patchouli,

Coffea arabica. Palms, papaya and bananas form a jungle outside, and the quarry is beautifully lit after sunset.

The rarest cacti are housed in greenhouses at the back of the garden, behind an area of ancient olive trees. Trays of tiny, rare cacti from Mexico sit alongside multi-coloured cacti from Thailand. The first greenhouse alone houses 1,000 different specimens. Dr Cezzi likes to create his own hybrids by pollinating chosen specimens with a brush. There are cacti here that can claim to be the only one of their kind in the world. Not surprisingly, such plants are carefully guarded.

The garden, tended by seven gardeners, is open to the public every day of the week. In April and May it plays host to hundreds of schoolchildren. As a further enticement for them, Dr Cezzi has created a miniature zoo at La Cutura, with Tibetan goats, miniature horses from Argentina and ornamental fowl.

Page 229 Part of the cactus collection of La Cutura.
Above The giant greenhouse, holding 2,000 cacti and other plants from Mexico, Africa and the deserts of South America, is the centrepiece of the garden.

SICILY

Dominated by Mount Etna, the highest active volcano in Europe, the landscape of the island of Sicily is mainly hilly, with coastal plains. The stony hillsides are covered with a characteristic *macchia* (*maquis*) of broom, cistus, myrtle and prickly pears. In spring, bee orchids and other wild flowers can be found. Citrus fruits, grapes, olives and hazelnuts are cultivated, while the almond blossom in spring is one Sicily's most beautiful sights.

Sicily has, historically, been the Mediterranean's richest prize, conquered and colonized by the Greeks, Romans, Byzantines, Saracens and Normans, and later ruled by Spain. The Bourbons of Naples then held the island until in 1861 it became part of a newly unified Italy.

In gardening, much is owed to the Arab settlement of the island from the ninth to the eleventh centuries. The Arabs introduced citrus trees, sugar cane, the date palm, pistachio nuts and papyrus. They instituted an irrigation system whereby water was channelled from *gebbie* (cisterns) through a series of channels and dykes moulded from earth to water the crops. In some Sicilian gardens remnants of this traditional Arab system are still in use today.

Orto Botanico di Palermo PALERMO, SICILY

This 200-year-old Botanic Garden is part of the University of Palermo. The garden first opened its gates to the public in 1795, but elsewhere an earlier small plot housed medicinal plants for teaching purposes: this was the first Botanic Garden. By 1786 the collection had outgrown its space and moved to a site near the newly laid-out gardens of Villa Giulia. It now covers 10 hectares/25 acres of tropical and subtropical plants, laid out according to Engler's and Linnaeus's plant classification systems. The garden's magnificent neoclassical buildings and many historic and rare specimens make for an exhilarating combination.

The 1795 Doric-columned Gymnasium originally housed the director's quarters and the Herbarium, with its collection of dried plants from all over the world. In a central room, a desk and bench served the 'demonstrators' who once stood and lectured students on the uses of medicinal plants. The two sphinxes in front of the Gymnasium are part of the Egyptian craze triggered by Napoleon's 1798 venture into Egypt. Sphinxes are also embossed on the Botanic Garden's own enviable flowerpots.

To the right of the main garden buildings, set out on benches, is some of the succulent collection – numerous tiny and curious denizens of the desert, now living happily in their sphinx-embossed pots. All shapes and sizes make up the collection. From India, *Euphorbia lactea* resembles a spiny tree; from Argentina, the cactus *Echinopsis thelegona* looks like writhing snakes; from Mexico, *Sedum morganianum* trails long, fleshy stems. Behind the benches, eighteen different frangipani in white, yellow and pink provide a fragrant backdrop.

Beyond the greenhouse, more cacti line up at the foot of a line of citrus trees, including the bitter orange (*Citrus* × *aurantium* Sour Orange Group) and *C. maxima*, resembling a large grapefruit, whose peel is currently being tested by scientists for antioxidant and anti-inflammatory properties. This is in line with the Botanic Garden's historic commitment to plants for medicinal and agricultural purposes.

A landmark of the garden is the long avenue of chorisia, the silk floss tree. These showy trees with their bulging, bottle-shaped, spine-studded trunks are resistant to drought, and have the ability to store water for dry periods. To the left of the avenue is an agave garden; to the right, separate glasshouses harbour carnivorous plants, bromeliads and papaya and banana trees. The Botanic Garden is a thriving place, with an atmosphere of careful bustle. Students can be seen working the beds. Round every corner, seedlings are being grown, plants potted up and school parties escorted.

An Australian corner includes the macadamia nut tree, and *Casuarina torulosa* with its feathery branches. Nearby, a fine, old *Paulownia tomentosa* from Japan is covered with violet foxglove-shaped flowers. Despite its fairytale appearance, paulownia has, through its deep root system, the ability to help reclaim compacted and contaminated soil – one of the reasons for the garden's interest in it. Among useful plants the garden has helped introduce into Europe are soya (*Glycine max*) and gossypium, used for cotton. Mandarins (*Citrus reticulata*) were first brought to the Mediterranean by the Botanic Garden, as was the loquat (*Eriobotrya japonica*).

The Palm Avenue makes a peaceful place to rest, with benches sited near by among the ruins of a fourteenth-century church. A good collection of cycads dates from one donated by Queen Maria Carolina of Naples and Sicily in 1793. She also donated one of the immense glasshouses.

Dominating a mount, above a pool with Egyptian papyrus, close to a bamboo grove, stands a magnificent dragon tree (*Dracaena draco*). Near by, euphorbias of every kind cover the ground. *Ephedra fragilis* grows in a mound, resembling a bad pudding-bowl haircut.

At the end of the main avenue, the large circular pond or Aquarium holds lush aquatic plants. It has recently been restored. Among the ficus collection is the giant of the garden: a massive *Ficus macrophylla* planted in 1845, with spectacular aerial roots. It has become the symbol of the Orto Botanico in Palermo.

Page 231 Grapefruit trees and *Euphorbia canariensis* in Il Giardino del Biviere.
Above Part of the succulents collection of the Orto Botanico.
Below The sphinx – part of the Egyptian craze triggered by Napoleon's 1798 venture into Egypt – is embossed on the Orto Botanico pots.

Villa Giulia

PALERMO, SICILY

The eighteenth-century gardens of Villa Giulia can claim to be the earliest public gardens in Italy. They were laid out by Niccolò Palma in 1777–8 to a formal, geometrical plan. Goethe, who visited shortly after the garden's opening, described this as 'the most wonderful spot on earth'. The nineteenth century introduced the fountains and charming cast-ironwork seats.

If the gardens feel unkempt now, with headless busts marring the pretty arched pavilions, there is still the sense of the sea around the corner, and the scent of citrus blossom in spring. Roses climb the palm trees, jacarandas and Judas trees flower among the araucarias and *Ficus benjamina*, and hibiscus and musa fill the box-edged beds. This is municipality, tempered with exoticism.

Left, above A chorisia – the silk floss tree with its bulging bottle-shaped, spine-studded trunk
Left, below *Yucca elephantipes* can grow to 6 metres/20 feet.
Below Potted succulents in the greenhouse.

Giardino della Kolymbetra

In a hidden ravine carved out between red limestone cliffs, this ancient orchard garden is reached by walking through the fifth-century-BC Greek Temple of Castor and Pollux, whose four Doric columns, re-erected as an 'ornamental ruin' in 1836, tower above it on the edge of the ridge. The garden, with its citrus and almond blossom, growing among centuries-old, bleached olive trees between boulders and crags, struck an eighteenth-century French tourist as resembling 'a new Eden'.

In the heart of the Valley of the Temples, within the ancient Greek settlement of Akragas, the gorge of Kolymbetra is thought to have held a reservoir known to the Greeks as 'the pool of the gods'. After the decisive victory against Carthage, won by these Greek settlers in 480 BC, Carthaginian prisoners were forced to dig the reservoir, and the tunnels which channelled water from underground springs, to provide a water supply for the citizens of Akragas. Some of these long trenches are still on display today, and still collect subterranean water to irrigate the Kolymbetra garden. They are known as *feaci*, probably after Feace, the Greek architect who designed them. In the first century AD the Kolymbetra pool was filled in and the valley was given over to agriculture.

With the Arab settlers of the ninth century came the citrus, the mulberry and the carob tree – the seeds of the latter being used as a measure (carat) for weighing gold and gemstones. Sugar cane, also introduced by the Arabs, is known to have been grown at Kolymbetra, along with a Sicilian staple, the prickly pear (*Opuntia ficus-indica*) with its edible fruit, the cactus fig. 'With about twenty prickly pear,' observed a French traveller eight centuries later, 'a Sicilian will manage to eat breakfast, have lunch, dine – and will sing in between meals.'

The ingeniously simple Arab method of irrigation is still in use in the garden, and their *gebbie* (cisterns) have been restored. In this thousand-year-old system, earth moulded into dykes and channels carries water to wherever it is needed among the rows of fruit trees. Only in the past few years has a modern irrigation system been added in order to save manpower.

The rehabilitation of this idyllic valley garden is the achievement of the Italian conservation body FAI, who took it on in a sorry state in 1999. Over the course of a year, volunteers helped clear rubbish out of the ravine. The orchard terraces were rebuilt and replanted, and the underground channels flowed again with water from the springs. With careful husbandry, FAI managed to save the larger part of the garden's flora, including such august specimens as a 200-year-old myrtle, a massive wild pistachio and a 200-year-old prickly pear. Of the nine different kinds of orange found growing here, some were unique and very old varieties, fruiting on trees 80 to 100 years old. The oldest olive tree at Kolymbetra is said to date back seven centuries.

As far back as the Middle Ages, Kolymbetra was already thought of as a 'garden', a reference, no doubt, to the beauty of its citrus groves with their scented spring blossom. Today it is a place of enchantment, the cliff walls draped with rosemary, its dry crags covered with a typical Sicilian *macchia* (*maquis*) of broom, prickly pears, fan palms (*Chamaerops humilis*), mulberries, myrtles and huge old olives. Cushiony banks of *Euphorbia dendroides* splash the rocks with gold each spring, and the castor oil plant (*Ricinus communis*) has naturalized in the valley.

Signora Antonietta is the welcoming gatekeeper to the garden. She will let you try some of the incomparable oranges picked straight off a tree.

Above, left and right Cliffs covered with the typical Sicilian *macchia* (*maquis*) – broom, prickly pears, euphorbia (*Euphorbia dendroides*), fan palms (*Chamaerops humilis*) and huge old olives.
Opposite, above The 1,000-year-old Arab irrigation system, with its dykes and channels and *gebbie* (cisterns) is still in use today.
Opposite, below Many of the olives at Kolymbetra are hundreds of years old. The oldest, it is said, dates back seven centuries.

Giardino di Villa Trinità

This unusual garden, made on volcanic soil high up on the slopes of Mount Etna, is part of an agricultural estate which has been in the Bonajuto family since 1428. The Bonajuto have an ancient pedigree, having arrived from Spain in the train of Blanche of Navarre, who became Queen of Sicily. Villa Trinità, their charming pink-washed manor house, has a date over the central arch to its courtyard of 1609. This was fifty years before the catastrophic eruption of 1669, in which a large part of Catania was flattened by lava flows.

In the nineteenth century, the estate was given over to the production of Etnean wine, most of which was shipped to Russia. In the manner of Sicilian aristocrats, the Bonajuto had a palace in Catania but journeyed to their country estate each summer to oversee the all-important grape harvest. The estate is 450 metres/1,476 feet above sea level, on the site of a Roman settlement, from which artefacts, ancient coins and tombstones have been found. Three generations of Bonajuto have gardened here on the fertile volcanic soil. Baron Salvatore Bonajuto's grandfather planted eucalyptus and palms, of which there are now more than twenty varieties. His father established the citrus orchards with their traditional, Arab-influenced irrigation system. Salvatore, an agronomist, recently planted an ornamental grove of citrus trees in open ground. Salvatore and his wife, Marina, restored the house as a full-time home in the 1980s; in 2009 Villa Trinità celebrated its 400th birthday.

The manor house, which has kept its timeless, rural charm, is enclosed within walls in the Sicilian–Arab fashion, and is surrounded by a 3-hectare/7½-acre botanical garden, stocked with indigenous and exotic species that reach luxuriant heights among the outcrops of volcanic stone. The oldest lava outcrops here are said to date back to 1382, when lava from the eruptions flowed down to reach the sea. The Mount Etna broom (*Genista aetnensis*) was, Salvatore says, one of the first plants to break up the lava with its roots. It is among the many plants here which characterize the Sicilian *macchia*.

A collection of succulents grows at one of the highest altitudes in Europe. Yuccas tower over borders of aloes and fleshy agaves, with *Dasylirion longissimum* adding its spiky charm. Among the trees are the Greek strawberry tree (*Arbutus andrachne*) and the Brazilian pepper tree (*Schinus terebinthifolius*). *Grevillea robusta*, *Melia azedarach* and the carob tree (*Ceratonia siliqua*) form part of the growing arboretum. Echiums, alliums and many different varieties of iris grow here, against a backdrop of euphorbia, fennel and the Sicilian staple, the prickly pear. The conditions may be harsh – three months of ash fell in 2001 – but the soil is rich. Pistachios, walnuts and persimmons are all used, as are the olives, citrus and summer fruits, in Villa Trinità's impressive kitchens. Here, Marina Bonajuto oversees the making of limoncello, mandarin liqueurs, orange blossom honey and home-made jams, while recreating old Sicilian recipes from her family's past. The red and white wine, from the family estates, is named Barone Antonio after the Bonajutos' son. This lush garden is a living demonstration of how beauty can emerge against the odds.

Above Zantedeschia banked up against an old agricultural building.
Opposite, above Phoenix canariensis, aloes, cypresses and (*right*) dasylirions thrive in the volcanic soil of the Villa Trinità garden.
Opposite, below Stone paths wind through the botanical garden, stocked with indigenous and exotic species, among the outcrops of volcanic stone.

Il Giardino del Biviere: Villa Borghese Catania, Sicily

Princess Miki Borghese calls her distinguished botanical collection 'the garden that wasn't'. Hewn from the rocky soil of a harsh and arid landscape, it expanded bit by bit, fuelled by hope and enthusiasm but with no overall plan. It is perhaps the only great Italian garden to be made on the site of what was once an ancient harbour; its swimming pool is built on what was the original lake floor. Biviere derives from the Arab word *vevere*, one of whose meanings was 'fish hatchery'. This land of lakes and marshes was granted to a Borghese ancestor by the King of Sicily in 1392. Malaria raged here until the 1930s, when work began on draining the Biviere lake; the reclaimed land from this dried-up lake was distributed to its former fishermen. By 1967, when Scipione and Miki Borghese arrived here, four small children in tow, Case del Biviere was uninhabited, waterless, treeless, a desolate terrain of 'stones and dust'. 'Once I realized my husband wanted to stay here to make a farm and plant orange trees,' recalls Miki Borghese, 'I knew I must love the place: I had to transform it.'

What she has achieved behind the tall, green gates of Case del Biviere is a kind of miracle – a flowering oasis. With no prior experience, she began to visit botanic gardens and read up on exotic and tropical plants. Her very first step was to plant succulents along the ancient harbour wall. Its good drainage guaranteed success, as did the intense Sicilian light and the fertile black volcanic soil. Il Biviere now is a lush and beautiful exotic garden with a splendid collection of succulents and rare specimens from all corners of the globe, gathered together in this very private garden through Princess Borghese's expert knowledge and love for tropical and subtropical plants.

What the Borghese family found in 1967 were three buildings – the house, its seventeenth-century chapel, and an inn, once used by hunters for duck shooting. The jetties of the former port surrounded them, the stones dispersed and scattered. Cavernous dips where the lake had been needed filling in and levelling. When this had been done and the jetties had been rebuilt, a layout began to emerge and Princess Borghese could begin to dream. What she envisaged was an informal garden, the framework provided by plants, the colour by extravagantly flowering trees and bushes. A smooth lawn would slope gently away from the house, while succulents – like 'green statues' – would add their strange, architectural shapes. Above all, there would be a palette of many differing shades of green.

The first trees to be planted were the Mediterranean boulevard palm (*Phoenix canariensis*). At the same time, behind the jetties, she placed white-flowered *Yucca elephantipes*. These giants, standing on stems like huge, pachyderm, wrinkled feet, give a sense of longevity to the garden.

The warm ochre walls of the house are set off by pale blue plumbago. Four grapefruit trees (*Citrus* × *aurantium* Grapefruit Group) scent the terrace and in one corner a thirty-year-old sculptural *Euphorbia canariensis* has reached the roof of the house. On the wide lawn the yellow-flowered Jerusalem thorn (*Parkinsonia aculeata*) is planted for early summer against blue jacaranda. *Grevillea robusta* follows with its golden blooms. In high summer, mysterious night-flowering cactus *Epiphyllum oxypetalum* opens its short-lived flowers after sunset. Stout-trunked chorisias brings up the rear, blooming for a month in September.

Nearer the pool, the garden becomes spikier and more exotic with agaves and yuccas among phormiums and palms, and the contorted shapes of *Cycas revoluta*, the Japanese sago palm. Clivia grows as ground cover in this garden, and near here, under a stand of pines, is a carpet of white iris.

At Il Biviere, under Miki Borghese's experienced eye, even roses grow in profusion, the Banksian roses and China roses especially relishing the Sicilian heat. *Rosa* × *fortuneana*, a Banksian relative and ancient Chinese hybrid discovered by Robert Fortune around 1848, covers itself each spring with scented, double pompons. This rampant rose does not do well in cold climates.

Beside the graceful little chapel is an old cypress *viale*, the dark trees lightened by the plumbago at their feet. Near by false pepper trees (*Schinus molle*) are curtained by drooping, green branches. The chapel is dedicated to San Andrea, patron saint of fishermen. The bell to summon the fishermen from the lake to attend Mass still keeps its place on Case del Biviere's terrace.

Above A thirty-year-old sculptural *Euphorbia canariensis* has climbed to the roof of the villa.

Above left Agaves including *Agave americana* 'Mediopicta Alba'.
Above right *Dasylirion longissimum.*
Below Succulents are planted along the original harbour wall.

San Domenico

This exquisite fifteenth-century monastery has been a hotel since 1896. From its garden terrace, the view takes in Mount Etna on one side, smoking lazily from its snow-capped summit, while on the other Taormina's ancient Romano-Greek theatre looks down from high up on its hill. Between it and the hotel is one of the few surviving untouched hillsides, where prickly pears, olives, broom and eucalyptus thrive amongst outcrops of volcanic rock. Straight ahead of the terrace stretches the deep blue Ionian Sea. It is a view which prompted even the saintly Cardinal Newman to declare that, observing it, '. . . you feel like reaching the closest step to heaven. For the very first time in my life I understand that. If I lived here I would be a better and deeply religious man.'

There is a turn-of-the-century flavour to this garden, which is shielded from the worst excesses of Taormina's building boom by the feathery branches of eucalyptus trees. Plants in nineteenth-century bravura colours are pressed together in riotous profusion. Vivid bougainvillea clothes the monastery walls and swathes the pergola of the central pathway. To the right, sturdy *Cycas revoluta* marks the edges of lavender parterres filled with California poppies, freesias and cineraria. In the middle, sweet peas climb citrus trees, and standard hibiscus and datura stand among marigolds and osteospermums, providing exuberant bursts of colour. There are geraniums and succulents in pots. Sedums spill over low walls. More pots, of agaves, mark a pillared walk. Even the towering araucaria is hemmed in by bedding.

The central avenue broadens out into a circle before entering an ivy tunnel. To the right is a charming nineteenth-century parterre, punctuated by mimosa trees, more *Cycas revoluta* and stately palms. The yellow of the mimosa is picked up by marigolds, California poppies and osteospermums in pale yellow, cream and gold. In the centre a giant strelitzia unfolds its exotic, bird-of-paradise flowers.

The left-hand side of the central pathway has a more haphazard, jungly appearance. *Yucca elephantipes*, callistemon, cannas, datura and strelitzia mingle with araucaria and banana palms. Under the citrus trees grow silvery cineraria and snowy-white zantedeschia (calla lilies). A dripping pipe gently waters clumps of colocasia, known as elephants' ears.

Downhill steps cross a pillared, tiled walk to a circular terrace overlooking the view. Parterre beds contain irises and freesias, and agaves cluster along the sea-facing wall. Within this lush and vibrant Sicilian garden, warmed by the hot, southern sun and scented by jasmine and orange blossom, are many such secluded corners.

Above and left There is a turn-of-the-century flavour to this garden, with its terraces planted in nineteenth-century bravura colours. It looks out over the deep blue of the Ionian Sea.

Racalia

Left The original *gebbia* is now the swimming pool. Newly restored terraces rise behind the villa.

The garden at Racalia, also known as Villa Ingham, lay largely undisturbed for many years. Rediscovery and large-scale renovation have been underway since 1999 under Alison Richards, sister of the present owner, William Richards. The property has been in the same English family for six generations, since Benjamin Ingham came here from Leeds in 1803 and founded a company producing and selling the fortified wine Marsala. Admiral Nelson ordered large quantities of Marsala for distribution to the British fleet. The company passed to Ingham's Whitaker nephews in 1861 and was sold to Cinzano in the 1920s.

The villa itself dates from the late eighteenth and mid-nineteenth centuries. In sits in 40.5 hectares/100 acres on a hill 5–6.5 kilometres/3–4 miles inland, overlooking the salt pans and the Egadi Islands, between Trapani and Marsala. The estate is in two parts – formal garden and woodland above, citrus groves and 3,000 olives below. There is a strong Arab influence throughout the whole area, and this evinces itself here in decorated tiles, ceramic pine cones on the balconies and Turks' heads around the swimming pool, which was the original *gebbia*.

The garden was laid out by Euphrosyne Whitaker, Alison's great-grandmother. She married in 1881, aged nineteen, planted a tree on her honeymoon and worked on the garden until the First World War. During the Second World War the villa became a military hospital. William Richards inherited the estate in 1977.

The original layout of the formal garden below the villa has been extended, although sadly none of the nineteenth-century plans survive. The Long Pergola, which is the boundary between the garden and the olive groves, was restored in 2005 and is planted with Banksian roses, jasmine, plumbago, passionflower, bougainvillea and *Podrana ricasoliana*. Alison seeks to maintain the spirit of the nineteenth-century garden while planting for the future with water-wise plants and trees from the Mediterranean, South Africa, Australia and South America.

Above the villa a large wood stretches along the limestone ridge, traversed by paths, terracing and long flights of stone steps. During the restoration the natural limestone cliffs and rockeries have re-emerged. This woodland provides a cool, shady refuge in the heat of the Sicilian summer.

This garden owes its existence to the natural spring that rises above the house and runs through several pools in the garden to irrigate the olives below. Racalia, in its superb setting, has a special atmosphere and the process of restoring it is a continuing journey of discovery.

Information for Travellers

Opening times and other details given here are accurate at the time of going to press, but may change subsequently. It is always wise to telephone or consult the website when planning a visit.
Primrose Bell

Castello di Agliè
Piazza Castello 2
10011 Agliè (TO)
Owner State
Tel 39 0124 330102
Location N of Turin; A5 Turin–Aosta exit S. Giorgio
Open Park May–October Tuesday–Sunday 8.30 a.m.–7.30 p.m. ;
guided tours by appointment
www.castellodiaglie.it

Isola Bella
288838 Stresa (VB)
Owner Borromeo family
Tel 39 0323 30556
Location From Verbania by boat and taxi boat
Open Daily end March–mid-October 9.00 a.m.–5.30 p.m.;
guided tours for groups (50 max.) by appointment
www.borromeoturismo.it
email info@borromeoturismo.it

Villa Rossi
Via Scodeggio 30
Venaria Reale (TO)
Owner Marchese Spinola
Location 10 km N of Turin centre
Open Groups by appointment
email lspinola@cersus.com

Isola Madre
228838 Stresa (VB)
Owner Borromeo family
Tel 39 0323 31261
Location From Verbania by boat and taxi boat
Open Daily end March–mid-October 9.00 a.m.–5.30 p.m.;
guided tours for groups (50 max.) by appointment
www.borromeoturismo.it
email info@borromeoturismo.it

Castello di Pralormo
Via Umberto I 26
10040 Pralormo (TO)
Owner Filippo and Consolata Beraudo di Pralormo
Tel 39 11 884870 or 39 11 8140981
Location 40 km S of Turin
Open For annual exhibition of tulips 'Messer Tulipano' in April
Monday–Friday 10.00 a.m.–6.00 p.m., Saturdays, Sundays and
holidays 10.00 a.m–7 p.m.; in May–July and September–October
Sundays and holidays 10.00 a.m.–6.00 p.m and daily for groups
by appointment: see website; closed August
www.castellodipralormo.com
messertulipano@castellodipralormo.com
email info@castellodipralormo

Giardino Botanico Alpinia
Via Alpinia
28838 Stresa (VB)
Owner State
Location By the Stresa–Mottarone cable car from Stresa Lido
every 20 minutes: the garden is 300 m from the first stop (Alpino
mid-way station); by car take the road to Mottarone peak.
Open Daily April–October 9.30 a.m.–6.00 p.m.
Entrance ticket included in return cable car ticket
www.giardinoalpinia.it
www.visitstresa.it

Giardino di Villa San Remigio
Via San Remigio 19
28048 Pallanza-Verbania (VB)
Owner Regione Piemonte
Tel 39 0323 503249 tourist office
Location On the Castagnola promontory by foot or car from
Verbania Pallanza
Open March–October; guided tours by appointment
www.verbania-turismo.it
email turismo@comune.verbania.it

Villa Cicogna Mozzoni
Viale Cicogna 8
821050 Bisuschio (VA)
Owner Cicogna Mozzoni family
Tel 39 0332 471134
Location Bisuschio 8.5 km N of Varese on SP 344 in direction
of Porto Ceresio
Open April–October Sundays and holidays 9.30 a.m.–12.00 p.m.
and 2.30–7.00 p.m.; open Easter Monday, 25 April, 1 May, 2 June,
15 August, closed Easter Sunday; guided tours (min. 20) daily
during the week by appointment
Lunch in the villa on request; for events see website
www.villacicognamozzoni.it
email info@villacicognamozzoni.it

Ente Giardini Botanici di Villa Taranto
Via Vittorio Veneto 111
28911 Verbania Pallanza (VB)
Owner State
Tel 39 0320 556667 ticket office 39 0323 404555
Location On Lake Maggiore between Intra (1.5 km) and Pallanza
(1.8 km)
Open Daily end March–1 November 8.30 a.m.–6.30 p.m. and
October 8.30 a.m.–5.30 p.m.
Tulip Week last week in April, Dahlia Maze late July to October
www.villataranto.it
email entevillataranto@tin.it

Giardino della Villa Bagatti Valsecchi
Via Galbiati 11
Cardano di Grandola ed Uniti (CO)
Owner Barone Architetto Pier Fausto Bagatti Valsecchi
Tel 39 0344 32120 (Grandola ed Uniti) or 39 02 76002034
(Milan)
Location Grandola N of Menaggio on Lake Como
Open On application by agreement with the owner or through
the tourist office in Menaggio (tel. 39 0344 30226); guided tours
arranged through tourist office
Apartments to let

Villa del Balbianello
Via Comoedia
22016 Lenno (CO)
Owner Fondo Ambiente Italiano (FAI)
Tel 39 0344 56110
Location By boat from Lido di Lenno; on Tuesdays, Saturdays,
Sundays and public holidays by foot from Lenno about 1 km
Open Daily mid-March–mid-November 10.00 a.m.–6.00 p.m.;
closed Mondays and Wednesdays except public holidays; guided
tours (max. 15) by appointment
www.fondoambiente.it
email faibalbianello@fondoambiente.it

Villa d'Este
Via Regina 40
22012 Cernobbio (CO)
Owner Villa d'Este S.p.A.
Tel 39 031 3481
Location Two minutes walk from Cernobbio
Open Daily March–November 10.30 a.m.–11.30 a.m. and
3.30–4.30 p.m.; groups (10 min., 30 max.) by appointment
Entrance ticket includes visit to the garden and tea at Villa d'Este
www.villadeste.it
email info@villadeste.it; food.beverage@villadeste.it.

Villa Carlotta
Via Regina 2
22019 Tremezzo (CO)
Owner State
Tel 39 0344 40405
Location Centre of Tremezzo, 30 km N of Como, 5.5 km S of
Menaggio
Open Daily mid-March to second week in November, March
and November 9.00 a.m.–4.00 p.m.,
April–mid-October 9.00 a.m.–6.00 p.m.,
mid-October–end October 9.00 a.m.–5.00 p.m.
For events see website
www.villacarlotta.it
email info@villacarlotta.it

Villa Melzi d'Eril
Via Lungolario Manzoni
22021 Bellagio (CO)
Owner Fulco Gallarati Scotti
Tel 39 339 4573838
Location By boat from Menaggio: on disembarking turn right
and walk ten minutes along the lake to the Bellagio entrance;
there is a second entrance in Loppia
Open Daily March–November 9.30 a.m.–6.30 p.m.; guided
tours (max. 50) by appointment
Holiday apartments to let
email loppiaappartamenti@alice.it

Il Pizzo
Via Regina 46
Cernobbio (CO)
Owner Paolo Lodigiani and Raimonda Sanna
Tel and fax 39 031 551262
Location 2 km N of Cernobbio along the lake on Strada Regina
Lungolago
Open By appointment: contact Marco Sala (39 338 8406580) or
email marcovpc@alice.it; guided tours (50 max.) on request
email raisanna@libero.it

Villa Cipressi
Hotel Villa Cipressi
Via IV Novembre 18
23829 Varenna (LC)
Owner Comune di Varenna
Tel 39 0341 830113
Location 15 minutes walk from station, 2 minutes from Piazza
della Chiesa
Open Daily 8.30 a.m.–7.30 p.m.
www.hotelvillacipressi.it
email info@hotelvillacipressi.it

Giardino di Villa Monastero
Viale Polvani 4
23829 Varenna (LC)
Owner Provincia di Lecco
Tel 0341 295450
Location 200 m from Piazza Centrale
Open Garden daily 9.00 a.m.–6.00 p.m.; guided tours by
appointment
www.villamonastero.it
email villa.monastero@provincia.lecco.it

Villa Sommi Picenardi
Viale Sommi Picenardi 8
Olgiate Molgora (LC)
Owner Sommi Picenardi family
Tel 39 039 508333
Location 17.5 km S of Lecco
Open By appointment April–October; guided tours (min.10,
max.50)
Light lunch/drinks on request
www.villasommipicenardi.com
email iredae@tin.it

Villa Borromeo Visconti Litta
Largo Vittorio Veneto 12
20020 Lainate (MI)
Owner Comune di Lainate
Tel 39 0293 598267
Location 20 km N of Milan
Open Guided tours of nymphaeum 2 May–October at various
times and dates, day and night: see website; guided tours for
groups (min. 20) by appointment (tel. 39 339 3942466)
www.amicivillalitta.it
email cultura@comune.lainate.mi.it

Giardino Botanico André Heller
Via Roma 2
25083 Gardone Riviera (BS)
Owner André Heller
Tel 39 336 410877
Location 36 km NE of Brescia
Open Daily March–October 9.00 a.m.–7.00 p.m.; guided tours
for groups (min. 15) by appointment
www.hellergarden.com
email info@hellergarden.com

Isola del Garda
Via Isola del Garda 1
25010 S Felice (BS)
Owner Borghese Cavazza family
Tel 39 328 3849226
Location Boats from various places on the lake: see website or
telephone 39 328 3849226
Open Guided tours daily except Saturday May–October
(booking advised); guided tours for groups (min. 15, max. 50)
by appointment
Estate olive oil for sale
www.isoladelgarda.com
email info@isoladelgarda.com

I Giardini di Limoni
Comune di Limone sul Garda (BS)
La Limonaia del Castel, 25010 Limone sul Garda
Owner Commune di Limone sul Garda
Tel 39 0365 954008 or 39 0365 954265
Location In centre of Limone sul Garda
Open April–October daily 10.00 a.m.–6.00 p.m. and
November–March Saturdays and Sundays 1.00 p.m.–4.00 p.m.
Ecomuseo Limonaia Pra'dela Fam,
Località Pra'dela Fam, 25080 Tignale (BS)
Tel 39 0365 73354
Location Strada Statale Gardesana Occidentale 45 bis
Open Wednesdays all year 10.00 a.m.–12.00 p.m., April–September
also Fridays 3.00–5.00 p.m. and Sundays 10.00 a.m.–12.00 p.m.
www.visitlimonesulgarda.com
email info@visitlimonesulgarda.com

Castel Trauttmansdorff
Via S. Valentino 51a, 39012 Merano (BZ), Alto Adige
Owner Provincia Autonoma di Bolzano
Tel 39 0473 235730
Location Follow signs from Merano (22.5 km from Bolzano) to
Scena for 2 km
Open 1 April–15 November daily 9.00 a.m.–6.00 p.m. and
15 May–15 September 9.00 a.m.–9.00 p.m. ; two 90-minute tours
daily without reservation in German and Italian; guided tours in
five languages (min. 10) by appointment two weeks in advance;
audio guides available; dragonfly tours first Sunday of month
For events see website
www.trauttmansdorff.it
email botanica@provincia.bz.it

Parco nell'Ombra del Paradeis
Cason Hirschprunn, Piazza S. Geltrude 5, 39040 Magrè (BZ)
Owner Alois Lageder
Tel 39 0471 809580
Location Magrè/Magreid 50 km N of Trento or 47 km S of
Bolzano on La Strada del Vino
Open Monday–Friday by appointment 9.00 a.m.–5.00 p.m.
(times can change according to the season); guided tours (min. 2,
max. 10) by appointment
Entrance includes a glass of wine; wine tasting, wine and food
products for sale; for events see website
www.aloislageder.eu
email paradeis@aloislageder.eu

Giardino di Pojega a Villa Rizzardi
Località Pojega, Via Poiega, 37050 Negrar (VR)
Owner Conti Rizzardi family
Tel 39 045 7210028
Location 15 km N of Verona
Open 1 April–31 October every Thursday and Saturday
3.00–7.00 p.m.; guided tours by appointment; guided
tours followed by wine and olive oil tastings (min. 15) by
appointment; for events see website
Concerts/ballets in the green amphitheatre during June/July
www.pojega.com
email info@pojega.com

Villa Arvedi
Via Valpantena
37023 Località Cuzzano
Grezzana (VR)
Owner Arvedi family
Tel 39 045 907045
Location 9 km N of Verona
Open Guided tours (min. 10) by appointment
www.villarvedi.it
email info@villarvedi.it

Parco Giardino Sigurta
Via Cavour 1
37067 Valeggio sul Mincio (VR)
Owner Enzo, Giuseppe and Magda Inga Sigurta
Tel 39 045 6371033
Location 37 km W of Verona
Open Daily March–November (see website for exact dates);
April–September 9.00 a.m.–6.00 p.m., March, October and
November 9.00 a.m.–5.00 p.m.; guided tours for groups by
appointment
Olive oil and wine tastings/sales; apartments to let, B&B: see
website
www.sigurta.it
email info@sigurta.it

Giardino Giusti
Via Giardino Giusti 2
37129 Verona
Owner Nicolo Giusti and Alessandra Giusti
Tel 39 045 8034029
Location In Verona near Il Teatro Romano and
La Chiesa di Santa Maria in Organo
Open Daily 9.00 a.m.–6.30 p.m; closed 25 December
email giardinogiusti@gmail.com

Villa da Schio
Piazza da Schio 4
36023 Costozza di Longare (VI)
Owner Giulio da Schio
Tel 39 340 48 54568
Location 12.5 km S of Vicenza
Open Daily except Mondays; guided tours of villa, gardens and
cellars (min. 10) by appointment
Flower show and market third weekend in May; for apartments
to rent and events see website
www.costozza-villadaschio.it
email info@costozza-villadaschio.it

Villa Trissino Marzotto
Piazza Giangiorgio 2
36070 Trissino (VI)
Owner The Marzotto family
Tel 39 0445 962029
Location 22 km W of Vicenza
Open Every Wednesday and Saturday 9.00 a.m.–12.00 p.m.;
closed August; other times by appointment
For events see website
www.villatrissinomarzotto.it
email info@villatrissinomarzotto.it

Ca' Marcello
Via dei Marcello 13
35017 Levada di Piombino Dese (PD)
Owner Count Vettor Marcello
Tel 39 049 9350340
Location 1 km from centre of Levada, 6 km from centre of Piombino Dese
Open April–October Sunday–Friday 9.00 a.m.–7.00 p.m.; guided tours with Count Marcello of villa and garden (min. 20) by appointment
For apartment to let and events see website
www.camarcello.it
email info@camarcello.it

Orto Botanico di Padova
Via Orto Botanico 15
35123 Padua
Owner University of Padua
Tel 39 0498 272119
Location Centre of Padua
Open April–October 9.00 a.m.–1.00 p.m. and 3.00–6.00 p.m. and November–March 9.00 a.m.–1.00 p.m.; closed public holidays
www.ortobotanico.unipd.it
www.horti.unimore.it/cd/padova

Villa Nazionale Pisani
Via Doge Pisani 7
30039 Stra (VE)
Owner Ministry of Cultural Heritage and Activities
Tel 39 040 502074
Location l6 km E of Padua, 36 km W of Venice, 5 minutes walk from centre of Stra
Open April–September 9.00 a.m.–7.00 p.m., October–March 9.00 a.m.–4.00 p.m.
Maze open April–September 9.00 a.m –1.30 p.m. , 2.15–7.15 p.m.
www.villapisani.beneculturali.it
email didatticavillapisani@libero.it

Villa Barbarigo-Pizzoni Ardemani
Via Diana 2
35030 Galzignano Terme (PD)
Owner Nobile Fabio Pizzoni Ardemani
Tel 39 0498 059224
Location 22.5 km S of Padua off SS 16
Open Daily March–end November 10.00 a.m.–1.00 p.m. and 2.00 p.m. to sunset; guided tours for groups (max. 40) by appointment: contact Dott. Giovanna Rossi (39 3286 482894) or email giovanna.rossi@valsanzibiogiardino.it
www.valsanzibiogiardino.it
email info@valsanzibiogiardino.it

Villa Emo
Via Rivella 4
35043 Monselice (PA)
Owner Marina Emo Capodilista
Tel 39 0429 781987
Location Monselice, 2 km S of Padua between Battaglia Terme and Monselice
Open April, May, June, September, October Saturdays 2.00–7.00 p.m., Sundays and holidays 10.00 a.m.–7.00 p.m.; daily for groups (min. 12) by appointment in writing or by telephoning number above

Castello di Duino
Via Castello di Duino 32
34011 Duino Aurisina Trieste
Owner Principi della Torre e Tasso
Tel 39 040 208120
Location 30 km N of Trieste
Open Daily except Tuesdays April–September 9.30 a.m.–5.30 p.m., March and October 9.30 a.m.–4.00 p.m; in winter open at weekends 9.30 a.m.–4.00 p.m.; guided tours by appointment
For events see website
www.castellodiduino.it
email visite@castellodiduino.it

Castello di Miramare
Viale Miramare
34014 Trieste
Owner State
Tel 39 040 224143
Location 8 km NW of Trieste
Open Park daily April–September 8.00 a.m.–7.00 p.m., March and October 8.00 a.m.–6.00 p.m., November–February 8.00 a.m.–5.00 p.m.
www.castello-miramare.it
email info@castello-miramare.it

La Mortola: Giardini Botanici Hanbury
Corso Montecarlo 43
18039 Ventimiglia (IM)
Owner State; managed by Università degli Studi di Genova
Tel 39 0184 229507
Location 6 km E of Ventimiglia, 28 km W of San Remo
Open Daily 1 March–15 June and 16 September–15 October 9.30 a.m.– 5.00 p.m.; 16 June–15 September 9.30 a.m.–6.00 p.m.; 16 October–28 February 9.30 a.m.–4.00 p.m.; closed 9 November–28 February and some Mondays: see website; guided tours (min. 20, max. 50) by appointment
www.giardinihanbury.com
email info@cooperativa-omnia.com

Villa Boccanegra: Giardino Piacenza
Corso Toscanini 49
18039 Ventimiglia (IM)
Owner Piacenza family
Tel 39 0184 229447
Location After the tunnel on the road from Ventimiglia towards France
Open By appointment: contact Dott. Ursula (39 335 7035185); guided tours for groups (min. 20) by appointment
email estero@piacenza1733.it

Villa Gavotti della Rovere
17011 Albisola Superiore (SV)
Owner Marchese Giovanni Maria Gavotti
Location Centre of Albisola
Open By appointment for groups (min. 20): contact Associazione Italia Nostra (39 019 820518) 5.00–7.00 p.m.

La Cervara
Abbazia di San Girolamo al Monte di Portofino
Lungomare Rossetti – via Cervara 10
16038 Santa Margherita (GE)
Owner Mapelli family
Tel 39 0185 293139
Location 36 km E of Genoa, 3 km from Santa Magherita station
Open March–October guided tours on first and third Sunday of
the month (see website for toll number to book); guided tours
for groups (min. 30) every day by appointment
www.cervara.it
email visite@cervara.it

Castello di Grazzano Visconti
Viale del Castello 2
29020 Grazzano Visconti (PC)
Owner Visconti di Modrone family
Tel 39 0523 870997
Location 12 km SW of Piacenza
Open Guided tours only mid-March–end June and
mid-August–end October (for exact dates, days and times see
website); guided tours for groups (min. 20, max. 40)
by appointment; for events see website
www.castellodigrazzanovisconti.it
email info@castellodigrazzanovisconti.it

La Pescigola
Località Pescigola, 54013 Fivizzano (MS)
Owner Tratech S.r.l.
Tel 39 0187 610312 or 39 340 8556213
Location 40km NE of La Spezia
Open Mid-March–mid-April for Tuscan Daffodil Festival (for
exact dates see website) every weekend 10.00 a.m.–7.00 p.m.;
during the week by appointment for groups and individuals;
guided tours available (min. 15); one weekend a month in May,
June, July, August (see website), other times by appointment
Lavender oil, honey, organic beauty products for sale; for events
see website
www.villapescigola.com
email info@villapescigola.com

Villa Grabau
Via di Matraia 269
55100 San Pancrazio (LU)
Owner Francesca and Federico Grabau
Tel 39 0583 406098
Location 7 km N of Lucca
Open Daily except Monday morning
Easter–1 November 10.00 a.m.–1.00 p.m. and 2.00–6.00 p.m.,
July and August 10.00 a.m.–1.00 p.m. and 3.00–7.00 p.m.,
2 November–Easter Sunday Sundays only 11.00 a.m.–1.00 p.m.
and 2.30–5.30 p.m.
Olive oil and wine tasting; apartment to let: see website
www.villagrabau.it
email info@villagrabau.it

Villa Oliva-Buonvisi
Via delle Ville 2034
55100 San Pancrazio (LU)
Owner Luisa Oliva and Gianni Oliva
Tel 39 0583 406462
Location 8 km N of Lucca
Open Daily 15 March–first week in November 9.30 a.m.–12.30 p.m.
and 2.00 p.m.–6.00 p.m.; other times by appointment
Concerts and operas during August; for apartment to let and
events see website
www.villaoliva.it
email info@villaoliva.it

Il Giardino di Palazzo Pfanner
Via deglie Asili 33
55100 Lucca (LU)
Owner Pfanner family
Tel 39 0583 954029
Location Centre of Lucca near Basilica di San Frediano
Open Daily 1 April–31 October 10.00 a.m.–6.00 p.m.; guided
tours by appointment
For events see website
www.palazzopfanner.it
email info@palazzopfanner.it

Villa Bernardini
Via di Vicopelago 573a
55057 Vicopelago (LU)
Owner Isabella Bernardini
Tel 39 0583 370327
Location 4 km S of Lucca towards Pisa
Open Daily 10.00 a.m.–12.00 p.m. and 3.00–6.00 p.m. by
appointment; guided tours (min.2) by a member of the family
For events see website
www.villabernardini.com
email info@villabernardini.it

Parco Villa Reale di Camigliano
Villa Reale
Marlia
55014 Lucca (LU)
Owner Pecci-Blunt family
Tel 39 0583 30108
Location 7 km N of Lucca
Open Daily 1 March–30 November 10.00 a.m.–1.00 p.m. and
2.00–6.00 p.m; closed Monday except holidays; guided tours by
appointment
www.parcovillareale.it
email info@parcovillareale.it

Villa Torrigiani di Camigliano
Via del Gomberaio 3
55010 Camigliano Santa Gemma (LU)
Owner Don Fabio Colonna dei Principi di Stigliano
Tel 39 0583 928041
Location 6.5 km NE of Lucca
Open Daily from second Sunday in March to end October
10.00 a.m.–1.00 p.m. and 3.00–6.00 p.m; from November to
March by appointment
Camellias in March; for events see website
www.villelucchesi.it
email villacamigliano@virgilio.it

Villa Massei
Via della Chiesa 53
55060 Massa Macinaia (LU)
Owner Paul Gervais and Gil Cohen
Tel 39 0583 90431
Location 13 km from Lucca
Open Groups (min. 20) by appointment
www.agardeninlucca.com
email info@agardeninlucca.com

Giardini di Agrumi e Orti Urbani di Buggiano Castello
Via dell'Indipendenza 45, Buggiano Castello, 51011 Buggiano (PT)
Owner There are 14 gardens each with a different name and owner; all are part of the Associazione Culturale Buggiano Castello
Tel 39 0572 30362
Location 45 km NW of Florence, 15 km SW of Pistoia, 1 km from Borgo a Buggiano
Open Only during 'La Campagna dentro la Mura', every two years on two spring Sundays (for dates and times see website), when there are musical entertainments and tastings of locally made limoncello and cakes; guided tours (max. 50): contact Giancarlo Panconesi Wine and olive oil tasting, products for sale; for accommodation and events see website
www.borgodegliagrumi.it
email acbc@katamail.com

Storico Giardino Garzoni
Via Garzoni, Piazza Vittoria 3, 51012 Collodi (PT)
Owner Villa e Giardino Garzoni S.r.l. and Gestione Sviluppo Turistico Collodi S.r.l.
Tel 39 0572 427314
Location 17 km N of Lucca
Open Daily 1 March–first Sunday in November 9.00 a.m.–dusk; November–February Saturdays and holidays only 10.00 a.m.–dusk; Collodi Butterfly House open 1 March–first Sunday in November 9.00 a.m.–dusk
For events see website
www.pinocchio.it
email giardinogarzoni@pinocchio.it

Giardino di Boboli
Piazza Pitti 1
50125 Firenze
Owner State
Tel 39 055 294883
Location In historic centre of Florence
Open Daily November–February 8.15 a.m.–4.30 p.m.; March 8.15 a.m.– 5.30 p.m.; April, May, September, October 8.15 a.m.–6.30 p.m.; June, July, August 8.15 a.m.–7.30 p.m; closed first and last Monday each month, 1 January, 1 May, 25 December
www.firenzemusei.it/00_english/boboli
email giardino.boboli@polomuseale.firenze.it

Giardino Bardini
Costa San Giorgio 6, 50125 Firenze
Owner State; restored and maintained by the Fondazione Parchi Monumentali Bardini e Peyron supported by Ente Cassa di Risparmio di Firenze
Tel. 39 055 2638599
Location SW of historical centre of Florence: Costa San Giorgio 2 (high entrance coming from Boboli); Via dei Bardi 1 (low entrance)
Open Daily November–February 8.15 a.m.–4.30 p.m.; March 8.15 a.m.– 5.30 p.m., April, May, September, October 8.15 a.m.–6.30 p.m., June, July, August 8.15 a.m.–7.30 p.m.; closed first and last Monday each month, 1 January, 1 May, 25 December; guided visits by appointment (39 055 20066206)
www.bardinipeyron.it
email info@bardinipeyron.it

Giardino Torrigiani
Via de' Serragli 146
50124 Firenze
Owner Marchesi Torrigiani
Tel 39 055 224527 or 055 2298200
Location Centre of Florence
Open By appointment only; guided visits by one of the owners
Lunch on request; for events see website
www.giardinotorrigiani.it
email vieri@giardinotorrigiani.it or elenasanminiatelli@virgilio.it

Giardino di Palazzo Corsini al Prato
Via del Prato 58
50123 Firenze
Owner Principe Filippo Corsini
Fax 39 055 268123
Location 7 minutes on foot from the Stazione di Santa Maria Novella
Open Daily 9.00 a.m.–12.00 p.m, 3.00 p.m.– 5.00 p.m. by appointment (contact Principessa Corsini by fax or email); closed Sunday; guided tours by appointment
Apartment to let; for events see website
www.artigianatoepalazzo.it/giardino
email psismano@tin.it

Villa Capponi
Via del Pian dei Giullari 3
50125 Firenze
Owner Aureliano and Maria Teresa Benedetti
Tel 39 055 2298609
Location 3 km S of Florence city centre
Open By appointment (min. 10)
Email mariateresabenedetti@yahoo.it

Giardino dell'Iris
Piazzale Michelangelo
50139 Firenze
Owner Comune di Firenze
Tel 39 055 483112
Location Centre of Florence, walking distance from Piazzale Michelangelo
Open Normally first three weeks in May daily (for exact dates see website) 10.00 a.m.–12.30 p.m., 3.00–7.00 p.m.; guided visits for groups by appointment with Iris Society
www.irisfirenze.it
email segreteria@irisfirenze.it

Villa Le Balze
Via Vecchia Fiesolana 26
50014 Fiesole (FI)
Owner Georgetown University, Washington, DC
Tel 39 055 59208
Location 8.5 km from Florence, 10 minutes walk from Fiesole bus stop
Open Monday–Friday during office hours by appointment (email smocali@villalebalze.org).; closed weekends, national holidays and August
www.villalebalze.org
email info@villalebalze.org

Villa La Pietra
Via Bolognese 120
50139 Firenze
Owner New York University
Tel 39 055 5007210
Location 2 km N of Florence
Open Guided tours Tuesday mornings by appointment (contact visit coordinator by telephone or email); guided tours of villa and garden Friday afternoons; third week in April and October free guided visits Monday–Saturday; garden closed August and 15 December–15 January
For events see website
www.nyu.edu/lapietra/visitor.information
email villa.lapietra@nyu.edu

Villa Peyron al Bosco di Fontelucente
Via di Vincigliata 2
50014 Fiesole (FI)
Owner La Fondazione Parchi Monumentali Bardini e Pyron
supported by Ente Cassa di Risparmio di Firenze
Tel 39 055 5003349
Location 2.5 km from Fiesole
Open Monday–Friday: appointment advised; Saturday and
Sunday groups only (max. 30) by appointment; guided tours
telephone (39 055 264321) or book on website
Olive oil tastings; for events see website
www.bardinipeyron.it
email info@bardinipeyron.it

Villa Guicciardini Corsi Salviati
Via Gramsci 462
50019 Sesto Fiorentino (FI)
Owner Seat of Universities of Wisconsin, Michigan and Duke
Tel 39 055 241586
Location 17 km NW of Florence, at entrance to Sesto Fiorentino
Open By appointment in writing: fax 39 055 2346863
email ghibellina@fastwebnet.it

Giardini di Villa Gamberaia
Via del Rossellino 72
50135 Settignano (FI)
Owner Dott. Luigi Zalum
Tel 39 055 697205
Location 7 km N of Florence
Open April–November Monday–Saturday 9.00 a.m.–5.00 p.m.
(6.00 p.m. in summer); Sundays and night visits by
appointment; guided tours (max. 20) by appointment
For apartments to let see website
www.villagamberaia.it
email info@villagamberaia.it

Poggio Torselli
Via Scopeti 10
50026 San Casciano–Val di Pesa (FI)
Owner Gianfranco Luzzetti (curator)
Tel 39 055 8290241 or 39 055 8229557
Location 23 km SW of Florence
Open By appointment Monday–Friday 8.00 a.m.–12.00 p.m.
and 1.00–5.00 p.m. ; Saturday by appointment; guided tours for
groups (min. 20, max. 50) by appointment
Old carriage room used for lunches, dinners and wine tasting;
wine/snack/buffet lunch on request; products on sale;
for events in April and May see website
www.poggiotorselli.it
email info@poggiotorselli.it

Villa I Tatti
Via di Vincigliata 26
50135 Firenze
Owner Harvard University
Tel 39 055 603251
Location 5 km NE of Florence
Open By appointment on written application (limited access);
guided tours of garden and house Tuesday and Wednesday
afternoons (max. 8): book well in advance.
www.itatti.it
email info@itatti.it

Vignamaggio
Via Petrolio 5, 50022 Greve in Chianti (FI)
Owner Gianni and Eleonora Nunziante
Tel 39 055 8546653
Location 30 km S of Florence, 42 km N of Siena, 5 minutes
from Greve by car
Open By appointment end of March–31 October Monday–
Saturday 11 a.m.–1.00 p.m. and 3.00–5.00 p.m. : contact Silvia
Mettini on telephone number above
Estate wine and olive oil tastings/sales; accommodation;
for events see website
www.vignamaggio.com
email agriturismo@vignamaggio.com

Villa della Petraia
Via della Petraia 40
Località Castello
50141 Firenze
Owner State
Tel 39 055 451208
Location 6 km NW of Florence
Open Daily November–February 8.15 a.m.–4.30 p.m.; March
and October 8.15 a.m.–5.30 p.m.; April, May, and September
8.15 a.m – 6.30 p.m.; June–August 9.00 a.m.–7.30 p.m.; closed
second and third Monday of each month, 1 January, 1 May, and
25 December
www.polomuseale.firenze.it/english/musei/petraia

Giardino di Bibbiani
Villa Bibbiani
50050 Capraia e Limite (FI)
Owner Giovanna and Donatella del Gratta
Tel 39 339 7157005
Location 43.5 km W of Florence, 0.8 km from Capraia
Open By appointment all year; guided tours for groups (max. 50)
Estate wine and olive oil tastings/sales
www.bibbianifattoria.it
email plmarchiafava@interfree.it

Villa Medicea di Castello
Via di Castello 47
Località Castello
50141 Firenze
Owner State
Tel 39 055 452691
Location 5 km N of Florence
Open Daily November–February 8.15 a.m.–4.30pm; March
and October 8.15 a.m.–5.30 p.m.; April, May and September
8.15 a.m.–7.30 p.m.; June–August 8.15 a.m.–7.30 p.m.; closed
second and third Monday of each month, 1 January, 1 May and
25 December
www.polomuseale.firenze.it

L'Apparita
Strada di Ginestreto 1
53100 Siena
Owner Paolo Giovanni Guiso
Tel 39 06 8557391
Location 3 km S of Siena
Open Groups by appointment
email paogiogui@libero.it

Badia a Coltibuono
Località Badia a Coltibuono
53013 Gaiole in Chianti (SI)
Owner Emanuela, Roberto, Paolo and Guido Stucchi-Prinetti
Tel 39 0577 74481
Location 6 km from Gaiole, 34 km N of Siena, 73 km S of
Florence
Open May–October every afternoon; guided tours at 2.00, 3.00,
4.00 and 5.00 p.m.
Wine tastings; cooking classes at the cookery school founded by
Lorenza de'Medici; accommodation; for events see website
www.coltibuono.com
email badia@colitibuono.com

Castello di Brolio
53013 Gaiole in Chianti (SI)
Owner Barone Ricasoli
Tel 39 0577 731 919 or 39 0577 7301
Location 13 km NE of Siena on SP 408, 1 km from Pianella
Open March–November 10.00 a.m.–6.30 p.m.; during winter
group visits only by appointment; guided visits by appointment.
Wine and olive oil tastings/sales; for events see website
www.ricasoli.it
email barone@ricasoli.it

Castello di Celsa
53018 Sovicille (SI)
Owner Livia Aldobrandini Pediconi
Tel 39 06 6861138
Location 20 km SW of Siena
Open By appointment Monday–Friday 9.00 a.m.–12.30 p.m.,
2.00–5.30 p.m., Saturday 9.00 a.m.–1.30 p.m.; guided tours for
groups (max. 30) by appointment
For accommodation see website
www.castellodicelsa.com
email info@castellodicelsa.com

Villa di Geggiano
Località Geggiano 1
53019 Pianella (SI)
Owner Boscu Bianchi Bandinelli family
Tel 39 0577 356879
Location 6 km NE of Siena (see website)
Open Guided visits by the owner (for groups of min. 6) by
appointment
Wine tasting/sales; lunch on request; for accommodation and
events see website
www.villadigeggiano.com
email info@villadigeggiano.com

Il Bosco della Ragnaia
53020 San Giovanni d'Asso (SI)
Owner Sheppard Craige
Tel 39 347 7049691 or 39 340 6617982
Location 40 km S of Siena between Pienza and Buonconvento
Open Every day dawn to dusk; guided tours (min. 15, max. 50)
by appointment
Truffle Festival first two weekends of November
No smoking in or near the woods
www.laragnaia.com
email frances@franceslansing.com

La Foce
Strada della Victoria 61
53042 Chianciano Terme (SI)
Owner Benedetta Origo
Tel 39 0578 69101
Location 5 km from Chianciano Terme
Open Every Wednesday afternoon, with guided tours every
hour April–September 3.00–7.00 p.m. and October–March
3.00–5.00 p.m.
Festival of Music at the end of July www.itslafoce.org
Estate olive oil tasting/sales; for accommodation see website
www.lafoce.com
email info@lafoce.com

Valle Pinciole
Strada di Vagliara 4
Cetona (SI)
Owner Federico Forquet
Tel 39 0578 238113
Location 2.5 km E of Cetona
Open April–October Tuesday and Friday
9.00 a.m.–1.00 p.m. and 2.30–6.00 p.m., by request on other
days: contact Signora Rita Trovato; groups (max. 40)
email rita.trovato@libero.it

Giardini di Villa Cetinale
Villa Cetinale
Anciano
Commune di Sociville
53018 Siena (SI)
Owner Società Casuarina Limited
Tel 39 0577 311147
Location 9 km SW of Siena
Open By appointment Monday–Friday 9.30 a.m.–12.30 p.m.
Olive oil tasting/sales; accommodation; for events see website
www.villacetinale.com
email info@villacetinale.com

La Porrona
Podere Porrona
Località San Giovanni D'Asso
53020 Montisi (SI)
Owner Pino Brusone
Location 15 km N of Pienza, 50 km SE of Siena
Open By appointment (max. 10)
www.laporrona.it
email gbrusone@hotmail.com

Il Giardino di Orlando
Castello di Argiano
53020 S. Angelo in Colle
Montalcino (SI)
Owner Signora Sarah Sesti
Tel 39 0577 844113
Location 12 km S of Montalcino
Open By appointment Monday–Friday: contact Sarah Sesti;
groups (max. 15)
Wine and olive oil tastings/sales; accommodation to let; for
events see website
email sarahsesti@gmail.com

Il Giardino Corsini:
Orto Botanico della Casa Bianca
Via Caravaggio 9
58018 Porto Ercole (GR)
Owner Marchese Alessandro Corsini
Tel 39 06 855 2536 or 39 338 1048119
Location On hill above Porto Ercole, 7 km from Orbetello, 42km
S of Grosseto
Open Daily by appointment; guided tours available
Music Festival end July–mid-August; for events see website
www.giardinocorsini.com
email papacxii@aol.com

La Ferriera
Grosseto
Owner Contessa Pietromarchi
Location Località Pescia Fiorentina
Open By appointment for groups
email giuppi.pietromarchi@tin.it

Villa Giardino Buonaccorsi
Contrada Giardino 9
62018 Giardino Buonaccorsi (MC)
Owner Villa Buonaccorsi S.r.l
Location 40 km S of Ancona
Tel & fax 39 0733 688189
Open Daily by appointment; guided visits by appointment:
contact Sig. Attilio Macellari by fax on the number above or tel
39 328 8868412.
For events see website
www.villagiardinobuonaccorsi.it
email info@villagiardinobuonaccorsi.it

Giardino Sgariglia
Via Sgariglia 1
63013 Grottammare (AP)
Owner Marchese Armida Cancrini Sgariglia
Location 43 km NW of Ascoli Piceno
Open Group visits (min. 8) by appointment through
L'Associazione Le Marche Segrete; contact Associazione Le
Marche Segrete, Via San Pancrazio 2, 63031 Castel di Lama (AP)
(39 335 6646182) or Giulia Panichi Pignatelli (39 0736 812552)
www.marchesegrete.it

Borgo Storico Seghetti Panichi
Via San Pancrazio 1
63031 Castel di Lama (AP)
Owner Principessa Giulia Panichi Pignatelli
Tel 39 0736 812552
Location 8 km E of Ascoli Piceno
Open Daily 10.00 a.m.–6.00 p.m. by appointment; guided visits
(min. 8) by appointment
'Maggio in Giardino' in May: see website
For accommodation in villa, apartments to let and events see
website
www.seghettipanichi.it
email info@seghettipanichi.it

Il Giadorto
Case Sparse 70
S. Arcangelo di Magione
06063 Perugia (PG)
Owner Daniela Fe d'Ostiani
Tel 39 075 848242
Location 12 km SW of Magione
Open By appointment for groups (min. 10, max. 30); guided
tours
Lunch in garden on request
email danielafedostiani@tiscali.it

Giardino all'Italiana di Villa Aureli
Via Luigi Cirenei 70
06132 Castel del Piano (PG)
Owner Count Sperello di Serego Alighieri
Tel 39 0755 140444 or 39 0552 752311
Location 10 km SW of Perugia
Open By appointment
Products for sale; for accommodation see website
www.villaaureli.it
email villa.aureli@libero.it

Orto e Giardino di Barbanera
Via San Giuseppe 1
006038 Spello (PG)
Owner Editoriale Campi
Tel 39 0742 391177
Location 1 km S of Spello
Open By appointment only: call Pia Fanciulli on 39 0742 391177
The Fondazione Barbanera 1762 archive can also be viewed by
appointment
www.barbanera.it
email segreteria@barbanera.it

Santa Maria in Portella
Santa Maria (Fraz. Torri)
06058 San Terenziano (PG)
Owner Helga Brichet
Tel 39 0742 99288
Location 3.5 km from Bastardo
Open By appointment; guided tours
Open day mid-May and annual Mass on the first Sunday of May
in the Chapel
Garden only contains old roses so visits before the end of May
are advisable.
email helga.brichet@virgilio.it

Castello Ruspoli-Vignanello
Piazza della Repubblica 9
01039 Vignanello (VT)
Owner Donna Claudia and Giada Ruspoli
Tel 39 0761 755338
Location Centre of Vignanello, 20 km SE of Viterbo
Open April–end October Sundays and public holidays
10.30 a.m.–1.00 p.m. and 3.30–6.00 p.m.; groups (min. 10)
by appointment during the week; guided tours in English for
groups by appointment.
For events see website
www.castelloruspoli.com
email castelloruspoli@libero.it

Sacro Bosco di Bomarzo
Località Giardino
01020 Bomarzo (VT)
Owner Bosco Sacro di Bomarzo S.r.l.
Tel 39 0761 924029
Location 20 km NE of Viterbo
Open Daily 8.00 a.m.–dusk; guided tours available
www.parcodeimostri.com
email info@parcodeimostri.com

Il Palazzo del Quirinale
Piazza del Quirinale
00187 Roma
Owner State
Tel 39 06 46991
Location On the Quirinale Hill
Open 2 June every year on the day of the Feast of the Republic;
applications to see the garden on other days must be made well
in advance and require a lot of documentation.
www.quirinale.it

Palazzo Farnese di Caprarola
Piazza Romeo Romei
Via Antonio da Sangallo
01032 Caprarola (VT)
Owner State
Tel 39 0761 646052
Location 19 km SE of Viterbo
Open Daily except Mondays 8.30 a.m.–7.30 p.m.; for guided
tours email sbaal@uni.it
www.caprarola.com/palazzo_farnese
email info@caprarola.com

Giardini Vaticani
00120 Stato della Città del Vaticano (RM)
Owner Stato della Città del Vaticano
Tel information 39 06 69884676 or 39 06 69883145
Location Ten minutes walk from Metro station
Open For updated details see website www.mv.vatican.va
Ticket includes entry to the Vatican Museums and guided
tour of the gardens; guided tours during opening hours for
individuals or small groups (max. 15) can be organized: email
visiteguidategruppi.musei@scv.va
www.vaticanstate.va and www.vatican.va

Villa Lante
Via Jacopo Barozzi 71
01031 Bagnaia (VT)
Owner State
Tel 39 0761 288008
Location 5 km E of Viterbo
Open Tuesday–Sunday, 1 November–28 February 8.30 a.m.–
4.30 p.m.; 1 March–15 April 8.30 a.m.–5.30 p.m.;
16 April–15 September 8.30 a.m. – 7.30 p.m.;
16 September–31 October 8.30 a.m.–5.30 p.m.; closed Monday,
1 January, 1 May, 25 December
email sbaal@uni.net

Villa Giulia
Piazzale di Villa Giulia 9
00196 Roma
Owner State
Tel 39 06 3222657 1
Location Centre of Rome
Open Tuesday–Sunday 8.30 a.m.–7.30 p.m.; closed 1 January
and 25 December
www.beniculturale.it
email villagiulia@arti.beniculturali.it

Giardino del Castello Orsini di Vasanello
Piazza Vittorio Veneto 23
01030 Vasanello (VT)
Owner Elena Misciattelli
Tel 39 0667 97835
Location Centre of Vasanello, 35.5 km E of Viterbo
Open By appointment; guided tours (min. 10)
For events see website
www.castellodivasanello.it
email elenamisciattelli@alice.it

Villa Madama
Via di Villa Madama 194
00195 Roma
Owner State
Tel 39 06 39614284
Location 3 km N of the Vatican Museum
Open By appointment with permission of the Ministry of
Foreign Affairs
email cerimoniale.segreteria@esteri.it

Palazzo Patrizi
Castel Giuliano
00062 Bracciano (RM)
Owner Marchese and Marchesa Patrizi
Tel 39 06 99802530
Location 52.5 km S of Viterbo, 40 km NW of Rome
Open By appointment; groups (min 15) by appointment
Rose Fair in May; for events see website
www.castel-giuliano.it
email info@castelgiuliano.it

Villa Medici
Viale Trinità dei Monti 1
00187 Roma
Owner Académie de France à Rome sponsored by the Ministry
of Culture and Communication
Tel 39 06 67611
Location On the Pincian Hill at the top of the Spanish Steps
Open Guided tours daily from 9.45 a.m.; for exact times and
tours in English, see website; group guided tours (min. 10, max.
35) by appointment
For events and festivals see website
www.villamedici.it
email standard@villamedici.it

Villa Wolkonsky
Piazza di Villa Wolkonsky
00185 Roma
Residence of British Ambassador to Rome
Location On the Esquiline Hill
Open Limited access; by appointment for groups; applications
in writing

San Liberato
Tenuta di San Liberato
Via Settevene Palo 33
00062 Bracciano (RM)
Owner Sanminiatelli Odescalchi family
Tel 39 06 9988384
Location 20 km NW of Bracciano
Open By appointment 1 May–15 June and 15 September–15
November: call 39 06 99805460
For events see website
www.sanliberato.it
email info@sanliberato.it or tenuta@sanliberato.it

Villa d'Este a Tivoli
Piazza Trento 5, 00019 Tivoli (RM)
Owner State
Tel 39 0774 312070
Location Centre of Tivoli, 35.8 km from Rome
Open Daily except Monday 8.30 a.m. to one hour before sunset;
closed 1 January, 1 May, 25 December; guided tours (max. 25)
by appointment
Call centre: 199 766 166 for telephone calls from Italy to book
tickets and tours; to book from abroad call 39 0445 230310 or
email villadestetivoli@telekottageplus.com
www.villadestetivoli.info
email info@villadestetivoli.info

Parco Villa Gregoriana
Piazza del Tempio di Vesta, Tivoli (RM)
Owner State; granted to FAI
Tel 39 0774 332650
Centre of Tivoli, 35 km E of Rome; two entrances: Piazza del
Tempio de Vesta and Largo Sant'Angelo
Open Every day except Monday (unless public holiday)
March and 16 October–30 November 10.00 a.m.–2.30 p.m.,
Sundays and holidays 10.00 a.m.–4.00 p.m.; 1 April–15 October
10.00 a.m.–6.30 p.m.; December–February by appointment only;
guided tours for groups by appointment call 39 06 39967701 or
see www.pierreci.it
For events see website www.fondoambiente.it
www.villagregoriana.it
email bookshopvillagregoriana@pierreci.it

Parco di Villa Belvedere Aldobrandini
Via G. Massaia 18
00044 Frascati (RM)
Owner Camillo Aldobrandini
Tel 39 06 9422560
Location 22 km SE of Rome
Open Monday–Friday summer 9.00 a.m–5.00 p.m.,
winter 9.00 a.m.–4.00 p.m.
Estate oil and wine for sale
email Algidosia@tiscalinet.it

Giardini di Castel Gandolfo
Via Carlo Rosselli
00040 Castel Gandolfo (RM)
Owner Stato della Città del Vaticano
Tel 39 06 69863111
Location 24 km S of Rome following directions to the Villa
Pontificia di Castel Gandolfo
Open By appointment at the discretion of the Vatican; guided
tours for small groups
www.vaticanstate.va/castelgandolfo

Giardini della Landriana
Via Campo di Carne 51
00040 Tor S. Lorenzo
Ardea (RM)
Owner Stefania Gallarati Scotti
Tel 39 039 6081532 or 39 06 91014140
Location 35 km S of Rome
Open March–November for guided tours at weekends: see
website; guided tours for groups on weekdays by appointment;
closed August
Lunch in garden on request
www.landriana.com
email info@landriana.com

Il Giardino di Ninfa
Direzione Giardino di Ninfa, Fondazione Roffredo Caetani
04010 Doganella di Ninfa (LT)
Owner Roffredo Caetani Foundation
Location Doganella 70 km S of Rome
Open April–October on the first Saturday and Sunday each month
and the third Sunday: April, May and June 9.00 a.m.–12.00 p.m.
and 2.30–6.00 p.m; July, August and September 3.00 p.m.–6.30 p.m.;
October 2.30 –4.00 p.m. ; tours are accompanied; for exceptional
opening hours see website; guided tours for groups (min. 30) on
other days by appointment. The management reserves the right
to cancel or reschedule public openings due to bad weather or
circumstances beyond its control.
www.fondazionecaetani.org
email caetani.giardinodininfa@panservice.it

Il Giardino di Torrecchia Vecchia
Cisterna di Latina (LT)
Owner Carlo Revelli Caracciolo
Location 10 km from Cisterna di Latina, SE of Rome
Open March–November by appointment (min. 6, max 20)
email carlo@revelli.com

Parco della Reggia di Caserta
e Giardino Inglese
Palazzo Reale
Via Dohuet 2
81100 Caserta
Owner State
Tel 39 0823 277111
Location Centre of Caserta
Open Daily except Tuesday; park open 8.30 a.m. to an hour
before sunset; English Garden open 10.00 a.m.to two hours
before sunset; guided tours (max. 30) by appointment: contact
www.arethusa.net. or tel. 39 0823 447147
www.reggiadicaserta.org
email Sopr.ambicebn@arti.beneculturali.it

Giardino dei Duchi Guevara di Bovino
Piazza della Repubblica 5
81020 Recale (CE)
Privately owned; managed by Giardini e Dimore dell'Armonia,
Via Novelli 5–81025 Marcianise
Tel 39 0823 442710
Location 37 km N of Naples, 4 km from Caserta
Open Daily by appointment; closed August; guided tours
(min. 20) available: contact Associazione Giardini e Dimore
Dell'Armonia Architetto Nicola Tartaglione (39 335 6099462)
For events see website
www.nicolatartaglione.it
email associazionegiada@yahoo.it

Il Chiostro di Santa Chiara
Via Santa Chiara 49
80134 Napoli
Owner Part of Il Complesso Monumentale di Santa Chiara
Tel 39 081 7971224 or Information 39 081 5516673
Location Centre of Naples
Open Weekdays 9.30 a.m.–5.00 p.m.,
holidays 10.00 a.m.–2.30 p.m.
For events see website
www.monasterodisantachiara.com
email info@monasterodisantachiara.eu

La Mortella
Via Francesco Calise 39
80075 Forio (NA)
Owner Fondazione William Walton e La Mortella
Tel 39 081 986220
Location 2.4 km N of Port of Forio, 5.5 km W of Port of Ischia
Open 1 April–end October Tuesday, Thursday, Saturday and
Sunday 9.00 a.m.–7.00 p.m.; guided tours by appointment
Spring and autumn concerts
For events see website
www.lamortella.org
email info@lamortella.org

Villa San Michele
Viale Axel Munthe 34
80071 Anacapri (NA)
Owner Swedish State
Tel 39 081 8371401
Location By bus or taxi from Piazza Vittoria then 5 minutes on foot,
45–60 minutes on foot from Marina Grande by La Scala Fenicia
Open January, February, November, December 9.00 a.m.–3.30p.m.,
March 9.00 a.m.– 4.30 p.m., April and October
9.00 a.m.–5.00 p.m., May–September 9.00 a.m. – 6.00 p.m.;
guided tours on request
For events see website
www.villasanmichele.eu
email museum@sanmichele.org

Villa Cimbrone
Via S. Chiara 26
84010 Ravello (SA)
Owner Veuilleumier family
Tel 39 089 857459
Location Centre of Ravello, 64 km S of Naples
Open Daily 9.00 a.m. to sunset; guided tours by appointment
For events: see website
www.villacimbrone.it
email info@villacimbrone.com

Villa Rufolo
Piazza Duomo
84010 Ravello (SA)
Owner Demanio, Ente Provinciale per il Turismo di Salerno
Tel 39 089 857621
Location Centre of Ravello, 64 km S of Naples
Open Daily 9.00 a.m. to sunset; guided tours by appointment
Ravello Festival June–September: see website
www.villarufolo.it
email info@villarufolo.it

La Cutura
Contrada Futura
73030 Giuggianello (LE)
Owner Salvatore Cezzi
Tel 39 0836 354164
Location 3 km on road to Palmariggi from Giuggianello
Open Daily winter 10.00 a.m.–1.00 p.m., 3.30 p.m.–7.30 p.m.,
summer 10.00 a.m.–12.30 p.m., 4.30–9.00 p.m.; guided tours
(min. 2, max. 55) by appointment
For events see website
www.lacutura.it
email info@lacutura.it

Orto Botanico di Palermo e Villa Giulia
Via Lincoln 2, 90133 Palermo
Owner Università degli Studi di Palermo
Tel 39 091 6238241
Location In the SE of Palermo, 500 m from the Central Station
Open Daily 1 November–28 February 9.00 a.m.–5.00 p.m.
Sundays 9.00 a.m.–2.00 p.m.; March 9.00 a.m.–6.00 p.m.; April
9.00 a.m.–7.00 p.m.; 1 May 9.00 a.m.–2.00 p.m.; 2 May–31 August
9.00 a.m.–8.00 p.m.; September 9.00 a.m.–7.00 p.m.; October 9.00
a.m.–6.00 p.m.; closed 1 January, Easter, 15 August, 25 December;
guided tours for groups (max. 50) by appointment
For events see website
www.ortobotanico.palermo.it
email ortobotanico@unipa.it

Giardino della Kolymbetra
Parco della Valle dei Templi di Agrigento, 92100 Agrigento
Owner Sicilian Government – granted to Fondo Ambiente Italiano
(FAI)
Tel 39 335 1229042
Location From Agrigento follow signs for Valle dei Templi; entrance
near the Dioscuri Temple
Open Daily October–March 10.00 a.m.–5.00 p.m.; April–June
10.00 a.m.–6.00 p.m.; July– September 10.00 a.m.–7.00 p.m.; closed
7–31 January; guided tours for groups (max. 50) by appointment
Olive oil, lemon and orange marmalades for sale; for events see
website
www.fondoambiente.it
email faikolymbetra@fondoambiente.it

Giardino di Villa Trinità
Via Trinità 34
95030 Mascalucia (CT)
Owner Salvatore and Marina Bonajuto
Tel 39 095 7272156 39 348 6521887
Location Near Mascalucia: see website for details
Open Daily by appointment; guided tours (min. 2)
Wine tasting/sales, lunch on request, B&B; for events see website
www.aziendatrinita.it
email info@aziendatrinita.it

Il Giardino del Biviere: Villa Borghese
Case del Biviere
96016 Lentini (SR)
Owner Maria Carla Borghese
Tel 39 095 7831449 or 39 348 3513110
Location Lentini, 32 km S of Catania, 3 km on SP 67 (Lentini–Valsavoia)
Open March–November by appointment; guided tours (min. 6, max. 50) by the owner
Products for sale; for apartment to let see website
www.ilgiardinodelbiviere.it
email biviere@sicilyonline.it

San Domenico
San Domenico Palace Hotel
Piazza San Domenico 5
98038 Taormina (ME)
Owner AMY Hotels
Tel 39 0942 613111
Location In historical centre
Open Daily
www.hotelsandomenicotaormina.it

Racalia
Marsala (TP)
Owner William Richards
Location 8 km N of Marsala
Open Groups (max. 20) by appointment, lunch by arrangement:
contact Alison Richards (44 (0) 207 2674881)
Estate olive oil for sale
www.racalia.com
email asmrichards@gmail.com

Other Gardens Worth Visiting

PIEDMONT

Parco Villa Pallavicino
Via Nazionale del Sempione Sud
28049 Stresa (VB)
www.parcozoopallavicino.it

La Venaria Reale
Piazza della Repubblica
10078 Venaria Reale (TO)
www.lavenaria.it

LOMBARDY

Villa della Porta Bozzolo
21030 Casalzuigno (VA)
www.fondoambiente.it

VENETO

Villa Fracanzan Piovene
Via san Francesco 2
36040 Orgiano (VI)
www.villafracanzanpiovene.it

Villa Pisani Bolognesi Scalabrin
Via Roma 19
35040 Vescovana (PD)
www.villapisani.it

Prato della Valle
Via Giosuè Carducci
35123 Padova
www.pratodellavalle.it

Villa Valmarana ai Nani
Via dei Nani 8
36100 Vicenza
www.villavalmarana.com

LIGURIA

Villa Durazzo Pallavicini
Via Pallavicini 13
16155 Pegli, (GE)
www.villapallavicini.info

Villa Negrotto Cambiaso Pallavicino
16011 Arenzano (GE)
www.comune.arenzano.ge.it

Palazzo Lomellino
Via Garibaldi 7
16124 Genova
www.palazzolomellino.org

TUSCANY

Castello di Vincigliata
Via di Vincigliata 21
50014 Fiesole (FI)
www.castellodivincigliata.it

Giardino della Gherardesca
Four Seasons Hotel
Borgo Pinti 99
50121 Firenze
www.fourseasons.com

Orto Botanico di Firenze
Via Micheli 3
50121 Firenze
www.museumsinflorence.com/musei/
botanical_garden

Villa di Vicobello
Viale Bianchi Bandinelli 14
53100 Siena
www.vicobello.it

Roseto Botanico Carla Fineschi
Località Casalone 76
52022 Cavriglia (AR)
www.rosetofineschi.it

Horti Leonini
53027 San Quirico d'Orcia (SI)
www.san-quirico.com

Villa Medici
Via Beato Angelico 2
50014 Fiesole (FI)
www.villa medicifiesole.it

LE MARCHE

Villa Caprile
Istituto Tecnico Agrario
Via Caprile 1
61100 Pesaro
iat.pesaro@regione.marche.it

Villa Imperiale
Via San Bartolo 63
61100 Pesaro
iat.pesaro@regone.marche.it

UMBRIA

Orto Medievale
Basilica di San Pietro
Borgo 20 Giugno 74
06121 Perugia
www.unipg.medievalgarden.it

Villa Fidelia
Via Flamina 70
06038 Spello (PG)
www.attivita.culturali@provincia.perugia.it

Castello Bufalini di San Giustino
Largo Crociani 3
06016 San Giustino (PG)
www.sangiustino.it

Civitella Ranieri Foundation
Località Civitella Ranieri
Umbertide
06019 (PG)
www.civitella.org

LAZIO

Villa Doria Pamphili
Via del Corso 305
00186 Roma
www.doriapamphili.it

Orto Botanico di Roma
Largo Cristina di Svezia 24
00165 Roma
www.italiantourism.com/botanici

PUGLIA

Villa Vergine
Strada Provinciale Collepasso – Noha
73020 Cutrofiano (LE)
www.villavergine.it

SICILY

Villa Palagonia
Piazza Garibaldi 3
Bagheria
90011 Palermo
www.villapalagonia.it

Giardino Pubblico
Via Roma 1
98039 Taormina
www.comune.taormina.me.it

Villa Malfitano
Via Dante 167
90141 Palermo
www.palermoweb.com/villa_malfitano

Also worth a visit

Aboca Herb Museum
Palazzo Bourbon del Monte
Via Niccolò Aggiunti 75
52037 Sansepolcro (AR)
www.abocamuseum.it

Glossary

Allée a walk bordered on either side by formally planted trees or clipped hedging

Barco park

Belvedere small lookout tower or pavilion for the enjoyment of a view

Berceaux trellising or pergola for climbing plants

Bosco, boschetto a small wooded area within the garden

Bowling green long level lawn near the house for the playing of games and the taking of exercise

Campagna low-lying area surrounding the city of Rome. The landscape was a source of inspiration for eighteenth- and nineteenth-century painters

Caryatid a sculpted figure serving as a support in place of a column and as an architectural motif

Casino a small pleasure pavilion in the grounds of a larger villa, sometimes standing on its own as a summer house for entertaining and day visits

Castelletto small castle, as, for example, in the grounds of the Castle of Miramare

Commedia dell' arte Form of Italian theatre with stock characters performed by troupes of travelling players from the sixteenth century

Cortile courtyard

Cryptoporticus semi-subterranean gallery; in Roman architecture, a covered passageway, often vaulted and serving as a support for structures above ground

Exedra semicircular screening wall or hedge often used to terminate an axis

Gebbia cistern (from Sicilian Arabic)

Giardino dei semplici garden of medicinal herbs

Giardino inglese a style of 'English' garden or landscape park which spread from England through Europe in the eighteenth- and nineteenth centuries, replacing many earlier formal gardens

Giardino pensile hanging garden

Giardino segreto small, private garden often placed near a Renaissance villa and intended for personal use or as a flower garden

Giochi d'acqua water jokes and games intended to drench unsuspecting visitors to the amusement of their hosts

Grotteschi fantastical human or animal figures, a style of Ancient Roman ornamentation rediscovered when Nero's Golden House was first explored in Renaissance Rome

Herm a sculpture in the form of a head or upper torso, supported by and as if growing out of a pillar

Hippodrome Renaissance conceit based on Roman 'hippodrome' gardens, as in Pliny's Tuscan villa which he described in a letter to a friend

Hortus cinctus garden within a circular enclosing wall as at Padua's Botanic Garden

Hortus conclusus enclosed pleasure garden, a version of the medieval enclosed garden

Laghetto pond

Limonaia building where citrus trees are sheltered during cold weather

Macchia Mediterranean scrub or *maquis*

Manège arena for training horses

Mascherone mask (*maschera*) often of a human or animal head, sculpted in grotesque style, whose function was to ward away evil spirits

Masseria fortified farmhouse found in southern Italy

Nymphaeum grotto, often with fountains and statues, inspired by Roman nymphaea (or shrines to the nymphs)

Parterre de broderie French-influenced parterre, often planted in box, of intricate, curving design, recalling embroidery patterns

Peschiera fish pond

Piano nobile main floor of a villa housing the grandest reception rooms

Pietra spugna calcareous stone used to decorate grottoes

Pomario a fruit orchard

Prato meadow

Putto cherub

Ragnaia small wood where nets were stretched between the trees in order to trap birds

Rocaille patterns made with shells or rocks, often decorating the walls of grottoes

Romitorio hermitage

Stanza di verzura garden room bounded by trees or hedges

Teatro di verzura green theatre

Vasca tank or basin

Viale avenue

Villeggiatura summer stay at a villa or country estate

Further Reading

Acton, Harold, *Tuscan Villas*, Thames & Hudson, 1973

– *Memoirs of an Aesthete*, Methuen, 1948

– *More Memoirs of an Aesthete*, Methuen, 1970

Agnelli, Marella, *Gardens of the Italian Villas*, Weidenfeld & Nicolson, 1987

Attlee, Helena, *Italian Gardens*, Frances Lincoln, 2006

Bellerini, Isabella Lapi, *The Medici Villas*, Giunti, 2003

Bedini, Gilberto, *The Villas of Lucca*, IdeArte, 2003

Black, Jeremy, *Italy and the Grand Tour*, Yale University Press, 2003

Bowe, Patrick, *Gardens of the Roman World*, Frances Lincoln, 2004

Boyden, Martha, and Alessandra Vinciguerra, *Russell Page, Ritratti di giardini italiani*, Electa, 1998

Caracciolo, Marella, and Giuppi Pietromarchi, *The Garden of Ninfa*, Umberto Allemandi, 1999

Campbell, Katie, *Paradise of Exiles*, Frances Lincoln, 2009

Cartwright, Julia, *Italian Gardens of the Renaissance*, Smith, Elder, 1914

Chatfield, Judith, *The Classic Italian Garden*, Rizzoli, 1991

– *A Tour of Italian Gardens*, Rizzoli, 1988

Clark, Ethne , 'A Biography of Cecil Ross Pinsent', *Garden History: the journal of the Garden History Society*, Winter 1998

Clark, Ethne and Raffaello Bencini, *The Gardens of Tuscany*, Weidenfeld & Nicolson, 1990

Coffin, David R., *The Villa in the Life of Renaissance Rome*, Princeton University Press, 1979

– *Gardens and Gardening in Papal Rome*, Princeton University Press, 1991

Dixon Hunt, John , *Garden and Grove: The Italian Renaissance Garden in the English Imagination 1600-1750*, University of Pennsylvania Press, 1996

Dixon Hunt, John (Editor), *The Italian Garden: Art Design and Culture*, Cambridge University Press, 1996

Evelyn, John, *The Diary of John Evelyn*, Dent, 1966

Farrar, Linda, *Ancient Roman Gardens*, Sutton Publishing, 1998

Gervais, Paul, *A Garden in Lucca*, Hyperion, 2000

Hobhouse, Penelope, *Gardens of Italy*, Mitchell Beazley, 1998

Hibbert, Christopher, *The Rise & Fall of the House of Medici*, Penguin, 1979

Howard, Esme, 'Beauty in Ruins', *Historic Gardens Review*, December 2009

James, Henry, *Italian Hours*, Penguin Classics, 1995

Lane Fox, Robin, *The Classical World*, Allen Lane, 2005

Larås, Ann, *Gardens of Italy*, Frances Lincoln, 2006

Lazzaro, Claudia, *The Italian Renaissance Garden*, Yale University Press, 1990

Lee, Hermione, *Edith Wharton*, Chatto & Windus, 2007

Listri, Massimo, and Cesare M. Cunaccia, *Italian Parks and Gardens*, Rizzoli, 1996

Masson, Georgina, *Italian Gardens*, Thames & Hudson, 1961

McEacharn, Neil, *The Villa Taranto*, Country Life, 1954

Medici, Lorenza de', *The Renaissance of Italian Gardens*, Pavilion Books, 1990

Moore, Alasdair, *La Mortola*, Cadogan, 2004

Moorehead, Caroline, *Iris Origo*, John Murray, 2000

Munthe, Axel, *The Story of San Michele*, Grafton, 1975

Nicholl, Charles, *Leonardo da Vinci*, Allen Lane, 2004

Origo, Benedetta, Morna Livingston, Laurie Olin and John Dixon Hunt, *La Foce*, University of Pennsylvania Press, 2001

Origo, Iris, *Images and Shadows*, John Murray, 1970

– *War in Val d'Orcia*, Allison & Busby, 2001

Page, Russell, *The Education of a Gardener*, William Collins, 1962

Platt, Charles, *Italian Gardens*, Harper & Brothers, 1894

Pozzana, Mariachiara, *Gardens of Florence & Tuscany*, Giunti, 2001

Quest-Ritson, Charles, *The English Garden Abroad*, Viking, 1992

– *Ninfa: The Most Romantic Garden in the World*, Frances Lincoln, 2009

Ramsay, Alex and Helena Attlee, *Italian Gardens*, Ellipsis, 2000

Rowdon, Maurice, *Lorenzo the Magnificent*, Weidenfeld & Nicolson, 1974

Russell, Vivian, *Edith Wharton's Italian Gardens*, Frances Lincoln, 1997

– *Gardens of the Riviera*, Little, Brown, 1993

Schama, Simon, *Landscape and Memory*, HarperCollins, 1995

Schinz, Marina, *A Tuscan Paradise*, Stewart, Tabori & Chang, 1998

Schinz, Marina and Gabrielle van Zuylen, *The Gardens of Russell Page*, Frances Lincoln, 2008

Shepherd, J.C. & G.A. Jellicoe, *Italian Gardens of the Renaissance*, Academy Editions, 1986

Strong, Roy, *The Artist and the Garden*, Yale University Press, 2005

Thacker, Christopher, *The History of Gardens*, University of California Press, 1979

Turner, A. Richard, *La Pietra*, Edizioni Olivares, 2002

Triggs, Harry Inigo, *The Art of Garden Design in Italy*, London, 1906

Vasari, Giorgio. *Lives of the Artists*, Penguin Classics, 1965

Wade, Judith, *Italian Gardens*, Rizzoli, 2002

Wharton, Edith, *Italian Villas and Their Gardens*, The Century Co., 1904

Woods, May, *Visions of Arcadia: European Gardens from Renaissance to Rococo*, Aurum Press, 1996

Index

NOTE: Illustrations generally appear on the same pages as the text. Illustrations and captions separated from the text are given page references in **bold**.